Global Aging and
Challenges to Families

D1566319

THE LIFE COURSE AND AGING
An Aldine de Gruyter Series of Texts and Monographs

SERIES EDITORS

Vern L. Bengtson, *University of South California*
Victor W. Marshall, *University of North Carolina, Chapel Hill*

Gerald Handel
Making a Life in Yorkville:
Experience and Meaning in the
Life Course Narrative of an Urban Working Class Man

Vern L. Bengtson and Ariela Lowenstein (eds.)
Global Aging and Challenges to Families

Walter R. Heinz and Victor W. Marshall (eds.)
Social Dynamics of the Life Course:
Transitions, Institutions, and Interrelations

Global Aging and Challenges to Families

editors

Vern L. Bengtson
Ariela Lowenstein

ALDINE DE GRUYTER
NEW YORK

About the Editors

Vern L. Bengtson AARP/University Chair in Gerontology and Professor of Sociology, University of Southern California

Ariela Lowenstein Associate Professor and Head, Department of Aging Studies, University of Haifa, Israel

ALDINE DE GRUYTER
A division of Walter de Gruyter, Inc.
200 Saw Mill River Road
Hawthorne, New York 10532

This publication is printed on acid free paper ∞

Library of Congress Cataloging-in-Publication Data

Global aging and its challenge to families / editors, Vern L. Bengtson and Ariela Lowenstein.
    p. cm. — (The life course and aging)
Includes bibliographical references.
    ISBN 0-202-30686-0 (alk. paper) — ISBN 0-202-30687-9 (pbk. : alk. paper)
    1. Aged—Family relationships. 2. Intergenerational relations. 3. Aged—Care. 4. Aging—Social aspects. I. Bengtson, Vern L. II. Lowenstein, Ariela. III. Series.

    HQ1061.G585 2003
    305.26—dc21
                                                                2003010497

Manufactured in the United States of America
10 9 8 7 6 5 4 3 2 1

CONTENTS

IV Intrasociety Changes in Intergenerational Support

V Intra- and Intersociety Differences and Social Change

Contributors

Isabella Aboderin
Institute for Development Policy and Management (IDPM), University of Manchester

Toni Antonucci
Program Director, Life Course Development Program of the Institute for Social Research; Professor of Psychology, University of Michigan

Claudine Attias-Donfut
Director, Research Department on Aging, CNAV (National French Retirement Fund)

Maria-Teresa Bazo
Professor of Sociology, University of the Basque Country, Spain

Vern L. Bengtson
AARP/University Chair in Gerontology and Professor of Sociology, University of Southern California

Simon Biggs
Professor, School of Social Relations, Keele University, United Kingdom

Svein Olav Daatland
Senior Research Fellow, Norwegian Social Research (NOVA), Oslo

Yuval Elmelech
Assistant Professor of Sociology, Bard College; Research Associate, Levy Economics Institute of Bard College; Assistant Director, Center for the Study of Wealth and Inequality, Columbia University

Ki-Soo Eun
Associate Professor of Sociology and Demography, Academy of Korean Studies, Korea

Daphna Gans
Doctoral candidate, Andrus Gerontology Center, University of Southern California

Iciar Ancizu Garcia
Doctoral candidate, University of the Basque Country, Spain

Roseann Giarrusso
Research Associate Professor of Gerontology and Sociology, Andrus Gerontology Center, University of Southern California

Haim Hazan
Professor of Social Anthropology and Sociology [need place of work]; Director, Herczeg Institute on Aging

Katharina Herlofson
Research Assistant, Norwegian Social Research (NOVA), Oslo

Ynez Wilson Hirst
Doctoral candidate, University of Southern California

James S. Jackson
University of Michigan: Daniel Katz Distinguished University Professor of Psychology; Professor of Health Behavior and Health Education, School of Public Health; Director, Research Center for Group Dynamics; Senior Research Scientist and Director, Program for Research on Black Americans, Institute for Social Research; and Director of the Center for Afroamerican and African Studies.

Ruth Katz
Head, Department of Human Services, The Center for Research and Study of the Family and The Center for Research and Study of Aging, Faculty of Welfare and Health Studies, University of Haifa

Kees Knipscheer
Professor of Social Gerontology, Free University in Amsterdam, The Netherlands

Martin Kohli
Professor of Sociology, Free University of Berlin, Germany

S. Hans-Joachim von Kondratowitz
Privatdozent and Affiliated Lecturer, Free University of Berlin, Germany

Wataru Koyano
Professor of Gerontology, Seigakuin University in Japan

Harald Künemund
Scientific Assistant, Department of Social Structure and Theoretical Bases of Sociology, Free University Berlin

Eugene Litwak
Professor of Sociology, Columbia University

Howard Litwin
Professor, Paul Baerwald School of Social Work, Hebrew University, Jerusalem

Ariela Lowenstein
Associate Professor and Head of the Department of Aging Studies, University of Haifa, Israel

David Mehlhausen-Hassoen
Research Assistant, Center for Study and Research of Aging, University of Haifa

Andreas Motel-Klingebiel
Scientist, German Centre of Gerontology (Deutsches Zentrum fuer Altersfragen, DZA)

Chris Phillipson
Professor of Applied Social Studies and Social Gerontology; Director, Institute of Aging, Keele University, United Kingdom

Jason L. Powell
Lecturer in Social Policy and Social Gerontology, University of Salford, United Kingdom

Dana Prilutzky
Social worker and Lecturer, Gerontology Department, Haifa University; Researcher, Center for Research and Study of Aging, Haifa and Faculty of Welfare and Health Studies, the University of Haifa, Israel

Norella M. Putney
NIH Ruth L. Kirschstein Postdoctoral Fellow and Research Associate, Andrus Gerontology Center, University of Southern California

Merril Silverstein
Professor of Gerontology and Sociology, University of Southern California

Seymour Spilerman
Julian C. Levi Professor of Sociology, Columbia University; Director, Center for the Study of Wealth and Inequality

Clemens Tesch-Roemer
Adjunct Professor, Free University of Berlin, Germany

Theo van Tilburg
Associate Professor, Department of Sociology and Social Gerontology, Vrije Universiteit Amsterdam, The Netherlands

Acknowledgments

We first wish to thank the European Community for its support of the OASIS project: Old age and autonomy: the role of service systems and inter-generational family solidarity. This was funded under the 5th Framework Programme of the European Community, contract number QLK6-CT-1999-02128. The participating countries and partners in the OASIS project are as follows: University of Haifa (Israel), Deutsches Zentrum für Altersfragen (Germany), Universidad del Pais Vasco in Bilbao (Spain), Keele University (UK), and NOVA the Norwegian Social Research Institute.

We are grateful to the University of Haifa for its financial support to the research conference on which this volume is based. We also thank the Alan E. Berlin and Frieda Berlin Philanthropic Fund and the Dennis and Edith Oberman Fund for a contribution at a most crucial time that enabled American scholars to attend the conference.

Two grants from the National Institute on Aging provided support in the preparation of this volume: 2-T32 AG00037, Multidisciplinary Research Training in Gerontology, and 5-RO1-AG07977, Longitudinal Study of Generations and Mental Health. The former supported three trainees who are coauthors of chapters in this volume: Norella Putney, Daphna Gans, and Ynez Wilson-Hirst. We are grateful to Dr. Robin Barr, Director of Training at NIA, for his leadership in supporting research training for students in the field of aging, and Dr. Richard Suzman, Associate Director of NIA, for his support of international research in aging.

Finally we thank Linda Hall, Program Manager, for her skillful assembly of the multinational chapters that make up this volume. This is the thirteenth volume Ms. Hall has helped Vern Bengtson to publish during the last twenty years. Her competence and tactful patience were invaluable.

Vern L. Bengtson
Ariela Lowenstein

| 1 |

Global Aging and the Challenge to Families

Vern L. Bengtson, Ariela Lowenstein, Norella M. Putney, and Daphna Gans

The recent explosion in population aging across the globe represents one of the most remarkable demographic changes in human history. Around the world today there is much concern about population aging and its consequences for nations, for governments, and for individuals. It has often been noted that population aging will inevitably affect the economic stability of most countries and the policies of most state governments. What is less obvious, but equally important, is that population aging will profoundly affect families. Who will care for the growing numbers of tomorrow's very old members of societies? Will it be state governments? The aged themselves? Their families?

Our purpose is to examine consequences of global aging for families and intergenerational support, and for nations as they plan for the future. We will be examining four remarkable social changes during the past fifty years:

- *Extension of the life course:* Over the past six decades there has been a remarkable increase in life expectancy, and an astonishing change in the normal, expected life course of individuals, especially in industrialized societies. A generation has been added to the average span of life over the past century.
- *Changes in the age structures of nations:* This increase in longevity has added a generation to the social structure of societies. Most nations today have many more elders, and many fewer children, than fifty years ago.

1

- *Changes in family structures and relationships:* Families look different today than they did fifty years ago. We have added a whole generation to the structure of many families. Some of these differences are the consequence of the expanding life course. Others are the result of trends in family structure, notably higher divorce rates and the higher incidence of childbearing to single parents. Still others are outcomes of changes in values and political expectations regarding the role of the state in the lives of individuals and families.
- *Changes in governmental responsibilities:* For most of the twentieth century, governmental states in the industrialized world increasingly assumed more responsibility for their citizens' welfare and well-being. In the last decade, however, this trend appears to have slowed or reversed as states reduce welfare expenditures.

How will families respond to twenty-first-century problems associated with population aging? Will families indeed be important in the twenty-first century, or will kinship and the obligations across generations become increasingly irrelevant, replaced by what Phillipson (see Chapter 2) calls "personal communities"?

In this chapter we first review population aging trends projected for the twenty-first century. While European nations have the most aged populations, the pace of aging is accelerating most rapidly in developing nations. In many nations, those aged 80 and over are the fastest growing portion of the total population. Second, we discuss the changes in the age structures of industrialized and developing nations, and the implications for governments and families. Third, we describe how these larger demographic changes are affecting the generational composition of families and the structures of kin availability. Fourth, we discuss the microlevel implications of these trends, as exemplified in family intergenerational relationships and behaviors. We present research addressing such issues as the strength and stability of intergenerational relations, the conflict or ambivalence that can characterize family relationships, and the increasing diversity of family relationships, a consequence of changing family structures. We conclude with some suggestions for future research and policy agendas—to be carried out by the next generation of scholars—concerning families, aging, and social change in the early twenty-first century.

THE REALITIES OF POPULATION AGING

Our global population is aging, and aging at an unprecedented rate. During the twentieth century we became aware of problems associated with the population "explosion" across the globe, and problems of migration

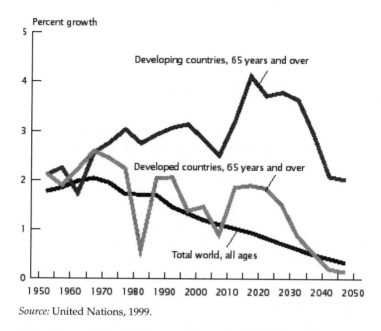

Source: United Nations, 1999.

Figure 1.1   Average Annual Percent Growth of Elderly Population in Developed and Developing Countries.

from rural to urban areas. But as we begin the twenty-first century, population aging is emerging as a preeminent demographic change. During 2000, the world's elderly population (aged 65 and over) grew by more than 795,000 people a month. Projections indicate that by 2010 the net gain will be 847,000 older people per month (U.S. Bureau of the Census, 2000).

Population Aging: A New Phenomenon

It should be noted that population aging represents a human success story. Societies now have the luxury of aging. But the incremental growth in life expectancy also poses many challenges. The numbers and proportions of elderly, especially the oldest old, will rise rapidly in most developed and many less developed countries over the next decades.

Population aging is occurring in both developed and developing nations.   This demographic phenomenon has been discussed most often in terms of its economic consequences for industrialized nation in Europe and Asia. What is less widely noted is that the absolute numbers of elderly in *developing* nations often are large and everywhere are increasing. In fact, less developed nations as a whole are aging much faster than their more developed counterparts (see Figure 1.1).

Many developing countries are now experiencing a significant downturn in rates of natural population increase (births minus death) similar to what has occurred in most industrialized nations. Well over half of the world's elderly (people aged 65 and over) now live in developing nations (59 percent, or 249 million people). By 2030, this proportion is projected to increase to 71 percent, or 689 million people (United Nations, 1999; U.S. Bureau of the Census, 2000). In Asia and the Latin America/Caribbean area, aggregate proportions of elderly are expected to more than double by 2030.

The current growth rate of the elderly population in the developing countries is expected to rise to above 3.5 percent annually from 2015 through 2030 before declining in subsequent decades (U.S. Bureau of the Census, 2000). While the aggregate numbers and proportions of elderly in developing nations are increasing faster than in developed nations, it is important to note that the elderly still comprise a significantly lower proportion of the total population in developing nations. As this aging process accelerates, in all nations age structures will change and the elderly will become an even larger proportion of individual nations' total populations.

Nations in Western Europe and Japan have the oldest populations in the world. Census projections show that by 2030, most of the Western European nations will have aged (65 and over) populations of 24 to 26 percent (U.S. Bureau of the Census, 2002). Japan is perhaps the most rapidly aging society in the modern world. Whereas in 2002 the elderly 65 and older were about 18 percent of the Japanese population, by 2030 this figure will rise to 29 percent (ibid.). By 2050 those aged 65 and over will represent about a third of Japan's total population (Kojima, 2000). It is not expected that historically low birth rates in Europe and Japan (with total fertility rates around 1.3) will recover in the next several decades, meaning that overall population levels in these nations will continue to decline (Population Reference Bureau, 2002). Currently, Australia, Canada, and the United States have moderately high aggregate percentages of elderly (13 percent), and these rates will increase to between 21 and 23 percent by 2030 (U.S. Bureau of the Census, 2002). In Israel, an industrialized nation that is relatively young, the 65 and older age group will constitute about 12 percent of the population in 2020 and 15 percent by 2030 (Brodsky, Shnor, and Be'er, 2000; U.S. Bureau of the Census, 2002). Figure 1.2 summarizes the projected changes between 2002 and 2030 in the percentage 65 and older in selected countries.

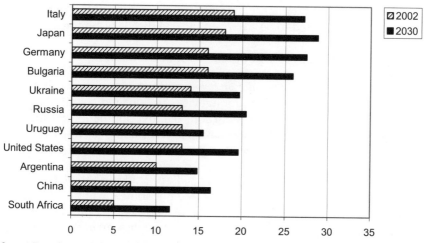

Source: Population Reference Bureau, 2002 and U.S. Bureau of the Census, 2002.

Figure 1.2   Percent 65 and Older in Selected Countries: 2002 and 2030.

The aging of the aged.   We must also consider the secondary aging process, sometimes termed the aging of the aged. Over time, a nation's elderly population will grow older on average as a larger proportion survives to 80 years and beyond. In many countries, the "oldest old" (people aged 80 and over) are now the fastest growing portion of the total population. In the mid-1990s, the global growth rate of the oldest old was somewhat lower than that of the world's elderly (65 and over), a result of low fertility that prevailed in many countries around the time of World War I. For example, people who were reaching the age of 80 in 1996 were part of a relatively small birth cohort. Thus the 1996 to 1997 growth rate of the world's oldest-old population was only 1.3 percent. Just a few years later, however, the fertility effects of World War I had dissipated. From 1999 to 2000, the growth rate of the world's 80 and over population had jumped to 3.5 percent (U.S. Bureau of the Census, 2000).

Until recently, Europe has had the highest proportions of population in the most advanced age categories. But in 2000, the North American oldest-old population aged 80 and over equaled that of Europe as a whole, probably as a result of small European birth cohorts around the time of World War I. By 2013, however, these percentages are again expected to be higher in Europe: in 2030, nearly 12 percent of all Europeans are projected to be age 75 and over, and 7 percent are projected to be age 80 and over (U.S. Bureau of the Census, 2002). In Japan, those 75 and over will constitute 17 percent of the total population in 2030, and 12 percent are projected to be age 80 and over (ibid.) On the other hand, in Israel, the percentage of the 80 and over population is projected to be 4 percent in 2030 (Brodsky, Shnor, and Be'er, 2000).

We can summarize these population trends as follows.

The world's total elderly population is increasing at a rapid pace. The combination of improved health and longevity and lowered fertility has generated growing numbers and proportions of older population throughout most of the world. The global population aged 65 and over was estimated to be 435 million people as of 2002, an increase of 15 million since 2000.

The elderly population is growing most rapidly in developing countries. Population aging has become a well-publicized phenomenon in the industrialized nations of Europe, the United States and Japan. But developing countries are aging as well, and at a much faster rate than in the developed world.

Europe is still the "oldest" world region, while Africa the "youngest." For many decades, Europe has had the highest proportion of population aged 65 and over among major world regions, and should remain the global leader well into the twenty-first century. However, Japan, with the highest life expectancy in the world, is projected to be the oldest *country* for the next several decades.

Elderly populations themselves are aging. An increasingly important feature of society aging is the progressive aging of the population itself. In the future, we can expect to see a sustained high growth rate of the oldest old. Between 1960 and 2040, all central and northern European countries are projected to experience an increase of at least 200 percent in the numbers of those 80 years and over, rising to over 400 percent in Switzerland and over 600 percent in Finland. However, even this rate "is dwarfed by that anticipated in the non-European countries, which is projected at a minimum of around 500 percent in New Zealand, over 800 percent in the United States, over 900 percent in Australia, and over 1,300 percent in Japan" (OECD, 1996, p. 15).

The Changing Age Structures of Societies: From Pyramids to Rectangularization

Population aging is altering the age structures of nations around the world. Age structures—representing age cohorts of different sizes relative to one another as they move through historical time—has profound implications for the economic, political, and social well-being of a nation and its people. The shape of an age structure tells much about dependency relationships between individuals and families, and their government, and the economic and social resources that may be available to meet the needs of the elderly. Figure 1.3 illustrates the historical and projected aggregate population age structure transitions in developing and developed countries.

Consider how much the age structures of populations in developed countries have changed over the past hundred years. At one time, most if not all countries had a youthful age structure similar to that of developing countries as a whole, with a large percentage of the entire population under the age of 15. In nineteenth-century America, for example, the shape of the population structure by age was that of a pyramid, with a large base (represented by children under age five) progressively tapering into a narrow group of those aged 65 and older. This pyramid shape has characterized the population structure by age in most human societies on record, from the dawn of civilization through the early Industrial Revolution and into the early twentieth century (Laslett, 1976; Myers, 1990). But by 1990 the age pyramid for America and other industrialized societies had come to look more like an irregular triangle.

Even as recently as 1950, among developed countries there was relatively little variation in the size of five-year groups between the ages of 5 and 24. The beginnings of the post–World War II baby boom can be seen in the 0–4 age group. By 1990, the baby boom cohorts were aged 24–44, and younger cohorts were becoming successively smaller. If fertility rates continue as projected through 2030, the aggregate pyramid will start to invert, with more weight on the top than on the bottom. The size of the oldest-old population (especially women) will increase, and people aged 80 and over may eventually outnumber any younger five-year-old group.

In OECD (Organization for Economic Cooperation and Development) nations, between 1960 and 2000 there was a sharp decline in the age group 0–14 and a considerable increase in the older age groups (66–79 and 80+). For example, in Spain the percentage of those 0–14 decreased from almost 28 percent of the total population in 1960 to only about 16 percent in 2000, with a projected further decrease to just 12 percent in 2040. On the other hand, the 65 and older age group increased from 8 percent in the 1960s to 16 percent in 2000, and by 2040 will constitute almost 29 percent of the population (OECD, 1996).

Thus, in the span of just one century, increases in longevity and decreases in fertility have caused the age pyramids to become rectangularized in most industrialized societies of the world. By 2030, age structures in developed countries will look more rectangular, with strikingly similar numbers in each age category, starting from children and adolescents and moving through those above the age of 60 (Treas, 1995a).

The picture in developing countries has been and will be quite different than that of developed countries. Given the relatively high rates of fertility

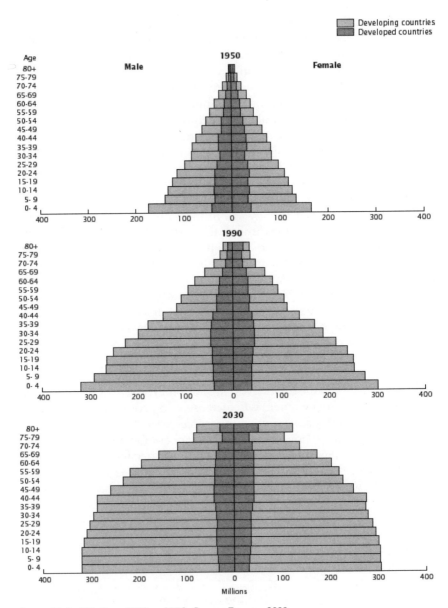

Source: United Nations, 1999 and U.S. Census Bureau, 2000.

Figure 1.3   Population by Age and Sex: 1950, 1990, and 2030.

that prevailed in most developing countries from 1950 through the early 1970s, the overall pyramid shape of their age structures had not changed greatly by 1990. However, the effects of fertility and mortality decline can be seen in the projected pyramid for 2030 (see Figure 1.3), which loses its strictly triangular shape as the size of younger five-year old cohorts stabilizes and the older age groups represent increasingly larger proportions of the total population.

Although the effect of fertility decline usually has been the driving force in changing population age structures, current and future changes in mortality will assume much greater weight, particularly in relatively "aged" countries (Caselli and Vallin, 1990), and are discussed further in the next chapter.

Shifts in population age structures generally result in new service demands and economic requirements. With an increasingly older age structure comes change in the relative numbers of people who can provide support to those who need it. In the early 1980s, Myers and Nathanson (1982) identified three prominent issues regarding population aging and the family: (1) The extent to which changes in social norms and responsibilities, driven by the secular processes of urbanization and modernization, alter traditional familial modes of caring for people. (2) The possible social support burden resulting from reduced economic self-sufficiency of aged people and the likelihood of heightened chronic disease morbidity and functional impairment related to longer life expectancy. (3) The ways in which countries develop funding priorities for public care systems given competing demands for scarce resources.

Research has demonstrated that the elderly population is diverse in terms of its resources, needs, and abilities (Bengtson, Rosenthal, and Burton, 1990). The stereotype of the elderly as a predominantly dependent group that drains a nation's economy is not supported by the evidence (Bengtson and Harootyan, 1994). It is important to keep in mind that not all elderly require support and not all working-age people actually work or provide direct support to elderly family members.

CONSEQUENCES OF POPULATION AGING FOR FAMILIES

Family Structures Have Changed: From Pyramids to Beanpoles

Consider the implications of these macrodemographic changes in age distribution for the generational structure of families. In the United States, for example, the population birth rate has decreased from 4.1 per female in 1900 to 1.9 in 1990 (Cherlin, 1999), while life expectancy has increased from 47 to 77 years. This means that the age structure of most American families has changed from a pyramid to what might be described as a "beanpole"—that is, a family structure the shape of which is long and thin with more family generations alive but with fewer members in each generation (Bengtson et al., 1990). Whether the "beanpole" structure adequately describes a majority of American families today has been debated (Farkas and Hogan, 1995; Treas, 1995b). Nevertheless, the changes in demographic distribution by age since 1900 are remarkable, and the progression "from pyramids to beanpoles" has important implications for family functions and relationships in the twenty-first century.

The "Kin Supply" Structure across Generations Has Changed

Macrodemographic trends have significant import for the composition of families, which in turn affects individual family members' well-being and their chances of receiving family support in time of need. For example, the "family decline" hypothesis of Popenoe (1993) suggests that American children are at greater risk today because of the breakdown of the nuclear family structure—specifically divorce—and the too-frequent disappearance of fathers from the lives of their children. However, the decrease in mortality rates over the last century implies a more optimistic scenario: The increasing availability of extended intergenerational kin—grandparents, great-grandparents, uncles, and aunts—are a resource for children as they grow up and move into young adulthood (Bengtson, 2001).

Peter Uhlenberg (1996) has examined the profound effects that mortality changes over the twentieth century have had on the "supply" of kin available for support of family members in American society. He noted that for children born in 1900, the chances of being an orphan (both parents dying before the child reached age 18) were 18 percent. However, for children born in 2000, 68 percent will have four or more *grand*parents still living by the time they reach 18. Further along the life course, by the time these children are themselves facing the responsibilities of rearing children, the effects of mortality declines on the availability of older kin for support are even more substantial. For those born in 1900, by age 30 only 21 percent had *any* grandparent still living. For those born in 2000, by age 30, 76 percent will still have at least one grandparent alive. Today it is more likely that 20-year-olds will have a grandmother still living (91 percent) than that 20-year-olds alive in 1900 still had their mother living (83 percent) (Uhlenberg, 1996).

Another perspective on this issue is provided by Wachter (1997) who used computer simulations to predict the availability of kin for twenty-first-century family members. He examined the implications of longevity, fertility, and divorce for families in the future. He found that while low fertility rates in the late twentieth century will lead to a shortage of kin for those reaching retirement around 2030, the effects of divorce, remarriage, and family blending are expanding the numbers and types of step-kin, thus "endowing the elderly of the future with kin networks that are at once problematic, rich, and varied" (ibid.:1181). The implications are that step-kin are increasing the kin supply across generations while also becoming potential sources of nurture and support for family members in need and that this may compensate in part for lower fertility rates (Amato and Booth, 1997).

There Are Longer Years of "Shared Lives" across Generations

Other implications of the demographic changes that have occurred over the twentieth century should be noted. First, we now have more years of "co-survivorship between generations" than ever before in human history (Bengtson, 1996; Goldscheider, 1990; Lowenstein, 2000). This means that more and more aging parents and grandparents are now available to provide for family continuity and stability across time (Silverstein, Giarrusso, and Bengtson, 1998). This also means a remarkable increase in multigenerational kin, representing a "latent network" (Riley and Riley, 1993) that can be activated to provide support and well-being for younger family members. The increased longevity of parents, grandparents, great-grandparents, and other older family members in recent decades represents a resource of kin available for help and support that can be, and frequently is, activated in times of need (King, 1994; Silverstein, Parrott, and Bengtson, 1995). These older kin will also be in better health than they might have been in the past (Hayward and Heron 1999).

At the same time, there are potentially negative consequences of the "longer years of shared lives" across generations. One involves protracted years of caregiving for dependent elders (Bengtson, Rosenthal and Burton, 1995). A second involves protracted conflict—what an 84-year-old mother in the Longitudinal Study of Generations termed a "life-long lousy parent-child relationship." Family researchers have not adequately addressed intergenerational conflicts throughout the adult years (Clarke, Preston, Raskin, and Bengtson, 1999; Lowenstein and Katz, 2000; Mabry, Takagi, and Bengtson, 2002). Because of longer years of shared lives, intergenerational relationships—in terms of help given or received and solidarity or conflict, or both—will be of increasing importance for family life in the future.

TRENDS IN INTERGENERATIONAL RELATIONSHIPS AND AGING

While there have been important changes in the demography of family structures and relations since the nineteenth century, population statistics about family and household structure tell only one part of the story. At the behavioral level, these changes have more immediate consequences in the ways family members organize their lives and pursue their goals in the context of increasing years of intergenerational "shared lives." We summarize below some research evidence on the consequences of "more years of shared lives" across generations. We do this by proposing three propositions that should be tested in future research.

Intergenerational Relationships Are Consistent and Strong over Time

The first proposition is that bonds between generations are surprisingly strong. Using longitudinal data from the Longitudinal Study of Generations (LSOG), we can now chart the course of intergenerational solidarity dimensions over several decades. One consistent result concerns the high levels of affectual solidarity (reflecting the strength of emotional bonds between generations) that appear over six times of measurement, from 1971 to 1997 (Bengtson et al., 2000; Bengtson, Giarrusso, Silverstein, and Wang, 2000). Results indicate that the average solidarity scores between grandparents and parents, parents and youth, and grandparents and grandchildren, are high—considerably above the expected midpoint of the scale. In addition, these scores have been remarkably stable over the thirty years of measurement; there are no statistically significant differences by time of measurement. Results also reflect a "generational bias" in these reports: Parents consistently report higher affect than their children do over time, as do grandparents compared to grandchildren. This supports the "intergenerational stake" hypothesis first proposed thirty years ago (Bengtson and Kuypers, 1971; Giarrusso, Stallings, and Bengtson, 1995). The older generation has a greater psychosocial investment, or "stake," in their joint relationship than does their younger generation, and this apparently influences their perceptions and evaluations of their common intergenerational relationships.

A different picture emerges when we consider normative solidarity as expressed in norms of filial obligations. In this case, an inverse relationship between age and support for such norms was found. Among LSOG respondents, the younger generation is more inclined to support strong filial responsibility than the older generation (also see Hamon and Blieszner, 1990; Logan and Spitze, 1995). The decline in obligation level was found to be progressive across age groups. One explanation may be that the younger generation is more dependent upon their parents today (Connidis, 2001; McGarry and Schoeni, 1997). This trend could press in the direction of recent cohorts of young adults feeling more obligation to parents than in the past, and, as a ripple-out effect, more obligation toward other kin than was the case for earlier cohorts (Rossi and Rossi, 1990). Findings from a study by Logan and Spitze (1995) suggest, however, that such age differences in the attitudes toward filial obligations actually highlight intergenerational solidarity: Older people's attitudes seem to give greater weight to the needs of younger generations and vice versa. The social norms held by older people may reflect their desire for autonomy and self-reliance, their sense that the proper role of parents is to be givers rather than receivers, and their wish to not become a burden to the younger generation. This is further elaborated in Chapter 12.

It should be noted, however, that not all intergenerational relationships display high levels of emotional closeness. Research based on the LSOG has found that about one in five relationships are characterized by either significant conflict or detachment (Clarke et al., 1999). Conflict may negatively influence the willingness of family members to assist each other, as well as their propensity for resolving issues, thereby affecting the overall quality of the relationship (Parrott and Bengtson, 1999). Studies on family relations, caregiving, and the well-being of family members living in multigenerational households point to issues of family conflict (Brody, Litvin, Hoffman, and Kleban, 1995; Lowenstein and Katz, 2000; Montgomery and Kosloski, 1994; Pruchno, Burant, and Peters, 1997). The ability of the family to cope with conflicts arising from caregiving responsibilities does in fact affect the quality of care, and the quality of the relations between caregiver and care receiver (Fisher and Lieberman, 1999; Merrill, 1996). However, it is important to recognize that the dimensions of solidarity and conflict do not represent a single continuum. Intergenerational solidarity can exhibit both high solidarity and high conflict or low solidarity and low conflict, depending upon family dynamics and circumstances (Bengtson, Giarrusso, Silverstein and Wang, 2000). Research on family relationships in later life so far has not adequately examined the issue of conflict, and more effort should be devoted to it (Clarke et al., 1999; Lowenstein, Katz, Prilutzky, and Melhousen-Hassoen, 2001).

Ambivalence is a new and potentially useful theoretical construct (Luescher and Pillemer, 1998), introduced by Luescher (2000) as another means for understanding parent-adult child relations in later life, especially in situations of elder care. This approach argues that because family life today is characterized by a multiplicity of forms, such as divorce, remarriage, or blended families, as well as other sources of stress, family relationships may be characterized by "intergenerational ambivalence," reflecting contradictions in relations between parents and adult offspring (Lowenstein et al., 2003). One of the major goals of the five-nation Oasis Project (Old Age and Autonomy: The Role of Service Systems and Intergenerational Solidarity) is to examine cross-nationally how intergenerational solidarity and ambivalence characterize and impact the caregiving behaviors and quality of life of elders and family caregivers (see Daatland and Herlofson, 2001;

Lowenstein et al., 2001). Connidis and McMullin (2001) propose that ambivalence can be viewed as a brokering concept between the solidarity paradigm and more problematic family relations such as divorce and its impact on intergenerational relationships (Kingston, Phillips, and Ray, 2001). The empirical evidence in this area is just emerging.

Intergenerational Relationships Are Increasingly Diverse

A second proposition is that there is considerable diversity and complexity in intergenerational relationships. For example, Silverstein and Bengtson (1997) used a nationally representative sample to examine the typological structure underlying measurements of intergenerational solidarity. They identified five types or classes of intergenerational family relationships. One type, the "tight-knit" relationship, is characterized by high emotional closeness, family members living fairly close to one another, frequent interaction, and high levels of mutual help and support (representing 25 percent of family relationships). At the other extreme is the "detached" type, with low levels of connectedness in all of the observed measures of solidarity (17 percent of family relationships). Between the tight-knit and the detached are three other classes of families. The "sociable" and "intimate-but-distant" types are similar to what Litwak (1960) described as the "modified extended family," in which functional exchange is low or absent but there are high levels of affinity, suggesting the potential for future support and exchange (representing 25 and 16 percent of family relationships, respectively). The "obligatory" type (16 percent of family relationships) suggests a high level of structural connectedness (proximity and interaction) with an average level of functional exchange but a low level of emotional attachment. No one type was dominant. The results suggest a considerable diversity of intergenerational relationships in contemporary American society.

Results shown in Figure 1.4 also revealed significant gender differences in the distributions of family relationship types. Relations with mothers were more likely to be tight-knit (31 percent) than were relations with fathers (20 percent). On the other hand, relations with fathers were four times as likely to be detached (27 percent) than those with mothers (7 percent). In fact, the detached represented the most frequent type of relationship between older fathers and their adult children. This may be a reflection of increased parental divorce.

Important ethnic differences in the distribution of intergenerational types by ethnicity were also found. Blacks and Hispanics were less likely than non-Hispanic whites to have obligatory relationships with mothers, and blacks were less likely than whites to have detached relationships with mothers. This corresponds to other studies, which have found

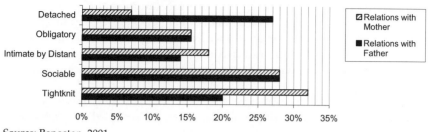

Source: Bengston, 2001.

Figure 1.4   Types of Intergenerational Relationships by Gender of Parent.

stronger maternal attachments in Black and Hispanic families than in white families. Moreover, findings are consistent with other studies that have focused on racial differences in filial norms. Lee, Peek, and Coward (1998) found Blacks to be more supportive of filial obligations than whites, and they attributed this to socialization to more collectivistic values in the African American community. Burr and Mutchler (1999) also found Blacks (and Hispanics) to be more supportive of filial responsibility norms than whites. These ethnic groups were more in favor of coresidence between generations than whites, but no difference in attitudes toward financial help and support were found. This is further elaborated in Chapter 12.

Intergenerational Relations Have Not Declined, Though Family Structures Have Changed

A third proposition is that while family structures have changed, inter-generational family relations remain strong. Situating multigenerational families in sociohistorical context allows us to broaden our inquiry into their importance and functionality. When we bring historical context into our analyses, several questions arise. How have intergenerational influences changed over recent historical time? Are families still important in shaping the developmental outcomes of youth? And what have been the effects of changing family structures and roles—the consequences of divorce, remarriage, and maternal employment—on intergenerational relationships?

Studies on the impact of parental divorce on parent-child relationships in later life suggest relations with father may be compromised. Where there is divorce, less adult child–parent contact is maintained, especially with fathers (Aquilino, 1994; Booth and Amato, 1994), and fathers are also less likely to consider their children as sources of support when in need (Uhlenberg, 1990). However, children of divorced parents who remain emotionally close to them also maintain greater contact (Cooney, 1994). Also, more positive ties to mothers have been reported, even though relationships with both parents are viewed more negatively than they are by children whose parents did not divorce (Kaufman and Uhlenberg, 1998). It is also the case, however, that divorced older parents generally provide less support to their adult offspring (White, 1992).

Regarding remarriage in later life, even though rates have declined since the 1970s, rates of cohabitation have increased (Cherlin, 1992). While earlier studies found that older remarried couples tend to enjoy positive support from their children (Vinick, 1978), more recent studies point to more problematic relations (Lowenstein and Ron, 1999). On the other hand, scholars have argued that the greater diversity of family structures that results from divorce and remarriage can form the basis for a new family structure, the "latent kin matrix" (Riley and Riley, 1996). These contemporary family structures and support arrangements place greater emphasis on the voluntary relationships between former in-laws and step–family members.

Examining families in changing historical contexts is an important research objective. Using a life course theoretical framework that focuses on the interplay of macroeconomic and microrelational processes, Bengtson, Biblarz, and Roberts (2002) examined the development of youths' achievement orientations—their educational and occupational aspirations, values, and self esteem. Achievement orientations are viewed as personal attributes that may be passed down, or "transmitted," from generation to generation in families, thus promoting continuity over multiple generations across many decades. Parent-child affective bonds can mediate this process. Knowing that Generation Xers were much more likely than their baby-boomer parents to have college-educated parents, fewer siblings, an employed mother, and to have grown up in a divorced household (40 percent for Generation Xers, 20 percent for their baby-boomer parents), the important question was how the two generations compared in terms of family solidarity and achievement orientations.

Results demonstrate that Generation Xers' achievement orientations are surprisingly similar to their baby-boomer parents at the same age, almost thirty years earlier. This suggests that despite changes in family structure and socioeconomic context, intergenerational influences remain strong. Generation Xers whose parents divorced were slightly less advantaged in terms of achievement orientations than Generation Xers who came from nondivorced families, yet they were higher on these outcome measures than were their baby-boomer parents at the same age, regardless of family structure. Maternal employment did not negatively affect the aspirations, values, and self-esteem of youth across these two generations, despite the dramatic increase in women's labor force participation over the past three decades. Finally, Generation X women were found to have higher educational and occupational aspirations in 1997 than their baby-boomer mothers had almost thirty years before. In fact, Generation X young women's educational aspirations were higher than Generation X young men's. These findings challenge the belief that families are declining in function and influence and that "alternative" family structures spell the downfall of American youth. American multigenerational families continue to perform their functions in the face of recent social change and varied family forms.

SETTING A FUTURE AGENDA FOR RESEARCH AND POLICY ON AGING: FAMILIES AND SOCIAL SUPPORT FROM AN INTERNATIONAL PERSPECTIVE

This volume brings together the contributions of twenty-five scholars from nine countries to discuss current research on aging, families, and social support. We present major issues concerning intergenerational family relations and social support in later-life families at the start of the twenty-first century. These issues include (1) rapid population aging; (2) changing structures of age and stratification; (3) globalization and migration; (4) changing family and network structures; and (5) the changing roles of the family vis-à-vis the state.

Supporting the aims of the Second World Assembly on Aging (Madrid, April 8–12, 2002), the authors provide comparative international perspectives on aging and changing families within Europe, Israel, the United States, South Korea, Japan, and the developing country of Ghana. These analyses consider the implications of cultural and social changes for intergenerational relations and support in later-life families within diverse societies and family structures and under changing family policies. Thus, a rich background is provided against which to further explore and develop theoretical and research questions and to set an agenda for future policy developments for aging families.

The conceptual and theoretical perspectives within which these issues are discussed expand upon Litwak's family task-specificity model (Litwak, 1985; Litwak and Messeri, 1989) to provide an understanding of the balance in care and support between informal and formal networks. When analyzing population aging vis-à-vis the impact of globalization and migration, the notion of the modified extended family (Litwak, 1960; Riley and Riley, 1996) and changes in family structures lead to the perception of personal communities and the importance of social capital. This brings us to consider the balance between governmental (formal) and family (informal) networks for care and support in light of changing cultural norms, as is occurring in South Korea and Japan, or developing countries like Ghana.

Specific topics deal with norms, perceptions, and attitudes with regard to filial obligations in different societies, intergenerational transfers, the role of offspring in constructing conjugal support in later life, issues of reciprocity and exchange, and relations between grandparents and grandchildren in societies experiencing changing family structures.

Many of the topics are analyzed within comparative and international perspectives. Comparative analyses are important for several reasons: First, research undertaken within a single society or a specific group often fails to reveal the influence of culture as a dynamic social force and does not allow enough room for the understanding of diversity. Second, such analyses lead to a broader understanding of social and familial processes and highlight the complex interplay between demographic changes, different societal systems, and policies that affect older people and their families. Third, comparative analyses provide an understanding of distinct societal and cultural influences, which allows us to learn about and develop new ways of responding to the changing interests and needs of older populations and diverse families in later life. For example, even though broad similarities have been found between many European countries, there remain variations within and between countries (Wenger, 1997).

Conducting comparative cross-national research on family relations, as in the OASIS Study (see Chapters 12 and 13), or looking at data from different family cultures such as Japan or Ghana, calls our attention to the importance of culture, ethnic diversity, the role of norms and values in shaping filial responsibility, and the ways filial responsibility is enacted. Such analysis also reflects the role of the state and its policies regarding elder care.

We see several research issues as central to setting a future agenda for research and policy formulations, and we hope that this volume will give rise to further debate, particularly on the following topics:

1. Will the effects of population aging on family structures cause changes that will weaken or strengthen family interactions and support exchanges?

2. Will the pattern of support and care from closer family network members be replaced by the extended family networks or even by personal communities? What will be the specific roles of grandparents and grandchildren in caring for the elderly?

3. Will patterns of intergenerational solidarity continue as a major determinant within family networks, or will we witness more conflicts and ambivalence in light of the more "vertical" family structures?

4. Will norms of filial obligation continue to play an important and universal role in care of aged family members in different societal structures and different family cultures? How shall we address diversity in family structures and social norms in view of global social changes?

5. What will be the proper balance of support and care between the state and the relevant informal networks? Will there or will there not be increased responsibility sharing between families and the state in support of aged family members?

CONCLUSION

Largely as a consequence of population aging, the changing societies of the twenty-first century are being confronted with profound yet not always recognized or understood changes in familial and network structures that will impact the future of family relations and social support into the distant future. The twentieth century witnessed an historical lengthening of the human life span. This aging of the population is without parallel in the history of humanity. If these trends continue, by the middle of the twenty-first century the number of older persons in the world will exceed the number of young for the first time in the history of mankind.

In this chapter we provided an overview of the phenomenon of population aging and its implications for families and nations. Our discussion addressed changes in the aggregate numbers and proportions of older populations in developed and especially developing countries, and the rapid aging of the elderly population itself. We showed how the age structure of a nation has significant consequences for dependency ratios, national economies, and policies, affecting the prospects that families and states will be able, or willing, to provide care for the elderly. Population aging is also reflected at the family level, where family structures are now characterized by four and even five generations, but with many fewer members in each generation. Within families, longer lives mean more years of cosurvivorship between generations. The changing composition of families, a consequence of longer lives as well as increased divorce and remarriage and single parenthood, may have the unintended but beneficial effect of expanding kin resources, increasing the potential that support and care will be available when needed. Finally, we presented research showing that intergenerational family relationships remain strong, and families continue to fulfill their functions for providing sustenance and social support to their members, even as families become increasingly diverse and complex.

ACKNOWLEDGMENTS

This research was funded by grants #R01AG07977 and #T32-AG00037 from Social and Behavioral Sciences program of the National Institute on Aging. Our thanks to Richard Suzman, Kathy Mann Koepke, Robin Barr, and Daniel Berch of NIA for their support and encouragement.

REFERENCES

Amato, P., and Booth, A. 1997. *A generation at risk: Growing up in an era of family upheaval.* Cambridge, MA: Harvard University Press.

Aquilino, W. S. 1994. Later life parental divorce and widowhood: Impact on young adults' assessment of parent-child relations. *Journal of Marriage and the Family* 56:908–22.

Bengtson, V. L. 1996. Continuities and discontinuities in intergenerational relationships over time. In V. L. Bengtson (ed.), *Adulthood and aging: Research on continuities and discontinuities.* New York: Springer.

Bengtson, V. L. 2001. Beyond the nuclear family: The increasing importance of multigenerational relationships in American society. The 1998 Burgess Award Lecture. *Journal of Marriage and Family* 63:1–16.

Bengtson, V. L., Biblarz, T. L., Clarke, E., Giarrusso, R., Roberts, R. E. L., Richlin-Klonsky, J., and Silverstein, M. 2000. Intergenerational relationships and aging: Families, cohorts, and social change. In J. M. Claire and R. M. Allman (eds.), *The gerontological prism: Developing interdisciplinary bridges* (pp. 115–47). Amityville, NY: Baywood.

Bengtson, V. L., Biblarz, T. L., and Roberts, R. E. L. 2002. *How families still matter: A longitudinal study of youth in two generations.* New York: Cambridge University Press.

Bengtson, V. L., Giarrusso, R., Silverstein, M., and Wang, H. 2000. Families and intergenerational relationships in aging societies. *Hallym International Journal of Aging* 2:3–10.

Bengtson, V. L., and Harootyan, R. A. 1994. *Intergenerational linkages: Hidden connections in American society.* New York: Springer.

Bengtson, V. L., and Kuypers, J. A. 1971. Generational difference and the "developmental stake." *Aging and Human Development* 2:249–60.

Bengtson, V. L., Rosenthal, C. J., and Burton, L. M. 1990. Families and aging: Diversity and heterogeneity. In R. Binstock and L. George (eds.), *Handbook of aging and the social sciences* (3rd ed., pp. 263–87). San Diego, CA: Academic Press.

Bengtson, V. L., Rosenthal, C. J., and Burton, L. M. 1995. Paradoxes of families and aging. In R. H. Binstock and L. K. George (eds.), *Handbook of aging and the social sciences* (4th ed., pp. 253–82). San Diego, CA: Academic Press.

Booth, A., and Amato, P. R. 1994. Parental marital quality, parental divorce, and relations with parents. *Journal of Marriage and the Family* 56(1):21–34.

Brodsky, J., Shnor, Y., and Be'er, S. 2000. *Elders in Israel: Statistical yearbook, 2000* (Hebrew). Jerusalem: JDC-Brookdale Institute of Gerontology and Human Development and Eshel.

Brody, E. M., Litvin, S. J., Hoffman, C., and Kleban, M. H. 1995. Marital status of caregiving daughters and co-residence with dependent parents. *Gerontologist* 35:75–85.

Burr, J. A., and Mutchler, J. E. 1999. Race and ethnic variation in norms of filial responsibility among older persons. *Journal of Marriage and the Family* 61:674–87.

Caselli, G., and Vallin, J. 1990. Mortality and population aging. *European Journal of Population—Revue Europeenne de Demographie* 6(1):1–25.

Cherlin, A. J. 1992. *Marriage, divorce, remarriage* (2nd ed.). Cambridge, MA: Harvard University Press.

Cherlin, A. J. 1999. *Public and private families*. Boston: McGraw-Hill.

Clarke, E. J., Preston, M., Raskin, J. and Bengtson, V. L. 1999. Types of conflicts and tensions between older parents and adult children. *Gerontologist*, 39(3):261–70.

Connidis, I. 2001. *Family ties and aging*. Thousand Oaks, CA: Sage.

Connidis, I., and McMullin, J. 2001. *Negotiating family ties over three generations: The impact of divorce*. Paper presented at the 17th World Congress of Gerontology, Vancouver, Canada.

Cooney, T. M. 1994. Young adults' relations with parents: The influence of recent parental divorce. *Journal of Marriage and the Family* 56:45–56.

Daatland, S. O., and Herlofson, K. (eds.) 2001. *Ageing, intergenerational relations, care systems and quality of life—An introduction to the OASIS project*. Oslo: NOVA—Norwegian Social Research.

Farkas, J., and Hogan, D., 1995. The demography of changing intergenerational relationships. In V. L. Bengtson, K. Warner Schaie, and L. M. Burton (eds.), *Adult intergenerational relations: Effects of societal change* (pp. 1–19). New York: Springer.

Fisher, L., and Lieberman, M. A. 1999. Longitudinal study of predictors of nursing home placement for patients with dementia: The contribution of family characteristics. *Gerontologist* 39(6):677–86.

Giarrusso, R., Stallings, M., and Bengtson, V. L. 1995. The "intergenerational stake" hypothesis revisited: Parent-child differences in perceptions of relationships 20 years. In V. L. Bengtson, K. W. Schaie, and L. M. Burton (eds.), *Adult intergenerational relations: Effects of societal change* (pp. 227–63). New York: Springer.

Goldscheider, F. K. 1990. The aging of the gender revolution: What do we know and what do we need to know? *Research on Aging* 23:531–45.

Hamon, R. R., and Blieszner, R. 1990. Filial responsibility expectations among adult child–older parents pairs. *Journal of Gerontology* 45(3):110–12.

Hayward, M. D., and Heron, M. 1999. Racial inequality in active life among adult Americans. *Demography* 36:77–91.

Kaufman, G., and Uhlenberg, P. 1998. Effects of life course transitions on the quality of relationships between adult children and their parents. *Journal of Marriage and the Family* 60:924–38.

King, V. 1994. Variation in the consequences of nonresident father involvement for children's well-being. *Journal of Marriage and the Family* 56:963–72.

Kingston, P., Phillips, J., and Ray, M. 2001. Conflict and ambivalence within intergenerational relations. In S. O. Daatland and K. Herlofson (eds.), *Ageing, intergenerational relations, care systems and quality of life: An introduction to the OASIS project* (pp. 31–40). Oslo: NOVA—Norwegian Social Research.

Kojima, H. 2000. Japan: Hyper-aging and its policy implications. In V. L. Bengtson, K.-D. Kim, G. C. Myers, and K.-S. Eun, (eds.), *Aging in East and West: Families, states and the elderly* (pp. 95–120). New York: Springer.

Laslett, P. 1976. Societal development and aging. In R. Binstock and E. Shanas (eds.), *Handbook of aging and the social sciences* (pp. 87–116). New York: Van Nostrand Reinhold.

Lee, G. R., Peek, C. W., and Coward, R. T. 1998. Race differences in filial responsibility expectations among older parents. *Journal of Marriage and the Family* 60:404–12.

Litwak, E. 1960. Geographic mobility and extended family cohesion. *American Sociological Review* 25:385–94.

Litwak, E. 1985. *Helping the elderly: The complementary roles of informal networks and formal systems.* New York: Guilford.

Litwak, E., and Messeri, P. 1989. Organizational theory, social supports, and mortality rates: A theoretical convergence. *American Sociological Review* 54(1):49–66.

Logan, J. R., and Spitze, G. D. 1995. Self-interest and altruism in intergenerational relations. *Demography* 32(3):353–64.

Lowenstein, A. 2000. Intergenerational family relations and social support. *German Journal of Geriatrics and Gerontology* 32:202–10.

Lowenstein, A., and Katz, R. 2000. Coping with caregiving in the rural Arab family in Israel. *Marriage and Family Review* 30(1):179–97.

Lowenstein, A., Katz, R., Prilutzky, D., and Melhousen-Hassoen, D. 2001. *The intergenerational solidarity paradigm.* In S. O. Daatland and K. Herlofson (eds.), *Ageing, intergenerational relations, care systems and quality of life: An introduction to the OASIS project* (pp. 11–30). Oslo: NOVA—Norwegian Social Research.

———. 2003. A comparative cross-national perspective on intergenerational solidarity. *Retraite et Societe* 38:52-80.

Lowenstein, A., and Ron, P. 1999. Tension and conflict factors in spousal abuse in second marriages of the widowed elderly. *Journal of Elder Abuse and Neglect* 11(1):23–45.

Luescher, K. 2000. *A heuristic model for the study of intergenerational ambivalence.* University of Konstanz, Arbeitspapier No. 29.

Luescher, K., and Pillemer, K. 1998. Intergenerational ambivalence: A new approach to the study of parent-child relations in later life. *Journal of Marriage and the Family* 60:413–25.

Mabry, J. B., Takagi, E., and Bengtson, V. L. 2002. *Long term "lousy" relationships: A life course perspective on intergenerational relationships.* Poster session presented at the annual meeting of the Gerontological Society of America, Boston.

McGarry, K., and Schoeni, R. F. 1997. Transfer behavior within the family: Results from the asset and health dynamics study. *Journal of Gerontology* Series B, 52B, Special issues, 82–92.

Merrill, D. M. 1996. Conflict and cooperation among adult siblings during the transition to the role of filial caregiver. *Journal of Social and Personal Relationships* 13:399–413.

Montgomery, R. J., and Kosloski, K. 1994. A longitudinal analysis of nursing home placement for dependent elders cared for by spouses vs. adult children. *Journal of Gerontology: Social Sciences* 49:S62–S74.

Myers, G. C. 1990. Demography of aging. In R. Binstock and L. George (eds.), *Handbook of aging and the social sciences* (3rd ed., pp. 19–44). San Diego, CA: Academic Press.

Myers, G. C., and Nathanson, C. 1982. Aging and the family. *World Health Statistic Quarterly* 35:225–38.

Organization for Economic Co-operation and Development 1996. *Caring for frail elderly people: Policies in evolution.* Social Policy Studies No. 19. Paris: OECD.

Parrott, T. M., and Bengtson, V. L. 1999. The effects of earlier intergenerational affection, normative expectations, and family conflict on contemporary exchange of help and support. *Research on Aging* 21(1):73–105.

Popenoe, D. 1993. American family decline, 1960–1990: A review and appraisal. *Journal of Marriage and the Family* 55:527–55.

Population Reference Bureau 2002. *2002 World Population Data Sheet.* Washington, DC: The Bureau. Retrieved February 2003 from the World Wide Web: http://www.prb.org//Content/ContentGroups/Datasheets/wpds2002.

Pruchno, R. A., Burant, C. J., and Peters, N. D. 1997. Coping strategies of people living in multigenerational households: Effects on well-being. *Psychology and Aging* 23:115–24.

Riley, M. W., and Riley, J. W. 1993. Connections: Kin and cohort. In V. L. Bengtson and W. A. Achenbaum (eds.), *The changing contract across generations* (pp. 169–90). Hawthorne, NY: Aldine de Gruyter.

Riley, M. W., and Riley, J. W. 1996. Generational relations: A future perspective. In T. K. Hareven (ed.), *Aging and generational relations: Life-course and cross-cultural perspectives* (pp. 283–91). Hawthorne, NY: Aldine de Gruyter.

Rossi, A. S., and Rossi, P. H. 1990. *Of human bonding: Parent-child relations across the life course.* Hawthorne, NY: Aldine de Gruyter.

Silverstein, M., and Bengtson, V. L. 1997. Intergenerational solidarity and the structure of adult child-parent relationships in American families. *American Journal of Sociology* 103:429–60.

Silverstein, M., Giarrusso, R., and Bengtson, V. L. 1998. Intergenerational solidarity and the grandparent role. In M. Szinovacz (ed.), *Handbook on grandparenthood* (pp. 144–58). Westport, CT: Greenwood.

Silverstein, M., Parrott, T. M., and Bengtson, V. L. 1995. Factors that predispose middle-aged sons and daughters to provide social support to older parents. *Journal of Marriage and the Family* 57:465–75.

Treas, J. 1995a. Older Americans in the 1990s and beyond. *Population Bulletin* 50:2–46.

Treas, J. 1995b. Commentary: Beanpole or beanstalk? Comments on "The demography of changing intergenerational relations." In V. L. Bengtson, K. W. Schaie, and L. M. Burton (eds.), *Adult intergenerational relations* (pp. 26–29). New York: Springer.

U.S. Bureau of the Census 2000. *International Data Base.* Washington, DC: Author.

U. S. Bureau of the Census 2002. *International Data Base.* Retrieved February 2003 from the World Wide Web: http://blue.census.gov/cgi-bin/ipc/idbagg.

Uhlenberg, P. 1990. How old are you? Age consciousness in American culture— H. P. Chudacoff. *Contemporary Sociology—A Journal of Reviews,* 19(5):669–70.

Uhlenberg, P. 1996. Mutual attraction: Demography and life-course analysis. *Gerontologist* 36:226–29.

United Nations 1999. *The sex and age distribution of the world populations* (1998 revision). New York: Author.

United Nations 2002. *World populations prospects.* New York: Author.

Vinick, B. H. 1978. Remarriage in old age. *Family Coordinator,* October, 359–63.

Wachter, K. W. 1997. Kinship resources for the elderly. *Philosophical transactions of the Royal Society of London.* 352:1811–17.

Wenger, G. C. 1997. Social networks and the prediction of elderly people at risk. *Aging and Mental Health* 1(4):311–20.

White, L. 1992. The effect of parental divorce and remarriage on parental support for adult children. *Journal of Family Issues* 13(2):234–50.

I

Theoretical Perspectives: Intergenerational Social Support in Multiple Contexts

| 2 |

Theories about Families, Organizations, and Social Supports

Eugene Litwak, Merril Silverstein, Vern L. Bengtson,
and Ynez Wilson Hirst

When researchers speak about the role of families in social supports, they often focus their analysis too narrowly. In caring for dependent members, for example, families must work in partnership with formal organizations and other primary groups. Trying to account for what families do without understanding this partnership leads to a misunderstanding of the family's role. In this chapter we will use a theory of organizational effectiveness, the task-specific theory (Messeri, Silverstein, and Litwak, 1993), to examine how this partnership works and under what conditions it works best.

We will suggest that the onset of modern industrial society has caused the traditional kinship unit to delegate some of its activities to a network of primary groups and formal organizations, but that it has retained many of its activities and in all cases works in close partnership with the outside groups (Anderson, 1977; Attias-Donfut and Arber, 2000; Bengtson, 2001; Fischer, 1982; Litwak, 1985; Litwak and Szelenyi, 1969). The notion that the family has "lost its functions" to formal organizations is false; instead, as we will argue, the family has retained all of the family functions in partnership arrangements with formal organizations.

With this framework in place, it is possible to accept statements that the nuclear family household has emerged in modern society as a major factor (Burgess, 1916; Parsons, 1944; Popenoe, 1993) while at the same time acknowledging that larger kinship systems continue to play a powerful role (Bengtson, 2001). Furthermore, it is possible to argue that large formal organizations have taken on activities formerly managed exclusively by the family (Burgess, 1916; Ogburn, 1932; Parsons, 1944; Popenoe, 1993), while rejecting the notion that the family has lost most of its traditional functions (Bengtson, 2001; Litwak, 1985; Litwak and Szelenyi, 1969). It is possible to agree with Weber (1957), Schumpeter (1947), and Parsons (1944) that larger formal organizations have structures that are contradictory to primary groups while also stating that formal organizations and primary groups typically work in partnership to optimally achieve their respective goals (Litwak, 1985; Litwak and Messeri, 1989; Litwak and Szelenyi, 1969). These paradoxes can be unraveled by the "task-specific theory of organizational effectiveness" (Litwak, 1985; Messeri et al., 1993).

Why do we use organizational effectiveness as a major variable? Theories of organizational effectiveness are important in understanding and predicting social behavior because effectiveness is one of the major causal factors motivating social behavior. The importance of organizational effectiveness depends upon other causal elements such as social class, where lack of resources prevents the use of the most effective groups; gender, where norms on male and female behavior prevent or enhance the use of the most effective groups; ethnicity, where social norms such as racism interfere with effectiveness; age, which defines who the caregiver is likely to be, i.e., adult child or parent; and health, where chronic illness makes the most effective design inoperative.

It should also be noted that measures of effectiveness often involve value judgments. This occurs when a situation leads to a conflict in values. For instance, the Catholic Church sees the use of condoms to achieve safe sex as a violation of its religious tenets. It only accepts abstinence and marital monogamy as modes for achieving safe sex, even if these methods are criticized as not likely to stop the spread of AIDS. Health educators often opt for just the opposite priority, that is, reducing the spread of AIDS through the use of condoms even if it means violating religious tenets. Organizational effectiveness theory can indicate what is the most useful form of organization to implement each of these positions, but it cannot state which position should be adopted. That is a value decision that is ultimately based on desirability and not effectiveness.

When organizational effectiveness is considered in conjunction with values and other causal factors, it provides an understanding of the family's role in contemporary society. In this chapter we first describe how notions of organizational effectiveness were used by traditional social theorists to explain the emergence of large formal organizations, the loss of functions leading to the decline of the extended family, and the emergence of the isolated nuclear family household. In the second section of the chapter we summarize empirical evidence showing that traditional family theories are inconsistent with the following two empirical findings: (1) that families work in partnership with large formal organizations in all functional areas and (2) that many primary groups beside the nuclear family are viable in contemporary society. The third section develops the task-specific theory of organizational effectiveness and shows how it accounts for these empirical trends. We then examine other major causal factors, which, in addition to the task-specific theory, facilitate an understanding of the variety of family types in contemporary society. Finally, in the conclusion, the paradoxes raised by the apparent contradiction between empirical data and traditional family theories will be revisited to show how the task-specific theory accounts for them.

TRADITIONAL FAMILY THEORIES AND ORGANIZATIONAL EFFECTIVENESS

There are several reasons to concentrate on organizational effectiveness when looking at the roles of families in social supports. One is that much of the traditional analysis of the family's roles relied on implicit theories of organizational effectiveness. Ogburn (1932) and Burgess (1916) spoke about formal organizations taking over many of the functions of the family, leaving only two: early socialization of the child and adult companionship. It is interesting to note that these arguments are echoed by Popenoe (1993). Implicit in their analysis was the assumption that formal organizations were more effective than primary groups in managing most functions. They never explained, however, why large-scale organizations were more effective, nor did they empirically document that families no longer played substantial roles when formal organizations took over some of their traditional functions. These researchers simply assumed a zero sum game. In other words, if formal organizations increasingly participated in a given function area, then it must mean that families were similarly decreasing their functioning in that area.

Parsons (1944) explicitly introduced group effectiveness as a major causal factor in explaining the emergence of the isolated nuclear family, large formal organizations that carried out traditional family activities, and the resultant declines of the extended family. He did this by drawing on the first version of organizational effectiveness theory, suggested by Weber (1957). Weber argued that the large monocratic bureaucracy was the most effective organization for achieving the majority goals in a modern society because it was better able to develop technical knowledge and resources. Parsons's justification for the survival of the nuclear primary household was very explicit in its focus on group effectiveness. He stated that the family was still the most efficient organization for managing two essential tasks for societal survival: early socialization of children and adult tensions management (Parsons and Bales, 1955). These, the authors argued, were functions that required optimization of emotional ties rather than technical knowledge. According to Parsons, the only form of the family that could simultaneously provide these two functions and exist side by side with the contradictory structures of the monocratic bureaucracy was the isolated nuclear family.

Parsons noted several points of conflict between primary groups such as families and bureaucracies. First, they had conflicting motivational foci. While the family motivated people through internalized commitments of duty and/or love—with priority given to preserving the relationship as an end in itself—formal organizations motivated staff by expedient economic incentives, so that if people did not have technical competence to do their jobs the formal organization put little value on the actual relationships. The contradiction between the two incentives is clearly seen when family norms are used in work situations, i.e., are they favoritism and nepotism or evidence of good parenting?

Second, Parsons suggested that the demands of formal organizations produce conflict with the extended family. The organizational requirement that people be assigned to jobs on the basis of their ability led to demands for differential mobility within the family. The traditional family could not exist with this requirement. The rationale for this conclusion was based on three considerations: (1) that all adult members of a primary group do not have equal ability, (2) that organizations are national and international in scope, and (3) that requirements that people be selected based on their ability could lead to different members of the primary group being assigned to different class positions and result in their living in different geographic areas. Parsons argued that the nuclear family (with only one major breadwinner in the work force) would face few barriers to differential geographic or occupational mobility. By contrast, the traditional extended family, including friends and neighbors, with multiple members in the labor force, would see differential mobility as destructive of their primary group ties and vigorously resist such pressures. Implicit in organizational effectiveness analysis was an eloquent theoretical justification for the traditional family theorist's view that nuclear families would emerge as the dominant family form in modern industrial society.

THE EMPIRICAL REALITY OF PRIMARY GROUP BEHAVIOR IN CONTEMPORARY SOCIETY

The traditional family theorist's view has been seriously questioned by modern empirical research in the following ways:

1. There is very strong evidence that extended families are viable and play exceedingly powerful roles in contemporary society—perhaps even more powerful than nuclear households.

2. There is strong evidence that families have not lost most of their functions, but rather have entered into a partnership with formal organizations in all functional areas.

3. There is strong evidence that the two functions reserved solely for the family by traditional family theorists—early socialization of children and adult tension management—are also managed in partnership with large formal organizations.

4. Finally, there is strong evidence that primary groups other than the family play a critical role.

Extended Kin Structures Are Powerful Factors in Contemporary Industrial Society

The assumption that the nuclear family has emerged as the sole survivor of the extended family structure has been challenged in recent time by Bengtson (2001) and others. Their conclusion that the extended family structure is stronger now than ever is based on two factors. First, people are now living far longer than they did in the past, which provides far greater opportunity for three- and four-generation families to form. Second, these researchers examined longitudinal data from a survey of three-generation families, whom they followed over twenty years, finding that family feelings of kinship solidarity, affection, and exchange of services have remained constantly high despite the vast social changes that have taken place over the same time period. For instance, parents in their later years live in a society with higher divorce rates and more women in the labor force, and a society in which both men and women have more education than their parents did twenty years before. Yet, the parents have continued to maintain a high level of identity and exchange with their adult children, just as their parents had displayed toward them. French researchers Attias-Donfut and Arber (2000), using a large random sample of three-generation families, provided similar evidence for strong kinship ties in France. Kohli, Kunemund, Motel, and Szydlik (2000) provided similar evidence for the strength of kinship systems in Germany.

These contemporary studies expanded on earlier work in gerontology, which showed that in 90 percent of cases kin and spouses, rather than formal organizations, supplied help for older people who were in need (Shanas, 1979). When spouses were not available, adult children predominantly supplied support. In even earlier work, Litwak (1985), in a series of studies in Buffalo, Detroit, New York, and Florida, and Sussman (1965) showed that kin maintain strong contact and exchange services among younger families.

The Family Has Not Lost Its Functions to Large Formal Organizations But Has Gone into Partnership with Them

Perhaps the most explicit contemporary studies dealing with the partnership of formal organizations and the family are Attias-Donfut and

Wolff (2000) and Kohli (1999). The former examined the relationship between support by governmental agencies set up to provide financial resources to families (e.g., pensions for retired older workers) and the amount of money the kinship members provided to each other. These researchers found a positive association, in that the more money older persons received from large governmental agencies the more likely they were to give money to their adult children. Kohli (1999) found the same relationship between government agencies and families in Germany. The thesis of partnership is further supported by the Attias-Donfut and Lapierre (2000) three-generation study in Guadeloupe. The investigators examined the impact of the French government provision of social security and family and health benefits to a preindustrial society. They found that the older people who now have pension money provide money and services to their children, who in turn provide money to their grandchildren.

In addition to the work of family theorists is the body of evidence provided by non–family theorists—specifically, epidemiologists and sociologists of health. Establishing the partnership relation between families and formal organizations in the field of health has been typically arrived at by showing the major role played by the family. The role of formal organizations, such as hospitals and the health care professions, is assumed to be self-evident. A series of remarkable prospective studies, each covering approximately ten years of the respondents' lives, found that families play a central role in reducing mortality (House, and Umberson, 1988). People with the least number of social supports (e.g., unmarried and few kin contacts) have approximately twice the chance of dying at an earlier age as those with strong social supports (Berkman and Breslow, 1983). Litwak and Messeri (1989) explicitly demonstrated the partnership role with formal organizations in their study of national mortality, in which they classified all causes of death by the degree of partnership required to reduce their rates. Further, they showed that being married provided an added measure of protection for individuals the more the disease required nontechnical services. Yet, in almost all instances there was some role played by both the family and formal organizations. In addition to highlighting the partnership relationship, these studies also questioned the loss of family function in the field of health.

In education, it has long been acknowledged that family characteristics are dominant predictors of educational success (Coleman et al., 1966). Blau (1981) examined the details of family socialization that enable families, in partnership with schools, to improve a child's reading and I.Q. scores. Litwak, Meyer, and Hollister (1977) showed how the joint cooperative efforts of families and schools can improve reading scores of children.

Today, it is very difficult to look at any of the functional fields identified by traditional family theorists as being lost to formal organizations without saying that the earlier research is quite simply wrong. The family continues to play a major role in all of these fields.

"Unique" Functions of the Family Are Also Partnered with Formal Organizations

It is important to note the empirical evidence that contradicts the assertions of traditional family theorists that early socialization of children and adult tension management/companionship are exclusively administered by the nuclear family unit. Adult companionship is enhanced by formal organizations that provide situations for optimizing companionship, such as theater, concert, and cruise ship organizations; other travel organizations; and builders of retirement communities whose major goal is to provide companions for free-time leisure activities. Similarly, the appearance on the scene of such resources as child development specialists, day care centers for children, early preschool programs, and pediatric medical specialties suggests a partnership relationship between formal organizations and mothers for the purpose of more effectively accomplishing early socialization of the child.

Friends, Neighbors, Work Friends, and Crisis Support Groups

In order to fully understand the role of the family, it is necessary to examine the reinforcing roles of other primary groups, including friends, neighbors, and semiprimary groups such as medically based social support groups. Katz and Lazarsfeld (1955), in their rediscovery of the primary groups, highlighted the role of different primary groups in different contexts. For instance, they pointed out that primary groups evolved within the very bowels of formal organizations. They cited the early studies by Mayo (Roethlisberger and Dickson, 1949) that showed that work primary groups played an essential role in regulating productivity. They then shifted to combat and showed that combat morale was highly associated with primary group development at the platoon and company level. A whole host of studies followed that showed that primary groups formed by work colleagues and supervisors provided significant social supports to individuals in the work situation (House, 1981; House and Cottington, 1986; LaRocco, House, and French, 1980). These researchers showed that tensions that arose in work environments could affect mental health and cardiovascular diseases and that one of the most effective ways of reducing job stress was having a primary group at work and not simply relying on the family. Starting in the early 1960s Litwak and colleagues, in a series of studies in Buffalo, Detroit, New York, Florida, and Hungary, showed that friends, neighbors, extended kin, and nuclear families played separate roles that were mutually supportive (Fellin and Litwak, 1963; Litwak, 1960a, 1960b, 1985; Litwak and Szelenyi, 1969; Messeri et al., 1993). Messeri et al. (1993), reviewing sixteen studies conducted in various communities and using meta-analysis statistics, powerfully reinforced this point.

In addition to more traditional forms of primary groups, a plethora of nontraditional primary groups has been identified based on the concept of social support groups in the field of health. One of the first was Alcoholics Anonymous, but many others followed, including Narcotics Anonymous, Weight Watchers, Alzheimer's caregiver groups, and AIDS buddy groups. Virtually every disease now has some type of support group. The main thing that characterizes these groups is the assumption that the goals of the group are achieved by the information, instrumental help, and emotional support that members provide to each other based on their everyday experience. It is also important to note that members of these groups are not motivated by economic rewards but by some internalized commitment of affection and duty. While these groups do have some of the attributes of traditional primary groups, they are clearly different in other ways. In that respect, they resemble the new forms of friends, neighbors, and kinship systems that we discuss below.

It is very important to understand the role of friends, neighbors, work friends, and other types of primary groups as providing a network of support for individuals. If these groups were ignored, it might seem that the traditional extended family functions have been completely lost and that they have been taken over by large formal organizations. In fact, what has happened is that the extended family has taken on a new form in which it has retained some key functions but has also gone into partnership with large formal organizations and a host of new primary groups.

TASK-SPECIFIC ORGANIZATIONAL EFFECTIVENESS THEORY AND THE PARTNERSHIP OF FORMAL ORGANIZATIONS AND PRIMARY GROUPS

Because the traditional formulations of family and organizational design do not seem to be adequate to explain the empirical findings, the question becomes: What are the theoretical alternatives? There are several formulations of organizational effectiveness theory used by sociologists. The one presented in this chapter is an expansion of organizational contingency theory that has been referred to as a task-specific approach (Litwak and Messeri, 1989; Messeri et al., 1993). An examination of this approach provides an explanation for the empirical patterning of behavior previously discussed.

Formal Organizations Optimize Tasks Requiring Technical Knowledge

The task-specific theory starts with an analysis of Weber's rationale for the effectiveness of monocratic bureaucracy (Litwak 1985; Litwak and Szelenyi 1969). It accepts Weber's view that the monocratic bureaucracy concentrates technical knowledge far more than the primary group. On the other hand, it rejects the idea that technical knowledge is always more effective than nontechnical knowledge. Furthermore, it rejects the assumption that formal organizations and primary groups are in complete conflict, which suggests that while their structures are in conflict they are mutually dependent upon each other for achieving common goals. The task-specific theory states that organizations and primary groups in partial states of conflict can exist in strong forms through the employment of linkages that permit the entities to coexist (Litwak 1985; Litwak and Meyer 1966; Litwak, Shiroi, Zimmerman, and Bernstein, 1970, ; Litwakand et al., 1977) and through moderation of the structure of the primary groups.

Central to Weber's formulation is his rationale for the monocratic bureaucracy's ability to concentrate technical knowledge, which enables the reader to understand why the primary group is most effective for managing nontechnical tasks. An expansion of Weber's logic that includes a new assumption about nontechnical tasks enables the reader to understand a larger variety of formal organizations, as well as a larger variety of primary groups. A review of Weber's assumptions that compares two extreme organizations, the monocratic bureaucracy and the nuclear family, will make this point clear.

Organizational Dimensions That Optimize Technical Knowledge: Comparing Monocratic Bureaucracies and Nuclear Families

Recruitment of Members on the Basis of Technical Knowledge. Monocratic organizations recruit members on the basis of their technical merit as measured by their educational training, their job experience, and/or their ability to pass an examination. By contrast, the nuclear family recruits members on the basis of birth or through courtship, both of which are heavily based on everyday knowledge.

Limits of Commitment Based on Technical Abilities. The monocratic bureaucracy limits its commitment to its members' technical abilities—that is, they must maintain the technological standards set for the job. If they do not, or if their technological skills are outmoded, they are expected to leave the job. By contrast, the nuclear family has virtually unlimited, lifelong commitments to the relationship as an end in itself. Expulsion is seldom, if ever, made on the basis of technical knowledge. Prototypical of such lifelong commitments are those between parents and children, which are heavily based on biological and legal definitions that have little if anything to do with technical knowledge. When the nuclear family does eliminate someone (e.g., through divorce), it does not typically use the degree of technical knowledge as the basis for expulsion.

Size, Division of Labor, and Degree of Specialization.   A third dimension of monocratic bureaucracy is on-the-job development of technical knowledge through commitment to large size and detailed division of labor. A detailed division of labor permits specialization, which allows staff to spend more time on a given topic by limiting the number of fields they must cover. This enables specialists to increase their technical knowledge in one particular field.

In addition, a detailed division of labor permits taking complex material and breaking it down to its simplest components, thus giving the staff advantages of speed and accuracy. This is typically illustrated by the automobile assembly line. A detailed division of labor also permits the standardization of idiosyncratic elements so that one specialist can handle a larger volume of services. This is illustrated in the typical nursing home, where one person can cook for one hundred if the institution can standardize the menu and the eating time and regulate who eats with whom. These functions of a division of labor are referred to as task simplification.

In comparison, the nuclear family is small, with only two adults and many different activities. It has what Cooley (1955) referred to as diffused relations. Division of labor, generally sex based, creates a general rather than a detailed division, which permits neither developing knowledge through detailed specialization nor greater speed through task simplification.

Motivation by Economic Market Incentives vs. Internalized Duty/Affection. Another dimension of group structure is the way in which groups motivate their members. The monocratic bureaucracy motivates its members in such a way as to preserve technical knowledge. Generally, such bureaucracies insist on emphasizing civil but impersonal relationships, because intense relationships of love or hate can distort objective judgments based on merit. Within that context, the main incentive used by the formal organization is an economic one. By contrast, the nuclear family motivates its members by internalized commitments of duty and/or affection to the relationship as an end in itself.

Importance of Nontechnical Tasks.   To comprehend why formal organizations have not taken over the functions of the primary groups, it is necessary to understand that there are circumstances under which technical knowledge is not always optimal for achieving life's goals. For instance, some services are so simple that individuals with everyday training can do them as well as a highly trained worker. Sometimes nontechnical services can be delivered more quickly than technical ones and speed of delivery is more important than less accessible technical ones. An example of both conditions would be lifting a cigarette out of the hand of an elderly person who has fallen asleep. Highly trained firemen provide no greater efficiency and they are less likely to be available in time to make a difference.

The task-specific theory states that when technical knowledge is no more effective than nontechnical training the primary group structure makes achievement less expensive and faster and motivates people better. This proposition is far from obvious, because the same people will occupy primary group and formal organizational roles. The question that arises is: Why can't people in their formal organizational roles manage nontechnical tasks as well as when they are in their primary group roles? The theoretical explanation lies in the structure of the primary group.

All dimensions of the nuclear family that make it an ineffectual group for managing technical tasks make it superior to formal organizations in managing nontechnical ones (Litwak, 1985). For instance, motivating individuals through internalized commitments of affection and duty will not reduce effectiveness if the task is nontechnical. It would, however, have the advantage over economic incentives by assuring high quality performance even when supervisors are not able to observe behavior. This theoretical formulation would explain the partnership role between formal organizations and primary groups if it could be shown that nontechnical aspects are intrinsic to science and technology and that they exist in all areas of life.

Science and Technology Require Partnership between Primary Groups and Formal Organizations

To address these questions, it is necessary to turn to an analysis of science and technology, a core element in modern industrial society. The theoretical rationale for stating that nontechnical tasks will be with society for the foreseeable future rests on the propositions expressed in the following three subsections.

Science and Technology Simplify as Well as Complicate Activities. Science and technology are focused on making things more effective. This can be done equally well by simplifying tasks so that the ordinary person can do them or by making things more technical so that only highly trained people can do them. In support of this conclusion we offer a brief review of things that have been simplified and given to the family and things that have been made more technical and taken away from the family.

Many things in the past would have been managed by highly trained people in formal organizations that have been simplified so that the ordinary individual with minor training can manage them. These include home testing for pregnancy, deciding on the daily regimen of insulin for patients with diabetes, and the conducting of home dialysis. Home health care is one of the fastest-growing health fields in the United States. Other activities that have been partly turned over to the family by science and technology are the making of home movies with editing capabilities, the taping of television programs, and home projection of rented movies. The development of personal computers, duplicating machines, and fax machines raises the possibility that for many the home will also become the place of work.

At the same time, there are few activities that are now handled at home that science and technology cannot devise ways to manage more effectively by turning them into technical tasks to be handled by a formal organization. For instance, it is now possible through the modern science and technology of cloning for doctors and formal organizations to make women pregnant without spouse, intercourse, or even the need for male sperm. In the past, procreation and the early socialization of children were thought to be functions still left to the family. It is possible that the family's function of monitoring health status and calling for ambulance services in case of an emergency will soon be replaced by a technological pendant that continuously monitors critical life functions and immediately calls for medical backup if any of them fail. It is easy to conceive of future scientific and technological developments that make it possible for formal organizations to provide daily meals and even to create clothes out of disposable materials, so that it will no longer be necessary to do laundry.

Scientific Advances Uncover New Uncertainties Even As They Close Down Old Ones.   The effects of science are not only understood by their capacity to explain what was previously unknown but also by the degree to which science uncovers new areas of the unknown. Exposing these new unknowns often reintroduces uncertainty and the nontechnical. For instance, it was a sociologist who discovered that AIDS was transmitted by sexual intercourse. This elevated the nontechnical tasks of the primary group (socialization of gender roles, safe sex, and courtship behavior) to the highest order of priority in the field of health. The discovery of the role of protease inhibitors to treat AIDS has also led to the discovery that the HIV virus can mutate and lead to a drug-resistant form of the virus. This, in turn, has forced health professionals to consider the primary group's daily routine. The most effective way to avoid drug resistance of the AIDS virus is to write medical regimens around the standardized daily patterns of the primary group, in order to assure that complex medications will be taken in a consistent way. Where individuals' primary group activities have no consistent daily patterns, they must be created before medication can be safely given.

Innovations Produced by Science and Technology Lead to Unanticipated Social Patterns. Yet a third basis for science and technology's stimulation of nontechnical events has to do with the uncertainties that arise from incorporating the new discoveries created by science and technology into social life. Major technological innovations, such as the introduction of the automobile, ultimately have impacts on social behavior that can never be fully anticipated. This leads to much uncertainty and a lack of technical knowledge on how to deal with the social ramifications of these new behaviors. For instance, the introduction of the automobile had a remarkable effect on cities' residential patterns. They changed from housing concentrated in limited areas around the centers of the cities to patterns of suburban sprawl. At the same time, the automobile led to new industries and the expansion of old ones—for example, automobile manufacturing, the tire industry, the steel industry, the oil and gas industries, the proliferation of gas stations, the motel industry, the automobile insurance industry, and the road construction industry. It also led to the development of specialized police units, such as the traffic unit, and the development of laws intended to govern driving.

In addition to these large formal organizational developments, the automobile affected the most intimate family relationships. For example, the car became an important factor in courtship behavior, providing a degree of privacy that previously could only be found in doorways and parks. It permitted extended kin and friends to live at greater geographic distances while still maintaining many kin and friendship exchanges. Consequently, the automobile was important in supporting the development of the modern form of extended family and friendship ties. We advance the hypothesis that it would have been very difficult for society to have anticipated the extent of changes brought about by this invention, and so consequently there were initially no ready social norms or laws that could guide behavior. This uncertainty meant that, initially, technical knowledge could not be developed to manage many tasks. Rather, reality was defined and optimally managed by the primary groups (Katz and Lazarsfeld, 1955).

From the perspective of organizational effectiveness theory, the rationale for why the growth of formal organizations did not eliminate the extended kin structure, as anticipated by traditional family theory, has now been explained. The expansion of technical tasks went along with the expansion of nontechnical ones, with the former requiring formal organizations and the latter requiring primary groups.

Task-Specific Theory: Matching Dimensions of Groups with Dimensions of Tasks

Parsons's central idea, the evolution of the isolated nuclear family household and the destruction of the extended family, is not consistent with the empirical data, which show that extended family ties, as well as other primary group associations, continue to play a powerful role in modern society. What theoretical explanation allows an understanding of this paradox? We will attempt to answer that question.

Modern Technology and the Modified Extended Family Solution.   Litwak and colleagues in a series of articles suggested that modern technology permits a variety of primary group structures that may not have been possible in the past (Fellin and Litwak, 1963; Litwak, 1960a, 1960b, 1960c, 1985; Litwak and Szelenyi, 1969). They suggest that the central underlying dimension for extended-kin families is long-term commitment based on biological and legal norms. Consequently, if kinship ties are to be maintained in the face of differential geographic mobility, they must give up propinquity (i.e., proximity). Science and technology—the telephone, e-mail, the World Wide Web, and fax capabilities—permit extended kin to provide advice, knowledge, and emotional and economic support across geographic distances. The advent of the train, the automobile, and the airplane allow most family members in the United States to reach each other in four hours or less (Litwak and Kulis, 1987). Consequently, despite the geographic dispersion of the family, kin can supply a substantial number of traditional extended family services.

At the same time, it is obvious that many key services have not been liberated from the demands of propinquity. These include such things as cooking meals, cleaning the house, doing the laundry, shopping for food, caring for and socializing children, providing first aid, calling the doctor in an emergency, providing temporary household help to a family member with an acute illness, and all of the other instrumental activities of daily living.

Consequently, the form of the extended family in a modern industrial society will be different from that of the past. First, the contemporary extended family no longer requires a common household or the close proximity of nuclear subunits, because services can be exchanged over geographic distances. Second, the nuclear family is now the chief household unit, managing all immediate household services. What cannot be ignored, however, is the reliance of the nuclear family on the extended family to manage other key services that require more than two adults. This new form of extended kin was called the "modified extended family" (Litwak, 1960a). Traditional family theorists, as well as the general public, focused on the household and assumed that the extended family had faded from existence.

This explanation still does not answer the question of how this kinship system could survive differential occupational mobility, with its implication of differential class culture and status. Actually, the answer was twofold (Litwak, 1960a). First, not all tasks (i.e., services) require a common lifestyle for effective delivery. Kin today can send money to be used by the recipients for any cultural activities they desire without requiring the giver and receiver to have a common lifestyle. Working-class families who provide money to support their child's advanced education, which ultimately leads to the child's rise into the middle class is an obvious illustration.

A question remains, however. If the new extended family structure is limited, in that it cannot provide services that require propinquity or a common lifestyle, does that indicate that the traditional family theorists were partially correct when they stated that there had been a loss of family functions? Our response is no. The supposedly "lost" functions were in fact taken over by the nuclear family household. Within that new context, both groups remain mutually supportive of each other. This is the theoretical rationale for Bengtson's conclusion (2001) that extended family structures have not only survived but may actually be a major source of support for the nuclear family.

The Nuclear Family Solution. At this point, we may ask: How did the structure of the nuclear family enable it to deal with the problems of geographic and occupational mobility? Parsons highlighted the critical dimension as the reduction of the household unit to two adults and dependent children. This smaller nuclear household unit could still manage many of the services of the traditional extended family household (cooking, daily house cleaning, caring for children, etc.), but it could not cover those services that required a larger family unit. That meant that the nuclear family unit was still dependent upon the extended family to cover services such as help with cash flow problems, help during periods of emotional crisis (e.g., conflicts between spouses), and help during health crises (such as a parent suffering an acute illness). Current studies show that these services are retained by the modified extended family and supplied to the nuclear family structure (Attias-Donfut and Wolff 2000; Bengtson 2001; Spilerman, 2000).

The Neighborhood Solution. The relationship of the modified extended family and the nuclear family household does not provide a solution to one set of tasks managed by the traditional extended family—services that require both large group size and proximity. For example, parents who want to know which teacher in the primary grades would be the best match for their child can often get this information from another parent whose child has had that teacher or even from neighborhood families who use the local public education system. Suppose individuals on a block feel that the traffic is too heavy on their street or that the nearby location of a bar endangers their children's welfare. When they seek help to petition city hall for resolutions, it is very likely that their neighbors will be a key support group. In other words, there are many services that in the past would have been managed by extended kin or larger family structures that were characterized by close geographic proximity. In today's society, neighbors, who generally are no longer kin, help each other to manage these activities. Thus, even though they are not kin, their services contribute greatly to the nuclear household. Furthermore, these associations remain in the domain of primary groups. The needs and services have not been completely lost to formal organizations, as traditional family theorists have assumed.

The Friends Solution. In order to further explore this line of reasoning, it is necessary to understand that there are some services that have traditionally required large group size and homogeneity of lifestyles. In the past, these services were covered by the traditional kinship system. These requirements often cannot be managed by the modified extended family nor by the nuclear household or the neighborhood primary group because members of the modified extended family do not necessarily have matching lifestyles, the nuclear family does not have the size, and neighbors may not have the emotional investment in the family necessary to help solve a particular problem. For instance, providing emotional support, knowledge, and instrumental help in locating a job or managing the stresses associated with a job is often best done by work colleagues who are friends (Granovetter, 1974; House, 1981; House and Cottington, 1986; LaRocco et al., 1980). Providing information on how to manage changes in roles, such as from being married to becoming a widow, is probably best handled by women who are widows and who previously shared a relatively common lifestyle (Lopata, 1979), while acquainting a new retiree with the nuances of how to manage his or her changed circumstances may best be handled by other retirees (Litwak, 1985).

The task-specific theory suggests that a network of mutually supportive primary groups—that is, the nuclear household, the modified extended family, friends, and neighbors—has replaced the traditional extended family primary group. What differentiates these primary groups is that each has some unique structural features while still retaining many of the traditional features of a primary group, such as making exchanges on the basis of internalized commitments rather than external economic rewards, dealing with nontechnical tasks, and having diffused rather than highly specialized interpersonal bonds. This theory is completely consistent with the empirical data on social supports, which show that different primary groups provide different services (Messeri et al., 1993), and this is a distinctive characteristic of modern industrial societies (Attias-Donfut and Rozenkier, 1996; Fischer, 1982; Litwak and Szelenyi, 1969).

This analysis goes a long way toward explaining the empirical pattern-ing of primary groups in our society. However, it does not explain new forms of primary groups, such as social support groups organized around illness, or the so-called weak-tie groups.

Connecting the Structure of the Group to Optimal Tasks.   To understand the full range of primary group networks and their partnership roles with formal organizations and each other, it is necessary to make explicit what was implicit in the above analysis, which is the relationship between the structure of a group and the services it can optimally deliver. Two propo-sitions form the core of the task-specific theory: (1) tasks can be analyzed using the same dimensions that characterize the structure of groups and (2) a group can optimally manage a task with a matching structure.

In fact, the above analysis of the differential roles of formal organiza-tions and primary groups matched up the technical attributes of the tasks with the dimensions of group structure that emphasized technical knowl-edge. When the task required technical knowledge, the structure with dimensions that provided technical knowledge was predicted to be most effective. When the task required everyday knowledge, the group dimen-sions that focused on nontechnical knowledge were predicted to be most effective. This analysis did not reveal the full complexity of task-specific theory because it assumed that all dimensions of formal organizations were focused on technical knowledge, while all dimensions of primary groups were focused on nontechnical knowledge. The full complexity of the task-specific theory emerges when an examination is made of the dis-tinction between tasks for different kinds of primary groups and different kinds of formal organizations.

Proximity or Continuous Face-to-Face Contact.   There are two factors that affect services characterized by proximity: (1) the degree to which they have been freed from geographic boundaries by science and technology and (2) the frequency of the services. Where a service has been freed and is infre-quent, it can be managed without proximity. For instance, emotional sup-port, knowledge, advice, and money can be exchanged over geographic distance through modern technology. Also, in situations in which services require face-to-face contact but it is normally a rare event, such as helping someone with household duties after the birth of a baby, modern means of transportation make this a feasible service for most families (Litwak and Kulis, 1987). On the other hand, there are some services that have not been freed by science and technology from geographic propinquity and that must be provided frequently. These are the daily household services such as feed-ing, cooking, toileting, help in walking, and daily straightening of rooms.

Long-Term or Short-Term Commitments.   Tasks can be classified in terms of their requirements for long-term or short-term commitments. Underlying this dimension are two considerations: (1) the amount of future time the individual must commit and (2) the extent of physical and economic resources required to deliver the service. However, the reasoning behind the need for long-term commitment for services requiring extensive physical and economic resources is not obvious. All exchanges involve reciprocity. The primary group's exchanges, unlike market exchanges, are based on internalized commitments. All things being equal, the more resources required to deliver a service, the greater the chances of reciprocity if there is a long-term commitment. Agreeing to provide daily food and other activities of daily living for long periods of time is a long-term commitment. By contrast, reporting to a parent that his or her infant has wandered into the street, reporting that a neighbor's house is on fire, or providing emergency first aid requires only short-term commitments. These acts, once performed, have no future obligations and involve so few resources that they can be easily repaid.

Homogeneous or Heterogeneous Lifestyles.   Some tasks can best be managed by those with common lifestyles. As indicated above, advice on how to manage new roles, such as those of widowhood, retirement, or marriage, are best given by individuals who have had experience in these new roles. On the other hand, some tasks require different lifestyles, such as providing household help for older people. This task is typically best managed by helpers who are younger and healthier. Then, again, some tasks can be carried out by either those with a common or different lifestyle— for example, providing money to meet a cash flow problem.

Size and Multiplexity.   Some services and tasks are best managed by small units rather than large ones and involve diffused relations rather than specialized ones. There are two underlying considerations with regard to size: (1) when the nature of the task provides no great advantages for a detailed division of labor, then diffused relations provide shorter and more flexible lines of communication; and (2) where the costs of coordinating a task are very small, then large groups have advantages over small groups. With many of the activities of daily living, such as making the beds, doing the laundry, cooking, shopping, and bathing, little is gained from a detailed division of labor, and thus attempts at specialization can actually lead to slower and more inflexible service. In contrast, a task that benefits from large size, because the costs of coordination are minimal, is dealing with a cash flow problem by borrowing money. In other words, the larger the kin network, the greater the chance of success. Without going into all the dimensions of the group, it becomes apparent that each dimension of group structure can be used to classify services, as well. To state that a group must match the dimensions of the task does not mean that there must be a simple one-to-one correspondence, but rather that the task probably requires matching bundles of dimensions (Litwak, 1985). Considering the dimensions independently can be highly deceptive.

The idea of classifying tasks by dimensions of groups is novel to the task-specific model. Establishing the principle of matching is also novel and critical because it enables the theorist to identify the solution that is organizationally most effective. The concept permits the social analyst to examine any primary group or formal organization, no matter what its characteristics, and predict which types of tasks it can optimally manage. It is this proposition that can be used to help explain the roles of all of the new forms of primary groups, as well as the alternative types of formal organizations, that exist in our society (Litwak, 1978, 1985).

DIVERSITY OF PRIMARY GROUPS AND EFFECTS VARIABLES OTHER THAN ORGANIZATIONAL DESIGN

While it is nice to speak about modal types such as the modified extended family, it is necessary to understand empirically that there is a range of extended family groups, a range of nuclear family households, and a range of formal organizations (Litwak, 1978, 1985; Silverstein and Bengtson, 1997). Departures from the modal types partly involve complexities of task-specific theory that have not been discussed (Litwak, 1985). More often, they also involve the intrusion of other causal factors such as economic status, health status, ethnic status, gender status, or age status.

Diversity from Modal Type

The analysis of group structures has assumed that science and technology lead to either technical tasks or nontechnical tasks, while in actuality science and technology may lead to any number of combinations of technical and nontechnical tasks. For instance, Litwak and Messeri (1989) showed empirically that health tasks can be classified by various degrees of technical and nontechnical tasks, which means that the importance of the primary group in reducing mortality in its partnership with health professionals also varies. Equally important, the combination of nontechnical and technical requirements can lead to a range of organizational structures (Litwak, 1978, 1985).

Paradoxically, some of these formal structures are consistent with the traditional kinship theories. For instance, science and technology can create organizations that require very little capital investment and are very labor intensive, in which the technical knowledge can be taught through apprenticeship training and the knowledge base is at a sufficiently low level that there is a good chance of staffing within a small labor pool. What is being described are family businesses such as vegetable markets, cleaning establishments, and some forms of plastics manufacturing. Evidence shows that small businesses continue to flourish now as they did in the past. It is this type of occupational niche that permits first-generation immigrants who have an education but who are not familiar with the language and customs of American society to succeed in small businesses (Portes, 1995).

Another factor to be taken into account in trying to understand the multiplicity of forms of kinship is the assumption of "perfect socialization." The requirement that the nuclear family take on a semiautonomous household role assumes that children and parents are socialized to understand the differences between semiautonomy and complete autonomy. But when children and parents have become extremely alienated from one another, some may adopt the isolated nuclear orientation. Litwak (1985), in a study of older people and their younger helpers, found, for instance, that approximately 20 percent of the older generation and 14 percent of the younger population helpers held to an isolated nuclear family norm, 8 percent of the older and 19 percent of the younger held to traditional family norms, and the majority (71 percent of the older and 64 percent of the younger) held a modified extended family orientation. Similarly, Bengtson (2001) found that approximately 70 percent of his population had very strong extended family identities.

Interaction of Task-Specific Theories and Other Causal Variables

The impact of other causal variables on organizational effectiveness also leads to a range of primary group types. For instance, Wilson (1987) and Wallace, Fullilove, and Wallace (1992) suggested that social class can lead to the breakup of primary groups (single-parent families and disorganized neighborhoods) among the truly disadvantaged. Young and Willmott (1957), Allan (1979), Litwak (1985), and Attias-Donfut and Rozenkier (1996) suggested that unskilled but working poor tend to have kinship structures resembling the traditional kinship system—that is, the kin are often also neighbors, friends, and work friends. The rationale behind this is that unskilled laborers do not have the same incentives for differential mobility, while they have greater incentives for propinquity because of their low economic status (Litwak, 1985; Litwak and Longino, 1987).

When social class and health have been introduced simultaneously as causal factors, it has led to the view that the modified extended family will have to coalesce geographically when older people become single or sick and require help with the instrumental activities of daily living (Litwak and Longino, 1987; Silverstein and Litwak, 1993). At the same time, the basic reason for kinship dispersal—that is, occupational demands—no longer holds true for retirees. Putney and Bengtson (2001) suggested that requirements for kinship coalescing arise because of more years given to education and delays in marriage, both of which leave adult children in the households of their parents for an extended period of time. This same reasoning could also explain various other times when the modified extended family coalesces. If younger people require help because of unemployment, chronic illness, or a desire to go back to college, they might solve their economic problems by moving in with their parents.

Studies on caregiving have made clear that gender is also a significant factor in defining primary groups. Traditional gender roles have dictated a sex-based division of labor with women in charge of family household functions and men as the main economic providers. Within this general category men have been responsible for some household roles, such as managing minor repairs in the house, mowing the lawn, and maintaining the car, while women have played an increasing role as economic providers. The distinctive roles have had significant impact on the way primary groups are structured and on the determination of who within them is most likely to provide leadership. Studies in the field of health have revealed that women are more likely to see themselves as caregivers (Umberson et al., 1996), are more likely to be caregivers (Attias-Donfut and Rozenkier, 1996), have more knowledge about health issues (Umberson, 1992), are more likely to see doctors, (Verbrugge, 1999), are more likely to see themselves as ill (ibid.), are more likely to be discriminated against by doctors (ibid.), and live longer then men (ibid.). The task-specific theory states that kin are the optimum primary group for managing everyday household services when the nuclear family becomes incapacitated, because these services require long-term commitment. At the same time, gender considerations suggest that women are often the best individuals to deliver these services. The confluence of these two causal considerations has been used to explain why it is that the frail elderly who have only male children are more likely to enter nursing homes at an earlier age (Townsend, 1965), why widowed women are more likely to live with adult children than widowed men (Attias-Donfut and Rozenkier, 1996; Lopata, 1979), and why marriage is likely to reduce morality rates more for men than for women (Berkman and Breslow, 1983; Litwak and Messeri, 1989).

This leads to still another paradox that has not as yet been fully explored by family theorists. If one examines the literature on health, it can be seen that marital status is strongly related to rates of morbidity and mortality (House et al., 1988). It is very possible that the larger society may not as yet be aware of the relationship between marital status, mortality, and morbidity (Waite, 1995). Once individuals become aware of the health virtues related to the marital role, another shift in social norms might take place in which marriage is again more highly valued (Litwak 1985; Litwak and Figueira, 1968). The rising demand of some gays and lesbians that they be given the right to marital status may be a forerunner of the larger society's feelings. Gays and lesbians have been exposed more clearly than the rest of the population to the virtue of marital status in caring for chronically ill partners.

BALANCING FORCES OF CONFLICTS AND COHESION

The analysis of primary groups in this chapter has concentrated on factors that promote cohesion despite the evidence that conflicts exist within these groups. The most public evidence of family conflict can be seen in the high rate of divorce in our society. Bengtson (2001) viewed family conflict as a critical problem in the study of kinship systems, as well. The task-specific theory provides a framework for understanding which forms of conflict are generated by the demands of organizational effectiveness and which by other variables. Any group that has internalized norms of affection and/or duty as the major mode of motivation must also consider dislike or hatred the opposite end of the same emotional continuum. This latter motivation can clearly work against the forces of organizational effectiveness that encourage family stability. For instance, the wife who dislikes her husband might carefully weigh ending a marriage against the emotional and effectiveness features of marriage, such as socialization of children, economic security, and status attainment.

In addition, demands for differential class status and geographic regions can affect various aspects of cultural and social lifestyles. These aspects can range from tastes in music, books, and theater, to forms of dress, speech patterns, food tastes, political views, health practices, housing preferences, and occupational aspirations for children. Stating that such differences need not rupture family ties because of the benefits of supportive services does not, unfortunately, remove these sources of friction, which can explode into open conflict if the mechanisms designed to bridge such conflicts work imperfectly. The importance of a task-specific framework is that it can highlight situations in which conflicts will inevitably exist. In so doing, the task-specific theory reveals the fault lines around which social dissension is likely to arise. Given the imperfect nature of socialization, the imperfect utilization of social mechanisms for bridging conflicts, and the intrusion of causal factors other than organizational effectiveness, a certain amount of conflict is guaranteed. What

Bengtson's observations make clear is that the task-specific theory should give greater attention to the likely failure of bridging mechanisms that deal with inevitable conflict, such as class differences, gender role ambiguity, and the use of formal organizations to substitute for the primary groups.

CONCLUSION

The answers to the paradoxes raised at the beginning of this chapter can now be addressed. It is possible to say that the nuclear family has replaced the extended family as the principal household unit, while at the same time stating that the extended family continues to exist in a stronger form as a nonhousehold structure. The task-specific theory argues that the extended · family continues to exist because (1) modern science and technology have made it possible for kin to exchange key services over large geographic distances and (2) these services contribute substantially to the well-being of the nuclear family household that has limited adult resources. Recognizing the limited adult resources of the nuclear family helps, in turn, to explain the nuclear family's increasing fragility (e.g., the rising rate of divorce and unmarried individuals), even as the evidence indicates extended kinship structures remain strong and stable.

At the same time, the task-specific theory also suggests that the extended family structure cannot fully substitute for the nuclear family structure (Messeri et al., 1993). The organizational effectiveness aspect of this theory suggests that there should be continuous, long-term pressure to stabilize divorce rates and/or to increase remarriage rates. Such pressure, though, depends upon society's recognition of the benefits of marriage, which so far do not seem to have not been widely recognized.

Another paradox is that the emergence of large formal organizations to manage family tasks has not resulted in the loss of family functions as predicted by traditional family theorists. Task-specific theory provides the rationale for unraveling this paradox. It argues that the logic of science and technology indicates that both technical and nontechnical resources are necessary to effectively achieve most goals in a modern industrialized society. The formal organization is optimal for managing technical tasks, and primary groups are optimal for managing nontechnical ones. Consequently, the effective management of most tasks requires a partnership between formal organizations and primary groups. That explains why, in most areas of life in contemporary society (be it health, education, work, leisure, safety, or religion), there is strong evidence of both primary group and formal organization participation. Furthermore, the logic of science and technology suggests that it will be this way for the foreseeable future.

A final paradox arises from the fact that formal organizations and primary groups have contradictory structures, which seem to negate the possibility that both can exist in society in a strong form (Schumpeter, 1947; Weber, 1957; Wirth, 1938). Yet, as just indicated, the empirical data show that both structures do exist in strong forms and in close partnership arrangements. The task-specific theory addresses this paradox by first showing that the conflicts between primary groups and bureaucratic organizations are muted by their dependence upon each other to achieve their respective goals. Task-specific theory also suggests that this intermediate state of conflict is further muted by the changes in structure of the traditional extended family structure. Finally, the theory posits the development of a "balance theory" of linkages between formal organizations and primary groups that can reduce conflict to the point where it is possible for the two types of structures to exist side by side, in spite of their real or apparent conflicts (Litwak et al., 1970, 1977).

The task-specific theory is an organizational effectiveness conception. To really understand the role of the family in contemporary life, however, it is necessary to consider this theory in conjunction with other causal variables, such as health status, class position, gender, and ethnicity. The task-specific theory can, for instance, predict when the modified extended family will move from geographically distant locations to ones with close proximity, depending upon the state of health or economic conditions of its members.

A consideration of the task-specific theory suggests that traditional family theory needs to develop a new way to define the family. Focusing on the isolated nuclear family, with the assumptions that kinship systems have disappeared and formal organizations have taken over most family functions, now seems inappropriate. To understand the role of the family in modern society, theorists should consider the partnership role between formal organizations and networks of supportive primary groups.

REFERENCES

Allan, G. A. 1979. *A sociology of kinship and friendship*. London: Allan and Unwin.
Anderson, M. 1977. The impact on the family relationships of the elderly of changes since Victorian times in government income maintenance provisions. In E. Shanas and M. B. Sussman (eds.), *Family, bureaucracy, and the elderly* (pp. 36–59). Durham, NC: Duke University Press.
Attias-Donfut, C., and Arber, S. 2000. Equity and solidarity across the generations. In S. Arber and C. Attias-Donfut (eds.), *The myth of generational conflict* (pp. 1–21). London: Routledge.
Attias-Donfut, C., and Lapierre, N. A. 2000. The welfare family: Three generations in Guadeloupean society, the history of the family. *International Quarterly* 5(30):329–46.

Attias-Donfut, C., and Rozenkier A. 1996. The lineage-structure social networks of older people in France. In H. Litwin (ed.), *The social networks of older people: A cross-national analysis* (pp. 31–53). London: Praeger.

Attias-Donfut, C., and Wolff, F.-C. 2000. Complementarity between private and public transfers. In S. Arber and C. Attias-Donfut (eds.), *The myth of generational conflict: The family and state in aging societies* (pp. 47–68). London: Routledge.

Bengtson, V. L. 2001. Beyond the nuclear family: The increasing importance of multigenerational bonds, The 1998 Burgess Award Lecture, *Journal of Marriage and the Family* 63:1–15.

Bengtson, V. L., Biblarz, T. Clarke, E. Giarrusso, R., Roberts, R. Richlin-Klonsky, J. and Silverstein, M. 2000. Intergenerational relationships and aging: Families, cohorts, and social change. In J. M. Clair and R. M. Allman (eds.), *The gerontological prism: Developing interdisciplinary bridges* (pp. 115–47). Amityville, NY: Baywood.

Berkman, L. F. and Breslow, L. M. 1983. *Health and ways of living: The Alameda county study*. New York: Oxford University Press.

Blau, Z. M. 1981. *Black children/white children: Competence, socialization, and social structure*. New York: Free Press.

Burgess, E. W. 1916. *The function of socialization in social evolution*. Chicago: University of Chicago Press.

Coleman, J., Campbell, E. Q., Hobson, C. J., McPartland, J. Mood, A. M., Weinfeld, F. D., and York, R. L. 1966. *Equality of educational opportunity*. Washington, DC: U.S. Government Printing Office.

Cooley, C. H. 1955. Primary groups. In P. Hare, E. F. Borgatta, and R. F. Bales (eds.), *Small Groups*. New York: Alfred A. Knopf.

Fellin, P., and Litwak, E. 1963. Neighborhood cohesion under conditions of mobility. *American Sociological Review*.

Fischer, C. S. 1982. *To dwell among friends*. Chicago: University of Chicago Press.

Granovetter, M. S. 1974. *Getting a job*. Cambridge, MA: Harvard University Press.

House, J. S. 1981. *Work stress and social support*. Reading, MA: Addison Wesley.

House, J. S., and Cottington, E. M. 1986. Health and the work place. In L. H. Aiken and D. Mechanic (eds.), *Applications of social science to clinical medicine and health policy* (pp. 392–416). New Brunswick, NJ: Rutgers University Press.

House, J. S., Landis, K. R., and Umberson, D. 1988. Social relationships and health. *Science* 241:540–45.

Katz, E., and Lazarsfeld, P. F. 1955. *Personal influence*. Glencoe, IL: Free Press.

Kohli, M. 1999. Private and public transfers between generations: Linking the family and the state. *European Societies* (pp. 81–104). London: Routledge.

Kohli, M., Kunemund, H., Motel, A., and Szydlik, M. 2000. Families apart? Intergenerational transfers in East and West Germany. In S. Arber and C. Attias-Donfut (eds.), *The myth of generational conflict* (pp. 88–99). London: Routledge.

LaRocco, J. M., House, J. S., and French, J. R. P., Jr. 1980. Social support, occupational stress, and health. *Journal of Health and Social Behavior* 21:202–18.

Litwak, E. 1960a. Occupational mobility and extended family cohesion. *American Sociological Review*, 25.

———. 1960b. Geographic mobility and extended family cohesion. *American Sociological Review*, 25.

_____. 1960c. Reference group therapy, bureaucratic career and neighborhood primary group cohesion. *Sociometry* 23.

_____. 1978. Organizational constructs and mega bureaucracy. In R. C. Sarri and Y. H. Hasenfeld (eds.), *The management of human services*. New York: Columbia University Press.

_____. 1985. *Helping the elderly: Complementary roles of informal networks and formal systems*. New York: Guilford.

Litwak, E., and Figueira, J. 1968. Technological innovation and theoretical functions of primary groups and bureaucratic structures. *American Journal of Sociology* 73:468–81.

Litwak, E., and Kulis, S. 1987. Technology, proximity and measures of kin support. *Journal of Marriage and the Family* 49:649–61.

Litwak, E., and Longino, C. 1987. Migration patterns among the elderly: A developmental perspective. *Gerontologist* 27(30):266–72.

Litwak, E., and Messeri, P. 1989. Organizational theory, social supports, and mortality rates: A theoretical convergence. *American Sociological Review* 54:49–66.

Litwak, E., and Meyer, H. 1966. Balance theory of coordination between bureaucratic organizations and community primary groups. *Administrative Science Quarterly*.

Litwak, E., Meyer, H. J., and Hollister, C. D. 1977. The Role of linkage mechanisms between bureaucracies and families: Education and health as empirical cases in point. In R. J. Lievert and A. W. Immershein (eds.), *Power, paradigms, and community research* (pp. 121–52). Beverly Hills, CA: Sage.

Litwak, E., Shiroi, E., Zimmerman, L., and Bernstein, J. 1970. Community participation in bureaucratic organizations: Principles and strategies. *Interchange* 1(4).

Litwak, E., and Szelenyi, I. 1969. Different primary group structures and their functions: Kin, neighbors, and friends. *American Sociological Review*.

Lopata, H. 1979. *Women as widows*. New York: Elsevier.

Messeri, P., Silverstein, M. and Litwak, E. 1993. Choosing optimal support groups: Review and reformulation. *Journal of Health and Social Behavior* 34(20):122–37.

Ogburn, W. F. (1932). The family and its functions. In W. F. Ogburn (ed.), *Recent social trends*. New York: McGraw Hill.

Parsons, T. 1944. The social structure of the family. In R. N Anshen (ed.), *The family: Its function and destiny* (pp. 173–201). New York: Harper.

Parsons, T., and Bales, R. F. 1955. *Family, socialization, and interaction process*. Glencoe: Free Press.

Popenoe, D. 1993. American family decline, 1960–1990: A review and appraisal. *Journal of Marriage and the Family* 55:527–55.

Portes, A. 1995. Economic sociology and the sociology of immigration: A conceptual overview. In A. Portes (ed.), *The economic sociology of immigration* (pp. 1–41). New York: Russell Sage Foundation.

Putney, N., and Bengtson, V. 2001. Women's midlife development: Families, intergenerational relationships and kinkeeping (unpublished manuscript). Andrus Center, University of California.

Roethlisberger, F. J. and Dickson, W. J., with assistance of H. A. Wright. 1949. *Management and the worker*. Cambridge, MA: Harvard University Press.

Schumpeter, J. A. 1947. *Capitalism, socialism, and democracy* (2nd ed.). New York: Harper.

Shanas, E. 1979. Social myth as hypothesis: The case of the family relations of old people. *Gerontologist* 19:3–9.

Silverstein, M., and Bengtson, V. L. 1997. Intergenerational solidarity and the structure of adult child-parent relationships in American families. *American Journal of Sociology* 103:429–60.

Silverstein, M., and Litwak, E. 1993. A task-specific typology of intergenerational family structure in later life. *Gerontologist* 33 (20:258–64.

Spilerman, S. 2000. A wealth and stratification process. *Annual Reviews of Sociology* 26:497–524

Sussman, M. B. 1965. The relationship between adult children and their parents in the United States. In E. Shanas and G. Streib (eds.), *Social structure and the family: Generational relations* (pp. 62–93). Englewood Cliffs, NJ: Prentice-Hall.

Townsend, P. 1965. The effects of family structure on the likelihood of admission to an institution in old age: The application of a general theory. In E. Shanas and G. Streib (eds.), *Social structure and the family: Generational relations* (pp. 163–87). Englewood Cliffs, NJ: Prentice-Hall.

Umberson, D. 1992. Gender, marital status and the social control of health behavior. *Social Science and Medicine* 34(80:907–17.

Umberson, D., Chen, M. D., House, J. S., Hopkins, K., and Slaten, E. 1996. The effect of social relationships on psychological well-being: Are men and women really so different? *American Sociological Review*, 61:837–57.

Verbrugge, L. M. 1999. Pathways of health and death. In K. Charmaz and S. Paterniti (eds.), *Society, social context, and self* (pp. 377–94). Los Angeles: Roxbury.

Wallace, R., M. Fullilove, and Wallace, D. 1992. Family systems and deurbanization: Implications for substance abuse. In J. Lowinson, P. Rluiz, and R. Millman (eds.), *Substance abuse, a comprehensive textbook* (pp. 944–55). Baltimore, MD: Williams and Wilkins.

Waite, L. 1995. Does marriage matter? *Demography* 32:483-507.

Weber, M. 1957. Max Weber: The theory of social and economic organizations (A. M. Henderson and T. Parsons (eds.), pp. 328–41). New York: Oxford University Press.

Wilson, W. J. 1987. *The truly disadvantaged: The inner city, the underclass, and public policy*. Chicago: University of Chicago Press.

Wirth, L. 1938. Urbanism as a way of life. *American Journal of Sociology* 64:8–20.

Young, M. and Willmott, P. 1957. *Family and kinship in East London*. London: Routledge and Kegan Paul.

| 3 |

From Family Groups to Personal Communities

Social Capital and Social Change in the Family Life of Older Adults

Chris Phillipson

Of course, for many people who grew up in the '70s, childhood was spent between parents, rather than with them. If parents didn't actually divorce, they certainly thought about it, often out loud, and sometimes requested their children's advice. I've heard horror stories about Christmas spent in airports, scenes at high school graduations, photo albums with one parent scissored out. I have heard so many of these stories that they are no longer remarkable—in fact, they have stopped being stories at all and have turned into cliches, and the more predictable the worse they are: the father remarries a witch who dislikes his children and turns him against them; the mother remarries a brute who likes her daughter too much. But any cliche has a fact for a heart, and the fact is that marriages, like political alliances, broke up all of this country in the 1970s. (Berne, 1997, p. 9)

This quotation from the American author Suzanne Berne's (1997) novel *A Crime in the Neighbourhood* reflects a common strand of contemporary thinking about personal relationships. From a haven of security, family life has become a dystopia for the twenty-first century: marriage, rather than for life, is increasingly viewed as an interlude before moving on to other social relationships. High divorce rates, the popularity of living alone (or going "solo"), and the dramatic growth of cohabitation are taken as key indicators of the challenge to traditional social relationships. In contrast, sociologists have challenged some of the more pessimistic forecasts about the future of family relations. What David Morgan (1996) defines as "family practices" may be changing, but the reality is more complex than one of abandonment of the family as an institution. Bonds may be loosening from one angle, but creating more options (and more potential partners) from another (Riley and Riley, 1993). More complex relationships (exemplified in the term "reconstituted families") may suggest uncertainty from one perspective, but represent a widening of choice from other points of view.

This chapter considers some of the issues running through current debates about the family life of older people. The argument developed will follow four main paths: First, the chapter will provide an interpretation of perspectives from social theory about changing family practices; second, as a means of clarifying issues relating to family practices and family support, a distinction will be drawn between generational relationships on the one side, and social networks on the other; third, the chapter will explore arguments relating to the role of social capital in the creation of social ties; fourth, the chapter will consider issues concerning the role of the state and the emergence of what is termed "global family relationships."

This first section discusses the main currents running through research on aging and family relationships, summarizing four main traditions: (a) the "isolated" nuclear family, (b) the extended family, (c) families and generations, and (d) families as personal communities. The argument developed is that these currents represent distinctive phases in the study of family life in old age, with a gradual widening in the range of relationships viewed as important to the lives of older people.

FAMILY CHANGE AND SOCIAL THEORY

Historically, a defining issue for social gerontology has been that of reconciling family change on the one hand, with family support on the other. Following in the tradition of Weber and Durkheim, and consolidated by Talcott Parsons (1943), social change (notably bureaucratization and industrialization) is seen to influence family life in a variety of ways (Cheal, 1999). As developed by Parsons, this led to the view that the nuclear family had become "structurally isolated," at least in the sense that individuals' responsibilities in adulthood were to their family of procreation first, and only then to parents, siblings, and other relatives (Allan and Crow, 2001). This argument found a parallel in theorists of urban society such as Louis Wirth (1938), who emphasized the emergence of a *Gemeinschaftlich* society of impersonal and instrumental social ties. According to this model, family networks were at best vulnerable to, and at worst pulled apart by, the rootlessness and anomie pervading modern urban life.

As an organizing principle for kinship practices, the Parsonian view was almost certainly correct (at least as regards Western kinship systems). However, its additional importance was in setting a challenge for gerontology, in its crucial phase of expansion during the 1950s and 1960s, to demonstrate the ways in which "structural isolation" could be more properly understood as an "ideal type" from which arose numerous qualifications and exceptions. Moreover, once the emphasis on family coresidence was dropped, sociologists could begin to ask interesting and practical questions about the degree to which wider family ties could be sustained in advanced industrial societies. Historical demographers such as Peter Laslett (1965), for example, in his pioneering study *The World We Have Lost,* had showed decisively that the nuclear family form (contrary to the argument from Talcott Parsons) had been dominant (in Western Europe) at least since the seventeenth century. As a result, the emphasis in research became that of documenting and describing the range of family ties maintained in the absence of coresidence, and in the context of geographical and subsequently social mobility.

The extent of such ties led researchers in the United States such as Marvin Sussman (1965) to emphasize the existence of "an extended family system," one that was "highly integrated within a network of social relationships and mutual assistance, operat(ing) along bilateral kin lines and vertically over several generations" (ibid.:63). Eugene Litwak (1960) developed the idea of the "modified extended family," which allowed nuclear families to develop coalitions to exchange services with each other (see Litwak, Silverstein, Bengtson, and Hirst, Chapter 2 in this volume). In Britain, the community studies tradition demonstrated the different ways in which groups of kin—working class and middle class—exchanged support in times of crisis and through different stages of the life course. Graham Allan (1996) noted from his review of this research, the degree to which in traditional working-class communities "kinship support was an unremarkable largely taken-for-granted feature of people's routine activities" (ibid.:29). British studies of middle-class couples by Bell (1968), and of a middle-class community by Willmott and Young (1960), also confirmed evidence from the United States and elsewhere, that occupational mobility did not impede the exchange of financial and other forms of assistance.

Much of this research concerned documenting exchanges across generations, even if the idea of "generations" was loosely and imprecisely defined. Sussman (1965) in the United States in the early 1950s, and Bell (1968) in England in the mid-1960s, showed how middle-class parents channeled aid to their children as a way of ensuring that lifestyles secured by one generation were passed to the next. And the studies by Young and Willmott (1957) and Townsend (1957) in Bethnal Green (London) illustrated generational support and exchange, in these instances built around the presence of "Mum" as a social and moral compass point (Phillipson, Bernard, Phillips, and Ogg, 2001). The message from this research seemed to be that despite the pressures involved in securing work and bringing up children, "strong ties of family" continued to provide support or "partial aid" to use Litwak's (1960) term, to groups such as older people. Urbanization (contrary to at least some of those from the Chicago School) did not appear hostile to family ties, which continued to thrive in some form or another.

It is relevant to note, however, a more "subversive" element in the expanding literature on family relationships. An aspect of this was captured by Streib and Thompson in their essay "The Older Person in a Family Context," published in 1960. These authors highlighted a number of studies demonstrating that the presence of children and grandchildren may not have a positive effect on the morale and adjustment of older people. Streib and Thompson noted studies reporting that "the level of morale is the same for those persons having no children and for those who see their children often and that the relationship holds for both high and low-status categories. . . . Moreover, among high-status older persons there is a tendency for morale to be higher among those persons who see their children and other relatives *less* frequently" (ibid.:463; emphasis in original). In their own study at Cornell, Streib and Thompson certainly found evidence for the importance of ties between retired respondents and their children and grandchildren, and the emphasis that older people placed on the importance of younger generations maintaining contact. On the other hand, the researchers also noted that "the kind of contact which the older person feels should be maintained is strictly of the "hands-off" variety. . . . Independence and non-interference [is] stressed as the key to successful inter-generational relationships" (ibid.:478).

The possible limits to assisting older people were brought out in a California study conducted in the early 1950s, and which found: "Two-thirds of the children, in spite of their ability to help, are ready for others to assume the responsibility for part or all of the support of their parents" (ibid.:481). This was an interesting finding in the context of a society with a weak welfare state, but it indicated the potential limits to support across generations. From a historical point of view, the evidence from countries such as France, the United States, and Britain is that parents were expected to maintain independence and autonomy for as long as possible (Haber and Gratton, 1993; Stearns, 1974; Thane, 2000). The desired state was subsequently codified in the phrase "intimacy at a distance" (Rosenmayr and Kockeis, 1963) although the implications of this phrase for wider issues of intergenerational solidarity have still to be fully explored.

FAMILIES AS GENERATIONS

Nonetheless, the idea of generations taking active responsibility for caring for each other was to become an important theme within gerontological research. A variety of studies in France, the United States, Germany, Britain, and elsewhere highlighted the extent to which intergenerational flows—downwards as well as upwards—were characteristic still of advanced capitalist societies (Arber and Attias-Donfut, 2000; Bengtson and Achenbaum, 1993; Walker, 1996). Contrary to predictions of conflict between "welfare generations" (a major theme in neoliberal and conservative thought in the 1980s and early 1990s) generations appeared to be maintaining their commitment to each other, through what Kohli and his coresearchers (2000) referred to as "multi-dimensional" forms of exchange. Attias-Donfut and Wolff (2000b) in France demonstrated the role of the "pivot" (middle-aged) generation in providing economic support to young people on the threshold to adulthood. Importantly, these researchers demonstrated the way in which public transfers reinforced rather than weakened family solidarities (see also Kunemund and Rein, 1999). This interweaving of the public and the private is presented as follows:

> Within the life course, individuals begin by receiving support from their mid-life parents which they in turn indirectly repay in their economically active years through their provision of pensions. During this period they also provide support to their adult children and receive private transfers from their elderly parents who in turn benefit from care as they enter later life. (Attias-Donfut and Wolff, 2000b, p. 65)

Longitudinal research reported by Bengtson, Giarrusso, Silverstein, and Wang, (2000) tracked feelings of emotional closeness and support across generations. The former they find as staying stable over a period of nearly two decades, with the maintenance of strong levels of affectual solidarity across generations. This is also reflected in intergenerational support, with adult children providing help to both mothers and fathers, although with the interesting findings that "the amount of support provided to mothers and fathers by adult children is higher when intergenerational affect is high. Further the amount of support provided to mothers is highest when mothers have greater need due to health problems" (ibid.:6).

The demographic shift toward a "beanpole" family structure (Bengtson, Rosenthal, and Burton, 1990) has also raised issues about the role of older adults as grandparents. Thompson (1999) views grandparenting as a distinctively modern experience: "In the past, because they died earlier, two-thirds of children grew up without any significant memory of a grandparent" (ibid.:476). Contrast this with the findings of the French study by Attias-Donfut and Wolff (2000a), where among the middle pivot generation: "Two out of three give care (i.e., spend time with their grand-children in the absence of the parents) whether on a regular basis or occa-sionally during the entire year and also often during vacations" (ibid.:35). A British survey of grandparents (conducted in 2000) found 36 percent reporting that on average they spend more than twenty-one hours a week looking after their grandchildren; more than one-quarter said they spent in excess of twenty-six hours (*Guardian,* 2000). Meredith Minkler's (Min-kler and Estes, 1999) research in the United States highlighted the dramatic rise in grandparenting care through the 1980s and 1990s, with more than one in ten grandparents having primary responsibility for raising a grand-child at some point, with this care often lasting for several years.

These findings may also reflect the shift in the resources and prospects of different generations. Bengtson et al. (2000, p. 9) express the view that increasingly older people are the "donors, not the net recipients" of gen-erational support. Kunemund and Rein (1999) make the important obser-vation that providing public resources to older people may assist in raising levels of emotional support within the family. They conclude: "When el-derly people have sufficient resources of their own, they are not forced by necessity to reply upon their families. Therefore interactions focused on intimacy and closeness have the potential to develop" (ibid.:97). More gen-erally, Bengtson has proposed that given an increase in longevity, multi-generational ties have assumed greater importance within Western societies. He argues from this that "for many Americans, multigenera-tional bonds are becoming more important than nuclear family ties for well-being and support over the course of their lives" (2001, p. 14).

PERSONAL COMMUNITIES AND THE PROVISION OF SUPPORT

To sum up the argument thus far: family relationships in their nuclear, extended, and generational forms have been the main focus for exploring the exchange of support in old age. Research has examined the social world of older people as dominated by families first of all; friends and neighbors second; and voluntary and bureaucratic organizations a distant third [to roughly paraphrase the formulation expressed in the late 1970s by Ethel Shanas (1979)]. This approach is, however, questioned by those working from a social network perspective, where the range of significant others is left for a more open-ended assessment. Antonucci and Akiyama (1987) draw upon the idea of the *convoy,* the group of "significant others" with whom support is exchanged through the life course. The researchers note that this formulation allows for broader conceptualization within which to consider specific individual experiences. They go on to argue:

This may be especially important among older people. Although, in most
cases, neighbours and friends might be expected to provide only a limited
amount of sick care for a chronically ill elderly person, a previous experience
of extended care provided by the older person to the friend or neighbour
may explain an unusual amount of sick care during a current illness. The
convoy concept provides a framework within which to understand these
specific supportive exchanges. (ibid.:519)

Barry Wellman (1990) suggests that while treating kinship networks as
discrete systems is useful for studying issues such as inheritance, it
wrenches out of context how ties with kin fit into everyday lives. Network
perspectives, he suggests: "Start with a set of all active or intimate relationships and only then ask if the *members* of such networks are kith or
kin" (ibid.:196; emphasis in original). Implicit in this approach is an
acknowledgment that some relationships are voluntary and freely chosen.
Bonvalet and her colleagues (1999) make this point well with the comment
from their French study:

> The "family circle" is thus a family system whereby the individual is not
> defined by already existing family ties, but creates his (or her) own circle of
> family and friends. This system of relationships, which is shaped and which
> changes over time, brings together two groups . . . on the one hand, the
> "legal" or "biological" kin; and on the other, the circle of "close persons," a
> complex network of affinities, contacts and mutual help involving blood rel-
> atives, in-laws and friends in variable proportions. (ibid.:243)

At one level, the findings from network studies reinforce the message
from family studies more generally: Kin provide the bulk of intimate ties;
primary or immediate kin are crucial for the provision of support; and
older people are active as donors as well as recipients of aid to their network. This theme has been reported in a range of empirical work in a number of different countries, for example: United States (Antonucci and
Akiyama, 1987), France (Bonvalet et al., 1999), Netherlands (Knipscheer et
al., 1993), England (Phillipson et al., 2001), Canada (Wellman, 1990), and
Wales (Wenger, 1992).

Network studies, however, also provide important qualifications to this
general picture. In the first place, the average number of intimate ties
reported by older people—8.4 in Antonucci and Akiyama (1987); 9.3 in
Phillipson et al. (2001)—should be placed within the context of the rather
small number of very close or important support providers—3.7 in
Antonucci and Akiyama (1987)—and the significant proportion reporting
relatively small personal networks overall. For example, in the Phillipson
et al., (2001) study, 30 percent of those interviewed ($n = 627$; men 65 and
over; women 60 and over) reported a network comprising five persons or

less. Among respondents with very small networks, men appear somewhat more frequently than women: 5 percent of men have networks of just one person or less, compared with 2 percent of women. Such figures raise issues about the vulnerability of networks to overload, and the difficulty individuals may face in spreading either the giving or receiving of care across a wide range of individuals. Moreover, many of these networks should more properly be viewed as "couple" rather than "family-centered." As Jamieson (1998, p. 136) has argued: "The historical shift from the 'family' to the 'good relationship' as *the* site of intimacy is the growing story of the couple relationship." Older people (men especially) see their partner both as a confidant and the key provider of sustained help and support. This is almost certainly not a new development, but one that stands out more prominently in the lives of people studied in the late twentieth and early twenty-first century.

A second important finding from network investigations concerns the specialist nature of the support provided by different network members. The argument is that while extended family ties and generations are important, they reveal only part of the picture in respect of the nature of support given and received by older people. In reality, people place themselves within a complex range of relationships, using different ties for different purposes, but often with limited overlap among them. Wellman and Wortley summarize the sociological basis of this in the following way:

> One segment of a network is composed of immediate kin whose relations are densely knit and broadly supportive, while other segments contain friends neighbours and workmates whose relations are sparsely knit, companionate, specialised in support, and connected with other social circles. . . . Strong friendships as well as immediate kin provide much emotional aid and services, while siblings are often good companions. Yet friends and relatives usually are members of different clusters of relationships within these networks. The combination of kith and kin supplies both stable support from ascribed ties with immediate kin and adaptive support from achieved ties with friends, neighbours, co-workers, and other organisational ties. (1990, p. 580)

Finally, and implicit in the above, network studies have opened up a debate on the importance of non–blood relationships in the lives of older people. Friends, for example, maybe especially important in the networks of urban couples, in some cases substituting for children or other relatives (Fischer, 1982). This appears to be the case with the current cohort of older people and may be even more characteristic of later cohorts. Pahl and Spencer (1997) argue that in some instances friends may even be taking over from families as new "families of choice." They suggest that as the proportion of marriages that end in divorce increases and as men and women move geographically, and perhaps socially from their families of origin, so friends come to provide continued support and security. The researchers note, for example, evidence from the British Household Panel Study, which shows that divorced men and women were more likely to have seen a close friend during the previous week than those who were married. A report in the British Social Attitudes Survey 1996 showed a general decline in the numbers seeing a relative or a friend at least once a week (in the period 1986 to 1995); but the decline in those who saw a best friend was down from 65 to 59 percent; while those who saw their mothers dropped from 59 to 49 percent. Summarizing the situation for adults of all ages, Pahl and Spencer find that

> respondents in 1995 were more likely to have seen their best friend during the previous week than any other relative or other family member (not sharing the same household). People grow up, parents die, children leave home, partners may come and go, but some friends continue to supply support in different ways throughout people's lives. (1997, p. 36)

THE NEW SOCIOLOGY OF FAMILY LIFE IN OLD AGE

In this section the above debates will be placed within a more general sociological context, and some issues and tensions identified between generational and network approaches to the study of family life. The purpose is to develop an argument about the need for a distinctive sociology of family life in old age, one that reflects both developments within the discipline, and the need for a robust linkage with relevant social theory. A starting point for the discussion must be to acknowledge the sheer diversity and range of experiences now contained within the institution of the family. Bernades (as cited in Allan and Crow, 2001) asks the question: "Do we really know what 'the family' is?" The answer is more uncertain than it was when Parsons (1943) was developing his approach in the 1930s and 1940s. Yet, in some ways, gerontology seems uneasy with the idea that family practices have become much less predictable. Shanas's (1979) "family first" model has become embedded within the core assumptions of the discipline. This is in part because the need to demonstrate the existence of family ties was a virtual mission statement for gerontology in the postwar period; in part also because it provided a coherent perspective against which empirical data could be modeled and tested.

This general approach was to be loosened by Finch and Mason's (1993) influential notion of family practices as a form of "negotiation." But the "negotiations" (still insufficiently detailed in empirical research) have been predominantly family- and generational-bound, even if the underlying argument from sociology has been toward a more fluid and open perspective on social relationships. Moreover, the issue of diversity has been somewhat sidelined by the main theoretical tradition used to explain family relationships. Social exchange theory, along with notions of reciprocity, has been used to underpin numerous studies of the family life of older people. Lowenstein, for example, notes:

> In the study of intergenerational relations, there is an increased emphasis on the interdependence of generations, that is the mutual exchange of resources between elderly parents and their adult children, based on social exchange theory. Social exchange theory deals with the balance between dependence and power as an important determinant of the satisfaction which two persons experience in their relationship. (1999, p. 400)

As broad principles underpinning social relationships, ideas about exchange and reciprocity continue to exert considerable force. They have been especially important in the debate about intergenerational equity, and have been used to explain a number of findings from researchers working in the area of family sociology. At the same time, these approaches may need some modification given a context of greater fluidity and instability in personal relationships. Reciprocity, in the kind of "risk society" outlined by Beck (1992) and Giddens (1994), may have a different quality when compared with the "environment of kin" (Frankenberg, 1966) into which older people's lives have traditionally been absorbed. Gouldner's (1960) view about the universality of reciprocity may still apply, but the mechanisms and outcomes in a world of "serial friendships" rather than "settled communities" will surely be different. Other factors such as migration and globalization also need to be taken into account as factors challenging traditional rules about reciprocity and exchange (Phillipson, 2001).

However, this process of "detraditionalization" is almost certainly a reworking rather than an abandonment of practices such as reciprocity, trust, and exchange. Giddens, for example, makes the following point:

> In a world of high reflexivity, an individual must achieve a certain autonomy of action as a condition of being able to survive and forge a life; but autonomy is not the same as egoism and moreover implies reciprocity and interdependence. The issue of reconstructing social solidarities should therefore not be seen as one of protecting social cohesion around the edges of an egoistic marketplace. It should be understood as one of *reconciling autonomy and interdependence* in the various spheres of social life. (1994, p. 13; emphasis in original)

Given this perspective of "reconstructing social solidarities," what are the main themes that a new family sociology of aging might need to take

into account? Three will be suggested here to open the discussion:
(1) reconfiguring family relationships as "personal communities;" (2)
exploring the role of social capital in promoting new forms of reciprocity;
(3) documenting the role of the state and globalization in influencing new
patterns of family life.

FAMILY LIFE AND PERSONAL COMMUNITIES

In the first place, the solidarities reproduced in old age are only partially
addressed through a focus on generations or cohorts. This point has been
developed by Riley and Riley (1993, p. 169) in their model of a *latent matrix*
of relationships, these reflecting greater complexity within the kinship system. This "emergent" type of kinship structure reflects the "fuzzy" edge to
kinship structures, and as well the less distinct boundaries set by age, generation or geographical proximity. The authors argue:

> . . . the emerging boundaries of the kin network may become more influ-
> enced by gender or even by race and ethnicity, than by age or generation.
> Instead, the boundaries of the kin network have been widened to encompass
> many diverse relationships, including several degrees of stepkin and in-
> laws, single-parent families, adopted and other "relatives" chosen from out-
> side the family, and many others. (ibid.:174)

The possibility of open or porous kinship boundaries is well-established
in the research literature. Carol Stack's (1974) study of a black urban community in the United States demonstrated how standard definitions of
nuclear or extended families often failed to capture the complex way in
which people lived their lives. Added to this is the importance of demographic changes such as later age of marriage, delayed childbirth, and
cohabitation, all of which underline the significance of the view that there
can be "little doubt that the network of potentially significant relationships
is becoming enlarged" (ibid.:187).

But a key point is the level of analysis to consider when exploring
changes in relationships. Generational and cohort perspectives are vital
when tracing developments at the macroeconomic and macrosocial levels,
as the debate around intergenerational equity and the link between family
and welfare generations demonstrate (Hills, 1996). But this must be complemented by approaches better able to explore microsocial developments, especially in respect of the process and dynamics of family and
community change. Here, the concept of "personal communities" (i.e., the
world of friends, leisure-associates, neighbors, and kin) has some merit
when attempting to capture the interplay of different kinds of social ties in
old age. Wellman and Wortley define a "personal community network" as

. . . a person's set of active community ties, [which] is usually socially diverse, spatially dispersed, and sparsely knit. . . . Its ties vary in characteristics and in the kinds of support they provide. Until now, community (and kinship) analysts have concentrated on documenting the persistence, composition, and structure of these networks in order to show that community has not been lost in contemporary societies. They have paid less attention to evaluating how characteristics of community ties and networks affect access to the supportive resources that flow through them. (1990, p. 560)

Placing people within the context of "personal communities" also bears upon an important sociological argument, namely, the development of a more "voluntaristic" element in personal relations. Instead of people locked into family groups, they may be more accurately perceived as "managing" a wide spread of relationships, with friends, kin, neighbors, and other supporters, exchanging and receiving help at different points of the life course (Pahl, 2000). Viewing people as "managers" of a network of relationships offers a different approach to that usually adopted within gerontology. Here, the traditional focus (as noted earlier) has been upon a preordained sequence starting with the family first, and leading outward toward other sets of relationships. However, an alternative approach is to view older people as active network participants, adopting a range of "strategies" in maintaining social ties (see also Litwak, Silverstein, Bengtson, and Hirst, Chapter 2 in this volume).

A further distinction may also be made between the two main levels at which support is exchanged. Typically, the focus of analysis has been upon *generational reciprocity*, comprising grandparents, adult children, and grandchildren. This type of reciprocity may be more or less prominent depending on the characteristics of the individual's total network. The latter, however, will display its own form of *network reciprocity* with the range of contacts open to numerous permutations. Moreover, the form of analysis will vary between the two levels. In generational reciprocity, the exchange of resources follows a more or less predictable pattern over the life course. To be sure, this is now viewed as a matter of give and take, "where the precondition of obedience has given way to a complex set of negotiations" (Segalen, 1997, p. 9). However, the exchange of support is still presented as a series of flows up and down the generational ladder. Network reciprocity, however, implies variation in the range of actors involved (for example, fictive kin, friends, neighbors, voluntary workers), and volatility in terms of their movement into and out of the network.

One implication of the above concerns the importance of placing generations in context, and understanding how they both affect and are affected by other social actors. Kith may not replace kin but they will almost certainly influence the range of help and support available to the older person. Clusters of friends and neighbors may "crowd in" or "crowd out" family support (using the terminology of Kunemund and Rein, 1999), with the possibility of substitution and/or withdrawal of different types of help.

SOCIAL CAPITAL AND SOCIAL SUPPORT

In one sense, the kind of argument developed thus far does no more than reengage with sociological perspectives from Weber, Durkheim, Simmel, and others. Wellman (1998), for example, notes that while this tradition highlighted the crisis in relationships accompanying the rise of modern capitalism, the potential for new communal ties was also acknowledged, for example, through the concepts of organic solidarity (Durkheim, 1933), and that of "sociation" (Simmel, 1950). The idea of relationships being reconstructed in an urbanizing society was, however, neglected within gerontology, given its preoccupation with families in their more traditional guise. However, the issue is not just the possibility of alternatives to kin, but the idea of new sources of power, and a wider spread of resources potentially available to the older person. One way in which this can be expressed is through the notion of social capital as developed in the writings of Bourdieu (1986), Coleman (1990), Putnam (2000), and others. In his review of this concept, Portes (1998, p. 7) suggests that: "(a) consensus is growing in the literature that social capital stands for the ability of actors to secure benefits by virtue of membership in social networks or other social structures." He goes on:

> Both Bourdieu and Coleman emphasize the intangible character of social capital relative to other forms. Whereas economic capital is in people's bank's accounts and human capital is inside their heads, social capital inheres in the structure of their relationships. To possess social capital, a person must be related to others, and it is those others, not himself who are the actual source of his or her advantage. (ibid.)

Ideas about social capital also draw upon Granovetter's (1973) distinction between "strong" and "weak" ties, the former referring to the "dense" ties to family and those similar to oneself, the latter to individuals dissimilar to oneself. A related distinction is between "bonding" and "bridging" forms of social capital. Putnam (2000, p. 22) summarizes this as follows:

> Some forms of social capital are, by choice or necessity, inward looking and tend to reinforce exclusive identities and homogenous groups. . . . Other networks are outward looking and encompass across diverse social cleavages. . . . Bonding social capital is good for undergirding specific reciprocity and mobilising social solidarity. Dense networks in ethnic enclaves, for

example, provide crucial social and psychological support for less fortunate members of the community. . . . Bridging networks, in contrast, are better for linkage to external assets and for information diffusion. . . . Bonding social capital is . . . good for "getting by," but bridging social capital is crucial for "getting ahead." Moreover, bridging social capital can generate broader identities and reciprocities, whereas bonding social capital bolsters our narrower selves.

Within gerontology, research has tended to focus upon the value of "strong ties," for example, those linked with immediate family and long-lasting friends and neighbors. Strong ties have the virtue of social inclusion; equally, reliance on these alone may risk people being marginalized or cut off from other groups. Just as people may need a spread of ties for accessing help in securing employment or promotion, scattered and episodic ties may also be helpful through periods such as retirement and old age. Pahl and Spencer make the general point that "those who have emphasised old-style ties based on gender, race or ethnicity as a way of empowering disadvantaged categories may unwittingly have added to their troubles by making it more difficult for such closer-knit groups to develop 'bridging' ties" (1997, p. 37). Such ties may be especially significant to the widow seeking alternatives to kin; to men and women entering retirement seeking to engage with new lifestyles; or to those needing help from abusive or exploitative relationships.

At a broader level, the argument also concerns older people's engagement with a "detraditionalized" world, with the reconstruction of later life as a period of choice on the one side, but one of risk and danger on the other (Phillipson, 1998). Inclusive ties fit well with inclusive institutions such as the welfare state, a stable intergenerational contract, and fixed-age compulsory retirement. Given the fragmentation of these into multiple pathways or privatized forms, a mix of strong and weak ties may become more advantageous. Empirically, the task becomes that of documenting the combination of ties generated in the diverse settings and communities in which people live their lives. Multigenerational ties will almost certainly be part of these, but may be complemented as well by other (non-blood) types of relationships.

POLITICAL ECONOMY AND SOCIAL SUPPORT

A final set of issues concerns the value of applying perspectives from critical gerontology to the analysis of family change. Critical gerontology has a number of variants in terms of political economy, humanistic, and biographical perspectives, all of which offer relevant insights into the question of support in later life (Cole, Van Tassel, and Kastenbaum, 1992;

Minkler and Estes, 1999; Phillipson, 1998). For our purposes, however, we shall focus on the contribution from political economy perspectives, exploring in particular the role of the state and the significance of a globalized economy for understanding the nature of social aging.

Generational and network-based relations, it may be argued, are shaped by external as much as internal forces, with the dominant institutions and ideologies associated with advanced capitalism playing a crucial role. In this context, the state, interacting with the spread of a global economy, is raising significant issues for the maintenance of traditional solidarities.

Estes (1999) views the state as having a central role in the construction of aging, in three main ways: (a) through the allocation of scarce resources; (b) through mediating between different segments and classes of society; and (c) through ameliorating social and economic conditions that could threaten the existing social order. However, the state also plays an ideological role in the transmission of beliefs concerning family care and support. This has been especially significant during the past two decades, a period of retrenchment in the production of welfare by the state (Estes and associates, 2001). Despite evidence for growing diversity in relationships and lifestyles, conventional ties, such as grandparenting, are increasingly valorized for sustaining women's presence in the labor market (see Biggs and Powell, Chapter 5 in this volume). At the same time, attempts by the state to roll back crucial services is itself in conflict with the wishes of a significant proportion of older people, whose preferences are for governments to expand provision in publicly funded social services (Phillipson, 1992). Family life has in many respects become part of the "crisis management" of aging, with governments resisting the idea of a realistic audit of the range of services which different generations are willing and able to provide.

The nature and maintenance of support is also affected by the location of the state within a globalized economy, and the impact of this on the construction of family life. In their study *Global Transformations*, David Held and his colleagues suggest the following:

> Today, virtually all nation-states have gradually become enmeshed in and functionally part of a larger pattern of global transformations and global flows. . . . Transnational networks and relations have developed across virtually all areas of human activity. Goods, capital, people, knowledge, communications and weapons, as well as crime, pollutants, fashions and beliefs, rapidly move across territorial boundaries. . . . Far from this being a world or "discrete civilisations" or simply an international order of states, it has become a fundamentally interconnected global order, marked by intense patterns of exchange as well as by clear patterns of power, hierarchy and unevenness. (1999, p. 49)

Carroll Estes (2000) argues that at the ideological level, globalization has assumed a power and force of its own, and that it has been especially important for promoting the inevitability of competitive global forces and the policies developed by corporations.

A globalized, corporate-driven, capitalist economy provides radically changed agendas and challenges in respect of achieving security in old age. In the first place, it is inappropriate to analyze responses and solutions to aging issues exclusively within national borders. John Urry's (2000) analysis of the new mobilities affecting the twenty-first century, and Manuel Castells's (1996) focus on the role of networks, rather than countries, providing the architecture for the global economy, come to the same conclusion in highlighting the various pressures affecting nation-states.

Increasingly, the sovereignty of nation-states is influenced to a greater or lesser extent by different kinds of transnational actors. Older people live in a global even more than a national society, and are increasingly contributing to, as well as depending upon, transnational chains of paid and unpaid labor. This new political economy is also creating "global families," these arising from the communities that emerge from international migration (Phillipson, 2000). Arlie Hochschild (2000) argues that most writing about globalization focuses on money, markets, and labor flows, with scant attention to women, children, and the care of one for the other. But older people might be added to this list. Elderly people are a part of the global flow: They grow old as migrants, are part of the care chain in receiving or giving care, or go backwards and forwards from one home to the other. In this context, globalization is producing a new kind of aging, one in which the dynamics of family life may be stretched across a number of continents (Phillipson, 2001).

This development produces greater diversity in respect of the social networks within which growing old is shaped and managed. Typically, older people's networks have been examined within national borders, and their experiences for care and support assessed within this context. But migrants bring important variations with responsibilities and resources that may stretch considerable physical distances. First-generation migrants, as well as later generations, from Bangladesh to Britain, to take one example, go backwards and forwards maintaining economic as well as social ties across different communities. This back-and-forth process in maintaining social ties has been noted for a number of migrant communities, with the creation of new opportunities for entrepreneurship as well the generation of "strong" [to use Granovetter's (1973) term] social ties and social networks. But equally there may be costs and distinctive inequalities as well. Gardner, in her study of Bangladeshi elders in Britain, captures this point in the following observation:

Migration involves profound contradiction and conflict and the [current] generation [of elders in Britain], more than others, embody and express the pain this causes. Caught between the opposing ideals of family togetherness and economic aspiration . . . and the practical needs for economic and medical support, it is hardly surprising that many feel an overwhelming sense of loss as they enter the last years of their lives. (1998, p. 176)

The globalization of family life is creating a major new research agenda in terms of tracking how generational and network-based ties are sustained across different nation-states (Phillipson, 2001). Some of the key questions include: Are there new means of contact and communication being developed to sustain traditional ties within families? What are the different ways in which men and women respond to the pressures of migration? Do distinctive types of reciprocity develop among families separated through time and space?

CONCLUSION

This chapter has reviewed sociological perspectives on the family life of older people. The main concern has been to highlight a number of distinctive approaches to this area of study. Particular emphasis has been placed upon the distinction between generational and network-based perspectives. The former remain of vital importance for studying topics such as inheritance and family-based obligations and rituals. A generational perspective is also central to macrosociological concerns, in particular those relating to issues about equity and solidarity. A network approach, however, emphasizes the way in which older people orchestrate a range of social ties, not all of which come under the rubric of families and generations. This broad spread of relations—part of the more fluid social world of late modernity—contributes to the production of support in ways requiring better documentation. One element of this may be older people developing a mix of "strong" and "weak" ties, these better suited to the risks and problems of daily living. Finally, an important element in the new conditions facing older people is the emergence of the "global family," a consequence of the acceleration in international migration over the past two decades. This new type of family is redefining social networks in the twenty-first century, with the building of more varied forms of reciprocity and exchange.

The changes described amount to a significant research agenda for gerontologists to consider in the new century. Demographic changes will almost certainly lead, as Bengtson (2001) suggests, to the increased salience of multigenerational ties, with bonds of friendship complementing these but also in some cases substituting for kin-based support. However, it is also the case that a broad range of social ties will be needed to cope with the pressures and conflicts affecting family relationships. Global changes associated with migration and increased mobility comprise one important element. Of additional importance is the tension between work relations on the one side, and family support on the other. Richard Sennett (1999), for example, has argued that the new flexibility and mobility associated with paid work may have a corrosive effect on long-term ties to friends and family. His analysis suggests that family relationships may be compromised by the insecurities and anxieties affecting people in employment. This raises the important question of the extent to which the social environment appropriate for an aging society may conflict with the economic goals of capitalism. Family groups and personal communities, as argued here, are traditionally associated with high levels of support to older people. However, this may be disrupted through work ties that encourage short-term forms of association rather the long-term connections characteristic of family ties.

The potential for support (through human longevity) is certainly greater than ever; but the pressure on relationships is also intense (as illustrated in the quotation that opened this chapter). How this conflict is reconciled will be a major issue for researchers to address over the next decade. Family and generational issues will certainly occupy a central place in the gerontological research agenda.

ACKNOWLEDGMENTS

The author thanks Ariela Lowenstein, Vern Bengtson, Simon Biggs, and David Morgan for their comments on earlier drafts of this chapter.

REFERENCES

Allan, G. 1996. *Kinship and friendship in modern Britain.* Oxford: Oxford University Press.

Allan, G., and Crow, G. 2001. *Families, households and society.* London: Palgrave.

Antonucci, T., and Akiyama, H. 1987. Social networks in adult life and a preliminary examination of the convoy model. *Journal of Gerontology* 42(5):519–27.

Arber, S., and Attias-Donfut, C. 2000. *The myth of generational conflict.* London: Routledge.

Attias-Donfut, C., and Wolff, F.-C. 2000a. The redistributive effects of generational transfers. In S. Arber and C. Attias-Donfut (eds.), *The myth of generational conflict* (pp. 22–46). London: Routledge.

_____. 2000b. Complementarity between private and public transfers. In S. Arber and C. Attias-Donfut (eds.), *The myth of generational conflict* (pp. 47–68). London: Routledge.

Beck, U. 1992. *Risk society*. London: Sage.

Bell, C. 1968. *Middle class families*. London: Routledge, Kegan and Paul.

Bengtson, V. 2001. Beyond the nuclear family: The increasing importance of multi-generational bonds. *Journal of Marriage and the Family* 63:1–16.

Bengtson, V. L., and Achenbaum, W. A. (eds.) 1993. *The changing contract across generations*. Hawthorne, NY: Aldine de Gruyter.

Bengtson, V. L., Giarrusso, R., Silverstein, M., and Wang, H. 2000. Families and intergenerational relationships in aging societies. *Hallym International Journal of Aging* 2(1):3–10.

Bengtson, V. L., Rosenthal, C., and Burton, L. 1990. Families and aging: Diversity and heterogeneity. In R. H. Binstock and L. George (eds.), *Handbook of aging and the social sciences* (3rd ed., pp. 263–87). San Diego, CA: Academic Press.

Berne, S. 1997. *A crime in the neighbourhood*. London: Penguin.

Bonvalet, C., Gotman, A., and Grafmeyer, Y. (eds.) 1999. La famille et ses proches: L'amenagement des territoire. *INED Cahier No. 143*. Paris: Presse Universitaire.

Bourdieu, P. 1986. Forms of capital. In J. G. Richardson, (ed.), *Handbook of theory and research for the sociology of education* (pp. 378–98). New York: Greenwood.

Castells, M. 1996. *The rise of the network society* Vol. 1. Oxford: Blackwell.

Cheal, D. 1999. The one and the many: Modernity and postmodernity. In G. Allan (ed.), *The sociology of the family: A reader* (pp. 56–86). Oxford: Blackwell.

Cole, T., Van Tassel, D., and Kastenbaum, R. 1992. *Handbook of aging and the humanities*. New York: Springer.

Coleman, J. S. 1990. *Foundations of social theory*. Cambridge, MA: Harvard University Press.

Durkheim, E. 1933. *The division of labour in society*. New York: Free Press.

Estes, C. 1999. Critical gerontology and the new political economy of aging. In M. Minkler and C. Estes (eds.), *Critical gerontology* (pp. 17–36). New York: Baywood.

_____. 2000. The globalization of capital: The welfare state and old age policy. Paper presented at the meeting of the American Sociological Association Annual Conference, Washington, D.C.

_____. (ed.) 2001. *Social policy and aging: A critical perspective*. Thousand Oaks: Sage.

Finch, J., and Mason, J. 1993. *Negotiating family responsibilities*. London: Routledge.

Fischer, C. 1982. *To dwell amongst friends*. Chicago: University of Chicago Press.

Frankenberg, R. 1966. *Communities in Britain*. London: Penguin.

Gardner, K. 1998. Identity, age, and masculinity amongst Bengali elders in East London. In A. Kershen (ed.), *A question of identity* (pp. 160–78). Aldershot: Avebury

Giddens, A. 1994. *Beyond left and right*. Oxford: Polity.

Gouldner, A. 1960. The norm of reciprocity: A preliminary statement. *American Sociological Review* 25(2):161–78.

Granovetter, M. 1973. The strength of weak ties. *American Journal of Sociology* 78:1360–80.

Guardian 2000. Poll reveals crucial role of grandparents in child care. December 14, p. 6.

Haber, C., and Gratton, B. 1993. *Old age and the search for security.* Bloomington: Indiana University Press.

Held, D., McGrew., A., Goldblatt, D., and Perraton, J. 1999. *Global transformations.* Cambridge: Polity.

Hills, J. 1996. Does Britain have a welfare generation? In A. Walker (ed.), *The new generational contract* (pp. 56–80). London: UCL.

Hochschild, A. 2000. Global care chains and emotional surplus value. In W. Hutton and A. Giddens (eds.), *On the edge: Living with global capitalism* (pp. 130–46). London: Jonathan Cape.

Jamieson, L. 1998. *Intimacy: personal relationships in modern societies.* Oxford: Polity.

Knipscheer, C. P. M., de Jong Gierveld, J., Van Tilburg, T. G., and Dykstra, P. A. (eds.) 1996. *Living arrangements and social networks of older adults.* Amsterdam: VU University Press.

Kohli, M., Kunemund, H., Motel, A., and Szydlik, M. 2000. Families apart? Inter-generational transfers in East and West Germany. In S. Arber and C. Attias-Donfut (eds.), *The myth of generational conflict* (pp. 88–99). London: Routledge.

Kunemund, H., and Rein, M. 1999. There is more to receiving than needing: Theoretical arguments and empirical explorations of crowding in and crowding out. *Ageing and Society* 19:93–121.

Laslett, P. 1965. *The world we have lost.* London: Methuen.

Litwak, E. 1960. Occupational mobility and extended family cohesion. *American Sociological Review* 25:9–21.

Lowenstein, A. 1999. Intergenerational family relations and social support. *Gerontologie und Geriatrie.* Key Note Lectures, Fifth European Congress of Gerontology (pp. 398–407). Darmstadt: Steinkopff.

Minkler, M., and Estes, C. 1999. *Critical gerontology.* New York: Baywood.

Morgan, D. 1996. *Family connections.* Cambridge: Polity.

Pahl, R. 2000. *On friendship.* Oxford: Polity.

Pahl, R., and Spencer, L. 1997. Friends and neighbours. *New Statesman,* September 26, pp. 36–37.

Parsons, T. 1943. The kinship system of the contemporary United States. *American Anthropologist* 45:22–38.

Phillipson, C. 1992. Family care of the elderly in Great Britain. In J. Kosberg (ed.), *Family care of the elderly* (pp. 252–70). London: Sage.

_____. 1998. *Reconstructing old age.* London: Sage.

_____. 2000. Globalisation and the reconstruction of old age: The role of transnational organisations and communities. Paper presented to the meeting of the American Sociological Association Annual Conference, Washington, D.C.

_____. 2001. Globalisation and intergenerational ties: New solidarities and relationships. Paper presented to the meeting of the World Congress of the International Association of Gerontology, Vancouver.

Phillipson, C., Bernard, M., Phillips, J., and Ogg, J. 2001. *The family and community life of older people: Social support and social networks in three urban areas.* London: Routledge.

Portes, A. 1998. Social capital: Its origins and applications in modern sociology. *Annual Review of Sociology* 24:1–24.

Putnam, R. 2000. *Bowling alone*. New York: Simon and Shuster.

Riley, M. W., and Riley, J. 1993. Connections: Kin and cohort. In V. L. Bengtson and W. A. Achenbaum (eds.), *The changing contract across generations* (pp. 169–90). Hawthorne, NY: Aldine de Gruyter.

Rosenmayr, L., and Kockeis, E. 1963. Propositions for a sociological theory of ageing and the family. *International Social Science Journal* 15(3):410–26.

Segalen, M. 1997. Introduction. In M. Gullestad and M. Segalen, *Family and kinship in Europe* (pp. 1–13). London: Pinter.

Sennett, R. 1999. *The corrosion of character*. London: W. W. Norton..

Shanas, E. 1979. The family as a social support system in old age. *Gerontologist* 19(2):169–74.

Simmel, G. 1950. *The sociology of Georg Simmel* (K. Wolff, ed. and transl.). Glencoe, IL: Free Press.

Stack, C. 1974. *All our kin: Strategies for survival in a black community*. New York: Harper.

Stearns, P. 1974. *Old age in European society: The case of France*. London: Croom Helm.

Streib, G., and Thompson, W. 1960. The older person in a family context. In C. Tibbitts (ed.), *Handbook of social gerontology* (pp. 447–89). Chicago: University of Chicago Press.

Sussman, M. 1965. Relationships of adult children with their parents in the United States. In E. Shanas and G. Streib (eds.), *Social structure and the family* (pp 62–92). New York: Prentice-Hall.

Thane, P. 2000. *Old age in English history*. Oxford: Oxford University Press.

Thompson, P. 1999. The role of grandparents when parents part or die: Some reflections on the mythical decline of the extended family. *Ageing and Society* 19:471–503.

Townsend, P. 1957. *The family life of old people*. London: Routledge, Kegan and Paul.

Urry, J. 2000. *Sociology beyond, societies*. London: Routledge

Walker, A. (ed.) 1996. *The new generational contract*. London: UCL.

Wellman, B. 1990. The place of kinfolk in personal community settings. *Marriage and Family Review* 15(1/2):195–228.

———. 1998. The network community. In B. Wellman (ed.), *Networks in the global village* (pp. 1–48). Boulder, CO: Westview.

Wellman, B., and Wortley, S. 1990. Different strokes from different folks: Community ties and social support. *American Journal of Sociology* 96:558–88

Wenger, G. C. 1992. *Help in old age: Facing up to change*. Liverpool: Liverpool University Press.

Willmott, P., and Young, M. 1960. *Family and class in a London suburb*. London: Routledge, Kegan and Paul.

Wirth, L. 1938. Urbanism as a way of life. *American Journal of Sociology*, 44(1):1–24.

Young, M., and Willmott, P. 1957. *Family and kinship in east London*. London: Routledge, Kegan and Paul.

| 4 |

Grandparents and Grandchildren in Family Systems

A Social-Developmental Perspective

Merril Silverstein, Roseann Giarrusso, and Vern L. Bengtson

There is little question that grandparents play valuable roles in providing time, labor, and financial and symbolic resources to other family members, which often enhances the equilibrium of families buffeted by stresses arising from social change. Social change (resulting from political, social, and economic transformations in society) may introduce uncertainty and turbulence into family systems and, at the extreme, cause the breakdown of competent family functioning. Assumed in the literature, but rarely articulated as a general principle, is the notion that grandparents are particularly valuable when social forces threaten to weaken the fabric of family life. This notion is rooted in the ideas and concepts of the life course perspective, a social-developmental framework that highlights historical, contextual, and systemic aspects of family development. In this chapter, we demonstrate how the elements of time, generational placement, culture, and place are key to our understanding of the role that grandparents play in the lives of their families.

Our basic proposition is that grandparent role enactment is a social construction that varies across personal and historical time, as well as across cultural and regional contexts. The premise of the life course perspective—that human development occurs at the intersection of biography, history, and social ecology—is key to making sense of the diverse ways in which the grandparent role is enacted. Further, the consideration of grandparenting from a family systems perspective makes it possible to appreciate the filial conditions to which grandparents respond, which are themselves shaped by temporal and ecological contexts. Data from the Longitudinal Study of Generations (LSOG) are used to illustrate some of these dynamics and their consequences for the healthy development of families.

BACKGROUND

The role of grandparents in both developed and developing societies has received increased scrutiny over the last fifteen years. In part, this trend can be seen as a response to the aging of societies and the greater availability of older adults in families (Uhlenberg, 1996), to the emergence of alternative family forms and household structures (Goldscheider, 1990), and changing labor market conditions and government policies that have compelled families to adapt to sometimes dire contingencies by increasing their reliance on private or internal resources such as grandparents. Classical sociological models of the family tended to relegate older generations to the periphery of family life (Goode, 1963) and even considered their presence to be detrimental to the economic well-being of the nuclear family (Parsons and Bales, 1955). More recent formulations of intergenerational family relations have stressed the importance of extended family cohesion for the successful adaptation of families exposed to stressful events and have documented the often heroic contributions made by grandparents especially toward ensuring the integrity of the nuclear family (see Hareven, 1994). One estimate is that grandparents provide $17–$29 billion annually in support to their children and grandchildren by means of unpaid supervision and child care (Bass and Caro, 1996). Indeed, the very process of population aging raises questions as to the kinds of roles grandparents will play in the future with respect to their families, as well the kinds of resources they are likely to provide to society in the twenty-first century. Increases in life expectancy—especially in the number of years of healthy aging—combined with greater amounts of shared lives across generations should alert social and behavioral scientists, as well as policymakers, to the emerging role of grandparents as caregivers and providers of support to family members in need.

Grandparents as Heroic Family Contributors

Why do grandparents serve as important resources for their grandchildren, particularly under conditions of family stress? It has been suggested that the significance of grandparents to the well-being of the family is so fundamental as to have an evolutionary basis. Evolutionary biologists contend that long-lived, healthy grandparents enhance the survival chances of their grandchildren by serving as surrogates for the biological parent in the event, for example, of maternal death, or in the presence of environmental threats to the grandchild (Hawkes, O'Connell, Jones, Alvarez, and Charnov, 1998; Pashos, 2000). If the grandchild has a better chance of surviving with grandparent-provided support, then the potential of that grandchild to reach puberty, reproduce, and pass that grandparent's "longevity" genes to the next generation will be enhanced. This bioevolutionary model has heuristic relevance today for appreciating the important role that grandparents play in maintaining the integrity—and in some cases the survival–of the contemporary family under conditions of social stress.

First, it is important to place the discussion of grandparenting in the context of contemporary discussions about the "decline of the American family" (Bengtson, Biblarz, and Roberts, 2002; Mutran and Reitzes, 1984; Stacey, 1991). The most prominent sociologist advancing the declining family functions argument is Popenoe (1988, 1993), who questions whether families today are capable of providing adequate support for their dependent members. However, nearly all of the evidence provided in support of this perspective is limited to the nuclear family consisting of parents with young children sharing a household. Empirical studies in family sociology suggest that family members in various generations continue to serve as "buffers," insulating individuals from the effects of potentially stressful or hazardous events (Allen and Walker, 1992; Bengtson and Silverstein, 1993; McLanahan and Sorensen, 1985; Silverstein and Bengtson, 1991; Umberson and Chen, 1994; Umberson, Wortman, and Kessler, 1992). Multigenerational families also buffer and protect individuals from the effects of macrosocial change (demographic changes, economic depressions and expansions, occupational downsizings, wars and threats of wars, and shifts in values) as demonstrated by Elder (1984), Conger, Elder, and Glen (1994), Elder, Rudkin, and Conger (1995), Elder and O'Rand (1995), Hareven (1982, 1995), and Broderick (1993).

Noteworthy in the context of this issue are what might be called "heroic" family interventions across generational lines that address nonnormative crises reflecting social change. One example is the case of grandparents stepping in to raise grandchildren in the face of parental incapacity through AIDS, drug or alcohol addiction, unemployment, divorce, single parenting, or imprisonment (Chalfie, 1994; Minkler and Roe, 1993). Although instructive, these findings of heroic support have done little to defuse the debate about "family decline." The contribution of grandparents is an important but often overlooked resource in promoting optimal family functioning. The literature on grandparents has lauded their contribution to the family system, calling them the "national guard" (Hagestad, 1985), the "silent saviors" (Creighton, 1991), and the "family watchdogs" (Troll, 1983) of the family. Implicit in these formulations is the notion that grandparents can fill in for parents who are no longer capable of or willing to fulfill their parental duties, or who need help doing so. Particularly noteworthy have been studies that document the complex ebb and flow of intergenerational support over time in families. While it is clear that family life is changing, families continue to provide significant sources of support to their members, so it remains less clear how intergenerational relations and their consequences differ from earlier decades within the same families, as well as how, when, and under what conditions these latent family intergenerational relationships become activated and with what effect (Riley and Riley, 1993).

Diversity in Grandparenting

Research suggests that the grandparent role is noteworthy for the diverse ways it can be performed and the indeterminate nature of the role (Bengtson and Robertson, 1985). Descriptions of grandparenting styles range from surrogate parenthood to being little more than a stranger to grandchildren (Cherlin and Furstenberg, 1986; Neugarten, 1964). Because there are few explicit expectations concerning the responsibilities and proscribed behavior of grandparents, the act of grandparenting is often fraught with uncertainty over the appropriate type and level of involvement grandparents ought to have with grandchildren. Scholars have often noted that grandparents' relationships with their grandchildren follow few social conventions and are tenuously maintained (Fischer and Silverman, 1982; Troll, 1983).

Much of the scholarly research on grandparents has tended to categorize styles of grandparenting into a set of distinct types (Baydar and Brooks-Gunn, 1998; Cherlin and Furstenberg, 1986; Neugarten, 1964). Although these studies used different sampling frames, focused on different aspects of the relationship, and considered different family life stages, they all point to substantial heterogeneity in the way that grandparent styles are adopted. In the most seminal of these studies, Cherlin and Furstenberg (1986) classified relationship styles between grandparents and their adolescent grandchildren into five types: (1) detached, (2) passive, (3) influential, (4) supportive, and (5) authoritative. Interestingly, they found that no one type of style constituted a clear majority. The absence of a modal type of grandparenting style implies substantial variability in the ways that grandparents enact their roles and suggests that there are few universal truths about this role. Indeed, there is evidence as well that grandparent roles have become more diverse over historical time.

Historical and demographic forces have also increased variation in the manner in which grandparent-grandchild relations are maintained.

Dramatic reductions in mortality rates in the United States over the twentieth century have produced an increase in the joint survivorship between generations in the family (Goldscheider, 1990). Uhlenberg (1996) has pointed out that grandparent availability has increased dramatically over the last century: only 24 percent of the 1900 birth cohort were born with all four of their grandparents alive, as contrasted with 68 percent today. Increasing longevity also means that it is not uncommon for grandparents to live long enough see a grandchild of theirs enter adulthood, and even middle age (Farkas and Hogan, 1994; Silverstein, Lawton, and Bengtson, 1994). Because the average age of first becoming a grandparent has roughly remained stable (45 years of age), the increase in longevity implies that grandparents today might expect to live almost half their lives in that role (Hagestad, 1985). Situating the lives of grandparents within the context of the family life cycle is essential for understanding the forms that this intergenerational relationship is likely to take.

Despite the great amount of attention recently devoted to studying the demographic characteristics of grandparents in the United States (see Szinovacz, 1998), we still know little about the grandparenting role over the life course. Research on grandparenting has tended to focus on discrete stages of the grandparent-grandchild life cycle and has usually been keyed to the age or residential circumstances of a particular grandchild or set of grandchildren (Cherlin and Furstenberg, 1986; Field and Minkler, 1988; Langer, 1990; Silverstein and Long, 1998). Other research has focused on special populations of grandparents, such as those who are raising their grandchildren (Fuller-Thomson, Minkler, and Driver, 1997), low-income African-American grandparents (Burton, 1995), Mexican-American grandparents (Silverstein and Chen, 1999; Strom, Buki, and Strom, 1997), and grandparents in farm families (King and Elder, 1995). Two recent studies have used the National Survey of Families and Households to make inferences about grandparent-grandchild relations at the national level. Uhlenberg and Hammill (1998) focused on the determinants of frequency of contact between grandparents and grandchildren who coreside with their parents, and Baydar and Brooks-Gunn (1998) developed a profile of grandmothers based on intergenerational caregiving. Yet, studies of grandparent involvement have largely been restricted to the study of involvement with younger, mostly nonadult children, and have been cross-sectional in design.

The Impact of Divorce on Grandparenting

Parental divorce tends to be an emotionally painful experience for grandparents if it disrupts relationships with grandchildren. Grandparents generally report a decline in relationship quality with their grandchildren when their offspring experience a divorce (Jaskowski and Dellasega, 1993). However, among grandparents of divorced adult children there are important variations. Grandparents tend to be more involved with their grandchildren when the grandparent is the maternal grandmother and when their own child is the grandchild's custodial mother who has not yet remarried (Clingempeel, Colyar, Brand, and Hetherington, 1992; Ahrons and Bowman, 1981; Hilton and Macari, 1997;). Grandparents at greatest risk of losing contact with grandchildren following a divorce in the middle generation are those on the paternal side (Kruk and Hall, 1995). From the perspective of the grandchildren, those from divorced families report less satisfactory relationships with their paternal grandparents than grandchildren from intact families (Ahrons and Bowman, 1981). Although some evidence shows that the negative effect of parental divorce on grandparent-grandchild relations appears to dissipate as grandchildren pass into adulthood (Cooney and Smith, 1996), the long-term effects of early disruption are not known. Achieving a better understanding of the relationship between grandparents and the offspring of their divorced children is important for explaining the apparent paradox that grandparent-grandchild ties have weakened (due to divorce) at the same time that the importance of grandparents has grown (due to divorce).

Effects of Grandparenting on Grandchildren in Crisis

With some notable exceptions, there is wide consensus in the field of sociology that family disruptions, most significantly parental divorce, have placed many adolescents and young adults at risk of psychological, social, and economic distress (Amato and Booth, 1997; Amato, Rezac, and Booth, 1995; Blankenhorn, 1995; Bumpass, 1990; Cooney and Uhlenberg, 1990; Glenn and Kramer, 1987; Popenoe, 1993; Schone and Pezzin, 1999). In the absence of additional social supports to families following divorce, all of these processes have the potential to undermine the healthy development of children. On the other hand, grandparents—who have sometimes been described as the "first line of support" for children following divorce—can (and often do) provide resources that may serve to offset, or buffer, the negative consequences of divorce on their grandchildren. To the extent that single mothers (and other distressed parents) experience role overload (e.g., forced to cover both market and nonmarket activities following divorce) the amount of time they have to spend with children will decrease (Astone and McLanahan, 1991). If grandparent involvement with children increases as parents' time with children declines, this compensatory effect could reduce the risk of negative outcomes for children in disrupted families.

Although there is evidence that grandparents may minimize the trauma caused by problems of divorce and drug addiction in the parental generation (for review, see Denham and Smith, 1989), this topic has been mostly studied in the context of grandparent-headed families. Solomon and Marx (1995), for instance, found that the health and school adjustment of grandchildren raised solely by grandparents was nearly equivalent to that of children who were raised by one biological parent. The contribution of grandparents to the emotional well-being of their grandchildren has been studied for young grandchildren (Lavers and Sonuga-Barke, 1997), but few studies have investigated how grandparents enhance the well-being of their grandchildren into adulthood. In summary, there have been few investigations of the effects of more normative styles of grandparenting on the long-term life chances, emotional states, and adaptive capacities of grandchildren.

A LIFE COURSE PERSPECTIVE ON GRANDPARENTING

Though rarely applied to grandparenting, the life course perspective can be a useful tool to organize predictions about the nature of grandparent roles, their change over time, and their variations across regions and cultures. The basic tenets of the life course perspective (Elder, 1994) are that human development (1) is dependent upon the exigencies of those with whom we have interpersonal relationships; (2) can be mapped over trajectories that are guided by multiple time clocks (individual, family, and historical time); (3) is the product of long-term antecedent events; and (4) is shaped by cultural contexts that give meaning to the roles and transitions experienced by individuals. We review these tenets below.

Linked Lives

The life course perspective implies that the life course transitions and trajectories of individuals are inextricably linked to the transitions and trajectories of significant others (Elder, 1994). One manifestation of the linked-lives phenomenon occurs within families when the fates of generations are interdependent. This occurs when the choices and options available to members of one generation are influenced by the needs and preferences of those in other generations. For instance, families in which grandparents are raising grandchildren form a dramatic example of how the fortunes of three generations in a family can be mutually interdependent. When grandparents adopt this new parenting role, grandchildren become the beneficiaries of such care, and parents are excused from the main responsibility to parent. In this way, the family is seen as a system of interlocking individuals who continually adapt both to their own needs and to those of others in the family system or kinship matrix (Riley and Riley, 1993). The role of the middle generation more generally—as a gatekeeper to grandchildren—forms the backdrop of mutual interdependence in the multigenerational family. Thus, the life course paradigm considers human development as a relational process of *linked lives* through time and stresses the importance of relationships in shaping the resources and well-being of individuals as they age (Bengtson, Biblarz, and Roberts, 2002; Elder, 1994).

Multiple Time Clocks

The life course perspective recognizes that human development is guided by multiple time clocks that are not always synchronized (Bengtson and Allen, 1993). These temporal dimensions include biographical time, family time, and historical time. Biographical time in this context refers to the developmental stage of the grandparent. Entry to the grandparent role most often occurs during the peak career years of the forties or fifties, when work roles may conflict with enactment of this new family role. Alternatively, as a result of delayed childbearing, grandparenthood may occur late in life when frailty may interfere with enacting the grandparent role. In addition, grandparents relate differently with grandchildren of different ages, with warmer and more involved relations occurring with younger grandchildren (Silverstein and Marenco, 2001).

Historical time refers to the secular societywide changes that establish the context for family interaction. For instance, the late twentieth century saw the beginning of what has been called the "divorce revolution" (Goldscheider, 1990). The dramatic alterations in family structure produced by this social change have potentially increased the importance of grandparents in some situations, such as when an adult child divorces (maternal grandparents may be especially significant) and have weakened the importance of grandparents in other circumstances (e.g., paternal grandparents). Other historical changes that may be influencing grandparenting include the improvement of the health and longevity of the older population (thus increasing the tenure of grandparenting), the expansion of stepgrandparenting, and increases in the flows of material and practical support from older to younger generations as a result of the changing balance of wealth between generations in recent times.

Long-Term Dynamics

The impact of grandparent involvement—in terms of both the long-term future of their grandchildren and long-term reciprocity—forms an important basis of a life course perspective on grandparenting. This perspective affirms that human relationships can be represented as stochastic processes in which outcomes are dependent upon earlier events. Long-term patterns in relationships between grandparents and their grandchildren are much less well understood than those between parents and children. Some evidence suggests that grandchildren who were more involved with their grandparents are more likely to support public programs serving the elderly (Silverstein and Parrott, 1997) and more willing to take a parent into the household as adults (Szinovacz, 1997). Longitudinal studies are rarely available to identify antecedents of relations between grandparents and their adult grandchildren or to track long-term changes in these relationships.

Social-Cultural Context

The life course perspective also stresses the cultural societal contexts within which family development takes place. The type and level of grandparent involvement have a basis in cultural norms that emphasize or downplay the role of grandparents and in the social and economic organizational aspects of the region that create or inhibit opportunities for grandparents to contribute to the family unit. For instance, the social ecology of grandparenting has been observed by King and Elder (1998), who found that paternal grandparents in rural Iowa communities tended to have stronger relations with their grandchildren than did maternal grandparents, a reverse of the pattern found in urban families (King and Elder, 1995). This feature of rural Iowa families is attributed to the unique organization of the farm family, with its strong patrilineal line of inheritance. Ethnic differences have also been observed with respect to African-American and Hispanic grandparents, who tend to be more involved than white grandparents in the lives of their grandchildren (Burton, 1990; Dilworth-Anderson, 1992; Hunter, 1997; Kennedy, 1990; Silverstein and Marenco, 2001).

Summary

In this section we have situated grandparenting activities within the context of historical time by assessing the responses, impacts, and needs of grandparents as products of the unique demands placed on families in particular sociohistorical periods. Further, we have considered the family as a system of mutually interacting actors by taking into account the interdependence of grandparents with members of other generations in the family. Last, we have assessed the impact of broad cultural, social, and economic trends by investigating the interaction between macrosocial change and family functioning. These approaches will further our understanding of the role played by grandparents in ensuring the well-being of families under various social conditions and contexts. Examining these issues is important because recent historical trends such as population aging, occupational restructuring, economic growth, and alterations in family forms have changed the microsocial contexts in which individuals negotiate the challenges of adulthood and aging and have, at the same time, increased the importance of grandparents to the well-being of the family.

Developmental theory has relevance as well within the context of a *family systems perspective*. The latter perspective expands the unit of analysis beyond even the relationship, to include the wider web of family interconnections. The basic premises of the systems approach is that the elements of a system are interconnected, that systems are best understood as wholes, and that systems adjust themselves through environmental feedback (Klein and White, 1996). Implicit in this formulation is the idea that, in the case of families, systems strive toward equilibrium through the transfer of resources (Broderick, 1993).

EMPIRICAL ILLUSTRATIONS OF THE LIFE COURSE APPROACH TO GRANDPARENTING

Contribution of Grandparents to the Well-Being of Grandchildren

Do grandparents mitigate disruptive family processes that would otherwise harm the well-being of grandchildren? The life course perspective—particularly its emphasis on early life experiences and cohort membership as social forces that shape life chances—is a useful conceptual device for organizing the analytic design used in studying this issue. When this paradigm has been applied to family processes it has principally been used to study how early parental attachment and investments affect the quality of adult parent-child relationships (Henretta et al., 1997; Rossi and Rossi, 1990; Whitbeck, Hoyt, and Huck, 1994). These findings suggest that past family experiences have a unique and enduring influence on intergenerational family behavior. However, the long-term effects of early grandparent attachments, activities, and investments on the development of grandchildren into adulthood have received little attention. If these efforts serve to stabilize the family unit by promoting overall family well-being, then both tangible and symbolic reward will likely flow to grandchildren as a result.

Research will be discussed below that focuses on grandchildren who came of age in the early 1970s, and on their children who came of age in the 1990s. The family lives of these two generations have differed considerably due to social change over these two decades. The change that was most dramatic and had the most implications for family life was the rapid increase in divorce in the parental generation (DaVanzo and Rahman, 1993; Goldscheider and Goldscheider, 1993). Evidence over the past thirty years shows that children raised in single-parent households generally have lower average levels of psychological well-being and achievement than those raised by two biological parents (Acock and Keicolt, 1989; Amato and Booth, 1997; Duncan and Duncan, 1969; McLanahan and Sorensen, 1985). Thus, these two generations have passed the threshold from adolescence to adulthood facing very different family stressors deriving from rapid social change over the last quarter century.

Despite the fact that relationships with grandparents might have weakened on some dimensions due to divorce in the parental generation (Cherlin and Furstenberg, 1986; Johnson, 1988; Matthews and Sprey, 1985), a competing perspective hypothesizes that the importance of grandparents is elevated by the greater needs of grandchildren today. Grandparent involvement is an especially important potential source of social support, because unlike daycare, after-school programs, babysitters, nannies, and other formal sources of help, grandparents are related family members who typically have a high level of concern for the interests of their children and grandchildren. Moreover, there has been tremendous improvement in grandparents' economic well-being and standard of living over the past twenty-five years. At the same time, more years, on average, are spent in active and healthy states after retirement today, and fewer years are spent with chronic illnesses and limiting disabilities. These positive trends may make grandparent involvement more important for grandchildren than ever before. Under this formulation, the potential for grandparents to ease the transition of their grandchildren to adulthood is even greater today than in the past. If grandparents truly serve a stabilizing function within the family system, then turbulent family experiences of contemporary grandchildren are more likely to be buffered, and the negative consequences of those experiences are more likely to be ameliorated, by interventions of grandparents.

Sample

We illustrate the issues raised above using data from the Longitudinal Study of Generations (LSOG). The baseline LSOG sample originated in 1971 and consisted of 2,044 individuals from 328 three-generation families: grandparents (G1s), their middle-age children (G2s), and their early adult or late-adolescent grandchildren (G3s) aged 16–26. Grandfathers in these families were selected via a multistage stratified random sampling procedure from a population of 840,000 individuals enrolled in southern

California's first large HMO (for further detail, see Bengtson, 1975, 1996). These grandfathers and their spouses, as well as their adult children and grandchildren and their spouses, were mailed a questionnaire to fill out. Since 1985, funding has allowed repeated assessments at three-year intervals.

The Wave-1 response rate for individual family members was 65 percent (2,044/3,160). This rate is comparable to initial response rates of other panel surveys of aging, even though response rates for mail self-administered surveys are usually much lower than those for face-to-face interviews. The eligible sample in subsequent waves of the LSOG (1985, 1988, 1991, 1994, 1997, 2000) has included all family members who were eligible at baseline (even if they did not respond at Wave-1), with the following adjustments: Participants became ineligible if they died or became mentally incapacitated ($N = 533$), or if they could not be located after the fourteen years between Wave-1 and Wave-2 ($N = 325$). Additions to the eligible sample have included new spouses (mostly G3s) and, since Wave-4 (1991), great-grandchildren (G4) who reached 16 years of age. Longitudinal participation rates were 67 percent between Wave 1 and Wave 2 and 85 percent, on average, between waves since 1985.

In the LSOG data, the reliability and validity of measurement scales have been extensively examined and found to exceed minimum levels necessary to assume their scalability and structural invariance over time (reliabilities range from .70 to .93). The most comprehensive analyses have been conducted on the dimensions of affectual solidarity (Bengtson and Roberts, 1991; Bengtson and Schrader, 1982; Mangen, Bengtson, and Landry, 1988; Roberts and Bengtson, 1993; Roberts, Richards, and Bengtson, 1991). Measurement properties of other key scales are reported in Bengtson (1996).

The LSOG affords data on the aging of successive generations over identical ages. Such a design represents an elaboration of the cross-cohort longitudinal designs described by Schaie (1965, 1977, 1994). Of special interest are two cohorts of grandchildren, the G3s and the G4s, who came of age in two different historical periods. Table 1 shows the match in age in adjacent cohorts in 1971 and 1997. Each generation of grandchildren averaged 19 years of age (G3s in 1971; G4s in 1997), while the parental generation was in their early forties (G2s in 1971; G3s in 1997) and the grandparental generation was in their early to midsixties (G1s in 1971; G2s in 1997). Because adjacent generations are measured at the same stage of life, it is possible to examine similarities and contrasts while holding age and family life stage constant, thereby allowing attribution of cross-generational differences to periodicity or historical factors. We call this a cross-generational design.

Table 4.1   Cross-Generational Design: Life Stage Comparisons across Two Historical Periods

	1971		1997	
Life Stage	*Average Age*	*Generation*	*Average Age*	*Generation*
Early Adulthood	19	G3	19	G4
Middle Adulthood	44	G2	42	G3
Late Adulthood	64	G1	62	G2

Although the LSOG does not well represent the poor or ethnic minorities, it represents a wide range of social classes, from the working poor to the upper middle class. Second, the prevalence of parental divorce in the sample roughly follows national trends, with 11 percent of grandparents, 20 percent of parents, and 43 percent of grandchildren having experienced a parental divorce. Third, the sample is unique in its long-term, longitudinal design and provides the opportunity to perform *cross-generational analysis* to investigate historical differences in family functioning.

Dimensions of Grandparent-Grandchild Relations

Relationships between grandchildren and their grandparents are conceptualized as consisting of three dimensions, deriving from the paradigm of intergenerational solidarity outlined by Bengtson and colleagues (see Roberts et al., 1991). First is the level of emotional attachment or *affectual solidarity* that the grandchild has for each grandparent. Second is the amount of contact with each grandparent, or *associational solidarity*. Third, is geographic distance, or *structural solidarity*. Fourth is agreement of opinions between grandparent and grandchild, or *consensual solidarity*. Fifth is social and emotional support, or *functional solidarity*. Each grandchild in the sample was asked about these dimensions with respect to their grandmothers and grandfathers on the maternal and paternal sides at each wave of the survey.

Cross-Generational Differences: Historical Effects

In this section we examine whether contemporary grandchildren have different relations with their grandparents than an earlier cohort of grandchildren. We present in Figures 4.1–4.4 levels of affection, association, distance, and consensus between grandparents and their adolescent and adult grandchildren in two similarly aged cohorts of grandchildren in

1971 and 1997. The first three figures show that contemporary grandchildren generally have weaker emotional attachments, have lower rates of contact, and live in less proximity to their grandparents than the cohort of grandchildren 26 years earlier. These findings suggest that relations between grandparents and their adolescent and young adult grandchildren have generally weakened over historical time on measures reflecting intimacy, interaction, and proximity. However, Figure 4.4 shows that more contemporary grandchildren perceive fewer differences in the opinions and values of their grandparents. Thus, generational cleavages—which may have been most deep during the turbulent 1960s—show much less of a gap today.

Long-Term Trajectories: Grandparents from Age 60 to 85

Figure 4.5 shows the long-term trajectories of affectual solidarity in grandparent-grandchild relationships in the 1971 cohort of grandparents (G1s) as they age 26 years. The average rate of change is shown for grandparents who age from about 60 to 85 years of age, while their grandchildren have passed from adolescence to middle age. Here we see a downward trend in the quality of the intergenerational bond over time, followed by a strengthening in later life. The downward trend has been demonstrated by other researchers, who have cited competing family and work demands on young adult grandchildren as potentially disruptive to their relationships with grandparents. However, the rise in the strength of these ties suggests that attachments between grandparents and grandchildren strengthen in the late old age of grandparents, when their position as family patriarchs or matriarchs has more meaning to middle-aged grandchildren, especially to those with children of their own.

Linked Lives Over Time: The Intergenerational Stake

By linking grandparent-grandchild dyads, we are also able to assess intergenerational differences in the perception of the common relationship. The "intergenerational stake phenomenon" (Giarrusso, Stallings, and Bengtson, 1995) is a pattern in which older generations perceive intergenerational relations in a more positive light than do younger generations. In Figure 4.6, we show that the older generation in all types of intergenerational dyads perceives a closer relationship than does the younger generation. This trend holds in G1–G3 dyads as well, which suggests that grandparents have a greater stake in the relationship than do the grandchildren, and that this gap actually widens over time, as the G3 grandchildren exhibit weakening emotional commitment and their grandparents exhibit strengthening emotional commitment. These results sug-

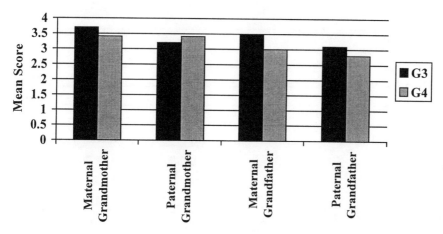

Figure 4.1 Affectual solidarity: Comparison of G3 in 1971 to G4 in 1997.

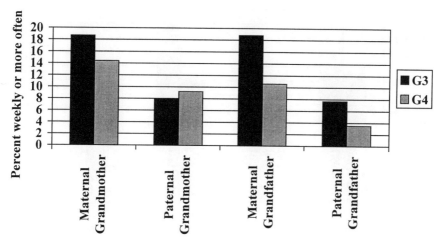

Figure 4.2 Associational solidarity: Comparison of G3 in 1971 to G4 in 1997.

gest that grandchildren are becoming increasingly more important to their grandparents than grandparents are becoming to their grandchildren. Such evidence highlights the importance of considering generational placement—whether higher or lower in the generational line—when assessing the quality of grandparent-grandchild relations.

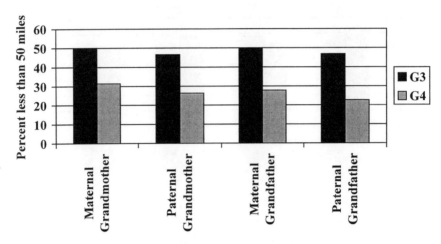

Figure 4.3   Structural solidarity: Comparison of G3 in 1971 to G4 in 1997.

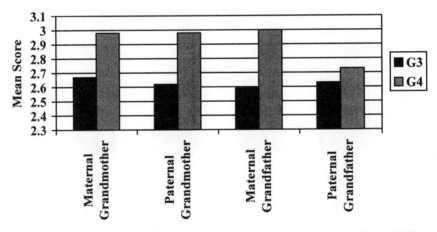

Figure 4.4   Consensual solidarity: Comparison of G3 in 1971 to G4 in 1997.

Ethnic Culture: Anglo vs. Mexican-American

In order to test the invariance in the intergenerational stake phenomenon across ethnic groups (Giarrusso, Feng, Silverstein, and Bengtson,
2001), a comparison was made between the LSOG and the Study of Mexican-American Families (see Markides and Krause, 1995), a data set with
the same measures as the LSOG and a similar design but consisting of only

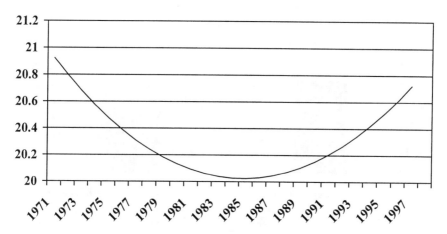

Figure 4.5   Estimated growth curve of affectual solidarity between grand-
8parents and grandchildren.

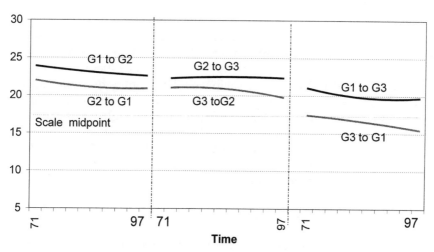

Figure 4.6   Affectual solidarity over time for linked generations, 1971–1997.

Mexican-American families. Since the intergenerational stake, as established in Anglo families, might be based on the preference of the younger
generation for autonomy from the older generation, this phenomenon
may be culturally circumscribed. In a cultural group with strong norms of
familism, such as Mexican-Americans, the incentive in the younger generation may be to minimize generational distance and stress generational

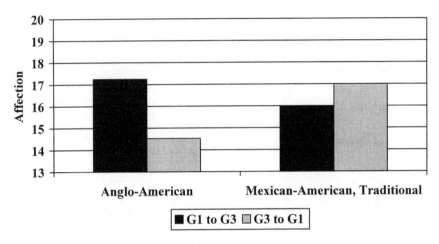

Figure 4.7 Grandparent-grandchild affection across two ethnic groups in linked generations.

continuity as an expression of filial piety. In Figure 4.7 we show the generational difference for grandparent-grandchild relations in Anglo families of the LSOG and in Mexican-American families that adhere more to traditional culture. We note the reversal in the relative strength of affectual solidarity between the two ethnic groups. In Mexican-American families, grandchildren express greater affection for their grandparents than their grandparents express toward them. Thus, when evaluating the cross-generational dyads, attention must be paid to the potential of culture to moderate the nature of intergenerational differences in the perception of grandparent-grandchild relations.

Social Ecology: Urban vs. Rural

Much has been written about the role of urban-rural context in structuring intergenerational relations. Here we compare our southern California families in the LSOG with those in the Iowa Study of Farm Families to identify differences in the extent to which grandchildren receive advice and guidance from their grandparents (see King, Silverstein, Elder, Bengtson, and Conger, in press). We see in Figure 4.8 that in Iowa farm, Iowa nonfarm, and southern California families, maternal grandmothers are most likely to provide advice and guidance. However, fewer than half as many Los Angeles grandchildren as Iowa grandchildren receive such advice across all types of grandparents. This difference is most pronounced among paternal grandfathers, which is likely the product of a

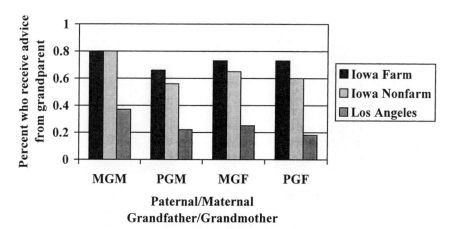

Figure 4.8 Percentage of grandchildren who receive advice from grandparents by urban-rural context.

patrilineal line of land inheritance that characterizes many farm families.
The results highlight the importance of considering social and economic
structures in the local ecology when examining the nature of the grandparent-grandchild bond.

Linked Lives: Effects of Divorce in the Middle Generation

The effects of parental divorce on grandparent-grandchild relations are
well-known, but less is known about the persistence of these effects when
children of divorce become adults. We examine differences between intact
and divorced families in terms of the strength of affective ties between
grandparents and grandchildren. From Figure 4.9, we see that the strength
of the bond is weaker in families with parental divorce than in those with
marriages intact. The disruptive effect appears to be most severe when the
parental divorce occurred in the teen years of the grandchild (13+). These
results further highlight the need to take into account the parental generation as gatekeepers between grandparents and grandchildren, as well as
the timing of divorce in the family life cycle.

Grandparents as Moderators of Grandchild Well-Being

Next, we examine the ability of grandparent involvement to buffer the
negative effects of divorce on the self-esteem of grandchildren. We first

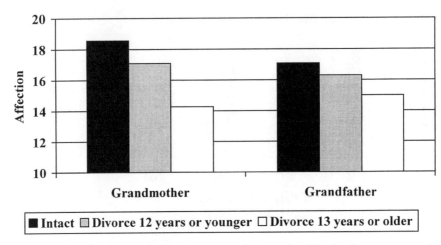

Figure 4.9   Effects of parental divorce on affectual solidarity between grandparents and grandchildren.

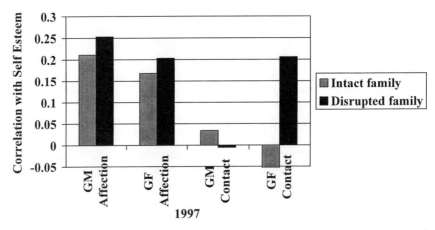

Figure 4.10   Contemporaneous correlations between affection/contact with
grandparents and self-esteem of grandchildren by parental status.

examine the contemporaneous influence of affection and contact on level
of self-esteem in grandchildren in 1997. Figure 4.10 shows these influences
as correlations between these two aspects of grandparent involvement and
self-esteem scores of grandchildren. We see positive correlations of affection with self-esteem. These correlations are somewhat higher for grandchildren whose parents have experienced a divorce. With regard to the

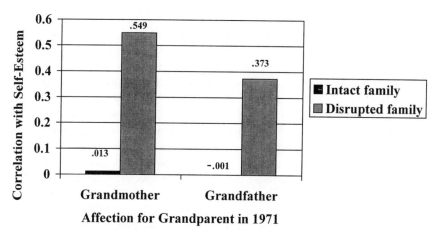

Figure 4.11 Correlations between affection for grandparents in 1971 and grandchildren's self-esteem in 1997 by parental status.

protective effects of contact with grandparents, only contact with grandfathers shows a similar pattern to affection, with greater grandparental contact associated with higher self-esteem among grandchildren from disrupted families. Thus, it appears that grandparental involvement has the ability to compensate for the negative effects of divorce on the self-esteem of adolescent and adult grandchildren.

In order to test for more enduring effects of grandparental involvement, we examine the relationship between affection from grandparents in 1971 and the self-esteem of grandchildren in 1997. Figure 4.11 shows almost no correlation among grandchildren whose parents' marriages were intact, but relatively high correlations among grandchildren who parents' marriages were disrupted. This effect holds for relations both with grandmothers and grandfathers. It is noteworthy that these correlations represent outcomes that are lagged by 26 years, which suggests that the effects of grandparents may be long-lasting, promoting the healthy development of grandchildren into their adults years.

CONCLUSION

In this chapter we have discussed a life course approach to the study of grandparent-grandchild relations in four-generation families and have provided some empirical illustrations of its application. In doing so, we have emphasized the importance of context—temporal, cultural, generational, and ecological—in promoting a fuller understanding of what has been called an "ambiguous" family relationship. Indeed, we suggest that the label "ambiguous," while relevant at the microlevel of family interaction, may not be relevant at the macro comparative level where distinct role patterning can be detected across various contexts.

We hope to accomplish two goals in advancing family science in this area of research. First, in outlining the importance of these contextual dimensions, we have potentially added greater complexity to the study of grandparent-grandchild relations. The requirements of cross-cultural, cross-generational, and cross-time hypotheses require that more elaborated models and hypotheses be developed to account for these added contingencies, as well as appropriate data to address additional hypotheses. However, any burden imposed on the researcher by this ambitious agenda is more than compensated for by the explanatory power that life course dimensions offer in terms of model building and testing. Our findings from the LSOG hint at the potential for uncovering important but "hidden" sources of structured variation in grandparenting that become apparent with appropriate data and theory to guide empirical models.

Second, we hope to add greater theoretical parsimony to the study of grandparenting by using a paradigm that relativizes grandparent-grandchild relations within the social-temporal contexts in which families function. Most studies of grandparents and grandchildren have tended to be nontheoretical, which has resulted in a volume of valuable but disparate findings that are difficult to synthesize. We believe that the evolution of a generalized theory of grandparenting requires integration of microlevel phenomena in the family with macrosocial, historical, and systemic forces that give shape to microinteractions. The life course perspective provides a set of organizing principles within which such an integration may evolve. How grandparents serve as adaptive resources to families across time and place will be the focus of research for some time to come and will provide a more complete rendering of the dynamic relationships between grandparents and grandchildren in the multi-generational family.

REFERENCES

Acock, A. C., and Keicolt, J. K. 1989. Is it family structure or socioeconomic status? Family structure during adolescence and adult adjustment. *Social Forces*, 68, 553–71.

Ahrons, C. R., and Bowman, M. E. 1981. Changes in family relationships following divorce of an adult child: Grandmother's perceptions. *Journal of Divorce* 5:49–68.

Allen, K. R., and Walker, A. J. 1992. Attentive love: A feminist perspective on the caregiving of adult daughters. *Family Relations* 41:284–89.

Amato, P. R., and Booth, A. 1997. *A generation at risk: Growing up in an era of family upheaval.* Cambridge, MA: Harvard University Press.

Amato, P. R., Rezac, S. J., and Booth, A. 1995. Helping between parents and young adult offspring: The role of parental marital quality, divorce, and remarriage. *Journal of Marriage and the Family* 57(2):363–74.

Astone, N. M., and McLanahan, S. S. 1991. Family structure, parental practices, and high school completion. *American Sociological Review* 56:309–20.

Bass, S. A., and Caro, F. G. 1996. The economic value of grandparent assistance. *Generations* 20:29–33.

Baydar, N., and Brooks-Gunn, J. 1998. Profiles of grandmothers who help care for their grandchildren in the United States. *Family Relations* 47(4):385–93.

Bengtson, V. L. 1975. Generation and family effects in value socialization. *American Sociological Review* 40(3):358–71.

———. 1996. Continuities and discontinuities in intergenerational relationships over time. In V. L. Bengtson (ed.), *Adulthood and aging: Research on continuities and discontinuities.* New York: Springer.

Bengtson, V. L., and Allen, K. R. 1993. The life course perspective applied to families over time. In P. Boss, W. Doherty, R. LaRossa, W. Schumm, and S. Steinmetz (eds.), *Sourcebook of family theories and methods: A contextual approach* (pp. 469–98). New York: Plenum.

Bengtson, V. L., Biblarz, T., and Roberts, R. E. L. 2002. *How families still matter.* New York: Cambridge University Press.

Bengtson, V. L., and Robertson, J. F. 1985. *Grandparenthood.* Beverly Hills, CA: Sage.

Bengtson, V. L., and Roberts, R. E. L. 1991. Inter-generational solidarity in aging families: An example of formal theory construction. *Journal of Marriage and the Family* 53:856–70.

Bengtson, V. L., and Schrader, S. S. 1982. Parent-child relations. In D. Mangen and W. Peterson (eds.), *Handbook of research instruments in social gerontology.* Minneapolis: University of Minnesota Press.

Bengtson, V. L., and Silverstein, M. 1993. Families, aging, and social change: Seven agendas for 21st century researchers. In G. Maddox and M. P. Lawton (eds.), *Kinship, aging, and social change,* Vol. 13, *Annual review of gerontology and geriatrics* (Vol. 13, pp. 15–38). New York: Springer.

Blankenhorn, D. 1995. Fatherhood. *New Republic* 213(23):4.

Broderick, C. O. 1993. *Understanding families.* Newbury Park, CA: Sage.

Bumpass, L. L. 1990. What's happening to the family? Interactions between demographic and institutional change. *Demography* 27:483–98.

Burton, L. M. 1990. Teenage childbearing as an altering life course strategy in multigeneration black families. *Human Nature* 1:123–43.

———. 1995. Inter-generational patterns of providing care in African-American families with teenage childbearers: Emergent patterns in an ethnographic study. In K. W. Schaie, V. L. Bengtson, and L. M. Burton, (eds.), *Adult intergenerational relations: Effects of social change* (pp. 79–96). New York: Springer.

Chalfie, D. 1994. *Going it alone: A closer look at grandparents parenting grandchildren.* Washington, DC: AARP.

Cherlin, A. J., and Furstenberg, F. F. 1986. *The new American grandparent: A place in the family, a life apart.* New York: Basic Books.

Clingempeel, W. G., Colyar, J. J., Brand, E., and Hetherington, E. M. 1992. Children's relationships with maternal grandparents: A longitudinal study of family structure and pubertal status effects. *Child Development* 63(6):1404-22.

Conger, R. D., Elder, J., and Glen, H. 1994. *Families in troubled times: Adapting to change in rural America.* Hawthorne, NY: Aldine de Gruyter.

Cooney, T. M., and Smith, L. A. 1996. Young adults' relations with grandparents following recent parental divorce. *Journals of Gerontology: Series B: Psychological Sciences and Social Sciences* 52B(2):S91–S95.

Cooney, T. M., and Uhlenberg, P. 1990. The role of divorce in men's relations with their adult children after mid-life. *Journal of Marriage and the Family* 52:677–88.

Creighton, L. 1991. Silent saviors. *U.S. News and World Report* December 16, pp. 81–89.

DaVanzo, J., and Rahman, M. O. 1993. American families: Trends and correlates. *Population Index* 59:350–86.

Denham, T. E., and Smith, C. W. 1989. The influence of grandparents on grandchildren: A review of the literature and resources. *Family Relations* 38:345–50.

Dilworth-Anderson, P. 1992. Extended kin networks in black families. *Generations* 16:29–32.

Duncan, B., and Duncan, O. D. 1969. Family stability and occupational success. *Social Problems* 16:273–85.

Elder, G. H. 1984. Families, kin, and the life course: A sociological perspective. In Ross D. Parke (ed.), *Review of child development research: The family* (pp. 80–136). Chicago: University of Chicago Press.

———. 1994. Time, human aging, and social change: Perspectives on the life course. *Social Psychology Quarterly* 57:4–15.

Elder, G. H., and O'Rand, A. 1995. Adult lives in a changing society. In K. S. Cook, G. A. Fine, and J. S. House (eds.), *Sociological perspectives on social psychology.* Needham Heights, MA: Allyn and Bacon.

Elder, G. H., Rudkin, L., and Conger, R. D. 1995. Inter-generational continuity and change in rural America. In V. L. Bengtson, K. W. Schaie, and L. M. Burton (eds.), *Adult inter-generational relations: Effects of societal change.* New York: Springer.

Farkas, J., and Hogan, D. 1994. The demography of changing inter-generational relationships. In V. L. Bengtson, K. W. Schaie, and L. M. Burton (eds.), *Adult inter-generational relations: Effects of societal change* (pp. 1–19). New York: Springer.

Field, D., and Minkler, M. 1988. Continuity and change in social support between young-old, old-old, and very-old adults. *Journal of Gerontology: Psychological Sciences* 43:P100–P106.

Fischer, L. R., and Silverman, J. 1982. Grandmothering as a tenuous role relationship. Paper presented at the annual meetings of the National Council on Family Relations, Portland, OR.

Fuller-Thomson, E., Minkler, M., and Driver, D. 1997. A profile of grandparents raising grandchildren in the United States. *Gerontologist* 37(3):406–11.

Giarrusso, R., Feng, D., Silverstein, M., and Bengtson, V. L. 2001. Grandparent-adult grandchild affection and consensus: Cross-generational and cross-ethnic comparisons. *Journal of Family Issues* 22(4):456–77.

Giarrusso, R., Stallings, M., and Bengtson, V. L. 1995. The "intergenerational stake" hypothesis revisited: Parent-child differences in perceptions of relationships 20 years. In V. L. Bengtson, K. W. Schaie, and L. M. Burton (eds.), *Adult intergenerational relations: Effects of societal change* (pp. 227–63). New York: Springer.

Glenn, N., and Kramer, K. B. 1987. The marriages and divorces of the children of divorce. *Journal of Marriage and the Family* 49:811–25.

Goldscheider, F. K. 1990. The aging of the gender revolution. *Research on Aging,* 12:531–45.

Goldscheider, F. K., and Goldscheider, C. 1993. *Leaving home before marriage: Ethnicity, familism, and generational relationships.* Madison: University of Wisconsin Press.

Goode, W. J. 1963. *World revolution and family patterns.* London: Free Press.

Hagestad, G. O. 1985. Continuity and connectedness. In V. L. Bengtson and J. F. Robertson (eds.), *Grandparenthood* (pp. 31–48). Beverly Hills, CA: Sage.

Hareven, T. K. 1982. *Family time and industrial time.* Cambridge, England: Cambridge University Press.

_____. 1994. Family change and historical change. In M. W. Riley, R. L. Kahn, and A. Foner (eds.), *Age and structural lag* (pp. 130–50). New York: Wiley.

_____. 1995. Historical perspectives on the family and aging. In R. Blieszner and V. H. Bedford (eds.), *Handbook of aging and the family* (pp. 13–31). Westport, CT: Greenwood.

Hawkes, K., O'Connell, J. F., Jones, N. G. B., Alvarez, H., and Charnov, E. L. 1998. Grandmothering, menopause, and the evolution of human life histories. *Proceedings of the National Academy of Sciences* 95:1336–39.

Henretta, J. C., Hill, M. S., Li, W., Soldo, B. J., and Wolf, D. A. 1997. Selection of children to provide care: the effect of earlier parental transfers. *Journals of Gerontology: Series B: Psychological and Social Sciences,* 52B(Special Issue):110–19.

Hilton, J. M., and Macari, D. P. 1997. Grandparent involvement following divorce: A comparison of single-mother and single-father families. *Journal of Divorce and Remarriage* 28(1–2):203–24.

Hunter, A. G. 1997. Counting on grandmothers: Black mothers' and fathers' reliance on grandmothers for parenting support. *Journal of Family Issues* 18(3):251–69.

Jaskowski, S. K., and Dellasega, C. 1993. Effects of divorce on the grandparent-grandchild relationship. *Issues in Comprehensive Pediatric Nursing* 16:125–33.

Johnson, C. L. 1988. *Ex familia: Grandparents, parents, and children adjust to divorce.* New Brunswick, NJ: Rutgers University Press.

Kennedy, G. E. 1990. College students' expectations of grandparent and grandchild behaviors. *Gerontologist* 30:43–48.

King, V., and Elder, G. H., Jr. 1998. Education and grandparenting roles. *Research on Aging* 20(4):450–74.

_____. 1995. American children view their grandparents: Linked lives across three rural generations. *Journal of Marriage and the Family* 57:165–78.

King, V., Silverstein, M., Elder, G. H., Jr., Bengtson, V. L., and Conger R. In press. Relations with Grandparents: Rural midwest versus urban southern California. *Journal of Family Issues.*

Klein, D. M., and White, J. M. 1996 *Family theories: An introduction.* Thousand Oaks, CA: Sage.

Kruk, E., and Hall, B. L. 1995. The disengagement of paternal grandparents subsequent to divorce. *Journal of Divorce and Remarriage* 23(1–2):131–47.

Langer, N. 1990. Grandparents and adult grandchildren: What do they do for one another? *International Journal of Aging and Human Development* 31:101–10.

Lavers, C. A., and Sonuga-Barke, E. J. S. 1997. Annotation: On the grandmothers' role in the adjustment and maladjustment of grandchildren. *Journal of Child Psychology and Psychiatry* 38:747–53.

Mangen, D. J., Bengtson, V. L., and Landry, P. H., Jr. 1988. *The measurement of intergenerational relations.* Beverly Hills, CA: Sage.

Markides, J. and Krause, N. 1985. Intergenerational solidarity and psychological well-being among older Mexican-Americans: A three-generation study. *Journal of Gerontology* 40:506–11.

Matthews, S. H., and Sprey, J. 1985. Adolescents' relationships with grandparents: An empirical contribution to conceptual clarification. *Journal of Gerontology* 40: 621–26.

McLanahan, S. S., and Sorensen, A. B. 1985. Life events and psychological well-being over the life course. In J. Elder and H. Glen (eds.), *Life course dynamics: Trajectories and transitions, 1968–1980.* Ithaca, NY: Cornell University Press.

Minkler, M., and Roe, K. M. 1993. *Grandmothers as caregivers.* Newbury Park, CA: Sage.

Mutran, E. J., and Reitzes, D. C. 1984. Inter-generational support activities and well-being among the elderly: A convergence of exchange and symbolic interaction perspectives. *American Sociological Review* 49:117–30.

Neugarten, B. L. 1964. The changing American grandparent. *Journal of Marriage and the Family* 26:199–204.

Parsons, T., and Bales, R. F. 1955. *Family, socialization and interaction process.* Glencoe, IL: Free Press.

Pashos, A. 2000. Does paternal uncertainty explain discriminative grandparental solicitude? A cross-cultural study in Greece and Germany. *Evolution and Human Behavior* 21(2):97–109.

Popenoe, D. 1988. *Disturbing the nest: Family change and decline in modern societies.* Hawthorne, NY: Aldine de Gruyter.

———. 1993. American family decline, 1960–1990: A review and appraisal. *Journal of Marriage and the Family* 55:527–55.

Riley, M. W., and Riley, J. W. 1993. Connections: Kin and cohort. In V. L. Bengtson and W. A. Achenbaum (eds.), *The changing contract across generations* (pp. 169–90). Hawthorne, NY: Aldine de Gruyter.

Roberts, R. E. L., and Bengtson, V. L. 1993. Relationships with parents, self-esteem, and psychological well-being in young adulthood: A further examination of identity theory. *Social Psychology Quarterly* 56:263–77.

Roberts, R. E. L., Richards, L. N., and Bengtson, V. L. 1991. Inter-generational solidarity in families: Untangling the ties that bind. *Marriage and Family Review* 16(1/2):11–46.

Rossi, A. S., and Rossi, P. H. 1990. *Of human bonding: Parent-children relationships across the life course.* Hawthorne, NY: Aldine de Gruyter.

Schaie, K. W. 1965. A general model for the study of developmental change. *Psychological Bulletin* 64:92–107.

―――. 1977. Quasi-experimental research designs in the psychology of aging. In J. E. Birren and K. W. Schaie (eds.), *Handbook of the psychology of aging*. New York: Van Nostrand Reinhold.

―――. 1994. Developmental designs revisited. In S. H. Cohen and H. W. Reese (eds.), *Life-span developmental psychology: Theoretical issues revisited* (pp. 45–64). Hillsdale, NJ: Erlbaum.

Schone, B. S., and Pezzin, L. E. 1999. Parental marital disruption and inter-generational transfers: An analysis of lone elderly parents and their children. *Demography* 36(3):287–97.

Silverstein, M., and Bengtson, V. L. 1991. Do close parent-child relations reduce the mortality risk of older parents? *Journal of Health and Social Behavior* 32:382–95.

Silverstein, M., and Chen, X. 1999. The impact of acculturation in Mexican-American families on the quality of adult grandchild-grandparent relationships. *Journal of Marriage and the Family* 61:188–98.

Silverstein, M., Lawton, L., and Bengtson, V., L. 1994. Types of inter-generational relations. In R. Harootyan, V. L. Bengtson, and M. Schlesinger (eds.), *Hidden connections: Inter-generational linkages in American society*. New York: Springer.

Silverstein, M., and Long, J., D. 1998. Trajectories of grandparents' perceived solidarity with adult grandchildren: A growth curve analysis over 23 years. *Journal of Marriage and the Family*, 60(4) 912–23.

Silverstein, M., and Marenco, A. L. 2001. How Americans enact the grandparent role. *Journal of Family Issues* 22:493–522.

Silverstein, M., and Parrott, T. 1997. Attitudes toward public support of the elderly: Does early involvement with grandparents moderate generational tensions? *Research on Aging* 19:108–32.

Solomon, J. C., and Marx, J. 1995. To grandmother's house we go: Health and school adjustment of children raised solely by grandparents. *Gerontologist* 35(3):386–94.

Stacey, J. 1991. *Brave new families: Stories of domestic upheaval in late twentieth century America*. New York: Basic Books.

Strom, R. D., Buki, L. P., and Strom, S. K. 1997. Inter-generational perceptions of English speaking and Spanish speaking Mexican-American grandparents. *International Journal of Aging and Human Development* 45(1):1–21.

Szinovacz, M. E. 1997. *Grandparenthood: Profiles, supports, and transitions*. Norfolk, VA: AARP Andrus Foundation.

―――. 1998. Grandparents today: A demographic profile. *Gerontologist* 38:37–52.

Troll, L. 1983. Grandparents: The family watchdogs. In T. Brubaker (ed.), *Family relationships in late life* (pp. 63–74). Beverly Hills, CA: Sage.

Uhlenberg, P. 1996. Mortality decline in the twentieth century and supply of kin over the life course. *Gerontologist* 36:681–85.

Uhlenberg, P., and Hammill, B. G. 1998. Frequency of contact with grandchild sets: Six factors that make a difference. *Gerontologist* 38:276–85.

Umberson, D., and Chen, M. D. 1994. Effects of a parent's death on adult children: Relationship salience and reaction to loss. *American Sociological Review* 59: 152–68

Umberson, D., Wortman, C. B., and Kessler, R. C. 1992. Widowhood and depression: Explaining long-term gender differences in vulnerability. *Journal of Health and Social Behavior* 33:10–24.

Whitbeck, L. B., Hoyt, D. R., and Huck, S. M. 1994. Early family relationships, intergenerational solidarity, and support provided to parents by their adult children. *Journal of Gerontology: Social Sciences* 49(2):S85–S94.

| 5 |

Older People and Family in Social Policy

Simon Biggs and Jason L. Powell

SOCIAL POLICY, AGING AND THE FAMILY

There has been an increasing interest in aging families within the social policy literature of recent years. This is a trend that has cut across both U.S. and European research (Bengtson, Giarrusso, Silverstein, and Wang, 2003; Lowenstein, 2003; Minkler, 1999; Walker and Naegele, 1999). The reasons for such growth are as much social and political, as they are academic. Western governments of left and right political persuasion recognize that the "family" is important for social and economic needs and this should be reflected in our understanding of family processes and in social policy associated with supporting families.

Conceptually, the notion of the "family" is often taken for granted and is not a term with a fixed meaning (Moen and Wethington, 1992; Silverstein and Bengtson, 1997). We can never be quite sure what "family" means unless we can understand the context in which it is used. Policymakers and politicians, for example, often use the idea of the family in their attempts to shape social relationships. In commonsense everyday language, people indicate what they mean by family when they are interacting with each other. As we become aware of the increasing fluidity of age-based roles and relationships and the multiple influences that impinge on family behavior, it has also become attractive to view families and family members as living by certain scripts or narratives.

To understand families and the social relations they represent, we must recognize that the meaning of the family changes in response to a wide variety of social, economic, political, cultural, and interpersonal conditions.

Policy both is an attempt to shape and is itself shaped by these meanings. Modern social systems depend upon families. One reason is that children come to be citizens because of the instruction and training provided in the private life of families (Giddens, 1993). Indeed, it is in families that people are expected to learn what it is to become a responsible citizen. Western governments generally assume an organization of society that requires families to perform work of caring, training, and socializing its members. In the United Kingdom, for example, much politicking has surrounded family life, including controversies over single parenting, financial support by absent fathers, and proposed legal reforms concerning divorce, domestic violence, and family homes (Williams, 1994). Policy narratives have centered on marking changes in the ways women, men, children, and "wider family" members interrelate, have relationships with one another, and the consequences of such changes for individuals and for society as a whole.

Narrativity has become popular in the human and social sciences, both as a method of undertaking and interpreting research (Holstein and Gubrium, 2000; Kenyon, Ruth, and Mader 1999;) and as a technique for modifying the self (McAdams, 1993; McLeod, 1997). Both Gubrium (1992) and Katz (1999) suggest that older people construct their own analytical models of personal identity based on lived experience and on narratives already existing in their everyday environments. By using a narrative approach, the meaning of family can be told through stories about the self as well as ones "at large" in public discourse.

"Discourse" itself is a phrase more often used to denote a relatively fixed set of stories to which individuals or groups have to conform in order to take up a recognized and legitimate role. Such an understanding of discourse can be found in the earlier work of Michel Foucault (1977) and others (Powell and Biggs, 2002). Self-storying draws attention to the ways in which family identities are both more open to negotiation and are more likely to be "taken in" in the sense of being owned and worked on by individuals themselves. Families, of course, are made up of interpersonal relationships within and between generations that are subject to both the formal rhetoric of public discourse, and the self-stories that bind them together in everyday life. The notion of family is, then, an amalgam of policy discourse and everyday negotiation and as such alerts us to the wider social implications of those relationships.

The rhetoric of social policy and the formal representations of adult aging and family life that one finds there provide a source of raw material for the construction of identity and a series of spaces in which such identities can be legitimately performed. It is perhaps not overstating the case to say that the "success" of a family policy can be judged from the degree to which people live within the stories or narratives of family created by it.

In fact, the relationship between families and older people has been consecutively rewritten in the social policy literature. Each time a different story has been told and different aspects of the relationship have been thrown into high relief. It might even be argued that the family has become a key site upon which expected norms of intergenerational relations and late-life citizenship are being built. This chapter explores the significance of such narratives, using developments in the United Kingdom as a case example that may also shed light on wider contemporary issues associated with old age.

The structure of the chapter is in four parts. We start by mapping out the emergence and consolidation of neoliberal family policy and its relationship to emphasis on family obligation, state surveillance, and active citizenship. Second, we highlight both the ideological continuities and discontinuities of the subsequent social democratic turn and their effects on older people and the family. Third, research studies are drawn on to highlight how "grandparenting" has been recognized by governments in recent years, as a particular way of "storying" the relationship between old age and family life. Finally, we explore ramifications for researching family policy and old age by pointing out that narratives of inclusion and exclusion often coexist. It is suggested that in the future, aging and family life will include the need to negotiate multiple policy narratives. At an interpersonal level, sophisticated narrative strategies would be required if a sense of familial continuity and solidarity is to be maintained.

A NEOLIBERAL STORY OF AGING AND THE FAMILY

Political and social debate since the Reagan/Thatcher years has been dominated by neoliberalism, which postulates the existence of autonomous, assertive, rational individuals who must be protected and liberated from "big government" and state interference (Gray, 1995). Indeed, Walker and Naegele (1999) claim a startling continuity across Europe in the way "the family" has been positioned by governments as these ideas have spread beyond their original "English speaking" base.

Neoliberal policies on the family have almost always started from a position of *laissez-faire*, except when extreme behavior threatens its members or wider social relations. Using the United Kingdom as a case example, it can be seen that that neoliberal policy came to focus on two main issues. While both only represent the point at which a minimalist approach from the state touches family life, they come to mark the dominant narrative through which aging and family are made visible in the public domain.

On the one hand, increasing attention was paid to the role families took in the care of older people who were either mentally or physically infirm. A series of policy initiatives (HMSO, 1981, 1989, 1990) recognized that families were a principal source of care and support. "Informal" family care became a key building block of policy toward an aging population. It both increased the salience of traditional family values and independence from government and enabled a reduction in direct support from the state.

On the other hand, helping professionals, following U.S. experience (Pillemer and Wolf, 1986), became increasingly aware of the abuse that older people might suffer and the need to protect vulnerable adults from a variety of forms of abuse and neglect (Biggs, Phillipson, and Kingston, 1995). Policy guidance, *No Longer Afraid: The Safeguard of Older People in Domestic Settings*, was issued in 1993 (HMSO, 1993), shortly after the move to seeing informal care as the mainstay of the welfare of older people. As the title suggests, this was also directed primarily at the family.

It is perhaps a paradox that a policy based ostensibly on the premises of leaving-be combines two narrative streams that result in increased surveillance of the family. This paradox is based largely on these points being the only ones where policy "saw" aging in families rather than ignoring it. This is not to say that real issues of abuse and neglect fail to exist, even though U.K. politicians have often responded to them as if they were some form of natural disaster unrelated to the wider policy environment (Biggs and Powell, 1999). To understand the linking of these narratives, it is important to examine trends tacit in the debate on family and aging, but central to wider public policy.

Wider economic priorities, to "roll back the state" and thereby release resources for individualism and free enterprise, have become translated into a family discourse about caring obligations and the need to enforce them. If families ceased to care, then the state would have to pick up the bill. It was not that families were spoken of as being naturally abusive. Neither was the "discovery" of familial abuse linked to community care policy outside academic debate (Biggs, 1996). Discourses on the rise of abuse and on informal care remained separate in the formal policy domain. However, a subtle change of narrative tone had taken place. Families, rather than being seen as "havens against a harsh world," were now easily perceived as potential sites of mistreatment, and the previously idealized role of the unpaid caregiver became that of a potential recalcitrant, attempting to avoid his or her family obligations. An attempt to protect a minority of abused elders thus took the shape of a tacit threat, hanging above the head of every aging family (Biggs and Powell, 2000). It is worth note that these policy developments took little account of research evidence indicating that family solidarity and a willingness to care had decreased in neither the United Kingdom (Phillipson, 1998; Wenger, 1994) nor the United States (Bengtson and Achenbaum, 1993). Further, it appeared that familial caring was actually moving away from relationships based on obligation and toward those based on negotiation (Finch and Mason, 1993). Family commitment for example, has been shown by

Pyke and Bengtson (1996), to vary depending upon the characteristic care-giving patterns within particular families. Individualistic families provided less instrumental help and made use of welfare services, whereas a second, collectivist pattern offered greater personal support. While this study focused primarily on upward generational support, Silverstein and Bengtson (1997) observed that "tight-knit" and "detached" family styles were equally common across generations. Unfortunately, policy developments have rarely taken differences in caregiving styles into account, preferring a general narrative of often idealized role relationships. It is not unfair to say that during the neoliberal period, the dominant narrative of family became that of a site of care going wrong.

A SOCIAL-DEMOCRATIC STORY OF AGING AND THE FAMILY

Social-democratic policies toward the family arose from the premise that by the early 1990s, the free-market policies of the Thatcher/Reagan years had seriously damaged the social fabric of the nation-state and that its citizens needed to be encouraged to identify again with the national project. A turn to an alternative, sometimes called "the third way," emerging under Clinton, Blair, and Schroeder administrations in the United States and parts of Europe, attempted to find means of mending that social fabric and, as part of it, relations between older people and their families. The direction that the new policy narrative took is summarized in Prime Minister Blair's (1996) statement, "The most meaningful stake anyone can have in society is the ability to earn a living and support a family." Work, or failing that, worklike activities, plus an active contribution to family life began slowly to emerge, delineating new narratives within which to grow old.

Giddens (1998) in the United Kingdom and Beck (1998) in Germany, both proponents of social democratic politics, have claimed that citizens are faced with the task of piloting themselves and their families through a changing world in which globalization has transformed our relations with each other, now based on avoiding risk. According to Giddens (1998), a new partnership is needed between government and civil society. Government support to the renewal of community through local initiative would gives an increasing role to "voluntary" organizations, encourages social entrepreneurship, and significantly supports the "democratic" family characterized by "equality, mutual respect, autonomy, decision-making through communication and freedom of violence." It is argued that social policy should be less concerned with "equality" and more with "inclusion," with community participation reducing the moral and financial hazard of dependence.

Through an increased awareness of the notion of ageism, the influence of European ideas about social inclusion, and North American social communitarianism, families and older people found themselves transformed into active citizens who should be encouraged to participate in society, rather than be seen as a potential burden upon it (Biggs, 2001). A contemporary U.K. policy document, entitled *Building a Better Britain for Older People,* is typical of a new genre of Western policy, restorying the role of older adults:

> The contribution of older people is vital, both to families, and to voluntary organisations and charities. We believe their roles as mentors—providing ongoing support and advice to families, young people and other older people—should be recognised. Older people already show a considerable commitment to volunteering. The Government is working with voluntary groups and those representing older people to see how we can increase the quality and quantity of opportunities for older people who want to volunteer. (Department of Social Security, 1998)

What is perhaps striking about this piece is that it is one of the few places where families are mentioned in an overview on older people, with the exception of a single mention of carers, many of whom, it is pointed out, "are pensioners themselves." In both cases the identified role for older people constitutes a reversal of the narrative offered in preceding policy initiatives. The older person, like other members of family structure, is portrayed as an active member of the milieu, offering care and support to others.

The dominant preoccupation of this policy initiative, is not however, concerned with families. Rather, there is a change of emphasis toward the notion of aging as an issue of lifestyle, and as such draws on contemporary gerontological observations of the "blurring" of age-based identities (Featherstone and Hepworth, 1993) and the growth of the gray consumer (Katz, 1999).

While such a narrative is attractive to pressure groups, voluntary agencies, and, indeed, social gerontologists, there is, just as with the policies of the neoliberals, an underlying economic motive that may or may not be of long-term advantage to older people and their families. Again, as policies develop, the force driving the story of elders as active citizens is to be found in policies of a fiscal nature. The most likely place to discover how the new story of aging fits the bigger picture is in governmentwide policy. In this case the document has been entitled *Winning the Generation Game* (U.K. Government, 2000). This begins well: "One of the most important tasks for twenty-first century Britain is to unlock the talents and potential of all its citizens. Everyone has a valuable contribution to make, throughout their lives." However, the reasoning behind this statement becomes clearer when policy is explained in terms of a changing demographic profile: "With present employment rates," it is argued, "one million more over-50s would not be working by 2020 because of growth in the older population. There will be 2 million fewer working-age people under 50 and 2 million more over 50: a shift equivalent to nearly 10 percent of the total working population."

The solution, then, is to engage older people not only in family life but also in work, volunteering, or mentoring. Older workers become a reserve labor pool, filling the spaces left by falling numbers of younger workers. They thus contribute to the economy as producers as well as consumers and make fewer demands on pensions and other forms of support. Those older people who are not thereby socially included can engage in the worklike activity of volunteering.

Most of these policy narratives only indirectly affect the aging family. Families only have a peripheral part to play in the story, and do not appear to be central to the lives of older people. However, it is possible to detect the same logic at work when attention shifts from the public to the private sphere. Here the narrative stream develops the notion of "grandparenting" as a means of social inclusion. This trend can be found in the United Kingdom, in France (Girrard and Ogg, 1998), Germany (Scharf and Wenger, 1995), as well as in the United States (Minkler, 1999).

In the U.K. context the most detailed reference to grandparenting can be found in an otherwise rather peculiar place—namely, the Home Office—an arm of the British government primarily concerned with law and order. In a document entitled *Supporting Families* (2000), "Family life," we are told, "is the foundation on which our communities, our society and our country are built." "Business people, people from the community, students and grandparents" are encouraged to join a schools mentoring network. Further: "The interests of grandparents, and the contribution they make, can be marginalized by service providers who, quite naturally, concentrate on dealing with parents. We want to change all this and encourage grandparents—and other relatives—to play a positive role in their families." By which it is meant: "home, school links or as a source of social and cultural history and support when nuclear families are under stress." Even older people who are not themselves grandparents can join projects "in which volunteers act as 'grandparents' to contribute their experience to a local family."

In the narratives of social democracy, the aging family is seen as a reservoir of potential social inclusion. Older people are portrayed as holding a key role in the stability of both the public sphere, through work and volunteering, and in the private sphere, primarily through grandparental support and advice. Grandparents, in particular, are storied as mentors and counselors across the public and private spheres.

While the grandparental title has been used as a catchall within the dominant policy narrative—bringing with it associations of security, stability and an in many ways an easier form of relationship than direct parenting—it exists as much in public as in private space. It is impossible to interpret this construction of grandparenthood without placing it in the broader project of social inclusion, itself a response to increased social fragmentation and economic competition. Indeed it may not be an exaggeration to refer to this construal of grandparenting as neofamilial. In other words, the grandparent has outgrown the family as part of a policy search to include older adults in wider society. The grandparent becomes a mentor to both parental and grandparental generations as advice is not restricted to schools and support in times of stress, but is also given through participation in the planning of amenities and public services (Better Government for Older People, 2000).

This is a very different narrative of older people and their relationship to families from that of the dependent and burdensome elder. In the land of policy conjuring, previously conceived problems of growing economic expense and social uselessness have been miraculously reversed. Older people are now positioned as the solution to problems of demographic change, rather than their cause. They are a source of guidance to ailing families, rather than their victims. Both narratives increase the social inclusion of a potentially marginal social group formerly known as the elderly.

THE UPS AND DOWNS OF "GRANDPARENTING" POLICY

There is much to be welcomed in this story of the active citizen elder, especially so if policy-inspired discourse and lived self-narratives are taken to be one and the same. There are also certain problems, however, if the two are unzipped, particularly when the former is viewed through the lens of what we know about families from other sources.

First, each of the roles identified in the policy domain—volunteering, mentorship, and grandparenting—has a rather secondhand quality. By this is meant that each is supportive to another player who is central to the task at hand. Rather like within Erikson's psychosocial model of the life cycle, the role allocated to older people approximates grand-generativity and is thereby contingent upon the earlier, but core life task of generativity itself (Kivnick, 1988). In other words it is contingent upon an earlier part of life and the narratives woven around it, and fails to distinguish an authentic element of the experience of aging.

When the roles are examined in this light, a tacit secondary status begins to emerge: volunteering becomes unpaid work; mentoring becomes support to helping professionals in their eroded pastoral capacities; and grandparenting, in its familial guise, becomes a sort of peripheral parent without the hassle. This peripherality may be in many ways desirable, so long as there is an alternative pole of authentic attraction that ties the older adult into social milieux. Either that or the narrative should allow space for legitimized withdrawal from socially inclusive activities. Unfortunately, the dominant policy narrative has little to say on either count.

Second, there is a shift of attention away from the most frail and oldest old, to a third age of active or positive aging, which, incidentally, may or may not take place in families. It is striking that a majority of policy documents of what might be called the "new aging," start counting from age 50, an observation that is true for formal government rhetoric and pressure from agencies and initiatives lead by elders (Biggs, 2001). This interpretation of the life course has been justified in terms of its potential for forming intergenerational alliances (Better Government for Older People, 2000) and fits well with the economic priority of drawing on older people as a reserve labor-force (U.K. Government, 2000).

Third, there is a striking absence of analysis of family relations at that age. Possibilities of intergenerational conflict as described in other literature (De Beauvoir, 1979), not least in research into three-generation family therapy (Hargrave and Anderson, 1992; Qualls, 1999), plus the everyday need for tact in negotiating childcare roles (Bornat, Dimmock, Jones, and Peace, 1999; Waldrop et al., 1999), appear not to have been taken into account. This period in the aging life course is often marked by midlife tension and multigenerational transitions, such as those experienced by late adolescent children and by an increasingly frail top generation (Ryff and Seltzer, 1996). Research has indicated that solidarity between family generations is not uniform, and will involve a variety of types and degrees of intimacy and reciprocity (Silverstein and Bengtson, 1997).

Finally, little consideration has been given to the potential conflict between the tacit hedonism of aging lifestyles based on consumption and those more socially inclusive roles of productive contribution, of which the "new grandparenting" has become an important part. While there are few figures on grandparental activity, it does, for example, appear that community volunteering among older people is embraced with much less enthusiasm than policymakers would wish (Boaz, Hayden, and Bernard, 1999). Chambre (1993) claims volunteering in the United States diminishes in old age. Her findings indicate the highest rates of volunteering occur in midlife, where nearly two-thirds volunteer. This rate declines to 47 percent for persons aged 65–74 and to 32 percent among persons 75 and over. A *Guardian*-ICM (2000) poll of older adults indicated that, among grandfathers, but not grandmothers, there was a degree of suspicion of child-care to support their own children's family arrangements. More than a quarter of men expressed this concern, compared with only 19 percent of women interviewed. The U.K. charity Age Concern stated: "One in ten grandparents are under the age of 56. They have 10 more years of work and are still leading full lives."

One might speculate, immersed in this narrative stream, that problematic family roles and relationships cease to exist for the work-returning, volunteering, and community-enhancing fifty-plus "elder." Indeed, the major protagonists of social democracy seem blissfully unaware of several decades of research, particularly feminist research, demonstrating the mythical status of the "happy family."

What emerges from research literature on grandparenting as it is included in people's everyday experience and narratives of self, indicates two trends. First, there appears to be a general acceptance of the positive value of relatively loose and undemanding exchange between first and third generations. Second, deep commitments become active largely in situations of extreme family stress or breakdown of the middle generation.

On this first count, Bengtson (1985) claims that grandparents have potential to influence and develop children through the transmission of values. Subsequently, grandparents serve as arbiters of knowledge and transmit knowledge that is unique to their identity, life experience, and history. Similarly, Levinson (1978) claims grandparents can become mentors, performing the function of a generic life guide for younger children. This "transmission" role is confirmed by Mills's (1999) study of mixed gender relations and by Waldrop et al.'s (1999) report on grandfathering. According to Roberto (Roberto and Stroes, 1992) early research on grandparenting in the United States has attempted to identify the roles played by grandparents within the family system and toward grandchildren. Indeed, much U.S. work on grandparenting has focused on how older adults view and structure their relationships with younger people.

Cherlin and Furstenberg (1986) found that African-American grandparents take a more active role, correcting the behavior of grandchildren and acting like "protectors" of the family. Accordingly, such behaviors are related to effects of divorce and under- or unemployment. Research by Kennedy (1990) indicates, however, that there is a cultural void when it comes to grandparenting roles for many white families, with few guidelines on how they should act as grandparents.

Girrard and Ogg (1998) report that grandparenting is a rising political issue in French family policy. They note that most grandmothers welcome the new role they have in child care of their grandchildren, but there is a threshold beyond which support interferes with their other commitments. Contact between older parents and their grandchildren is less frequent than with youngsters, with financial support becoming more prominent.

Two reports, explicitly commissioned to inform U.K. policy (Hayden, Boaz, and Taylor, 1999; andBoaz et al., 1999), classify grandparenting under the general rubric of intergenerational relationships. Research evidence is cited that "when thinking about the future, older people looked forward to their role as grandparents" and that grandparents looked after their grandchildren and provided them with "love, support and a listening ear," providing childcare support to their busy children and that they were enthusiastic about these roles. Hayden et al. (1999) used focus groups and qualitative interviewing and report: "Grandparenting included spending time with grandchildren both in active and sedentary hobbies and pursuits, with many participants commenting on the mental and physical stimulation they gained from sharing activities with the younger generation." Coupled with this, the Beth Johnson Foundation (1999) found that older people as mentors had increased levels of participation with more friends and engendered more social activity. With the exception of the last study, each has relied on exclusive self-report data, or views on what grandparenting might be like at some future point.

In research from the tradition of examining social networks, and thus not overtly concerned with the centrality of grandparenting or grandparentlike roles as such, it is rarely identified as a key relationship and could not be called a strong theme. Studies on the United Kingdom (Phillipson, Bernard, Phillips, and Ogg, 2000), Japan (Izuhara, 2000), the United States (Schreck, 2000; Minkler, 1999), Hispanic-Americans (Freidenberg, 2000), and Germany (Chamberlayne and King, 2000) provide little evidence that grandchildren, as distinct from adult children, are prominent members of older people's reported social networks.

Grandparental responsibility becomes more visible if the middle generation is for some reason absent. Thompson (1999) reports from the United Kingdom that when parents part or die, it is often grandparents who take up supporting, caring, and mediating roles on behalf of their grandchildren. The degree of involvement was contingent, however, on the quality of emotional closeness and communication within the family group. Minkler (1999) has indicated that in the United States, one in ten grandparents has primary responsibility for raising a grandchild at some point, with care often lasting for several years. This trend varies between ethnic groups, with 4.1 percent white, 6.55 percent Hispanic, and 13.55 African-American children living with their grandparents or other relatives. It is argued that a 44 percent increase in such responsibilities is connected to the devastating effects of wider social issues, including AIDS, drug abuse, parental homelessness, and prison policy. Thomson and Minkler (2001) note that there is an increasing divergence in the meaning of grandparenting between different socioeconomic groups, with extensive caregivers (7 percent of the sampled population) having increasingly fewer characteristics in common with the 14.9 percent who did not provide child care. In the United Kingdom, a similar split has been identified with 1 percent of

British grandparents becoming extensive caregivers, against a background pattern of occasional or minimal direct care (Duckworth, 2001).

It would appear that grandparenting is not, then, a uniform phenomenon, and extensive grandparenting or grandparentlike activities are rarely an integral part of social inclusion. Rather, while it is seen as providing some intergenerational benefit, it may be a phenomenon that requires an element of unintrusiveness and negotiation in its nonextensive form. When extensively relied on it is more likely to be a response to severely eroded inclusive environments and the self-protective reactions of families living with them. Minkler's analysis draws attention to race as a feature of social exclusion that is poorly handled by policy narratives afforded to the family and old age. There is a failure to recognize structural forms of inequality, and action seeking to socially include older people as a category appears to draw heavily on the occasional helper and social volunteer as a dominant narrative.

LIVING WITH MULTIPLE NARRATIVES

Each phase of social policy, be it the Reagan/Thatcherite neoliberalism of the 1980s and early 1990s, the Clinton/Blairite interpretation of social democracy in the late 1990s, or the millennial Bush administration, leaves a legacy. Moreover, policy development is uneven and subject to local emphasis and elision, which means that it is quite possible for different, even conflicting narratives of family and later life to coexist in different parts of the policy system. Each period generates a discourse that can legitimate the lives of older people and family relations in particular ways, and as their influence accrues, creates the potential of entering into multiple narrative streams.

A striking feature of recent policy history has been that not only have the formal policies been quite different from one another in their tenor and tacit objectives, they have also addressed different areas of the lives of aging families. Where there is little narrative overlap, there is the possibility of both policies existing, however opposed they may be ideologically or in terms of practical outcome. Different narratives may colonize different parts of policy, drawing on bureaucratic inertia, political inattention, and convenience to maintain their influence. They have a living presence, not least when they impinge on personal aging.

Also, both policy discourses share a deep coherence, which may help to explain their coexistence. Each offers a partial view of aging and family life while downloading risk and responsibility onto aging families and aging identities. Neither recognizes aging that is not secondary to an independent policy objective. Both mask the possibility of authentic tasks of aging.

If the analysis outlined above is accepted, then it is possible to see contemporary social policy addressing diverse aspects of the family life of older people in differing and contradictory ways. Contradictory narratives for the aging family exist in a landscape that is at one and the same time increasingly blurred in terms of roles and relationships and split off in terms of narrative coherence and consequences for identity. Indeed in a future of complex and multiple policy agendas, it would appear that a narrative of social inclusion through active aging can coexist with one emphasizing carer obligation and surveillance. Such a coexistence may occasionally become inconvenient at the level of public rhetoric. However, at an experiential and ontological level, that is to say at the level of the daily lives of older adults and their families, the implications may become particularly acute. Multiple coexisting policy narratives may become a significant source of risk to identity maintenance within the aging family.

One has to imagine a situation in which later lives are lived, skating on a surface of legitimizing discourse. For everyday intents and purposes this surface supplies the ground on which one can build an aging identity, and relate to other family members and to one's immediate community. However, there is always the possibility of slipping, of being subject to trauma or transition. Serious slippage will provoke being thrown onto a terrain that had previously been hidden, an alternative narrative of aging with entirely different premises, relationship expectations, and possibilities for personal expression.

Policy narratives, however, are also continually breaking down and fail to achieve hegemony as they encounter lived experience. Indeed, it could be argued that a continuous process of reconstitution takes place via the play of competing narratives. When we are addressing the issue of older people's identity in later life we can usefully note Foucault's (1977) contention that there has been a growth in attempts to control national populations through discourses of normality, but at the same time this has entailed increasing possibilities for self-government.

Part of the attractiveness of thinking in terms of narrative, that policies tell us stories that we do not necessarily have to believe, is the opening of a critical distance between description and intention. Policy narratives describe certain, often idealized, states of affairs. Depicting them as stories, rather than realities, allows the interrogation of the space between that description and experience.

CONCLUDING COMMENTS

What does this examination of policy discourse and everyday stories of family and aging selves tell us, and what are the lessons for future applied research?

First, we are alerted to the partial nature of the narratives supplied by policy, which affects our perception of families as well as of older people. The simplifying role of policy discourse tends to highlight certain politically valued aspects of experience to the exclusion of other possibilities. These are also the discourses most likely to be reflected in policy-sponsored research.

Second, the inclusion of certain roles, activities, and age bands in policy discourse has a legitimizing role. In other words, it not only sanctions the direction of resources and the action of helping professionals—important though that is—it also contributes to the legitimated identities afforded to people in later life. This includes at least two factors key to aging identity: the creation of social spaces in which to perform aging roles and be recognized as so doing, and the supply of material with which explicit yet personal narratives of self and family can be made.

Third, a significant element in the "riskiness" of building aging and family identities under contemporary conditions may arise from the existence of multiple policy discourses that personal narratives, of family, self, and relations between the two, have to negotiate. Research on the management of identity, should, then, be sensitized to the multiple grounds on which identity might be built and the potential sources of conflict and uncertainty that may occur.

Fourth, attention should be paid to the relationship between tacit and explicit influences on identity management in late-life families. The multiple sources for building stories "to live by" and the tension between legitimizing discourses and alternative narratives of self and family would suggest that identities are managed at different levels, for different audiences, and at different levels of awareness. There are implications here for both the conceptualization of familial and policy relations and for the practice of research. The story that the researcher hears and then records may be tapping a particular level of disclosure, depending in part upon how the research itself is perceived, and indeed, perceives itself.

In summary, we have argued that future developments in policy analysis will have to take both tacit and explicit themes in social policy into account. They will also have to more closely examine the relationship between personal storymaking and formal policy discourse. Policies provide narrative templates within which certain categories of person or group are encouraged to live out their lives. However, this legitimized performance may differ significantly from an individual or family's everyday experience of that same role, function, or social space, leading to conflict between different levels of narrative. We are left in the end with a question: How far will it be possible for aging families to use often deeply ambivalent policy material, which nevertheless provides opportunities for positive growth and resistance?

REFERENCES

Beck, U. 1998. *Democracy without enemies*. Cambridge: Polity.

Bengtson, V. L. 1985. Diversity and symbolism in the grandparent role. In V. Bengtson and J. Robertson (eds.), *Grandparenthood* (pp. 11–25). Beverly Hills, CA: Sage.

Bengtson, V. L., and Achenbaum, W. (eds.) 1993. *The changing contract across generations*. Hawthorne, NY: Aldine de Gruyter.

Bengtson, V. L., Giarrusso, R., Silverstein, M., and Wang, H. 2003. Families and intergenerational relationships in aging societies. *Hallym International Journal of Aging* 2(1):3–10.

Beth Johnson Foundation. 1999. *Intergenerational programmes*. Stoke: Author.

Better Government for Older People. 2000. *Better Government for Older People*. Wolverhampton: Author.

Biggs, S. 1996. A family concern: elder abuse in British social policy. *Critical Social Policy* 16(2):63–88.

Biggs, S. 2001. Toward critical narrativity: stories of aging in contemporary social policy. *Journal of Aging Studies,* 15(1):1–14.

Biggs, S., Phillipson, C., and Kingston, P. 1995. *Elder abuse in perspective*. Buckingham: OUP.

Biggs, S., and Powell, J. 1999. Surveillance and elder abuse: The rationalities and technologies of community care. *Journal of Contemporary Health* 4(1):43–49.

Biggs, S., and Powell, J. 2000. Managing old age: The disciplinary web of power, surveillance and normalisation. *Journal of Aging and Identity* 5(10):3-13.

Blair, T. 1996. *New Britain: My vision of a young country*. London: Fourth Estate.

Boaz, A., Hayden, C., and Bernard, M. 1999. *Attitudes and aspirations of older people*. DSS research report, 101. London: CDS.

Bornat, J., Dimmock, B., Jones, D., and Peace, S. 1999. Stepfamilies and older people. *Ageing and Society* 19(2):239–62.

Chamberlayne, P., and King, A. 2000. *Cultures of care*. London: Policy.

Chambre, S. M. 1993. Volunteerism by elders: Past traditions and future prospects. *Gerontologist* 33:221–28.

Cherlin, A., and Furstenberg, F. F. 1986 Grandparents and family crisis. *Generations: Journal of the American Society on Aging* 10(4):26–28.

De Beauvoir, S. 1979. *Old age*. London: Penguin.

Department of Social Security 1998. *Building a better Britain for older people*. London: HMSO.

Duckworth, L. 2001. Grandparents who bring up children need more help. *Independent,* 13(9),18.

Featherstone, M., and Hepworth, M. 1993. Images of positive ageing. In M. Featherstone and A. Wernick (eds.), *Images of ageing* (pp. 304–32). London: Routledge.

Finch, J., and Mason, J. 1993. *Negotiating family responsibilities*. London: Routledge.

Foucault, M. 1977. *Discipline and punish*. London: Tavistock.

Freidenberg, J. 2000. *Growing old in el barrio*. New York: NYUP.

Giddens, A. 1993. *Sociology*. Cambridge: Polity.

———. 1998. *The third way*. Cambridge: Polity.

Girrard, I., and Ogg, J. 1998. Grandparenting in France and England. Presentation to the British Society of Gerontology, Sheffield.

Gray, J. 1995. *Enlightenment's wake*. London: Routledge.

Guardian-ICM Poll. 2001. *Grandparenting and retirement activities*. London: ICM.

Gubrium, J. F. 1992. *Out of control: Family therapy and domestic disorder*. Thousand Oaks, CA: Sage.

Hargrave, T., and Anderson, W. 1992. *Finishing well: Aging and reparation in the inter-generational family*. New York: Brunner and Mazel.

Hayden, C., Boaz, A., and Taylor, F. 1999. *Attitudes and aspirations of older people: A qualitative study*. DSS Research report 102. London: CDS.

HMSO 1981. *Growing older*. London: Author.

HMSO 1989. *Community care: An agenda for action*. London: Author.

HMSO 1990. *NHS and Community Care Act*. London: Author.

HMSO 1993. *No longer afraid: The safeguard of older people in domestic settings*. London: Author.

Holstein, J., and Gubrium, J. 2000. *The self we live by*. Oxford: OUP.

Home Office 2000. *Supporting families*. London: HMSO.

Izuhara, M. 2000. *Family change and housing in post-war Japanese society*. Singapore: Ashgate.

Katz, S. 1999. Busy Bodies: Activity, aging and the management of everyday life. *Journal of Aging Studies* 14(2):135–52.

Kennedy, G 1990. College students expectations of grandparent and grandchild role behaviours. *Gerontologist* 30(1):43–48.

Kenyon, G., Ruth, J., and Mader, W. 1999. Elements of a narrative gerontology. In V. L. Bengtson, and K. Schaie (eds.), *Handbook of theories of aging* (pp. 40–58). New York: Springer.

Kivnick, H. 1988. Grandparenthood, life review and psychosocial development. *Journal of Gerontological Social Work* 12(3):63–82.

Levinson, D. 1978. *The seasons of a man's life*. New York: Ballentine.

Lowenstein, A. 2003. Contemporary liter-life family transitions: Revisiting theoretical perspectives on aging and the family: Toward a family identity framework. In S. Biggs, A. Lowenstein, and H. Hendricks (eds.), *The need for theory*. Amityville: Baywood.

McAdams, D. 1993. *The stories we live by*. New York: Morrow.

McLeod, J. 1997. *Narrative and psychotherapy*. London: Sage.

Mills, T. 1999. When grandchildren grow up. *Journal of Aging Studies* 13(2):219–39.

Minkler, M. 1999. Intergenerational households headed by grandparents: Contexts, realities and implications for policy. *Journal of Aging Studies* 13(2):199–218.

Moen, P., and Wethington, E. 1992. The concept of family adaptive strategies. *Annual Review of Sociology* 18:233–51.

Phillipson, C. 1998. *Reconstructing old age*. London: Sage.

Phillipson, C. Bernard, M., Phillips, J., and Ogg, J. 2000. *The family and community life of older people*. London: Routledge.

Pillemer, K., and Wolf, R. 1986. *Elder abuse: Conflict in the family*. Dover: Auburn House.

Powell, J., and Biggs, S. 2002. Bio-ethics and technologies of the self: Understanding aging. *Journal of Medical Humanities*.

Pyke, K. D., and Bengtson, V. L. 1996. Caring more or less: Individualistic and collectivist systems of family eldercare. *Journal of Marriage and the Family* 58:1–14.

Qualls, S. 1999. Realising power in intergenerational hierarchies. In M. Duffy (ed.), *Handbook of counselling and psychotherapy with older adults* (pp. 228–41). New York: Wiley.

Roberto, K., and Stroes, J. 1992. Grandchildren and grandparents: Roles, influences, and relationships. *International Journal of Aging and Human Development* 34:227-39.

Ryff, C., and Seltzer, M. 1996. *The parental experience in midlife*. Chicago: CUP.

Scharf, T., and Wenger, G. 1995. *International perspectives on community care for older people*. Aldershot: Avebury.

Schreck, H. 2000. *Community and caring*. New York: UPA.

Silverstein, M., and Bengtson, V. L. 1997. Intergenerational solidarity and the structure of adult child-parent relationships in American families. *American Journal of Sociology* 103(2):429–60.

Thompson, P. 1999. The role of grandparents when parents part or die; some reflections on the mythical decline of the extended family. *Ageing and Society* 19(4):471–503.

Thomson, E., and Minkler, M. 2001. American grandparents providing extensive childcare to their grandchildren: prevalence and profile. *Gerontologist* 41(2):201–9.

U.K. Government 2000. *Winning the generation game*. Cabinet-Office.gov.uk.

Waldrop, D., Weber, J., Herald, S., Pruett, J., Cooper, K., and Jouzapavicius, K. 1999. Wisdom and life experience: How grandfathers mentor their grandchildren. *Journal of Aging and Identity* 4(1):33–46.

Walker, A., and Naegele, G. 1999. *The politics of old age in Europe*. Buckingham: OUP.

Wenger, C. 1994. *Support networks for older people*. Bangor: CSPRD.

Williams, F. 1989. *Social policy: A critical introduction. Issues of race, gender and class.* Cambridge: Polity.

II

Theoretical Perspectives: The Role of Intergenerational Social Support

| 6 |

Intergenerational Transfers in the Family

What Motivates Giving?

Martin Kohli and Harald Künemund

INTRODUCTION

Private transfers between adult generations in the family are an important part of the intergenerational link in modern societies. The sociological imagination was long truncated by the emphasis of classical modernization theory on the emergence of the nuclear family. This restrictive view has first been transcended by research on the emotional and support relations between adult family generations. But it is only during the last decade that sociology has discovered again the full extent of the family as a kinship and especially a generational system beyond the nuclear household (Bengtson, 2001), which includes massive monetary relations and flows as well.

In the meantime we have become aware of the salience of intergenerational transfers not only for the family as such—how the family distributes its resources among and assures the well-being of its members—but also for the broader issues of social policy, social inequality, and social integration (Attias-Donfut, 1995; Szydlik, 2000). Of special interest is the articulation between the private transfers in the family and the public transfers in the welfare state. In the conventional story of modernization, the emergence of the nuclear family and of the public old-age security system were seen as parallel and mutually reinforcing processes. The basic assumption was that the development of the welfare state would crowd out the private support within families. Recent evidence, however, points to the opposite conclusion: Welfare state provisions, far from crowding out family support, enable the family in turn to provide new intergenerational support and transfers (Kohli, 1999; Künemund and Rein, 1999).

While intergenerational family transfers beyond the nuclear household are thus still a new field of inquiry, some of their basic patterns are by now well-known, at least for the countries where the relevant data exist:[1] There is a net flow of material resources from the older to the younger generations, i.e., from the elderly in retirement to their adult children and grandchildren, in the opposite direction of the public transfers through the old-age security system. The former is partly a result of the latter: The pensions paid to the elderly through the public "generational contract" enable them to make transfers to their descendants (Kohli, 1999). The flow is by *inter vivos* transfers as well as by bequests. The intrafamily distribution of these two forms seems to be different: Bequests are to a large extent distributed equally across all children in the family (even in countries such as the United States, where there are very few restrictive rules regarding the disposition of one's estate), while *inter vivos* transfers are made unequally and seem to go in higher proportion to the more needy children.

In other respects, there is less clarity. For example, the effects of transfers are still under dispute. With regard to their effects on wealth accumulation among the recipients, a few years ago Gale and Scholz noted that "even the most fundamental factual issues remain unresolved" (1994, p. 146). An even more striking example is the lack of clarity about the motives for transfer giving. As McGarry (1997) has observed, much of the economic literature on transfers seeks to explain the motivation behind these intergenerational linkages, with special emphasis on the issue of altruism vs. exchange, in order to understand their distributional effects; but despite this substantial amount of research, "a consensus has not yet been reached about the importance of these alternative models" (ibid.:1). One of the reasons for this disappointing state of affairs is that most research so far has relied on a static instead of a dynamic framework for testing these models (McGarry, 2000). Another reason, however, may be that the motives themselves and the relations among them have not been adequately specified.

In this chapter, we empirically assess the structure and consequences of transfer motives. First we discuss the (nontrivial) question of why we should be interested in motives and the range of motives described in the literature. Second we analyze the empirical structure of motives based on data from the German Aging Survey, a large nationally representative survey of the German population aged 40–85. In the third part we focus on two motives that stand for different motivational clusters, conditional versus unconditional giving, and examine their sociodemographic correlates as well as their impact on the giving of transfers or other kinds of support.

TRANSFER MOTIVES: AN OVERVIEW

Why Ask for Motives?

Why should we be interested in the motives for transfer behavior as long as we have sufficient information on that behavior itself and on its objective correlates? It may be feasible to explain transfer giving by sociodemographic variables such as income and wealth of givers or need of recipients, and by relational variables such as geographical or emotional closeness or frequency of contact between the two. This is the explanatory strategy that we (like most other sociologists) have pursued so far, with results that have clearly demonstrated the significance of these variables (Kohli, Künemund, Motel, and Szydlik, 2000; Motel and Szydlik, 1999).

So why should motives be included? The question is not rhetorical, particularly since past research on motives (or attitudes) and behavior has led to the conclusion that the correspondence between the two is far from perfect, and necessarily so.

A first answer would be that an explanation of transfer giving on the basis of the sociodemographic characteristics of givers and recipients and other objective criteria alone remains incomplete. A "full" explanation requires encompassing the level of action as well, which means that the orientations that the actors bring to their situations have to be considered.

But this only begs the question: Why do we need such a "full" explanation? Why is it not sufficient to be parsimonious, and to take a shortcut from the objective variables directly to behavior? The answer here can be given in terms of a formal theory of action, decision, or choice, such as in the rational choice perspective (Esser, 1999). According to this perspective, different motives or preferences will result in different evaluations of the situation, and thus in different behavioral responses to situational changes. Motives therefore are necessary for predicting the effect of such situational or contextual changes.

This argument is analogous to that of most economists who have studied transfers and other family behavior. Their interest in motives stems from their view that motives are critical for assessing the likely impact of changes in resource conditions (and in the policy measures that create these changes) on transfer behavior. Whether transfers to children are motivated by altruism or by exchange considerations makes a difference for predicting the likely consequences of, e.g., changes in tax (dis-)incentives or in public transfers such as pensions.

In fact, motives are usually *defined* by economists in terms of differential reactions to changing situational conditions, and not in terms of psychological or sociopsychological realities. As an example, Masson and Pestieau (1996) state that the purpose of their classification of transfer motives is not to offer a full psychological explanation, but to assess how people will react to changing incentives, e.g., those of economic policy. Becker (1991), whose work has pioneered the economics of the family, has made a similar emphasis: "I am giving a definition of altruism that is relevant to behavior—to consumption and production choices—rather than giving a philosophical discussion of what, really 'motivates people'" (ibid.:279).

Of course, if these conceptual constructions are too far from how people are really motivated (with or without quotation marks), or how motives are negotiated in interaction, they will not be very useful in predicting behavioral responses. And it has to be acknowledged that even if the motives held by a person are adequately measured, we cannot assume that behavior exactly follows from them, i.e., that under equal situational conditions a given motive will always result in the same behavior. This is due to the fact that situational conditions as well as motives are interpreted and negotiated among the participants to a situation (Finch and Mason, 1993). We thus have to brace ourselves for different evaluations of these conditions. This means that the explanatory power of models even if they include motives necessarily remains limited.

The main problem, however, is that the assumption of each individual having a single well-defined motive is unrealistic. There is competition and overlap among motives, and a person may hold several motives simultaneously that seemingly contradict each other (Finch and Mason, 1993; Künemund and Motel, 2000). In order to determine the effect of motives on transfer behavior, we need to analyze the motivational space in its empirical structure, allowing for the fact that several motivational tendencies may coexist within the same individuals. For this, imputing motives from behavior (as is usually done in the economic literature) will not do. Instead, motives must be assessed directly, such as through appropriate questioning.

Another reason for studying motives stems from their role in the structure of social relations. There is, for example, good reason to believe that motives are important not only for the incidence and size of transfers but also for their "quality." For recipients, it makes a difference whether transfers from their family members are motivated by self-interest (only) or (also) by love, benevolence, generosity, or a sense of personal obligation. For example, a gift of money has a different quality if given unconditionally, "without strings attached," or if given conditional on compliance with expectations of exchange, reciprocity, control, or status. There may be some cynics who would say of their parents, "I don't care what they think as long as they hand over the goods." But in most cases, the motive for giving will be highly salient to the recipient because it carries not only explicit expectations but hidden ones as well. Even if the transfer behavior as such does not change as a function of whether these hidden expectations are fulfilled or not, the latter will affect the quality of the transfer in terms of the moral burden that it constitutes, or the conflicts that it brings forth.

Finally, on a more general level, transfer motives can serve to address the theoretical controversy in sociology about the autonomy or embeddedness of economic exchange. In a structuralist perspective, money can be seen as a specific code of communication, or as part of the "language" of social interaction, and motives are among its important signifiers. In what is perhaps a more common way of framing this controversy, motives are critical for determining the scope of utilitaristic versus normative or interpretive approaches to social relations. While we will not go into this theoretical discussion here, we want to note that family transfers are an especially appropriate field for it because the family potentially partakes in different logics of action (Kohli, 1997).

The Range of Transfer Motives

With regard to the economic analysis of bequests, Masson and Pestieau (1996) propose a general distinction into three families: accidental, voluntary, and capitalist ones. "Accidental" bequests occur as a consequence of precautionary savings and deferred consumption: Because of the uncertainty of one's life span and the imperfections of capital markets (pertaining to, e.g., annuities or housing), individuals and households cannot—contrary to what is claimed in the life-cycle savings model—smooth out the differences between their current income flows by optimizing their saving and dissaving behavior over the life span. Thus, unspent wealth remaining at the end of life represents an information deficit: the inability to exactly predict one's time of death and the funds needed to reach it (for example, with regard to medical costs or the duration of expensive institutionalization when disabled). Perfectly efficient capital markets should be able to solve this problem; it would then be rational to hand over all one's wealth to a capital fund in return for a corresponding lifetime annuity. "Voluntary" bequests (or *inter vivos* transfers) range from pure altruism to paternalistic behavior to self-interested strategic exchange. For individuals interested in maximizing their own personal utility only, bequests are rational insofar as they result in a better treatment by the descendants (the "strategic bequest motive," Bernheim, Shleifer, and Summers, 1985), i.e., give the bequeathing persons some control over the behavior of their descendants. On the other hand, many economists accept the possibility of altruism, or even see it as the primary motive in intergenerational family relations (Becker, 1991). Finally, "capitalist" or entrepreneurial bequests (or *inter vivos* transfers) are directed to "accumulation for its own sake," or more precisely, to creating and conserving an estate beyond one's own personal existence.[2]

"Accidental" bequests are not really motives per se in terms of purposeful action; what is motivated here is the precautionary saving that lies behind them, and does not include an intention to give.[3] "Capitalist" bequests refer to specific motivations that are not directed at the descendants as persons but only at their role as entrepreneurs and bearers of the family fortune. In the following discussion we will therefore restrict ourselves to the middle one of these three families of bequests, those labeled "voluntary." It is here that the core issues of how motives impact on transfer behavior arise.

As noted above, the economic literature has not yet been able to resolve the debate about altruism versus exchange motives. In the sociological literature, there is even more unresolved complexity as these types of motives are complemented by various forms of reciprocity. Altruism, exchange and reciprocity are broad categories that all comprise a range of different motivational tendencies that may or may not occur in conjunction. Moreover, it is not sufficient to enumerate the motives for giving alone; we also need to examine the reasons for not giving, such as conflicts or motives of independence and separation.

This complexity makes a full overview of the range of motives almost impossible; but an attempt can be made to draw out some of the basic points of agreement and disagreement (Künemund and Rein, 1999). The altruism theory assumes affection, or a moral duty, or obligation as a basis for providing help in situations of need. Altruism requires no further instrumental explanation. The exchange theory, on the other hand, posits that one gives to others because one expects them to give in return. Kotlikoff and Morris (1989) offer a radicalization of the logic of exchange by proposing that transfers from the aged to their adult children are simply a bribe. They interpret the finding that the aged parents give money to their adult children and grandchildren as an active inducement to get their children to provide them with services. Consistent with the logic of the strategic bequest motive (Bernheim et al., 1985), we might also simply assume that when the level of surplus is substantial, the children extend help in the expectation of acquiring some portion of these surplus resources. Where such exchange expectations are in effect, it follows that the more resources the elderly have, the more they can receive in turn.

By positing an indirect exchange motive, Stark (1995) provides something of a bridge between the economic literature on altruism and exchange and the sociological literature on reciprocity. The basic idea behind the "demonstration effect" is to identify a mechanism by which children get socialized to accept a general normative pattern of obligation to help the elderly. Stark finds that adult children who have young children are likely to visit or call their aged parents ten more times a year than adult children who are childless. The interpretation is that the middle generation treats their aged parents well in order to demonstrate to their children how they would like to be treated when they are aged. Stark assumes stronger demonstration effects from visits, telephone calls, and the provision of everyday services than from the giving of money because the children can see and understand what is happening. The demonstration theory thus proposes an extension of the exchange motive in the direction of indirect reciprocity: namely, that you give to a person other than the one from whom you expect the benefit of the exchange.

The economic literature tends to confirm that pure altruism is not the dominant motive, but as noted above the evidence remains inconclusive. The concept of pure altruism is not the only one, however. For example, altruism may be associated with a "joy of giving" or a "warm glow;" here giving may persist even when the need of the recipient is met, or giving takes place even if there is no need at all. This has been labeled "impure altruism" (Andreoni, 1989). The same applies when the donor expects to get valued social approval from the act of giving or from signaling income (Glazer and Konrad, 1996).[4]

All these various forms of altruism can be contrasted to those of exchange. As to the latter, the evidence is again mixed. Many authors find empirical support for exchange while others such as Boersch-Supan et al. (1990) and McGarry and Schoeni (1997) conclude that there is only weak or no evidence that monetary transfers from the aged to their children are an implicit payment for services that these children give to their aged parents.

In the sociological literature, it is especially the norm of reciprocity that has been subject to numerous studies on the exchange relationships of elderly people and adult children (for overviews see Antonucci and Jackson, 1990; Hollstein and Bria, 1996). In general, it is assumed that giving places an obligation to get something back in return for what was given, and that the values exchanged should be broadly equivalent. The recipient may avoid this obligation either by refusing the gift or by repaying it immediately. Gouldner assumes that "the norm of reciprocity cannot apply with full force in relations with children, old people, or those who are mentally or physically handicapped" (1960, p. 178) because these groups are less able to reciprocate. As a result, fewer individuals will establish relations with them. From this argument we may conclude that having more resources enables the elderly to stay involved in reciprocal giving and receiving and also places them in a position to initiate an exchange.

Where the relationship is more intimate and stable, such as, for example, the relationship between aged parents and their adult children, the rules of exchange allow for reciprocity to take place over a long period of time and as a spot transaction. The implicit rules also allow for an asymmetry between what is initially received and what is later given, and the exchange may involve different types of transfers and support. Antonucci and Jackson (1990, p. 178) use the metaphor of "deposits" placed in a "support bank" that can be drawn on in future times of need. The availability of resources—not only current ones but also those that have earlier been placed in the "support bank"—thus reinforces autonomy and self-respect by placing the elderly in a position where they can maintain their social status by being able to give to their adult children. Where the parents become passive recipients, they incur a loss of status.

Another field of sociological inquiry is the norms of responsibility and of family obligations (Cantor, 1979; Qureshi, 1990). Family obligations have a special weight in societies with a (neo-)Confucian background (Chen and Adamchak, 1999; Koyano, 2001), but contrary to many popular assumptions they are also (still) pertinent in Western societies. Finch and Mason (1993) present one of the most interesting analyses of obligations between adult children and aged parents. They argue that "norms about family obligations do get taken into account" (ibid.:28) and that the principle of reciprocity is usually accepted as well but that the outcome remains open. Whether and how the obligation to give help is felt is the result of a "process of negotiation, in which people are giving and receiving, balancing out one kind of assistance against another, maintaining an appropriate independence from each other as well as mutual interdependence" (ibid.:167). Obligations to help one's aged parents thus do not simply follow from an abstract normative principle but are created concretely through interaction over time. This implies that they may also be rejected, for example if the support from the other side that one feels entitled to has not come forth. Obligations are thus not unconditional; whether they are accepted and seen as legitimate depends on other dimensions of the relationship or on its earlier history.

Based on these considerations, it is now possible to construct the contours of a broader motivational space for intergenerational transfers and support than either the economic or the sociological literature has used so far, and to conceptualize some of its main lines. We conceive of these motives as a series of basic orientations including altruism (concern for the well-being of others), direct exchange (concern for one's own interest in getting some return), delayed or indirect or generalized reciprocity (concern for giving back what one has received earlier, or for giving it to others such as the next generation, or for giving so that the recipient may give to others), sense of duty (internalized normative obligation), and separation (concern for keeping autonomy or distance). There are additional possible motives that we have not tried to operationalize, such as control or power (concern for making recipients comply with one's wishes—a motive that may be distinguished from that of "buying" services in return for giving transfers) status (concern for one's social honor), or compliance with external norms (concern for being accepted or for getting valued social approval).

It needs to be stressed again that the task at hand is not to determine which single motive is the dominant one in a population or in each of its subgroups. Many studies show that the single motive assumption is not valid and that overlap and coexistence (or conflict) of several motives even within the same individual is the norm. Our task therefore is to first examine the empirical structure of motives in order to arrive at empirically grounded typologies of combinations of motives (Künemund and Motel, 2000; Silverstein and Bengtson, 1997) as a prerequisite for assessing the impact of motives on transfer behavior.

THE EMPIRICAL STRUCTURE OF MOTIVES

Our empirical study is based on the German Aging Survey, a large representative survey of the 40–85-year-old German nationals living in private households collected in the first six months of 1996. The sample ($n = 4838$) was stratified according to age groups, gender, and East and West Germany. Interviews were conducted orally at the respondents' homes; in addition, a "drop-off" questionnaire was left to the respondents for self-administration. The survey program comprised sociological measures of the various dimensions of life situations and welfare—among them, intergenerational relations and transfers—as well as psychological measures of self and life concepts (Dittmann-Kohli et al., 1997; Dittmann-Kohli, Bode, and Westerhof, 2001).[5]

The following analysis is restricted to the retired part of the sample, i.e., those above age 55 with neither the respondent nor the spouse fully participating in the labor force. We thus focus on those persons who are the prime recipients of the public generational contract. The demographic and socioeconomic characteristics of the sample are shown in Table 6.1.[6] The giving and receiving of transfers refer to money and larger gifts in kind to or from kin during the twelve months before the survey as well as to large gifts or support any time before (excluding inheritance). "Support" includes these material transfers plus three forms of services: care for disabled persons, taking care of children or grandchildren, and instrumental help (e.g., with household chores) during the last twelve months. The descriptive results confirm the well-known pattern that intrafamily transfers and support are to a large extent confined to the generational lineage—there are few transfers to other kin.

In order to assess transfer motives directly (instead of imputing them from behavior), we have constructed a series of statements referring to the various motivational dimensions discussed above. These items were contained in the self-administered drop-off. The items were introduced by telling the respondents, "The following statements concern the support for kin [*Angehörige*], e.g., parents and children." We have thus taken account

Table 6.1   Sociodemographic Characteristics of the Sample and Frequency of
Transfers and Support

Sex: female (%)	59.0
Age: mean/standard deviation	69.0/7.1
Region: former GDR (%)	18.5
Community (%): <2,000	9.3
2,000–5,000	6.5
5,000–20,000	17.0
20,000–50,000	10.2
50,000–100,000	4.3
100,000–500,000	16.3
>500,000	36.4
Living alone (%)	30.8
Health (%): no difficulties	52.0
minor difficulties	31.5
considerable difficulties	16.5
Education (%): low	26.9
Middle	52.5
High	20.6
Equivalence income (DM): mean/standard deviation	1.930/1.197
Occupational prestige: mean/standard deviation	66.0/28.8
Has received transfers from parents, parents-in-law, or grandparents (%)	5.7
Has given transfers to kin (%)	30.2
Has given transfers to children or grandchildren (%)	27.2
Has given any kind of support to kin (%)	51.2
Has given any kind of support to children or grandchildren (%)	43.8

Note: German Aging Survey 1996, *n* = 2.205, weighted (respondents aged 55–85; neithe respondent nor spouse participating in labor force).

of the fact that transfer motives may apply to the kinship system as a whole but that its most salient part is usually the generational lineage. For each item, respondents were given a choice of four answers: fully agree, agree somewhat, disagree somewhat, and fully disagree.

It should be noted that motives in the psychological sense would be difficult or even impossible to assess through simple questionnaire items of this sort. What we obtain are rather values, attitudes, and beliefs that may correspond to more deeply ingrained motivational bases for acting toward one's family members. For reasons of simplicity, however, we use the term "motive," thus retaining the standard terminology of the transfer literature.

Table 6.2 presents these various statements on support for kin ranked in descending order of agreement. At this point already, the overall pattern of rates of (full or partial) agreement shows that there must be a high amount of overlap among different and sometimes seemingly contradictory motives (Künemund and Motel, 2000). The statement that draws the highest agreement ("If my family members need help I will always be

Table 6.2 Motives for Family Support

Items	Fully agree (%)	Agree somewhat (%)	Disagree somewhat (%)	Fully disagree (%)
If my family members need help I will always be there.	52.0	40.5	4.8	2.7
I would like to pass on to the next generation what my parents have given me.	41.5	44.0	7.5	7.0
I think that it is simply my duty to help my family members.	40.0	44.1	11.2	4.7
My parents have done so much for me that I would like to give them back some of it.	39.0	38.6	9.9	12.5
If I help my family members, I can expect help from them in return.	27.1	47.7	16.4	8.8
Grown-up children should be able to stand on their own two feet, and not expect support from their parents.	32.3	41.2	21.3	5.2
If someone wants to inherit from me, he/she should do something for it.	18.0	38.2	28.9	14.9
At my age why should I still save money? My family members can make much better use of it.	16.5	32.2	34.7	16.6
If I dislike a family member, I am not going to help them.	12.2	25.2	37.2	25.4
There is no need for me to help my family members because there is enough public support.	5.0	15.4	46.0	33.6

Note: German Aging Survey 1996, $n = 1.837$, weighted.

there") is one that expresses family help as a matter of course—in other words, one of self-evident and unconditional ("pure") altruism. More than half of our respondents declare themselves fully and another two-fifths somewhat altruistic with regard to family members. However, the feeling of normative obligation to help ("I think that it is simply my duty . . .") follows closely, with 84 percent agreeing fully or somewhat. In terms of behavior, this would in most cases also be categorized as altruistic, but the motivational properties of these two statements are different. The second most widely shared motive, with 85 percent full or partial agreement, is one of indirect reciprocity (the desire to give to the next generation what one has received from the previous one), and the fourth, of delayed reciprocity (the desire to give back to one's parents some of what one has received from them). The fifth motivational statement ("If I help my family members, I can expect help from them in return") is somewhat ambivalent: It may denote an expectation of direct or "pure" reciprocity, but it may also be a simple description of what is likely to happen. It may in other words be either a requirement for reciprocity or a factual statement of its operation. It is closely followed by an assertion of separation in the sense of individualization and autonomy ("Grown-up children should be able to stand on their own feet . . .").

An exchange motive in the sense of strategic bequest (that it is right for parents to try to manipulate their children by threatening to disinherit them) splits the respondents in two groups of about equal size. The same applies to a statement that expresses the uselessness of savings in old age. Here again there is some ambivalence: The statement may be read as an indicator of altruism, but it may also mean that by refusing to take precautions one compromises one's future autonomy. That helping should be conditional on having a close affective tie to the recipient—a statement denoting a particular kind of exchange or separation—meets with an approval rate of less than two-fifths. Least frequent is the agreement to our indicator of "crowding out" processes (Kohli, 1999; Künemund and Rein, 1999): that there is no need to help because the state provides enough support.

The pattern that emerges at this point is one of a strong propensity to help, be it for reasons of altruism, normative obligation, or reciprocity. A clear majority also requires that adult children should stand on their own feet. There is in other words a readiness to help when help is needed, but also an expectation that the children do everything they can to not let such situations of need arise. Motives of exchange (such as strategic bequest) or separation are less widely shared.

From the economic literature, we might expect that these items represent a one-dimensional continuum from altruism to exchange. From the sociological literature, on the other hand, we would expect a multidimensional space of motives that overlap and interact in specific decisions to provide help, i.e., norms of responsibility and obligation, reciprocity, affection, altruism, as well as exchange expectations (Künemund and Rein, 1999). Unfortunately, space and time limitations of the German Aging Survey allowed only for single indicators for most of the theoretically expected motives. But even on this limited basis we can examine the full motivational space, and address the question to what extent its dimensions reproduce the expected motives.

An exploratory nonlinear principal components analysis reveals three dimensions that do not correspond to either of these expectations (Table

Table 6.3   Structure of Motives (Nonlinear Principal Components Analysis)

	Component loadings		
Items	Dimension I (Eigenvalue .27)	Dimension II (Eigenvalue .18)	Dimension III (Eigenvalue .13)
My parents have done so much for me that I would like to give them back some of it.	.56		
I think that it is simply my duty to help my family members.	.79		
If my family members need help I will always be there.	.80		
I would like to pass on to the next generation what my parents have given me.	.70		
If I help my family members, I can expect help from them in return.	.50	−.54	
If I dislike a family member, I am not going to help them.		−.53	
If someone wants to inherit from me, he/she should do something for it.		−.74	
There is no need for me to help my family members because there is enough public support.		−.54	
Grown-up children should be able to stand on their own two feet, and not expect support from their parents.		−.63	.53
At my age why should I still save money? My family members can make much better use of it.			−.80

Note: German Aging Survey 1996 (only component loadings ≥.5; total fit: .59).

6.3).[7] With one exception, the statements that load high on the first dimension indicate a readiness for unconditional giving (be it for reasons of an altruistic orientation, reciprocity, or a normative obligation to help family members in need) while the statements that load high on the second dimension contain an explicit condition that has to be met. These conditions also cover a wide range of motives: direct exchange, affective closeness, autonomy, and the (non-)availability of public support. The exception is the statement of direct reciprocity ("If I help my family member . . ."). As noted above, this statement has indeed a double meaning, and this also applies to the distinction of conditional vs. unconditional giving: It can be understood as either a reason to give or a result of giving, i.e., as either a precondition or a description of an outcome that is not critical for one's decision to provide help. The (less important) third dimension shows high loading for two statements that express autonomy and separation between the generations: that adult children should be able to stand on their own feet and that parents should continue to save for their own future benefit and independence.

The main structural pattern is thus the contrast between unconditional and conditional solidarity. For the remaining analyses we focus on the two statements with the highest component loadings on these two dimensions. They can also be directly interpreted as indicators of altruism and exchange. In a first step, we examine the predictors of the two contrasting types of solidarity. Table 6.4 presents the results of ordinal logistic regressions on the degree of agreement to these statements in terms of odds ratios.[8] The models show a strong effect of social stratification and gender. The odds to agree to the "strategic bequest" statement, and with that, to conditional giving, decrease significantly with socioeconomic variables such as occupational prestige (Wegener, 1985) and education. Women are less likely than men to be motivated by an instrumental exchange orientation. On the other hand, respondents with considerable difficulties in daily activities due to health problems are less disinterested, i.e., more inclined to tie their giving to the condition of direct exchange: The odds to agree to this statement increase by one-third with poor health. Agreement is also higher in the former GDR compared to the former FRG, even when all other independent variables are held constant. Having received transfers from one's own parents, parents-in-law, or grandparents decreases the inclination for maintaining a direct exchange condition, but the effect is not significant.

For our statement on unconditional giving ("If my family members need help I will always be there"), the East-West divide is again highly salient, while gender and social stratification are not significant, with the exception of a moderate effect of household equivalence income where those in the highest quintiles are more likely to give without strings attached. Health is also again a highly significant predictor—being in poor health decreases the odds of being unconditionally available for help.

In sum, it seems that having insufficient resources and/or a need for help results in a preference for conditional giving, and vice versa. But the variables of social stratification and gender do not only indicate a resource differential; they also stand for different family styles in terms of emotional closeness and unconditional support, and for different personal inclinations to care for others. The fact that both statements receive higher agreement in East Germany may indicate a style where family solidarity is self-evident and mandatory but where there is also an obligation to reciprocate—where solidarity is seen as necessarily two-way.

As a second step, we ask whether these motives are a relevant predictor of the process of giving between generations (holding other factors constant). Table 6.5 presents the results of separate logistic regressions on giving transfers and giving any kind of support to kin. In line with our previous research (Kohli, 1999; Kohli et al., 2000; Motel and Szydlik, 1999)

Table 6.4   Predictors of Motives (Ordinal Logistic Regressions)

	"Inherit"		"Always"	
	Univariate	*Multivariate*	*Univariate*	*Multivariate*
Sex: female (reference: male)	0.72***	0.59***	1.01	1.01
Age group: 70–85 (55–69)	0.94	0.93	1.08	1.15
Region: former GDR (FRG)	1.51***	1.70***	1.89***	2.05***
Community:				
2.000–5.000 (<2.000)	0.78	0.87	0.97	1.07
5.000–20.000	0.68*	0.87	1.11	1.33
20.000–50.000	0.64**	0.80	1.06	1.06
50.000–100.000	0.56**	0.62*	1.19	1.05
100.000–500.000	0.47***	0.61**	1.28	1.34
>500.000	0.53***	0.72*	1.06	1.18
Living alone (living with others)	0.99	1.11	0.96	0.88
Health: minor difficulties (none)	1.00	0.98	0.89	0.93
considerable difficulties	1.36**	1.33**	0.64***	0.61***
Education: Middle (low)	0.82	0.72**	1.28*	1.07
High	0.44***	0.50***	1.32*	1.01
Equivalence income: 2nd quintile (lowest quintile)	0.91	0.88	1.35*	1.17
3rd quintile	0.72**	0.80	1.57***	1.33
4th quintile	0.67***	0.89	1.56**	1.36*
Highest quintile	0.56***	0.95	1.42**	1.53**
Occupational prestige	0.99***	0.99***	1.01**	1.00
Received transfers from parents, parents-in-law, or grandparents earlier (no)	1.30	1.25	0.74	0.69
Constant (B): $\alpha = 1$	—	2.92***	—	3.44***
$\alpha = 2$	—	1.29***	—	2.36***
$\alpha = 3$	—	–0.52*	—	–0.19
Pseudo R^2 (McFadden)	—	0.03	—	0.03
N		1.399		1.399

Note: German Aging Survey 1996. ***, $p < .01$; **, $p < .05$; *, $p < .1$.

the results show that the odds of transfer giving increase significantly with socioeconomic resources as measured by equivalence income and occupational prestige (while the effect of education is absorbed in these other variables). Living alone strongly decreases the odds of giving monetary transfers, indicating the fact that many of those living alone do not have children or other kin. A similar predictive pattern holds for providing any kind of support to kin.

But the main result for our present purpose is the massive effect of the transfer motives. Controlling for all other variables, agreeing to the unconditional (altruistic) orientation increases the odds to provide monetary transfers by a factor of 6, while agreeing to the direct exchange (strategic

Table 6.5   Predictors of Transfer and Support Giving (Binary Logistic Regressions)

	Giving transfers		Any kind of support	
	Univariate	Multivariate	Univariate	Multivariate
Sex: female (reference: male)	0.82*	0.87	1.01	1.15
Age group: 70–85 (55–69)	1.21	1.16	0.80**	0.80*
Region: former GDR (FRG)	0.99	1.03	1.22*	1.23
Community: 2.000–5.000 (<2.000)	1.42	1.28	0.89	0.86
5.000–20.000	1.14	0.91	0.80	0.72
20.000–50.000	1.20	0.86	0.71	0.55**
50.000–100.000	1.28	0.94	0.82	0.66
100.000–500.000	1.69**	1.22	1.04	0.88
≥500.000	1.09	0.73	0.78	0.66*
Living alone (living with others)	0.66***	0.57***	0.53***	0.50**
Health: minor difficulties (none)	1.01	1.29	0.93	1.01
considerable difficulties	1.01	1.21	0.62***	0.75*
Education: middle (low)	1.21	0.84	0.97	0.77
High	1.83***	0.86	1.27	0.80
Equivalence income: 2nd quintile (lowest quintile)	1.43*	1.52*	0.88	0.93
3rd quintile	2.03***	1.96***	1.30	1.31
4th quintile	2.20***	2.18***	1.31	1.35
Highest quintile	3.34***	3.50***	1.36*	1.54**
Occupational prestige	1.01***	1.01***	1.01***	1.01***
Agree to "Inherit" (disagree)	0.72***	0.78**	0.67***	0.71***
Agree to "Always" (disagree)	6.35***	6.07***	4.83***	4.56***
Constant (B)	—	–3.12***	—	–0.94***
Pseudo R^2 (McFadden)	—	0.08	—	0.07
N		1.394		1.398

Note: German Aging Survey 1996. ***, $p < .01$; **, $p < .05$; *, $p < .1$).
"Any kind of support" includes financial transfers, care for the disabled, child care, and instrumental (household) support.

bequest) orientation has a strongly significant negative effect. With regard to the more inclusive category, providing any kind of support to kin, the two orientations have a similar impact. Thus, it is not only needs and resources[9] that determine intergenerational support in the family but also the motivation of the givers as assessed by direct questioning.

CONCLUSIONS

The first conclusion to be highlighted is that that the motivation for giving monetary and other support to kin consists of a complex pattern with a large amount of overlap and interaction among different motives. Based on our assessment of the range of the motives that have been conceptualized so far through a limited number of questionnaire statements, we have been able to show that the search for single or dominant motives is misguided, and that we need to search instead for the combinations of motives that typically occur. This should apply both to a person's general attitudes and to concrete single transactions.

Our own search by means of an exploratory nonlinear principal components analysis has resulted in a structure of the motivational space that does not correspond to the commonly assumed altruism-exchange dichotomy nor to its extension into a trichotomy with reciprocity included. What we have found instead is a dichotomy of unconditional vs. conditional giving, with a third (less prominent) dimension denoting independence and separation between the generations. Both unconditional and conditional giving comprise several specific motives, with the former emphasizing altruism, reciprocity, and normative obligation, and the latter, direct exchange. The distinction between these two motivational types is reminiscent of similar distinctions in the literature on types of parent-child relationships and styles of socialization.

By focusing on one motive statement for each of these two types it has been possible to determine which sociodemographic conditions have an impact on them, and what impact they themselves have in turn on transfer and support giving. The motives are socially stratified, again corresponding to the stratification of family relationship types. They also vary along gender lines, with women leaning more toward unconditional and less toward conditional giving than men.

As a final step, we have shown that motives contribute in a highly significant way to the explanation of transfer behavior. We cannot ascertain yet whether motives and motivational types make a difference for the meaning and quality of intergenerational transfers in the family, but they do have a strong impact on the incidence of transfer giving. It is therefore not sufficient to infer motives from transfer behavior, or to pass from objective sociodemographic variables and resource conditions directly to the behavior under scrutiny. Motives have to assessed independently, and to be integrated into any attempt at a fuller explanation of transfer giving.

ACKNOWLEDGMENTS

Preliminary versions of this chapter were presented at the *Conference on International Perspectives on Families, Aging and Social Support* (University of Haifa, Israel, May 17–20, 2001), and at the *International Meeting on Age Structure Transitions and Policy Dynamics* (Academia Sinica, Taipei, Taiwan, December 6–8, 2001). We are grateful to the organizers and participants of these conferences—especially to Eugene Litwak and Sy Spilerman—for their helpful comments. The first author is indebted to the Hanse Institute for Advanced Study (Delmenhorst/Bremen) for being invited as a Fellow during the academic year 2000–2001. Completion of the chapter was supported by the Ford Foundation (Grant No. 1000-1729-1).

NOTES

1. See for France: Attias-Donfut (1995); for Germany: Motel and Szydlik (1999), Kohli (1999); for Israel: Spilerman, Lewin-Epstein, and Semyonov (1993); for the United States: Soldo and Hill (1993) and McGarry (1997).

2. Masson and Pestieau (1996, p. 17) mistakenly claim that this type of bequest "concerns only the well-to-do." The main historical model, however, and one that is still found today is the family farm. Here, the "estate thinking" (*Hofdenken*) has meant that the life of the farm takes primacy over the individual lives of the succeeding generations of family members.

3. There may of course be a combination with considering the well-being of descendants. For example, if precautionary saving is motivated by the desire not to burden the children with one's need, or to be able to cover one's own living *and* leave a bequest.

4. The question of whether there is "pure" altruism or whether the motive is the joy of giving may seem a moot one as long as we find that the concern is for the well-being of the recipient and not for one's own. Where giving continues even in the absence of need, however, it does seem warranted to speak of "impure" altruism.

5. The German Aging Survey has been designed and analyzed jointly by the *Research Groups on Aging and the Life Course* at the Free University of Berlin and the *Research Group on Psychogerontology* at the University of Nijmegen (Netherlands) together with *infas Sozialforschung*, Bonn, and financed by the Federal Ministry for Families, Elderly, Women and Youth. The sole responsibility for the content of this paper lies with the authors.

6. See Künemund, Motel, and Szydlik (2000a) for a detailed description of all variables and the whole sample.

7. For the nonlinear principal component analysis we use the PRINCALS procedure of the SPSS package. For details see de Leeuw and van Rijckevorsel (1980); all variables are treated as ordinal.

8. For details on logistic regression, see, for example, DeMaris (1992). Since education, income, and prestige are correlated, not all of these variables remain significant in the multivariate model.

9. In a different context we have shown that such orientations prove to be significant even when examining parent-child dyads where characteristics of the recipients and of the relationship between the two are included in the model (Künemund and Motel, 2000). We will extend our present analysis in this direction at a later point.

REFERENCES

Andreoni, J. 1989. Giving with impure altruism: Applications to charity and Ricardian equivalence. *Journal of Political Economy* 97:1447–58.

Antonucci, T. C., and Jackson, J. S. 1990. The role of reciprocity in social support. In B. R. Sarasin, I. G. Sarasin, and G. P. Pierce (eds.), *Social support: An interactional view* (pp. 173–98). New York: Wiley.

Attias-Donfut, C. 1995. Le double circuit de transmission. In C. Attias-Donfut (ed.), *Les solidarités entre générations: Vieillesse, familles, état* (pp. 41–82). Paris: Nathan.

Becker, G. S. 1991. *A treatise on the family* (enlarged ed.). Cambridge, MA: Harvard University Press.

Bengtson, V. L. 2001. Beyond the nuclear family: The increasing importance of multigenerational bonds. *Journal of Marriage and the Family* 63:1–16.

Bernheim, D. B., Shleifer, A., and Summers, L. H. (1985). The strategic bequest motive. *Journal of Political Economy* 93:1045–76.

Boersch-Supan, A., Ghokale, J., Kotlikoff, L. J., and Morris, J. 1990. *The provision of time to the elderly by their children* (NBER working paper No. 3363). Cambridge, MA: National Bureau of Economic Research.

Cantor, M. H. 1979. Neighbors and friends: An overlooked resource in the informal support system. *Research on Aging* 1:434–63.

Chen, S., and Adamchak, D. J. 1999. The effects of filial responsibility expectations on intergenerational exchanges in urban China. *Hallym International Journal of Aging* 1:58–68.

De Leeuw, J., and van Rijckevorsel, J. 1980. HOMALS and PRINCALS: Some generalizations of principal component analysis. *Data Analysis and Informatics* 2:231–42.

DeMaris, A. 1992. *Logit modelling*. Newbury Park: Sage.

Dittmann-Kohli, F., Bode, C., and Westerhof, G. J. (eds.). 2001. *Die zweite Lebenshälfte: Psychologische Perspektiven. Ergebnisse des Alters-Survey.* Stuttgart: Kohlhammer.

Dittmann-Kohli, F., Kohli, M., Künemund, H., Motel, A., Steinleitner, C., and Westerhof, G. 1997. *Lebenszusammenhänge, Selbst- und Lebenskonzeptionen. Erhebungsdesign und Instrumente des Alters-Survey.* Forschungsgruppe Altern und Lebenslauf (FALL), Freie Universität Berlin (Forschungsbericht 47).

Esser, H. 1999. *Soziologie: Spezielle Grundlagen. Band 1: Situationslogik und Handeln.* Frankfurt/M: Campus.

Finch, J., and Mason, J. 1993. *Negotiating family responsibilities*. London: Routledge.

Gale, W. G., and Scholz, J. K. 1994. Intergenerational transfers and the accumulation of wealth. *Journal of Economic Perspectives* 8:145–60.

Glazer, A., and Konrad, K. 1996. A signalling explanation for charity. *American Economic Review* 86:1019–28.

Gouldner, A. W. 1960. The norm of reciprocity: A preliminary statement. *American Sociological Review* 25:161–78.

Hollstein, B., and Bria, G. 1996. *Reciprocity in parent-child relationships.* Paper presented at the 91st Annual Meeting of the American Sociological Association, New York, August.

Kohli, M. 1997. Beziehungen und Transfers zwischen den Generationen: Vom Staat zurück zur Familie? In L. A. Vaskovics (ed.), *Familienleitbilder und Familienrealitäten* (pp. 278–88). Opladen: Leske and Budrich.

_____. 1999. Private and public transfers between generations: Linking the family and the state. *European Societies* 1:81–104.

Kohli, M., and Künemund, H. (eds.) 2000. *Die zweite Lebenshälfte. Gesellschaftliche Lage und Partizipation im Spiegel des Alters-Survey.* Opladen: Leske and Budrich.

Kohli, M., Künemund, H., Motel, A., and Szydlik, M. 2000a. *Grunddaten zur Lebenssituation der 40–85 jährigen deutschen Bevölkerung. Ergebnisse des Alters-Survey*. Berlin: Weißensee.

Kohli, M., Künemund, H., Motel, A., and Szydlik, M. 2000b. Families apart? Intergenerational transfers in East and West Germany. In S. Arber and C. Attias-Donfut (eds.), *The myth of generational conflict: Family and state in ageing societies* (pp. 88–99). London: Routledge.

Kotlikoff, L. J., and Morris, J. N. 1989. How much care do the aged receive from their children? A bimodal picture of contact and assistance. In D. A. Wise, (ed.), *The economics of aging* (pp. 149–72). Chicago: University of Chicago Press.

Künemund, H., and Motel, A. (2000). Verbreitung, Motivation und Entwicklungsperspektiven privater intergenerationeller Hilfeleistungen und Transfers. In M. Kohli and M. Szydlik (eds.), *Generationen in Familie und Gesellschaft* (pp. 122–37). Opladen: Leske and Budrich.

Künemund, H., and Rein, M. 1999. There is more to receiving than needing: Theoretical arguments and empirical explorations of crowding in and crowding out. *Ageing and Society* 19:93–121.

Masson, A., and Pestieau, P. 1996. *Bequests and models of inheritance: A survey of the literature* (Document no. 96–20). Paris: DELTA.

McGarry, K. 1997. Inter vivos transfers and intended bequests (NBER working paper No. W6345). Cambridge, MA: National Bureau of Economic Research.

———. 2000. Testing parental altruism: Implications of a dynamic model (NBER working paper No. W7593). Cambridge, MA: National Bureau of Economic Research.

McGarry, K., and Schoeni, R. F. 1997. Transfer behavior within family: Results from the Asset and Health Dynamics Study. *Journals of Gerontology* 52B(special issue):82–92.

Motel, A., and Szydlik, M. 1999. Private Transfers zwischen den Generationen. *Zeitschrift für Soziologie* 28:3–22.

Qureshi, H. 1990. A research note on the hierarchy of obligations among informal carers: A response to Finch and Mason. *Ageing and Society* 10:455–58.

Silverstein, M., and Bengtson, V. L. 1997. Intergenerational solidarity and the structure of adult child-parent relationships in American families. *American Journal of Sociology* 103:429–60.

Soldo, B. J., and Hill, M. S. 1993. Intergenerational transfers: Economic, demographic, and social perspectives. *Annual Review of Gerontology and Geriatrics* 13:187–216.

Spilerman, S., Lewin-Epstein, N., and Semyonov, M. 1993. Wealth, intergenerational transfers, and life chances. In A. B. Sorensen and S. Spilerman (eds.), *Social theory and social policy* (pp. 165–86). New York: Praeger.

Stark, O. 1995. *Altruism and beyond. An economic analysis of transfers and exchanges within families and groups*. Cambridge: Cambridge University Press.

Szydlik, M. (2000). *Lebenslange Solidarität? Generationenbeziehungen zwischen erwachsenen Kindern und Eltern*. Opladen: Leske and Budrich.

Wegener, B. (1985): Gibt es Sozialprestige? *Zeitschrift für Soziologie* 14:209–35.

| 7 |

Family Characteristics and Loneliness among Older Parents

Kees Knipscheer and Theo van Tilburg

Loneliness among older people is an intriguing issue in aging research, policy, and practice. Many disciplinary perspectives and approaches have been used in an attempt to understand and explain well-being and loneliness among older adults. Dykstra (1990), with reference to House and Kahn (1985), found three approaches in the study of the association between types of relationships and well-being with loneliness as a component of an overall measure of well-being: (a) the social integration approach, (b) the social network approach, and (c) the social support approach. In the social integration approach the focus is on the existence of relationships such as marital relationship, availability of family members or friends, and memberships in church or volunteer associations. Researchers in the social network tradition examine the structure of the relationships in which individuals are embedded. Their hypothesis is that the structure and composition of the network have an impact on the pattern of interactions and flow of resources within the network with consequences on well-being. Within the social support approach, researchers focus on what is provided to an individual by others (i.e., emotional or instrumental support) and how this is appreciated. Each of these traditional approaches has been productive in understanding well-being and loneliness among older people (Dykstra, 1990; de Jong Gierveld and Tilburg, 1995).

In this study we intend to expand this tradition and add a somewhat different approach to explain loneliness—a family system approach. A starting point in this approach is the notion that the family as a whole has its own impact on the behavior and subsequently on the well-being of its individual members. The family is viewed as a cultural entity that establishes a common ground for interaction and exchange, and defines a family style of dealing with ongoing family issues. The focus may be on the functioning of the total set of family relationships including their interrelatedness and not on separate dyadic relationships. These notions are based on fundamental social-psychological and sociological arguments that social system characteristics impact human behavior. Our question is, therefore, whether we can show the specific impact of the type of family characteristics as a collectivity on the well-being of older parents.

CHARACTERISTICS OF A FAMILY AS A WHOLE

The literature discusses several approaches that view the family as a cultural entity. Handel (1967) discussed "family themes" as typical family-bounded patterns of feelings, motives, fantasies, and conventionalized understandings that organize a family's view of reality. Ford and Herrick (1974) took a somewhat different perspective and talked about "family rules"—binding directives concerning the ways in which family members should relate to one another and to the outside world. Family rules provide a family with character and style. In 1981, Reiss introduced the notion of "family construct," suggesting that a family creates its own paradigm— a set of shared assumptions that make sense of the world and coordinate the actions of the family members. Bennett et al. (1988) tried to cover each of these notions under the umbrella concept of "family identity"—a group psychology phenomenon that has its foundation in a shared system of beliefs, including implicit assumptions about roles, relationships, and values that govern interaction in families. According to the authors, a fundamental component of family identity is the beliefs about family membership—who is in and who is out of the family—both now and in the past. Recently, Widmer et al. (1999) and Widmer (1999) reconsidered the component of family membership. While earlier discussions assumed, explicitly or implicitly, that a family includes those who share a household or a limited set of family roles, Widmer et al. (1999) prefer to talk about family contexts—a rather large and unbounded set of kin. They argue that recent findings about strong emotional bonds between adults and their siblings and parents, about divorce and the extension of remarriage, and about pseudokinship ties show the existence of complex family groupings, referred to as family contexts, a type of cognitive network. This is important to our approach in this study, because we also suggest considering older parents and their adult children as a cultural entity with a specific type of interrelatedness, despite the fact that they mostly live in separate households. We suggest that this interrelatedness originates about thirty years prior to the study time from two kinship systems. It is based in early educational and developmental experiences, is still dealing with a number of common orientations, beliefs, and perceptions, and demonstrates a number of commonalities in the style of behavior. We suggest calling this typical cultural family characteristic the family ambience of older parents and their adult children. Family ambience ranges from a positive coherent family ambience to a diverse incoherent family ambience.

Another perspective on the family as a whole took a more functional orientation. Several family sociologists (Alexander, Johnson, and Carter, 1984; Epstein, Bishop, and Levin, 1978; Moos and Moos, 1981; and Olson et al., 1982; Olson, Russell, and Sprenkle, 1983; and Olson, Sprenkle, and Russell, 1979; Sprenkle and Olson, 1978) introduced, during the second half of the twentieth century, measurement instruments, procedures, and tools to typify families as a functioning social system. This approach was developed in order to relate the quality of family functioning to the outcome of educational processes and/or relational experiences. Scholars tried to identify family characteristics that distinguish between problem and non–problem families, i.e., families with and without schizophrenics, neurotics, runaway adolescents, and/or sex offenders. Similarly, quality of relational functioning between marital partners has been related to outcomes such as divorce, level of communication, and affection. Touliatos, Perlmutter, and Straus (1990) published an early overview and Tutty (1995) presented a comparative analysis of the methodological quality of six measures of family functioning.

Olson, Sprenkle, and Russell (1979) considered two dimensions of family functioning as crucial: cohesion and adaptability. They considered extreme scores on both adaptability and cohesion as dysfunctional for educational outcomes. They introduced the self-report measure, the Family Adaptability and Cohesion Evaluation Scales (FACES), from which a Clinical Rating Scale version was later developed (Olson and Killorin, 1985). Moos and Moos (1981) included nine dimensions of family functioning; among them were cohesion, expressivity, norms and values, and organization and control. Again, these dimensions of family functioning were expected to be related to outcomes of family and relational functioning (Moos, 1990; Holahan and Moos, 1987; Billings, Cronkite, and Moos, 1983). The McMaster Model of Family Functioning, developed by Epstein, Bishop, and Levine (1978) and originally designed as a clinical rating scale, consists of six dimensions: problem solving, communication, roles, affective responsiveness, affective involvement, and behavior control. Later a sixty-item self-report instrument was developed to assess the six identified dimensions of family functioning (Epstein, Baldwin, and Bishop, 1983).

In this chapter, we intend to take a comparable functional approach of the family system in order to examine whether we can expand our understanding of loneliness among older parents. However there are a few important differences. The families we study do not live as nuclear families anymore. Most children have had their own nuclear families for quite a long time and live geographically apart from their parents. Moreover, we are not interested in the outcome of educational processes among children, but rather in experienced loneliness among the older parents. Based on a qualitative study, Pyke and Bengtson (1996) introduced a distinction between individualist and collectivist systems of family elder care. To qualify the distinction between the two family systems the authors "identified three sets of traits, among which there was a high level of congruency: family ethics, the level of contact and interdependence that family members expect and receive from one another, and responses to the caregiving needs of aging family members" (Pyke, 1999, p. 662). Interestingly, these traits present a clear combination of the cultural and functional dimensions of family systems. Both Pyke and Bengtson (1996) and Pyke (1999) demonstrate that factors at the family level appear to be important in understanding outcomes at the individual level: aging parents.

The data of a substudy of the NESTOR "Living Arrangements and Social Networks of Older Adults" program enables us to construct characteristics of the family and to examine to what extent these characteristics are related to older parent's experience of loneliness. In this case we consider older parents and their adult children—living at home or independently—as a family. We intend to determine to what extent both family ambience and family functioning are interrelated and whether they are related to the level of loneliness of older parents, controlling for individual and relational determinants.

METHOD

Sample

In 1992–1993, 277 older adults, referred to as the focal parents, participated in a study on characteristics of personal networks. These focal parents, 144 men and 133 women, were between 55 and 89 years old (average 68.1; SD = 8.3); 194 lived with a partner (191 were married, 1 divorced, and 2 widowed) and the others had no partner (1 married and separated, 10 divorced, and 72 widowed). Other participants in the study were focal parents' partners and a selection of the children. The focal parents were a selection from all respondents (n = 580) in the study. Excluded were childless respondents and respondents with step-, foster, or adoptive children (n = 144), and respondents with a partner outside the household (n = 4). Furthermore, data on family ambience had to be available from the focal parent (35 respondents were excluded), from the partner, if there was a partner (exclusion of 40 respondents), and from at least one child (exclusion of 63 respondents). Next, 17 focal parents were excluded due to missing data on loneliness.

The focal parents in the study comprised a probability sample from another sample. The initial sample consisted of 4,494 respondents with whom face-to-face interviews were conducted in 1992 (de Jong Gierveld, van Tilburg, and Dykstra, 1995). The initial sample was stratified, with equal numbers of men and women born from 1903 to 1937, and was randomly taken from the registers of eleven municipalities in the Netherlands. The response rate was 62 percent.

In the beginning of the initial interview, all the children of the parents were identified. The focal parents (and their partners) had 1 to 11 children (on average 3.0; in total 835). Questionnaires were mailed to the parents and the children who were identified as network members and were among the eight network members with whom the contact was most frequent. The procedure has been described in detail elsewhere (Klein Ikkink, van Tilburg, and Knipscheer, 1999). Data on family ambience was available from 1 to 6 children (on average 1.8; in total 488).

Measurements

Family ambience was measured by a number of statements describing how family members used to deal with each other as a "team" of family members. Each family member was invited to react to a number of statements about his/her family's ambience from his/her own perspective. Following Moos and Moos (1986) and Jansma (1988), who translated earlier Moos's Family Climate Scale in Dutch, we selected a set of fourteen (see Appendix) items referring to reciprocal concern and commitment, getting along, affective responsiveness, and openness of communication. Answering categories were *no!, no, more or less, yes,* and *yes!* with corresponding values of 1 to 5 assigned. The scale had a range of 14 to 70 and was homogeneous (Loevinger's coefficient of hierarchical homogeneity $H = 0.44$) and reliable ($\rho = 0.90$).

To measure loneliness, five positive and six negative items were used (de Jong Gierveld and Kamphuis, 1985). The positive items assessed feelings of belonging, for example, "I can rely on my friends whenever I need them." The negative items applied to aspects of missing relationships, for example, "I experience a sense of emptiness around me." Answering categories were *no!, no, more or less, yes,* and *yes!* Answers on positive items were reversed. To improve scale homogeneity, the answers were dichotomized, assigning the median category to the value indicating loneliness. The scale had a range of 0 (not lonely) to 11 (extremely lonely). The scale had been used in several Dutch surveys and proved to be a robust, reliable, and valid instrument (van Tilburg and de Leeuw, 1991). The homogeneity (H = 0.45) and reliability (ρ = 0.87) of the scale were sufficient.

A scale for the capacity to perform activities in daily life (ADL) was constructed as a sum score of four items: walking up and down stairs, walking for five minutes outdoors without resting, getting up from and sitting down in a chair, and getting dressed and undressed. The response options were "not at all," "only with help," "with a great deal of difficulty," "with some difficulty," and "without difficulty," with corresponding values of 1 to 5 assigned. The scale was homogeneous (H = 0.64) and reliable (ρ = 0.87). The range was 4 to 20; a higher score indicated a better capacity.

With respect to relationship characteristics, the questionnaires were completely personalized. The names of the children and other network members were included on the list for the parents, and the names of the parent(s) and the other children were on the list for the children. Three questions were posed about instrumental support received: "How often in the past year did the following people help you with daily chores in and around the house, such as preparing meals, cleaning the house, transportation, small repairs, or filling in forms?," " . . . gave you advice (e.g., on an important decision or on filling out forms)?" and " . . . gave you help when you needed it, e.g., when you were ill?" For emotional support received, three questions were posed: "How often during the past year did it occur that the following persons gave you a present?," " . . . showed you they cared for you?" and "How often during the past year did it occur that you told the following persons about your personal feelings?" Six similar questions were asked about support given. The response options were *never, seldom, sometimes,* and *often,* and these responses were scored on a scale from 1 to 4. For each relationship, four sum scores of instrumental and emotional support received and given were computed. The scores of the four scales range from 3 to 12. The four scales are homogeneous ($H \geq$ 0.55) and reliable ρ (0.76).

Procedure

First, focal parent's view on family ambience and loneliness was compared with partner's and children's scores. For 149 focal parents, data from more than one child was available. The children's scores were averaged, and the variation across children was computed by taking the standard deviation. Second, focal parent's loneliness was regressed on family ambience, controlled for sex, age, focal parent's and partner's ADL capacity, and the number of children. For family ambience, six variables were selected: focal parent's and partner's view, the average and standard deviation across the children, and in order to evaluate whether incongruencies between family members were of importance, the difference between focal parent's and partner's view and between focal parent's and children's view. The control variables were entered into the equation, while the significance of the six variables on family ambience was evaluated by a forward stepwise procedure ($p < 0.10$) in order to avoid multicollinearity problems. The analysis was conducted for focal parents with and without a partner separately. Third, variables on the exchange of support within the family (three on instrumental and three on emotional support) were introduced and extended the equation. Two types of variables were on the instrumental and emotional support received from the partner and the average support received from the children. The reports by the focal parent (support received) and by the others (support given) were both taken into account by taking their average. Data on support received from the partner was missing for two respondents who were excluded from the analysis. For six focal parents, the partner's report on support provided to the focal parent was missing. For the others, the scores of both reports were averaged. Of the 835 relationships between the focal parents and their children, reports were missing for 295 relationships; for 464 relationships both reports from the parent and the child was available, for 70 only parent's report was available, and for 6 only child's report was available. Since we were interested in family support and wanted to take into account supportive exchanges between children, the third type consisted of the average intensity of support across all relationships between children, not taking into account the direction of the support provided. Consequently, only respondents with more than one child ($n = 239$) were included. However, due to the selection, children data on relationships between children were missing for 61 respondents, leaving 47 focal parents without a partner and 131 with a partner. The sex, age, marital status, and average loneliness and family ambience of those 61 focal parents did not differ significantly from the 178 respondents included in the analysis. Since there were strong correlations between instrumental and emotional supportive exchanges, a forward stepwise procedure was adopted, with $p < .10$ due to the small number of respondents. Knowing that loneliness is strongly related to partner status we executed all the analyses for focal parents with and without partner separately.

RESULTS

Our explorative analysis focused on the explanation of the focal parent's loneliness. First we present descriptive findings. Respondents with a partner and without a partner differed significantly in loneliness (M 2.1 versus 3.9; SD 2.6 versus 3.4; $t = 4.3$; $p < 0.001$) and perceived family ambience

Table 7.1   Differences in Intensity of Supportive Exchanges

	No partner (n = 47)		With partner (n = 131)		
	M	SD	M	SD	t
Instrumental Support					
Support received from partner			9.7	2.0	
Support received from children	7.4	1.7	6.4	1.7	2.6**
Intensity within relationships between children	4.4	1.5	5.1	1.7	2.4*
Emotional Support					
Support received from partner			10.4	1.2	
Support received from children	9.7	1.0	9.1	1.2	2.9**
Intensity within relationships between children	7.2	1.7	7.7	1.8	1.7+

+, $p < 0.10$; *, $p < 0.05$; **, $p < 0.01$; ***, $p < 0.001$.
Note: Focal parents with two or more children only.

(M 53.9 versus 50.8; SD 6.6 versus 7.5; $t = 3.5$; $p < 0.001$). Among respondents with a partner there were no significant differences between focal parents and their partners in loneliness (M 2.1 versus 2.5; $t = 1.9$; $p > 0.05$) as well as in perceived family ambience (M 53.9 versus 54.0; $t = 0.1$; $p > 0.05$). Parents' loneliness correlated 0.45 and their family ambience correlated 0.55. Loneliness did not differ between the children and the focal parent (M 2.5 versus 2.6; $t = 0.6$; $p > 0.05$; $r = 0.22$). However, the average perceived family ambience among adult children was lower than perceived ambience among their parent being focal respondent (M 47.6 versus 53.0; $t = 10.8$; $p < 0.001$; $r = 0.27$).

Six support measures have been constructed, three for instrumental support and a parallel three for emotional support. In general, focal parents report to get emotional support more often than instrumental support (Table 7.1). The intensity of received partner support—for those with a partner—as perceived by the focal parent and as given by the partner is higher (more frequently given) than children support. Interestingly, on average, support from children to focal parents without a partner, including the "received" perspective of the focal parent and the averaged "given" perspective of the children, is significantly higher than for those with a partner, for both instrumental and emotional support. It seems that both focal parents without a partner (being in majority widowed or divorced) and their children reciprocally acknowledge the children's investment in parental support. However, looking at the third measure of support, taking the average intensity of giving and receiving support among children only, it appears that the level of exchange of instrumental as well as emotional support is somewhat higher among children of focal parents with a partner.

Table 7.2 Correlations of Intensity of Supportive Exchanges and Focal Parent's Perspective on Family Ambience

	No partner (n = 47)	With partner (n = 131)
Instrumental Support		
Support received from partner		0.16+
Support received from children	0.18	0.17*
Intensity within relationships between children	0.13	0.17*
Emotional Support		
Support received from partner		0.31***
Support received from children	0.06	0.28***
Intensity within relationships between children	0.19	0.26**

+, $p < 0.10$; * $p < 0.05$; ** $p < 0.01$; *** $p < 0.001$.
Note: Focal parents with two or more children only.

Correlations of the support measures and the focal parent's perspective on family ambience are presented in Table 7.2. A remarkable finding is that among focal parents with a partner emotional support is more strongly related to the perspective on family ambience than instrumental support. Furthermore, correlations with emotional support are higher among focal parents with a partner than among those without a partner. This is interesting because the level of emotional support from children among focal parents without a partner is the highest support level of children as was shown in Table 7.1. It seems that a high level of emotional support of children among parents without a partner does not always allow for the perception of a homogeneous and balanced family ambience.

Model 1 in Table 7.3 presents the results of the regression of focal parent's loneliness on six measures of perceived family ambience, controlling for well-known determinants as sex, age, ADL capacity, and number of children. Family ambience as perceived by the focal parent was by far the best predictor of his or her experience of loneliness, although it did not enter the equation among focal parents without a partner. Partner's perceived family ambience is considerably related to loneliness of the focal parent, but did not contribute to the regression. Neither children's perceived family ambience nor the variability among the children was related to the focal parent's loneliness. Focal parent's loneliness was lower when there was more variability of focal parent's, partner's, and children's perspectives on family ambience, as indicated by the difference scores. However, these variables did not contribute to the regression.

The regression equations were extended with the support data (Model 2 in Table 7.4). Unfortunately, due to missing data on support, the number of families represented in the analysis has been considerably reduced. In

Table 7.3   Regression of Focal Parent's Loneliness: Model 1

	No partner (n = 83)		With partner (n = 194)	
	r	β	r	β
Sex	−0.03	−0.04	−0.10	−0.08
Age	−0.01	−0.03	0.09	0.06
ADL capacity				
Focal parent	−0.17	−0.17	0.02	−0.03
Partner	†		−0.04	−0.05
Number of children	−0.01	−0.02	−0.04	−0.08
Family ambience as perceived by[a]				
Focal parent	−0.24*		−0.36***	−0.37***
Partner	†	−0.23***		
Children (average score)	−0.01		−0.09	
Variability in family ambience a				
Among children (SD)	−0.00		−0.05	
Difference between focal parent and partner†			−0.21**	
Difference between focal parent and children	−0.20		−0.15*	
R^2		0.03		0.15**

+, $p < 0.10$; *, $p < 0.05$; **, $p < 0.01$; ***, $p < 0.001$.
†, Not included in the equation.
[a]Forward stepwise procedure.

these analyses 18 and 19 percent of the variation in loneliness among the focal parents has been explained, however with a surprising similarity and a typical difference between the two types of parents. In both equations the focal parents perspective on family ambience contributes in explaining loneliness, be it among parents with a partner more significantly. Among focal parents without a partner ADL capacity of the focal parent has a considerable contribution in explaining loneliness. Among focal parents with a partner, in contrast, emotional support received from children contributes significantly in explaining loneliness, even when taken into account the contribution of the focal parents perspective on family ambience. High intensity in received emotional support from children (according to parent and children) seems to prevent older people's loneliness.

DISCUSSION

In this chapter, we explored the contribution of family characteristics in explaining loneliness among older parents. We developed a family system approach by constructing two types of family characteristics: family ambi-

Table 7.4 Regression of Focal Parent's Loneliness: Model 2

	No partner (n = 47)		With partner (n = 131)	
	r	β	r	β
Sex	0.12	0.02	–0.05	0.02
Age	–0.01	–0.04	0.12	0.12
ADL capacity				
Focal parent	–0.31*	–0.24	–0.00	–0.08
Partner	†		–0.05	–0.02
Number of children	0.07	–0.00	–0.01	–0.08
Family ambience as perceived by a				
Focal parent	–0.37**	–0.31+	–0.35***	–0.31***
Partner	†		–0.20*	
Children (average score)	–0.31*		–0.23**	
Variability in family ambience a				
Among children (SD)	0.00		–0.06	
Difference between focal parent and partner	†		–0.16+	
Difference between focal parent and children	–0.12		–0.09	
Instrumental support a				
Support received from partner	†		–0.06	
Support Received from Children	–0.03		–0.21*	
Intensity within relationships between children	0.11		–0.22*	
Emotional support a				
Support received from partner	†		–0.10	
Support received from children	0.08		–0.28**	–0.21*
Intensity within relationships between children	–0.03		–0.24**	
R^2	0.19		0.18**	

+, $p < 0.10$; *, $p < 0.05$; **, $p < 0.01$; ***, $p < 0.001$.
†, Not included.
[a]Forward stepwise procedure.
Note: Focal parents with two or more children only.

ence and family functioning. Family ambience refers to the family as a cultural identity with a specific type of interrelatedness that is based on a number of shared orientations, beliefs and perceptions with a behavioral impact on family interaction patterns. A set of fourteen statements, describing how family members are used to dealing with each other, has been utilized to measure family ambience. All these statements had their focus on the family as a whole. Family functioning refers to the way the family functions as a social system in adaptability to new situations, in organization of activities or in exchange of support. In this study we construed "group-measures" of exchange of support between individual family members as an indices of family functioning.

Because parents with a partner were very significantly less lonely than those without a partner, analyses were conducted for the two groups separately. Parents with a partner were more positive in their perspective on family ambience than parents without a partner, while there was no difference between these parents and their partners. In general children were lower on family ambience. Such a difference in perspective between parents and children appears not to be unusual. Parents often register fewer conflicts and disagreements in their family relationships, easily neglect violations of family rules, and prefer to stress a common commitment to the family style of life (Knipscheer and Bevers, 1985; Luescher and Pillemer, 1998).

Children of focal parents without partner focused their instrumental and emotional support on their parent, this support being more intensive than among focal parents with a partner. It appears that children and divorced or widowed parents in old age agree on their acknowledgement of the support needed by and given to the parent. Given this focus on the parental support in the case of focal parent without a partner, exchange of support—both given and received—among children themselves appears to be considerably lower. In this case, family functioning in the area of support has a clear focus on focal parent without a partner.

The exchange of support between family members is related to the focal parent's perspective on family ambience, with a considerably higher correlation among parents with a partner. The parents' positive view on their family's ambience is related to a higher level of exchange of support among family members. Family functioning in the area of support and perceived family ambience seem to have a reciprocal relationship. This particularly pertains to the exchange of emotional support among families of focal parents with a partner.

Focal parents with a partner, who have a positive view on their family's ambience, are much less lonely than others (both focal parents with a partner, who have a less positive view on their family's ambience and focal parents without a partner). While the partner's family ambience score and several family ambience indices are significantly related to the focal parents loneliness, they do not contribute in the regression on loneliness. This means that none of the family indices on family ambience, the average of the children, the variability among the children's score, the difference between focal parent and partner, nor the difference between focal parent and children contribute systematically to the explanation of the focal parent's loneliness. From this analysis it is clear that it is the individual focal parent's perspective on the ambience of the family collective that appears to be the best predictor of the focal parents experience of loneliness, especially when this parent still has a partner. In other words, there appears to be a connection between a parent's perception of his or her family ambience and his or her experience of loneliness.

Adding the support data to the regression analyses increased the explanatory power of the regression analyses. Still the focal parent's perspective on his/her family's ambience appears to be the most crucial one, in this case irrespective of the focal parent having a partner or not. For the parents without a partner, ADL capacity turns out to be second important explanatory factor. For focal parents with a partner, however, the intensity of the emotional support received from children appears to be the second important factor, as was previously reported by Long and Martin (2000). This is the only factor of family functioning construed at a family system level, which contributes significantly in the explanation of the focal parent's loneliness. In reviewing the explanatory power of about 19 percent, we have to consider that the difference between parents without and with a partner was not taken into account since analyses were conducted separately for each group. Furthermore, it is remarkable that we were able to model differences in loneliness among parents with a partner, given the low variability in scores.

Finally, we have to comment on three specific aspects of the design of this study on the family system. First, when studying the family from the perspective of family members it is preferable to have data collected from all members (Mangen, 1995). Since we analyzed data collected within the framework of a network study, including partners, children, other kin and nonkin, the number of children included was relatively small. Furthermore, nonresponse from family members resulted in a smaller number of families for which data from different members was available. Second, methodological developments have resulted in improved techniques for the analysis of characteristics of individual family members and their relationships while taking into account contextual family characteristics by means of multilevel analysis (Snijders, 1995). However, tools to study the family as a whole while taking into account the variability in family perspectives of individual family members and characteristics of their relationships are still very limited (Tutty, 1995). Our approach to studying differences in the loneliness of a specific parent from aggregated characteristics and perspectives of children and their mutual relationships might neglect specific family dynamics. Third, we introduced two types of family characteristics—family ambience and family functioning—and construed for each of them a number of variables at the family level to see to what extent family variables would explain loneliness of a specific family member—the focal parent. The two family variables that turned out to contribute in explaining loneliness among the focal parents appear to be directly or more or less indirectly the focal parents' perspectives on family ambience and family functioning. In the second model only the focal parents' family ambience score of the six ambience measures contributed to the explanation of loneliness, while in family functioning only emotional support received from children contributed, this support measure being a combination of the support as received according to the parent and given according to the children. None of the other "collective" measures contributed to the explanation of loneliness. As for family ambience, as measured in this study, this may suggest that there are as many perspectives on family ambience as there are family members. This idea is supported by Widmer's (1999) concept of individually cognitive contexts. As for family functioning, it suggests that the real experience of emotional support, as measured in the emotional support received from children, moderates the focal parents' loneliness. These limited findings may question our ambition to develop family characteristics that explain loneliness or our achievement in the construction of adequate family characteristics.

ACKNOWLEDGMENTS

This study is based on data collected in the context of the Living Arrangements and Social Networks of Older Adults research program, conducted at the Vrije Universiteit in Amsterdam and the Netherlands Interdisciplinary Demographic Institute in The Hague. The research has been funded by a program grant from the Netherlands Program for Research on Ageing (NESTOR).

APPENDIX: ITEMS ON FAMILY AMBIENCE

1. We can get along very well.
2. In our family we are very open about our experiences.
3. We always have an easy understanding about what we are expected to do.
4. We can cooperate quite well.
5. Criticism about each other is always settled in our family.
6. We are strongly attached to each other.
7. We criticize each other if necessary.
8. We make considerable effort to see and talk to each other.
9. Sometimes we hug each other spontaneously.
10. If one of us is believed to misbehave, the family comments on this.
11. We are very reliable in meeting arrangements/commitments.
12. When we are together, the atmosphere is very relaxed.
13. If something has to be done, we will get things done.
14. We sympathize very much with each other.

REFERENCES

Alexander, B., Johnson, S., and Carter, R. 1984. A psychometric study of the Family Adaptability and Cohesion Scales. *Journal of Abnormal Child Psychology* 12: 199–288.

Bennett, L. A., Wolin, S. J., and McAvity, K. J. 1988. Family identity, ritual, and myth: A cultural perspective on life cycle transitions. In C. J. Falicov (ed.), *Family transition; Continuity and change over the life cycle* (pp. 211–34). New York: Guilford.

Billings, A., Cronkite, R., and Moos, R. 1983. Social environmental factors in unipolar depression: Comparisons of depressed patients and nondepressed controls. *Journal of Abnormal Psychology* 92:119–33.

de Jong Gierveld, J., and Kamphuis, F. 1985. The development of a Rasch-type loneliness scale. *Applied Psychological Measurement* 9:289–99.

de Jong Gierveld, J., and van Tilburg, T. G. 1995. Social relationships, integration and loneliness. In C. P. M. Knipscheer, J. de Jong Gierveld, T. G. van Tilburg, and P. A. Dykstra (eds.), *Living arrangements and social networks of older adults* (pp. 155–72). Amsterdam: Free University Press.

Dykstra, P. A. 1990. *Next of (non)kin.* Amsterdam: Swets and Zeitlinger.

Epstein, N. B., Baldwin, L. M., and Bishop, D. S. 1983. The McMaster Family Assessment Device. *Journal of Marital and Family Therapy* 9:171–80.

Epstein, N. B., Bishop, D. S., and Levin, S. (1978). The McMaster model of family functioning. *Journal of Marriage and Family Counseling* 4:19–31.

Ford, F. and Herrick, J. 1974. Family rules: Family life styles. *American Journal of Orthopsychiatry* 44(1).

Handel, G. (1967). *The psychosocial interior of the family.* Chicago: University of Chicago Press.

Holahan, C. J., and Moos, R. 1987. The personal and contextual determinants of coping strategies. *Journal of Personality and Social Psychology*, 52:946–55.

House, J. S., and Kahn, R. L. 1985. Measures and concepts of social support. In S. Cohen and S. L. Syme (eds.), *Social support and health* (pp. 83–108). Orlando, FL: Academic Press

Jansma, J. B. M. 1988. De gezinsklimaatschaal. In P. M. Schoorl, A. K. de Vries, and M. C. Wijnekus (eds.), *Gezinsonderzoek: Methoden in de gezinsdiagnostiek.* Nijmegen: Dekker en van de Vegt.

Klein Ikkink, K., van Tilburg, T. G., and Knipscheer, K. 1999. Support exchanges in relationships between elderly parents and their adult children: Normative and structural explanations. *Journal of Marriage and the Family* 61(4):831–44.

Knipscheer, C. P. M., and Bevers, A. 1985. Older parents and their middle aged children: Symmetry and asymmetry in their relationship. *Canadian Journal on Aging* 4:145–59.

Knipscheer, C. P. M., de Jong Gierveld, van Tilburg, T. G., and Dykstra, P. A. (eds.). 1995. Living arrangements and social networks of older adults. Amsterdam: Free University Press.

Long, M. V., and Martin, P. 2000. Personality, relationship closeness, and loneliness of oldest old adults and their children. *Journal of Gerontology* 55B, 311–19.

Luescher, K., and Pillemer, K. 1998 Intergenerational Ambivalence: A new approach to the study of parent-child relations in later life. *Journal of Marriage and Family* 60:413–25.

Mangen, D. J. 1995. Method and Analysis of Family Data. In R. Blieszner, and V. H. Bedford (eds.), *Handbook of aging and the family* (pp. 148–77). London: Greenwood.

Moos, R. 1990. Conceptual and empirical approaches to developing Family-based Assessment Procedures: Resolving the case of the Family Environmental Scale. *Family Process* 29:199–208.

Moos, R., and Moos, B. 1986. *Family environment scale manual*, second edition. Palo Alto, CA: Consulting Psychologists.

Moos, R., and Moos, B. 1981. *Family environment scale manual*. Palo Alto, CA: Consulting Psychologists.

Olson, D. H., and Killorin, E. 1985. *Clinical rating scale for the circumplex model of marital and family systems*. St. Paul: Department of Family Social Science, University of Minnesota.

Olson, D. H., McCubbin, H. C., Barnes, H., Larsen, A., Muxen, M., and Wilson, M. 1982. *Family inventories: Inventories used in a national survey of families across the family life cycle*. St. Paul: Department of Family Social Science, University of Minnesota.

Olson, D. H., Russell, C. S., and Sprenkle, D. H. 1983 Circumplex model of marital and family systems: VI. Theoretical update. *Family Process* 22:69–83.

Olson, D. H., Sprenkle, D. H., and Russell, C. S. 1979. Circumplex model of marital and family systems I: Cohesion and adaptability dimensions. Family types and clinical applications. *Family Process* 18:3–28.

Pyke, K. 1999. The micropolitics of care in relationships between aging parents and adult children: Individualism, collectivism, and power. *Journal of Marriage and the Family* 61:661–72.

Pyke, K. D., and Bengtson, V. L. 1996. Caring more or less: Individualistic and collectivist systems of family elder care. *Journal of Marriage and the Family* 58:1–14.

Reiss, D. 1981. *The families construction of reality*. Cambridge, MA: Harvard University Press.

Snijders, T. A. B. 1995. Multilevel models for family data. In J. J. Hox, B. F. van der Meulen, J. M. A. M. Janssens, J. J. F. ter Laak, and L. W. C. Tavecchio (eds.), *Advances in family research* (pp. 193–208). Amsterdam: Thesis.

Sprenkle, D. H., and Olson, D. H. 1978. Circumplex model of marital systems: IV. Empirical study of clinic and non-clinic couples. *Journal of Marriage and the Family Counseling* 4:59–74.

Touliatos, J., Perlmutter, B. F., and Straus, M. A. (eds.) 1990. *Handbook of family measurement techniques*. Newbury Park: Sage.

Tutty, L. M. 1995. Theoretical and practical issues in selecting a measure of family functioning. *Research on Social Work Practice* 5:80–106

van Tilburg, T. G., and de Leeuw, E. D. 1991. Stability of scale quality under different data collection procedures: A mode comparison on the "de Jong-Gierveld Loneliness Scale." *International Journal of Public Opinion Research* 3:69–85.

Widmer, E. D. 1999. Family contexts as cognitive networks: A structural approach of family relationships. *Personal Relationships* 6:487–503.

Widmer, E., Romney, A. K., and Boyd, J. 1999. Cognitive aspects of step-terms in American kinship. *American Anthropologist* 101(2):374–78.

| 8 |

Disposable Children

On the Role of Offspring in the Construction of Conjugal Support in Later Life

Haim Hazan

In a recently published book on aging and popular culture the author aptly defines the old problem of continuity versus discontinuity in the lives of old people as "the struggle of memory against forgetting" (Blaikie, 1999). Notwithstanding the proverbial allusion to the decline of cognitive competence in later life, the implication of that statement is that identity is premised on a sense of certitude marred and challenged by disruptive experiences and processes of denial. This observation bears no novelty since the leading assumption in gerontological writings is marked by the stamp of the management of duration and the construction of temporality. Even in ethnographies of age class systems that apparently defy the notion of the "ageless self" (Kaufman, 1986) there is a distinct bias towards the intergenerational scheme as a guiding principle for the organization of the life course (Fry, 1999). The latest trends in constructivist theory, whose core themes throw into relief the autonomy of subjectivity in writing its own version of cultural interpretation, extol the genre of narrativity as a major source of both recounting and producing meaning (Kenyon and Mader, 1999) and in effect selfhood (Bruner, 1999). The practice of storytelling is indeed a reenactment of lifelong purview revolving around the interweaving of personal reflections into the memorized repertoire of the past as anchored in and constrained by the present (Myerhoff, 1978). It would appear that even seemingly postmodern views of aging such as those held by Featherstone and Hepworth (1991), Rosenau (1992), Hazan (1994), and Gubrium and Holstein (1999) are trapped in the stipulation that the self—

real or spectral—is a kaleidoscope of its social antecedents and perceived prospects. In that sense Bengtson's following assertion is an intriguing and challenging observation: "Issues of continuity and contrast between generations have been important to many theories in sociology and developmental psychology during the past half century. Yet we have had very little empirical data by which to assess these issues, and we have lacked data to examine long term consequences of generational continuity and contrast for either younger or older generation family members" (Bengtson, 1996, p. 271). It presumes the dichotomy of continuity and disjuncture while lamenting the deficient database for offering a sound theoretical perspective on intergenerational relationship. This candid admission of doubtfulness does not cast an aspersion on gerontological thinking but gives license to alternative and further deliberations.

One such reconsideration of both social reality and its conceptual framing is the recurrent trope juxtaposing old age to childhood. This analogy, which draws on structural similarities of dependency and marginality (Hockey and James, 1993), also suggests another common denominator. That is the tendency to regard both children and the elderly as occupying distinct cultural spaces of identity consisting of exceptional symbolic languages, of mythlike properties and self-referent nonlinear dynamics (Hazan, 1996). This sets both childhood and old age as discrete categories separated from other imagined stages of life, hence rendering them unique provinces of knowledge and study. Such perspective requires methodological fortitude as well as an epistemological shift since the prevalent developmental approach to the understanding of life enforces a continuity slant geared to the cumulatively oriented epoch of modernity steering toward predestined upward routes of progress (Bauman, 1991, 1992).

The purpose of this chapter is partly to deviate from that path of research and to pose some questions as to the relations between intergenerational patters of continuity and discontinuity and intragenerational structures of exchange. Since the scope of this discussion does not permit a well-deserved theoretical exposition of this stance, I shall pursue the matter within the limits of one issue—that of the interplay between conjugal support and the role of offspring in the construction of codes of care within kinship networks.

THE ARGUMENT

The argument to be presented is that in later life a shift might take place from filial support to conjugal care giving and that such a transition is accompanied by a change in terms of endearment from the putative bonding of love to a more disenchanted yet realistic and pragmatic concept of care.

Furthermore, the accomplishment of conjugal care is enabled through the long-term commitment to the bond cum bondage of rearing children. Children therefore can be of use to parents; but their instrumental value rests with their cultural presence as icons of ultimate parental investment rather than with their expected returns. As parents expend various shared and usually massive resources in their offspring sometimes inconsequentially and frequently to the detriment of their prospective financial security, they also forge a set of working relationship between themselves. This mutual transaction performed and rationalized under the guise of love and concern for the next generation might generate in turn a partnership that in and of itself becomes a viable support system regardless of its explicit intended object.

Such reinforced mutual bonds as by-products of normative preoccupation with children are not necessarily contingent upon actually having them. Edward Albee's *Who's Afraid of Virginia Wolf* fictionally demonstrates how a turbulent marriage is nevertheless shakily sustained through the invention of an imaginary dead child.

Children could indeed serve as a conjugal cementing force no matter whether they are dead or alive and in that respect their position, as successors to their begetters must be reconsidered.

Sociobiological wisdom has it that procreation preserves the continuous survival of a species. However, culture, be it Western, Oriental, or otherwise, is rife with reported cases of infanticide (Hausfater and Hrdy, 1984; Hrdy, 1996; Sheleff, 1981) and other variations on the theme of dispensable children. The biblical prototype of child sacrifice in the binding of Isaac is echoed by symbolic resonance of the deliberate or inadvertent killing of an offspring. Bloch's (1978) *So the Witch Won't Eat Me: Fantasy and the Child's Fear of Infanticide* and Sheleff's (1981) *Generations Apart: Adult Hostility to Youth* are just two examples of avid, comprehensive, and insightful investigations into the respective psychology and sociology of human desire and the practice and notion of infanticide. Sheleff even coined a term to label that condition named after the mythological Persian hero Rustum. Sheleff suggests that in contrast to the Oedipal complex, the mental state involved in the occurrence of filicide should be called the Rustum complex. He adds that the killing of offspring, particularly female, indicates that "the pressures to be rid of children are however, more than just economic and utilitarian. . . . The advent of a child, particularly of a first child, causes tensions between husband and wife" (ibid.:191). A dead child or an estranged one, however, is no longer a bone of contention between spouses. Rather, full attention can then be given to the dyadic set of relationships that, according to Simmel (1950) are in any case much less intricate and more manageable than the triad's incessantly permutable balance of power.

Yet notwithstanding the demographic trends of decline in childbirth and a slowdown in population growth, particularly in more developed nations (see, for example, Johnson, 1995) the ethos of child-rearing is still rampant in the Western world. Moreover, a multitude of studies suggests that the socioeconomic value of children to parents follows a downward trend of decreasing filial support and commitment (Bigner, 1989); de Regt, 1995; Beck and Beck-Gernsheim, [1990] 1995). Caregiving therefore is transferred from the intergenerational system to alternative sources such as social institutions, welfare agencies, and intragenerational contacts. The latter might include age-homogeneous communities, friendship networks, and—first and foremost—spouses.

This process of social change is largely due to the invisible hand of macrosocial forces such as age classification and their behavioral consequences as expressed in forms of normative obligations and in images of old age in consumer popular culture (Bellah et al., 1985; Featherstone, 1995). Rather than attributing this shift in exchange to cohort effect and to cultural commonalities, I propose that reliance on one's generational contemporaries could be accounted for in terms of the awareness of the mutability and lability of children's' commitment coupled with the rising use of long-term financial planning. In that sense the "inter-generational stake" phenomenon (Bengtson, 1996), which was found to be consistent over time, is an indication of this cultural change.

LOVE AND CARE

With culture at the core and change in mind, Beck and Beck-Gernsheim (1995) and Willen and Montgomery (1996) take up the idea of conjugal love superseding the child-parent bond and maintain that in a postmodern age the conjugal relationship is solidified and sustained by the opportunity of joint self-realization. Having eliminated most traditional causes for rearing children as relevant to our age, the authors conclude that the sharing of the enterprise of bringing up offspring furnishes the mutual experience of love and bonds spouses in a way that other social institutions cannot do. However, from this point of view, the investment in a child sucks up energy from that project of marital love, thereby interfering with the production of a meaningful partnership between parents. Our approach is nevertheless not to explore sources of meaning and the social construction of love nor does it presuppose the need for intergenerational continuity as embodied in children. Our contention is founded on the pragmatic anthropological precept of practical reasoning as manifested in rational choice of investment and expected returns. The project of childrearing is thus indeed an energy generator and expender but the time and resources consumed are certainly not a waste. They enable the couple to uphold a future transaction through a laborious yet continuous performance of mutual interaction.

What makes that investment worthwhile as a long-term perspective is the discrepancy between the still prevalent legacy of sanctified marriage in the traditions of the great religions, on the one hand, and the nature of fragmented, fluid, and noncommittal associations of the late and post-modern era, on the other. While marriage falls under the former category, filial attachment falls under the latter. Relationships with children thus become a less trustworthy safety net than that ensured and enshrined by the ethos of the durable and reliable institution of marriage, however anachronistic it might appear to some generations of offspring.

Evidently such an assertion requires two methodological prerequisites: a longitudinal course of controlled observations and a follow-up of conjugal decision-making. Both caveats cannot be adequately addressed here and hence neither systematic data nor properly devised research design are presented. Exploratory and conjectural though it might seem, the study is based on cases anchored in solidly investigated contexts whose ethnographic scopes were documented and analyzed in a series of monographs. Each study conveys self-reported narratives of elderly spouses whose viewpoint on cross-generational relationships could provide the overall perspective on the role of offspring as dispensable carriers of tenuous continuity and fragile conjugal bonds. Such confessional reflections are of primary importance to our argument since they were elicited from a hindsight position where no further gains could be accrued from a no longer operable and negotiable set of filial relationship.

The following cases are cues for the plausible transformations from modes of temporally regulated reciprocity to patterns of lateral exchange. The ordering of commitment and obligation alters from expectations across generations to care practices prevailing within the age group. The accounts studied represent a shift in codes of accountability from offspring to cohort in general and to spouses in particular. Hence, perhaps the most striking evidence for such mobilization of resources is the change in the attitude toward children. As indicated at the beginning of this chapter, the culturally embedded ambivalence toward offspring takes a turn to a more critical and disillusioned position where filial involvement in caring for parents is no longer taken for granted. The result is a revised stance toward the efficacy and indeed the value of intergenerational benefits.

CASES IN POINT

The ethnographic reflections enlisted to corroborate our thesis are drawn from my own research into four old–age homogeneous settings. Even though this methodological restraint predetermines to a large extent the nature of the findings, it follows the framing of the discourse within generational rather than intergenerational bounds and their corresponding

social milieux. The elderly populations discussed greatly varied both culturally and socioeconomically but could be placed on relatively the same
level of need of care.

(1) The trigger for the first inquiry was first provided by a woman in a
day care center in London, who volunteered the following self–observation
regarding her relationship with her husband. While joining him for a bingo
afternoon, she remarked: "I don't really love him any more but I wouldn't
let one hair of his fall." When asked to explain she added that her prime
concern was to care for her spouse under any circumstances and that that
obligation was unrelated to what she felt toward him. The couple, whose
children, like most of their fellow poverty-stricken Center members' offspring, were alienated from their parents. Therefore, the parents could not
rely on filial support and hence were forced to resort to each other and to
the local system of care. That system was based on the obliteration of past
attachments and on the fostering of a present-bound view of human interaction as a pool of available resources drawn and distributed according to
need rather than debt or investment (Hazan, 1980).

This social form of generalized reciprocity revolved around a consensual awareness of the fallacy of long-term obligations and the futility of
emotional bonds. The expressions of this disillusionment were myriad
and included the sardonic rejection of the notion of children's presence in
their parents' lives through dismissive comments such as "paper children"
in reference to photographs of their children, or in black humor describing
the purpose of stones set by children on their parent's graves as a preven-
tive measure against a possible resurrection. Insisting that their only resort
was to each other, they endorsed the assertion of the woman quoted by
denying love as the cause for conjugal commitment and ascribing it to
rational, practical exigency. Thus, a couple who was seen hugging in a pas-
sionate manner and was asked about the nature of this unexpected conduct apparently replied: "We only support each other so that we don't fall
down."

(2) Another ethnographic field revealed a complementary aspect of that
denial of children. In this instance the elderly concerned came from an
opposite social status category. They were members of the University of
the Third Age in Cambridge, England (Hazan, 1996). This voluntary
organization, founded and run by the elderly themselves, consisted of
socially established and economically well-to-do members whose academic and professional background was manifested and promoted in the
various activities of the university. The age identity developed among
them distinguished between younger age groups (under sixty) and the
incapacitated old—"the fourth age" as they termed it. Between these two
categories emerged their own enclave, "the third age" of mentally and
physically fit retirees. The self-consciousness of belonging to that category

was expressed in the conviction that knowledge of old age can only be acquired by the aged, who are endowed with "a third age eye" whose gaze alone can capture the experience of aging.

Being relatively affluent, members were able to fend for themselves. Talk of offspring therefore was rare and aloof. Even children's accomplishments were hardly mentioned and when asked to comment on their families they preferred to focus on general matters of principles of education, on cultural aspects of the generation gap, and on human universals rather than on specific members of their own families. An example of this attitude was an exchange of snapshots taken during Christmas holiday, showing only landscapes, gardens, and interiors of houses or gatherings with friends. When they were asked to describe at some length the family atmosphere at Christmas dinner, the absence of children was palpable.

Married couples among that group seemed to lead a life of shared interests and cooperation, and their general ability to function enabled them to participate jointly in outings, trips, classes, and parties. The mode of exchange marking this social profile was of mutual reciprocity based on lifelong partnership but generated and sustained by the pragmatism of everyday life. This state of relationship was encouraged by the fact that most couples had retired to Cambridge from other places in the United Kingdom and were thus away from kith and kin, and hence forced into greater dependency on each other.

(3) The third case does not provide direct observations on conjugal relationship but considers an option of intragenerational identification with shared fate while rendering other life worlds irrelevant. This process of deculturation (Anderson, 1972) cultivates a common ground for setting the scene for obviating the importance of children and reinforcing cohort "we feeling" and ties with spouses.

The research took place in an urban renewal neighborhood in Israel (Hazan, 1990). The neighborhood's elderly residents constituted only a secondary target for the renewal project. A large and active day center had been opened for them, but their status within the "community" was problematic. They were seen as representatives of the former, preproject ethnic neighborhood identities, and many of them received welfare support. The welfare services were perceived as a threat to the creation of the idiom of community within the project, since their existence perpetuated the stigma of poverty. It had thus been decided to separate physically the community center from the welfare office, which had been moved to another street. Nevertheless, a series of activities for the elderly were initiated, aimed at integrating them into the community. The first and most important of these was a literacy program.

The idea of integration was presented as the wish to develop intergenerational relationships between grandparents and their grandchildren, by means of enabling the former to assist the latter with their homework and in reading stories. Only elderly women participated in the course, since the neighborhood's old men were literate in Hebrew and spent most of their time in local synagogues, which served as social centers. The participants did not attach much importance to the stated objective of learning to read and write. Some even ridiculed the idea, claiming that the grandchildren did not need their assistance anyway, adding that the relationship with them was based, as one woman put it, on "what's in the heart and what's in the pot." As is usual in literacy classes for new immigrants, the course material was very simple, consisting mainly of fairy tales. At the end of the course the participants were asked by their instructor to write an essay that would demonstrate their command of the language by describing the particular story that had made the strongest impression on them. The essays were collected and published in a booklet form for local distribution. Without exception the women chose one story, "The Disguised Egg," by a well-known Israeli poet and writer. This story recounts the adventures of an egg that became fed up with its eggy identity and decided to seek its fortune in other roundish forms in which it hoped to find true happiness. This journey of self-revelation passes through a balloon, an apple, a ball, and other objects, but brings only disappointment. The egg eventually reaches the conclusion that it cannot change into something else, returns with relief to its egg shape, and hatches a chick.

The women, each in her own words, offered almost identical explanations as to why the story had struck a chord with them. They saw the text of the story as an allegory of their own fate. They had immigrated to Israel from the countries of their birth, whose culture they had internalized. In Israel they had passed through various phases, in each of which an attempt had been made to transform their basic identity into something else. In the immigrants' camp they had been expected to become Israelis, and later on in the neighborhood others had tried to impart a culture foreign to them. They claimed, however, that their true selves were to be found only in their origins, in their undisguised ethnic heritage. Some went still further in developing this theme, remarking in their essays that only once it had accepted itself for what it was could the egg become fertile. In their case, too, only once they had resigned themselves to what they were, not through necessity but by choice, would they be of any use to their grandchildren.

The main lesson to be learned from the parable of the disguised egg is therefore that one's mask must be removed before one can know her true self and view herself as a complete person. Removal of these disguises, however, means the abrogation of Israeli reality in general and that of the neighborhood in particular. Paradoxically, it is the formal support system of welfare services and community institutions that facilitated that declaration of generational independence and of authentic identity. Under the guise of literacy and learning both husbands and wives found sanctuary in what they deemed to be their primordial origin—the former in synagogues and the latter in the classroom. This sequestered haven of old age reflects not only a recourse to intragenerational affiliation but also a rejection of the immediate context for a unison with core cultural themes. This abandonment of the present to the mythical immutability of the eternal now is emphatically demonstrated in the fourth ethnographic case.

(4) The study was situated in an Israeli old age home (Hazan, 1992) for able-bodied and mentally alert residents. This criterion of entry and exit prescribed the rules of the local social arena, which demanded a constant publicly displayed management of the impression of good functioning. Those whose abilities could not conform to the expected standards of autonomous conduct ran the risk of being removed from the institution. Married couples enjoyed an edge of mutual care that forestalled visible incapacitation and hence inspection and interference by members of staff. While most singles as well as couples were subjected to the same regime of monitoring behavior and facing crucial decisions accordingly, others were exonerated from this fate by virtue of their special standing in the home and outside it. One such resident was a woman who became one of Israel's most celebrated figures in the pantheon of nation-building. Having lost both her sons in the War of Independence, she and her husband dedicated the rest of their years to the education of newcomers, particularly children from North African countries. They settled among the immigrants in a frontier region of the country, set up schools and helped in their "absorption." These legendary paragons of Zionism were immortalized in literature, their story was included in the state's school curriculum, and their presence was prominent in public events. Needless to say, their residence in the home was regarded by management and other residents alike as a great privilege.

However, the woman in the couple explained their stay in the home in terms of her awareness of their impending frailty:

> The time has come that we cannot look after ourselves anymore. I possibly could but my husband needs care. It doesn't really matter where we stay because we live only in one place—with our children, all of them, our two sons and the thousands of the others we made into Israelis. They all tell me that our place is not in an old age home, but I disagree, we are not different from anybody else betrayed by their own body. This aging body is not us, we just happen to lodge in a rundown house. We are what we accomplished. Whenever a class of children comes to visit us [the couple was a focus of school pilgrimages], I know where we really belong, we belong with them.

A striking feature of this rendition of the blurred divide between private and collective selves is the presentation of the children as the raison d'être of the couple's life. Hence the fallen children were reincarnated in the next generation of the childlike newcomers whom the couple inducted into the Zionist ethos and in the younger visitors who treated them as objects of ancestral worship. Thus the sacrificial loss of their sons made the couple both an icon of national revival and an indivisible unit representing inter-generational continuity enshrined in collective memory.

DISCUSSION: MODERNITY AND INTRAGENERATIONAL TIES

A few ethnographic illustrations serve only to hint at sociological sub-stance and evidently the four examples are no more than a descriptive teaser for the development of a better argued case for dissecting the link-age between conjugal ties and cross-generational cleavage. However, a macroscopic view of that interplay implies that the project of modernity is the driving force behind the cultural transformations from reliance on fil-ial support to leaning on spousal care. The vagaries of the postindustrial epoch not only reshuffle normative codes and deconstruct selves (Gergen, 1994) but mainly turn what Moore (1978) coined "life term arena" into "a limited term arena" of associations and ensuing obligations. The change in exchange therefore is from the sequential to the transversal, from the ten-uous cross-generational to the available, albeit not necessarily desirable, intragenerational. This shift in the mechanism of securing interests and caring for old age transforms the value of having children from a prospec-tive resource to a current template of the conjugal bond, which in itself becomes a prominent keystone for planning the future and mainly safe-guarding the present. The notion of such a sense of security is a compre-hensive one, namely that not only are sustenance and health matters protected but other concerns such as autonomy, identity, and meaning are considered as worthwhile resources to be drawn from a pool encapsulated in the intragenerational world of old age.

The sociocultural prerequisites enabling the age-based classification necessary for this construction were widely described and discussed in the socioanthropological literature of the 1980s (for example, Keith, 1980, 1982; Kertzer and Keith, 1984; Riley, Hess, and Bond, 1983). While empha-sis was placed on principles of stratification and cultural comparisons with other age-graded societies were made, very little attention was paid to the spirit of the times, which in today's terms would be called "high modernity" or "late modernity" (Giddens, 1991), "reflexive modernity" (Beck, [1986] 1992), or simply modernity. I would like to suggest that the four aforementioned ethnographic cases attest to the prevalence and per-vasiveness of that spirit, hence confining the phenomenon of old age iden-tification within the parameters of life in a modern era.

Modernity, being a controversial concept and a multifaceted one at that, lends itself to multiple interpretations. However, four emergent properties of modernity are projected onto the conduct of the elderly actors presented in our four-act play.

The Center people are the unadulterated product of the welfare state with its ravages and advantages. The relative security of essential provisions granted by welfare policies engenders a double effect of continuity of existence and discontinuity of existentialism, i.e., life divorced from socially approved meaning. Within that vacuous space a redefined form of symbolic codes and ensuing social rules emerged as a lateral exchange system of nonmutual care. That territory of exclusion is not merely another manifestation of ageism but an untoward implementation of major culture forces positioning people within fields of social distinction (Bourdieu, [1979] 1984) and in the case of the impoverished elderly it reflects the effects of consumer society from which they are banished.

The membership of the University of the Third Age revealed a complementary aspect of modernity embedded in late capitalism, that is, the opportunity of some elderly to select at will their desired style of retirement. As elaborated by the founder of the University of the Third Age, the emergence of a third age is "a fresh map of life" drawn by the forces of self-enterprise and freedom of choice (Laslett, 1989). Such elective living is made possible by long-term planning and the use of personal means accrued during a lifetime of operating in a capitalist system.

The third case of the neighborhood's women is evidence of the growing spread of multiculturalism and of the social license to claim various origins of identity. Israel, being a society in transition from a value system dominated by one culture of Eastern European nation-builders to a more pluralistic sociopolitical fabric, facilitates and even encourages that variable statement of belonging. The transcendence of national boundaries, which could be interpreted in terms of the upsurge of global trends, stands in contradictory relations to the following.

The fourth dimension of modernity is the nation-state whose imagined community (Anderson, 1991) is founded on a solidarity of collective memory and myths. The couple whose fallen sons symbolized that national identity were by virtue of that both representatives and generators of the modern ethos of nationalism epitomized in the hero cult of the dead soldier.

Those grand narratives of modernity constitute the macroforces that regulate and shape the microcosmos of each of our local stories, hence rendering them nonanecdotal and linking them as sociologically instructive. The main lesson that could be learned from juxtaposing these cases is that the seemingly circumstantial contexts accounting for the uniqueness of each field are different shades of the same picture that portrays modern old age not as a developmental outcome of intergenerational continuity but as a reflection of cross-generational schism. Having fulfilled their function of scaffolding the otherwise ramshackle construction of marriage, children can vacate the family arena so that the two lifelong wrestlers may engage in their last embrace.

REFERENCES

Anderson, B. 1972. The process of deculturation: Its dynamics among United States aged, *Anthropological Quarterly* 45(4):209–16.

_____. 1991. *Imagined communities: Reflections on the origin and spread of nationalism.* London: Verso.

Bauman, Z. 1991. *Modernity and ambivalence.* Cambridge: Polity.

_____. 1992. *Mortality, immortality and other life strategies,* Cambridge: Polity.

Beck, U. [1986] 1992. *Risk society.* Cambridge: Polity.

Beck, U., and Beck-Gernsheim, E. [1990] 1995. *The normal chaos of love.* Cambridge: Polity.

Bellah, R. N., et al. 1985. *Habits of the heart: Individualism and commitment in American life.* Berkeley: University of California Press.

Bengtson, V. L. 1996. Continuities and discontinuities in intergenerational relationships over time. In V. L. Bengtson (ed.), *Adulthood and aging: Research on continuities and discontinuities.* New York: Springer.

Bigner, J. J. 1989. *Parent-child relations: An introduction to parenting.* New York: Macmillan.

Blaikie, A. 1999. *Aging and popular culture,* Cambridge: Cambridge University Press.

Bloch, D. 1978. *So the witch won't eat me: Fantasy and child's fear of infanticide.* Boston: Houghton Mifflin.

Bourdieu, P. [1979] 1984. *Distinctions: A social critique of the judgement of taste.* London: Routledge and Kegan Paul.

Bruner, J. 1999. Narrative of aging. *Journal of Aging Studies* 13:7–10.

De Regt, A. 1995. Costs and benefits of changes in parental care. *Netherlands Journal of Social Sciences,* 31(1):64–75.

Featherstone, M. 1995. Post-bodies, aging and virtual reality. In M. Featherstone and A. Wernick (eds.), *Images of aging* (pp. 227–44). London: Routledge.

Featherstone, M., and Hepworth, M. 1991. The mask of aging and the post-modern life course. In M. Featherstone, M. Hepworth, and B. Turner (eds.), *The body: Social processes and cultural theory* (pp. 370–89). London: Sage.

Fry, C. L. 1999. Anthropological theories of age and aging. In V. Bengtson and K. W. Schaie (eds.), *Handbook of theories of aging* (pp. 271–86). New York: Springer.

Gergen, K. J. 1994. *Realities and relationships: Soundings in social construction.* Cambridge, MA: Harvard University Press.

Gubrium, J. F., and Holstein, J. A. 1999. Constructivist perspectives on aging. In V. Bengtson and K. W. Schaie (eds.), *Handbook of theories of aging* (pp. 287–305). New York: Springer.

Hausfater, G., and Hrdy, S. B. (eds.) (1984). *Infanticide: Comparative and evolutionary perspectives*. Hawthorne, NY: Aldine de Gruyter.

Hazan, H. 1980. *The limbo people: A study of the constitution of the time universe among the aged*. London: Routledge and Kegan Paul.

———. 1990. *A paradoxical community*. Greenwich, CT: JAI.

———. 1992. *Managing change in old age: The control of meaning in an institutional setting*. Albany: State University of New York Press.

———. 1994. *Old age: Constructions and deconstructions*. Cambridge: Cambridge University Press.

———. 1996. *From first principles: An experiment in aging*. Westport, CT: Bergin and Garvey.

Hockey, J., and James, A. 1993. *Growing up and growing old: Ageing and dependency in the life course*. London, Newbury Park, New Delhi: Sage.

Hrdy, S. B. 1996. Infanticide. In D. Levinson and M. Ember (eds.), *Encyclopedia of cultural anthropology*. New York: Henry Holt.

Johnson, S. P. 1995. *World population: Turning the tide: Three decades of progress*, London and Boston: Graham and Trotman/Martinus Nijhoff.

Kaufman, S. R. 1986. *The ageless self: Sources of meaning in late life*. Madison: University of Wisconsin Press.

Keith, J. 1980. The best is yet to be: Toward an anthropology of age. *Annual Review of Anthropology* 9:339–64.

———. 1982. *Old people as people: Social and cultural influences on aging and old age*. Boston and Toronto: Little, Brown.

Kenyon, G. M., Ruth, J.-E., and Mader, W. 1999. Elements of a narrative gerontology. In V. Bengtson and K. W. Schaie (eds.), *Handbook of theories of aging* (pp. 40–58). New York: Springer.

Kertzer, D., and Keith, J. (eds.) 1984. *Age and anthropological theory*. Ithaca, NY: Cornell University Press.

Laslett, P. 1989. *A fresh map of life: The emergence of the Third Age*. London: Wendengeld Nicolson.

Moore, S. F. 1978. Old age in a life-term social arena: Some Chagga of Kilimanjaro in 1974. In B. Myerhoff and A. Simic (eds.), *Life's career-aging: Cultural variations on growing old*. Beverly Hills, CA: Sage.

Myerhoff, B. 1978. *Number our days*. New York: Dutton.

Riley, M. W., Hess, B. B., and Bond, K. (eds.) 1983. *Aging in society: Selected reviews of recent research*. Hillsdale, NJ: Lawrence Erlbaum Associates.

Rosenau, P. M. 1992. *Postmodernism and the social sciences*. Princeton, NJ: Princeton University Press.

Sheleff, L. 1981. *Generations apart: Adult hostility to youth*. New York: McGraw-Hill.

Simmel, G. 1950. *The sociology of George Simmel*. Translated, edited, and with an introduction by Kurt H. Wolff. New York: Free Press.

Willen, H., and Montgomery, H. 1996. The impact of wish for children and having children on attainment and importance of life values. *Journal of Comparative Family Studies* 27(3):499–518.

III

Intrasociety Diversity in
Intergenerational Support

| 9 |

Israeli Attitudes about
Inter Vivos Transfers

Seymour Spilerman and Yuval Elmelech

INTRODUCTION

With the accumulation of household wealth in Western countries since the conclusion of World War II, there has been a growing interest in the transmission of financial assets across generations. This is a theme of some importance in stratification research because it taps a central mechanism in the replication of inequality. It is also a topic of interest in the family literature since the timing and volume of parental transfers are a potential source of strain in the relationship between generations.

The most common approach by sociologists to understand the replication of inequality involves an examination of the paths by which parental labor market attainment influences the income of offspring (Duncan, 1968; Duncan, Featherman, and Duncan, 1972). Yet, narrowly speaking, it is not an income stream that is transferred, though parental education and occupational position have a considerable, albeit indirect, impact on the earnings of children (Jencks et al., 1972; Sewell and Hauser, 1975). Rather, transfers are made from the stock of parental assets, in some mix of *inter vivos* gifts and bequests. Estimates of the importance of parental transfers suggest that it accounts for some 43 percent of current household wealth (Gale and Scholz, 1994), though variant calculations range from 20 percent (Modigliani, 1988) to 80 percent (Kotlikoff and Summers, 1981, 1988).

Accompanying recent research into the features of the transmission process—the parental decision on how much to transfer during their lifetimes, the division among offspring when there are several children, and the extent of backward flow from children to elderly parents [see Spilerman

(2000) for a review of this literature]—there has been a corresponding interest in the formation of attitudes on these matters, especially in regard to transfer "motives" and parental views of their responsibility for assisting adult children (Holtz-Eakin and Smeeding, 1994; Ribar and Wilhelm, 2001). Can transfer decisions be understood as altruistic expressions of concern for children or are parents purchasing services from their offspring? Are parents using gifts to instill a sense of guilt or obligation, hoping for repayment in later years (Stark, 1995)? In the main, attempts to uncover parental motives have sought to infer them from observed transfer flows, examining the financial needs of recipient children and the services provided to parents, in the form of shopping, cleaning, and visitation (Cox, 1987; Cox and Rank, 1992, McGarry and Schoeni, 1997).

In contrast, there has been little research that directly examines values and attitudes about intergenerational transfers, either from the point of view of parental motives, or from the perspective of parental feelings of obligation toward offspring (for an exception, however, see Ribar and Wilhelm, 2001). The values that are maintained on these matters can be an important determinant of the decision to transfer resources within parental lifetimes and of the volume and timing of the *inter vivos* transmissions. Yet, we know little about the distribution of these attitudes in the population—the extent to which they are aligned with class, ethnicity, and racial membership—or of how they are formed—whether molded by prior life experiences, by the perceived needs of adult children, by the availability of parental resources, or by deeper norms of community or filial obligation.

In this chapter we examine attitudes in Israel about intergenerational assistance and investigate the impact of these attitudinal dispositions on transfer decisions by parents. It should be noted that views about parental obligations are probably not independent of a country's economic and social organization. In a country with an extensive program of public assistance for young adults, for example, there may be less need for private family transfers, and less of a sense of parental responsibility for providing support. Similarly, where young couples face severe liquidity constraints, or otherwise require substantial resources in order to begin a new household, parental feelings of obligation might be heightened. For the reasons summarized in the next section, Israel is a country in which the need for parental support is high and the level of parental involvement in the financial lives of young adults can be considerable.

The data for the study come from the 1994/95 Survey of Families in Israel, in which 1,607 respondents were interviewed on topics relating to work behavior, household income, wealth, assistance received from parents and given to children, and views about financial responsibilities between parents and children. The data cover the urban, Jewish population of the country. Israeli Arabs were excluded because the basis of social obligation in that community is more rooted in tradition and local village arrangements, and a different study design would have been required to probe these intergenerational linkages. Additionally, to be included in the survey, respondents had to be in their first marriage, with at least one spouse between the ages of 30 and 65, and at least one spouse having resided in Israel during the prior ten years.

ATTITUDES IN ISRAEL ABOUT INTERGENERATIONAL TRANSFERS

The cost of establishing a household in Israel is high, relative to average family income (Spilerman, 2003). In large part, this is a consequence of the absence of rental housing in the country, compelling young couples to purchase an apartment early in their marital careers. Although the government seeks to facilitate housing purchases by providing young couples with subsidized mortgages, the amounts offered are insufficient for acquiring a home in one of the main cities, where young adults often prefer to reside and where the better jobs are located (Elmelech, 1992). As a result, it is not unusual for young Israelis, contemplating marriage, to turn to their parents for assistance with an apartment purchase—as well as with the other expenses of beginning a household. Israeli parents, in turn, often accept this expense as a responsibility of parenthood.

Responses are reported in Table 9.1 to two questions from the survey that tap perceptions of the magnitude of the problem facing young couples and convey a sense of the views about parental responsibility to provide financial assistance. Question 1 is a scale item, assessing the difficulty of coping in Israel without financial support from parents. Fully 90 percent of respondents believe that this is very difficult, if not impossible. Question 2 inquires about the duration of a parent's financial responsibility. Some 57 percent of respondents believe that the obligation extends beyond a child's marriage year, indeed, until the time that assistance is no longer required. These responses provide the context for investigating parental attitudes about aid giving in several focused areas of potential need by adult children.

In the first section of the chapter we examine the determinants of transfer attitudes with respect to four sorts of assistance that may be requested of parents: a home purchase, schooling expenses, the purchase of a car, and ongoing financial support in the years following marriage. The responses come from a question that inquired in a common manner about the above domain areas:

"For each of the following items, do you think it is a parent's responsibility to finance the bulk of the expenditure?

(a) Yes, even if it means that parents have to work longer hours or take an additional job.

(b) Yes, but only if parents have the funds.

(c) No, it is the child's responsibility to finance this expenditure."

Table 9.1   Parental Values in Regard to the Provision of Financial Assistance to Adult Children (*N* = 1606)

---

1. How important is it for parents in Israel to provide financial assistance to their children? (%)

a. Impossible to manage without parental assistance	24.5
b. Extremely difficult to manage without parental assistance	38.5
c. Very difficult without parental assistance	27.2
d. Not very difficult to manage without parental assistance	8.1
e. Easy to get by without parental assistance	1.7
	100.0

2. Until when, in your opinion, should parents provide financial support to their adult children? (%)

a. Until the child reaches age 18	2.7
b. Until the completion of military duty	5.6
c. Until the child leaves home	7.5
d. Until the completion of studies	7.9
e. Until the time of marriage	15.0
f. Until the adult child no longer requires financial support	56.7
g. Other, don't know	4.6
	100.0

Two of the questionnaire items refer to parental assistance with a home purchase—before and subsequent to marriage. To enhance reliability, a single measure was created by summing their scores. Four items inquired about schooling—two about after-school study while in high school (art, dance, etc.), and two about assistance with the cost of higher education. These items were summed to create a variable that taps attitudes about assistance with schooling. The car purchase measure is also based on two questions, referring to the parental obligation before and after marriage. Last, the ongoing assistance measure is based on two questions, relating to the period immediately following marriage and to the provision of aid in later years. Each of the constructed measures was coded so that a low value indicates child's responsibility, and a high value signifies that the expense is a parental obligation. The distribution of responses on the four measures is reported in Table 9.2.

The responses indicate a broad acceptance of parental responsibility to assist with the acquisition of a home and with the costs of schooling, along

Table 9.2   Distribution of Expressions of Parental Responsibility (%)[a] for Assisting Adult Children[b] (High Value = Greater Parental Responsibility)

	Low					High
	1	2	3	4	5	6
1. Assistance with a home purchase (N = 1594)	3.1	14.4	46.5	23.6	12.4	
2. Assistance with expenditures for education (N = 1599)	3.6	7.8	12.3	23.0	29.4	24.0
3. Provision of continuous support (N = 1601)	24.2	13.7	46.2	6.4	9.5	
4. Assistance with the purchase of a car (N = 1598)	24.9	24.2	40.2	6.9	3.8	

[a]Row sum equals 100.
[b]Categories relabeled after addition of component items (see text) so that low = 1. In expression 2, which is based on four items, the low category is the sum of four cells, each having a small N.

with a lesser sense of obligation to provide aid for the purchase of an automobile or in an ongoing manner—note the greater proportion of responses in the high categories of the former items. The stronger expressions of parental obligation probably reflect the centrality in Israel of home ownership and educational attainment for living standards and family welfare.

One intent of the present study is to ascertain the etiology of attitude formation in regard to parental obligations in the four domain areas. How are the attitudes generated in the population? Do they derive from ethnic values and perhaps inform the disparity in living standards in Israel between Ashkenazim and Sephardim? To what extent are they conditioned by the experience of having received transfers from one's own parents? Are they influenced by a respondent's available resources and consequent ability to assist his or her children? We now consider an explanatory formulation of the process of attitude development.

The Analytic Strategy

Three sets of variables are introduced in a regression framework as potential determinants of the transfer attitudes: (1) terms that tap a respondent's receipt of parental aid in the early years of his/her marriage; (2) terms that reflect a respondent's financial resources at the current time (1995); and (3) dummy variables for ethnicity and time period of the marriage. The analytic approach is to first examine the impact of a respondent's receipt of early assistance (exogenous variables in this formulation) on transfer attitudes, and then to enter the variables for current resources.

Ethnicity and year of marriage are introduced as controls—contextual terms that may affect transfer attitudes and are correlated with the variables of more central concern—though they are not without intrinsic interest themselves.

The appeal of this approach is that it permits the indirect effects of early transfer receipts to be measured, along with the possible direct effects on attitudes. For example, if parental assistance was provided at the time of the respondent's marriage—for the purchase of a home or to cover other start-up expenditures—this could influence a respondent's attitudes in two ways: (a) via a modeling process:[1] "I should help my children because I received parental aid," or (b) through the promotion of wealth accumulation by the respondent, which in turn might predispose him/her to a more favorable view of assisting children. In the first instance, the addition of terms for *current* assets to the regression would have no effect on the coefficient for receipt of early transfers; in the second, we expect a lessening in the magnitude of the coefficient because it is the wealth level that is influencing attitudes.

Transfers received from parents in the early years of a respondent's marriage are measured by two variables: ongoing assistance in the first three years of marriage, and home ownership at time of marriage.[2] In the Israeli context, early home ownership is highly dependent upon the availability of parental aid for this purpose (Spilerman, 2003). We use early home ownership as a proxy for parental aid, in place of a direct measure, because of the complexity of the transfer process with respect to this form of assistance, which can involve outright gifts, loans under different terms, cosigner obligations, and the possibility of assistance with the down payment or with mortgage payments.

The financial resources of a household at the current time (1995) are measured by three variables: (a) Objective standard of living—a composite variable constructed from a sum of Z-scores for number of household items (refrigerator, washing machine, etc.), amount of vacation travel outside Israel, and frequency of paid household help; (b) subjective standard of living—a scale item that requested a comparison with the "average" living standard in Israel; and (c) a count of number of children of the respondent. If the availability of resources influences a respondent's attitudes about intergenerational assistance, we would expect the first two variables to have a predisposing effect toward transfers, whereas number of children—a measure of demands on the resources—may have a negative impact because of the burden of accommodating the financial needs of multiple children.

Three additional substantive regressors were introduced: education and age of the respondent, and receipt of ongoing assistance by the respondent—not just in the period following marriage. The first two are established as determinants of values and attitudes in a variety of domain areas (e.g., Kiecolt, 1988; Silver and Muller, 1997). Since educational attainment would have been completed early in the life course, the schooling variable is entered together with the terms for early transfers—all refer to attitude formation by young adults. Respondent's age is viewed as a proxy for the effects of a variety of maturation events, unmeasured in the model, which lie behind many sorts of attitude shifts over the life course. Since it is current age that is relevant to the attitudinal dispositions, this variable is entered along with the contemporaneous living standards measures. The third regressor—receipt of ongoing assistance[3]—is also introduced with the living standard variables and provides a measure of the impact of long-term "modeling" experiences on attitude formation.

The final variables in the model are dummy terms for ethnicity and year of marriage. The rationale for the former is that there may exist distinctive ethnic views about parental responsibility, beyond those generated by ethnic differences in the values of the substantive regressors. Five ethnic terms were created, based, for convenience, on the geographic origin of the male householder: Israel, Western Europe, Eastern Europe, Africa, and Asia. To better reflect cultural background, Israel-born males were coded in terms of father's country of birth. With respect to year of marriage, this set of terms captures the economic climate in the country at the time the respondent had to contend with the expenses of establishing a household. Much like the receipt of early parental transfers, this cohort effect might predispose an individual to a particular view about supporting adult children.

DETERMINANTS OF THE TRANSFER ATTITUDES

Each of the four attitudinal constructs was regressed against the sets of explanatory variables described above. Because the dependent variables are ordinal, OLS estimates would be biased since the assignment of numerical values to the responses is arbitrary as long as the rank order of the categories is maintained. Instead, ordered logit regression was employed.

Assistance with a Home Purchase

Column (1) of Table 9.3 reports the impact of the background terms—ethnic affiliation, year of marriage, and educational attainment—along with the indicators of early receipt of parental assistance (owned home at marriage, received continuous assistance in the first three years of marriage). The last two have strong effects and suggest that a respondent who received early aid is more likely to be predisposed to the view that it is a parent's responsibility to assist children with a home purchase. Educational

Table 9.3   Determinants of Attitudinal Support for Parental Assistance with a Home Purchase—Ordered Logit Regression, Standard Errors in Parentheses

Variable:	(1)		(2)	
Ethnicity:[a]				
Western Europe	.0847	(.2353)	.0090	(.2370)
Eastern Europe	.0655	(.2096)	−.0076	(.2120)
Africa	−.0432	(.2148)	.0323	(.2163)
Asia	−.1718	(.2172)	−.1211	(.2188)
Year of marriage:[b]				
1960–69	−.4660**	(.1791)	−.3999	(.2055)
1970–78	−.5435**	(.1776)	−.7418**	(.2572)
1979–86	−.3623	(.1855)	−1.0092**	(.3519)
1984–94	−.4466*	(.1992)	−1.0932**	(.3926)
Early transfers received/education:				
Continuous assistance[c]	.3670**	(.1331)	.2404	(.1418)
Home ownership at marriage	.3294**	(.1044)	.2765**	(.1058)
Educational attainment	.0530**	(.0177)	.0238	(.0191)
Current SOL/related measures:				
Age of respondent			.0062	(.0107)
Ongoing assistance over the years[d]			.1212*	(.0509)
Objective SOL			.1444*	(.0615)
Subjective SOL			−.0719	(.0860)
No. of children			−.2760***	(.0606)
−2LL	3714		3682	
N	1401		1401	

$*p < .05; **p < .01; ***p < .001.$
[a]Omitted term is for Israel origin.
[b]Omitted term is for marriage before 1960.
[c]Assistance received by respondent in first three years of marriage.
[d]Assistance received by respondent subsequent to first three years of marriage.

attainment has a similar import, possibly because of the effect of education on values (Silver and Muller, 1997), though perhaps because educational attainment, like the receipt of early parental aid, improves a family's prospects for higher income, greater asset holdings, and a higher standard of living in later years.

These competing explanations are partially clarified by equation (2) , in which terms have been introduced for current standard of living of the respondent and for the continued receipt of parental assistance. Two of the indices of current living standard are significant—ongoing assistance, the objective measure—while number of children (a proxy for demands on the parental resources) has an expected negative effect. Only the subjective term fails to reach significance. At the same time, the terms for receipt of early support are much reduced in magnitude from their values in column (1). Assistance received in the first three years of marriage is no longer significant and the coefficient of home ownership at marriage is smaller by some 20 percent. This suggests that much of the effect of early transfer receipts on the attitude, noted in equation (1), works through the impact of this aid on the living standard terms.

The fact that the educational attainment term also becomes insignificant in equation (2) is in line with this interpretation. Viewed as a determinant of attitude formation, its effect should not be attenuated by the introduction of measures for current living standard. But, if educational attainment is seen as influencing attitudes through its effect on income and living standards in later years, its impact would be muted by the introduction of the intervening variables—which is what we find.

Two other results from equation (2) deserve mention. First, there is evidence of a modeling effect from receipt of parental transfers. The regressor for home ownership at marriage remains significant, though reduced in magnitude. Moreover, the term for receipt of ongoing support is significant. Since these effects are net of current living standards, they suggest that the fact of having received transfers from parents influences one's attitudes toward helping offspring with a home purchase. Second, although there are no significant ethnic effects, there is a clear trend in the year of marriage terms to a lessening in feelings of responsibility for assisting children with a home purchase. Possibly this relates to the positive trend in economic development in Israel; possibly the attitude change reflects a shift in views toward greater individual responsibility. With the data at hand these alternative explanations cannot be distinguished.

Parental Support for Schooling, Ongoing Assistance, and a Car Purchase

Regression results for these attitudinal constructs are presented in Tables 9.4–9.6. With respect to schooling and ongoing support, there is a considerable correspondence between the findings and those for assistance with a home purchase, but also some notable differences. In equations (1) of Tables 9.4 and 9.5, there is, again, evidence that respondents who received an early transfer are more inclined to the view that parents should assist their children. However, with the introduction of the terms for contemporaneous living standard (equations 2)—a measure of the family's resource base that would be available for transfer—the effect is much reduced.

The modeling effects of parental transfers are somewhat different for the two attitudes, schooling and ongoing assistance. They are stronger for the latter (equation 2 of Table 9.5), with the terms for transfers received in the first three years of marriage and receipt of assistance subsequent to

Table 9.4   Determinants of Attitudinal Support for Parental Assistance
with Schooling Expenses—Ordered Logit Regression, Standard
Errors in Parentheses

Variable:	(1)		(2)	
Ethnicity:[a]				
Western Europe	.0308	(.2221)	−.0073	(.2227)
Eastern Europe	.3334	(.1974)	.2824	(.1989)
Africa	.4031	(.2043)	.4570*	(.2057)
Asia	.0127	(.2042)	.0950	(.2056)
Year of marriage:[b]				
1960–69	−.1911	(.1703)	−.0742	(.1936)
1970–78	−.0993	(.1709)	−.0216	(.2449)
1979–86	−.2364	(.1765)	−.2559	(.3327)
1984–94	−.2061	(.1883)	−.1582	(.3720)
Early transfers received/education:				
Continuous assistance[c]	.0596	(.1288)	.0262	(.1372)
Home ownership at marriage	.3057**	(.1005)	.2240*	(.1018)
Educational attainment	.0456**	(.0169)	.0130	(.0181)
Current SOL/related measures:				
Age of respondent			.0106	(.0102)
Ongoing assistance over the years[d]			.0542	(.0490)
Objective SOL			.1529**	(.0589)
Subjective SOL			.2190**	(.0784)
No. of children			−.1057	(.0578)
−2LL	4507		4477	
N	1401		1401	

*$p < .05$; **$p < .01$; ***$p < .001$.
[a]Omitted term is for Israel origin.
[b]Omitted term is for marriage before 1960.
[c]Assistance received by respondent in first three years of marriage.
[d]Assistance received by respondent subsequent to first three years of marriage.

this time period both having significant effects. By comparison, in the case
of the schooling regression, it is only the early home ownership term that
is significant in the presence of the living standard variables (equation 2 of
Table 9.4). The living standard variables, in turn, have a considerable
impact on the two attitudes, in each case predisposing the economically
better off respondents to a stronger expression of parental responsibility.

The final measure, attitudes toward financing an automobile purchase,
provides different results (Table 9.6). While there is some indication that
educational attainment and the receipt of early support raises one's sense
of responsibility to provide assistance (equation 1), the effects become
insignificant in the presence of the living standard variables (equation 2).
The term for number of children does remain significant, though barely so;

Table 9.5   Determinants of Attitudinal Support for Ongoing Assistance by
Parents—Ordered Logit Regression, Standard Errors in Parentheses

Variable:	(1)		(2)	
Ethnicity:[a]				
Western Europe	−.2204	(.2335)	−.2350	(.2351)
Eastern Europe	.0097	(.2081)	.0270	(.2110)
Africa	.0468	(.2130)	.1215	(.2150)
Asia	−.4276*	(.2140)	−.3442	(.2162)
Year of marriage:[b]				
1960–69	−.2051	(.1821)	−.2111	(.2073)
1970–78	−.0825	(.1808)	−.1156	(.2572)
1979–86	−.1231	(.1899)	−.1814	(.3489)
1984–94	−.3470	(.2041)	−.4128	(.3915)
Early transfers received/education:				
Continuous assistance[c]	.4911***	(.1343)	.3734**	(.1425)
Home ownership at marriage	.2480**	(.1039)	.1875	(.1055)
Educational attainment	−.0011	(.0174)	−.0217	(.0187)
Current SOL/related measures:				
Age of respondent			−.0031	(.0106)
Ongoing assistance over the years[d]			.1258*	(.0518)
Objective SOL			.1281*	(.0608)
Subjective SOL			.0957	(.0800)
No. of children			.0061	(.0585)
−2LL	3808		3791	
N	1401		1401	

$*p < .05; **p < .01; ***p < .001.$
[a]Omitted term is for Israel origin.
[b]Omitted term is for marriage before 1960.
[c]Assistance received by respondent in first three years of marriage.
[d]Assistance received by respondent subsequent to first three years of marriage.

in essence, this equation suggests a weak determination of the attitude by
variables that tap a respondent's transfer experience or financial resources.
It may well be the case that economically better off parents are more likely
to assist with a car purchase, but it would appear that this aid does not
come about from a more favorable view of the parental responsibility. Possibly, the weaker sense of obligation is due to the fact that automobile ownership in Israel is less crucial to family welfare than the other living
standard items.

ATTITUDES AND BEHAVIOR

There remains a question of the impact of the attitudes on parental behavior. In particular, to what extent do favorable views about assisting

Table 9.6   Determinants of Attitudinal Support for Parental Assistance
            with a Car Purchase—Ordered Logit Regression, Standard Errors in
            Parentheses

Variable:	(1)		(2)	
Ethnicity:[a]				
Western Europe	−.2275	(.2320)	−.2757	(.2327)
Eastern Europe	.0087	(.2047)	−.0375	(.2064)
Africa	.1110	(.2085)	.1616	(.2094)
Asia	−.0872	(.2105)	−.0409	(.2112)
Year of marriage:[b]				
1960–69	−.2542	(.1817)	−.1816	(.2070)
1970–78	−.1869	(.1786)	−.2028	(.2564)
1979–86	−.0016	(.1860)	−.1944	(.3489)
1984–94	−.1679	(.2000)	−.3412	(.3898)
Early transfers received/education:				
Continuous assistance[c]	.2645*	(.1337)	.1977	(.1417)
Home ownership at marriage	.0472	(.1021)	−.0017	(.1035)
Educational attainment	.0484*	(.0174)	.0275	(.0187)
Current SOL/related measures:				
Age of respondent			.0062	(.0107)
Ongoing assistance over the years[d]			.0824	(.0512)
Objective SOL			.1171	(.0604)
Subjective SOL			.0143	(.0786)
No. of children			−.1207*	(.0601)
−2LL	3798		3786	
N	1401		1401	

*$p < .05$; **$p < .01$; ***$p < .001$.
[a]Omitted term is for Israel origin.
[b]Omitted term is for marriage before 1960.
[c]Assistance received by respondent in first three years of marriage.
[d]Assistance received by respondent subsequent to first three years of marriage.

children with the acquisition of particular items, or with providing ongoing support, translate into a greater likelihood of making *inter vivos* transfers?

This question cannot be addressed by simply regressing transfer behavior on measures of the expressed views of parents and their resources. The attitudinal information in the survey captures the views of respondents in 1995, whereas the questions about transfers inquire about assistance that was provided prior to that year. As a consequence there is the possibility of movement toward "cognitive consistency" (Festinger, 1957) on the part of a respondent. Having made a transfer, a parent might adjust his/her views on the desirability of assistance in order to bring the attitudes into line with the behavior. Similarly, if a parent has refused a request for finan-

cial support, there might be an erosion in the expressed commitment to provide assistance.

The technical problem this creates is that the attitudes are no longer
exogenous and their effects on parental transfers cannot be estimated by
OLS regression. In this section we therefore consider a simultaneous equation model,

$$y_1 = \beta_1 y_2 + \gamma_1' X_1 + \varepsilon_1 \tag{1}$$
$$y_2 = \beta_2 y_1 + \gamma_2' X_2 + \varepsilon_2 \tag{2}$$
$$E(\varepsilon_1 \varepsilon_2) = \sigma_{12}$$

in which y_1 = assistance provided to children, y_2 = attitude about the
parental obligation, X_1 and X_2 are vectors of explanatory variables, and $\gamma 1$
and $\gamma 2$ are coefficient vectors. To provide consistent estimates of the coefficients the equations are estimated by two-stage least squares (2SLS).

The first equation, for assistance provided, is specified in terms of the
variables presumed to directly influence a transfer decision: Expressed
attitudes about the parental obligation, the living standard measures, and
number of children of the respondent who are older than 25—the last an
indicator of demands for parental resources. To secure model identification, we omit from this equation the terms for respondent's education and
financial assistance received in the early years of his/her marriage. These
variables are presumed to influence the transfer decision only indirectly,
either through their contribution to current living standards or via their
effect on the attitudinal variable, as described in the prior section.

The second equation, for attitudes about the parental obligation, is
specified as a function of the provision of assistance and variables that
would have directly influenced the attitude formation: respondent's education, aid received early in marriage from parents, ethnicity, year of marriage, and number of children. Omitted from the equation, for model
identification reasons, are the living standard terms that would have influenced transfer attitudes indirectly, through their impact on the decision to
provide aid.

Note that two different measures of number of children are employed.
Number of children older than 25 is used in the first equation, for transfer
behavior, as an indicator of the current demand for transfers since these
children are likely to have established their own households. Total number of children, in comparison, appears in the attitudinal equation as a
measure of potential demand for assistance. It is this long-term exposure
to significant expenses that is presumed to influence attitudes of parental
responsibility.

The most important type of support that Israeli parents can provide
is to assist with the purchase of an apartment. We therefore turn to an

Table 9.7   Two Stage Least Squares Estimation Of Parental Attitude And Provision Of Assistance For Home Purchase,[a] Standard Errors In Parentheses

Variable	(1) Assistance Provided[b]		(2) Parental Obligation to Assist	
Constant	−1.2584***	(.3689)	3.2657***	(.2874)
Parents obligation	.4240***	(.0947)		
Assistance provided			.2839	(.3133)
No. of children older than 25	.1550**	(.0621)		
Objective SOL[c]	.0876**	(.0348)		
Subjective SOL[d]	.1199***	(.0411)		
Marriage after 1960	−.1537**	(.0609)	−.2184	(.1427)
Africa/Asia ethnicity			.1117	(.1154)
Education			.0225	(.0164)
Continuous assistance early in marriage			−.0901	(.1681)
Home ownership at marriage			.2824**	(.1003)
No. of children of respondent			−.1477***	(.0454)
R^2	.208		.108	
N	417		417	

*p < .05; **p < .01; ***p < .001.
[a]Sample restricted to respondents with at least one child older than 25.
[b]Asistance provided with apartment purchase to at least one child.
[c]Composite variable, constructed from sum of Z-scores for number of household items, amount of vacation travel, frequency of household help.
[d]Scale item that requests respondent to compare own standard of living with that of the average Israeli family.

exploration of the relation between views of parental responsibility for assisting with this expense and the parental decision to participate in the purchase. For this investigation the sample is restricted to respondents with at least one adult child, since only these individuals are "at risk" of being asked to provide aid for an apartment purchase. This specification—limiting the analysis to respondents with one or more children older than 25—reduces the sample size[4] to N = 417.

In Table 9.7 results are reported for the 2SLS estimates. Column 1 presents the equation for provision of assistance; column 2 reports estimates for the attitudinal regression. In the first equation, not surprisingly, the provision of aid is strongly influenced by the living standard measures—economically better off parents are more likely to make transfers—and by number of children older than 25; the latter is significant because the transfer question asked about assistance to "at least one child," and a positive association with number of children would therefore be expected. Net of these variables, the significant attitudinal term indicates that a disposition to assist has an independent effect on the decision to provide support; this inclination is not a mere reflection of the availability of parental resources.

The equation for the attitudinal expression (column 2) is consistent with the earlier findings (Table 9.3). We again find support for a modeling effect, in that early home ownership (a proxy for aid received by the respondent for this purpose) appears to encourage an attitude of parental obligation. Note that family size has the opposite effect. This result is particularly interesting because, according to equation 1, the number of *adult* offspring increases the likelihood of a transfer (to at least one child). However, the two findings are not inconsistent in that, while there is a greater likelihood of parental aid when there are several adult children, one's view of parental responsibility might be adversely affected by the realization that the current and future needs of several children can be considerable.

Finally, beyond this determination of the attitudinal variable, the lack of significance in equation (2) of the term for transfers provided by the respondent argues against a cognitive consistency thesis. Specifically, we do not find evidence for the view that parental feelings of obligation, at least with respect to a home purchase, are influenced by the knowledge that one has, in fact, provided such assistance to children in past years.

A More General Structural Model

Having singled out for consideration the provision of assistance for a home purchase and parental attitudes on this matter, we turn to a more general structural model of the determination of attitudes and transfers. Instead of considering each kind of assistance as a separate issue, with its own process of attitude determination, we estimate a model with an unobserved attitudinal construct—"parental responsibility for assisting children financially." Four indicators were used to identify the construct: The parental obligation to provide aid for (a) a home purchase, (b) education, (c) continuous assistance, and (d) the purchase of an automobile.

Similarly, since parents may assist children financially in a variety of ways and with different goals, we created a summary, unobserved construct—"financial assistance provided to adult children"—for which three indicators were constructed from the survey data: (a) Number of types of help provided (for a car, schooling, ongoing support), (b) the transfer of at least $10,000 to children in the past 10 years, and (c) provision of assistance for a home purchase.

Using LISREL notation (Joreskog and Sorbom, 1993) this model can be written as

$$Y = \Lambda\eta + \varepsilon \tag{3}$$
$$\eta = B\eta + \Gamma X + \zeta \tag{4}$$

where Y is a column vector of indicators of the latent variables η, Λ is a matrix of factor loadings relating the indicators to the latent variables, X is a vector of the exogenous "causes" of η, and B and Γ are matrices of structural parameters. The ε and ζ are error terms and are assumed to be mutually uncorrelated. The model structure, together with the parameter estimates, is reported in Figure 9.1.

Because the indicators of the endogenous variables are categorical, weighted least squares was used instead of maximum likelihood estimation. The fit of the model is quite good. Although the model chi-square (=90.789) is significant at $p < .01$, the CFI and TLI measures are .939 and .928, respectively, and RMSEA = .054—all of which indicate a satisfactory fit to the data. The unobserved constructs are identified by setting the loadings of the home acquisition terms equal to one; the remaining factor loadings are all positive and significant, suggesting that each of the latent variables is well-defined by its set of indicators.

In sign and significance, the parameter estimates in the structural portion of the model are almost identical with the 2SLS coefficients in Table 9.7. This is not surprising. In the analyses reported in Tables 9.3–9.6, in which the individual attitudes were examined separately, a considerable similarity in causal structure was noted for the different attitudes. This commonalty is reflected in the estimates of the current model.

We conclude that parental attitudes toward providing assistance and the transfer decisions of parents are best viewed as single constructs, at least in the Israeli context. It does not appear that there is much to be gained by analyzing the relationship between attitudes and behavior separately for the different kinds of transfers. Rather, the structure is effectively represented by one construct for a willingness to provide transfers (for whatever purpose) and a second representing a diffuse sense of parental responsibility.

The main findings from the model are that (a) the attitudinal disposition and the respondent's standard of living—a measure of resource level—both have a considerable impact on the transfer decision, and (b) the attitudinal disposition, itself, is not affected by the fact of having made a transfer in the past—note the insignificant coefficient from the latent transfer variable to the latent attitude (–.009). In short, the evidence is strong that attitudes influence behavior, even aside from the availability of resources for making a transfer, but there is no support for a cognitive consistency argument.

As to attitude formation, there is evidence that educational attainment and, to some extent, modeling behavior (receipt of parental assistance in the past) affect the dispositional variable. Support for the latter effect, however, is mixed—the early home ownership term is significant, suggesting a

191

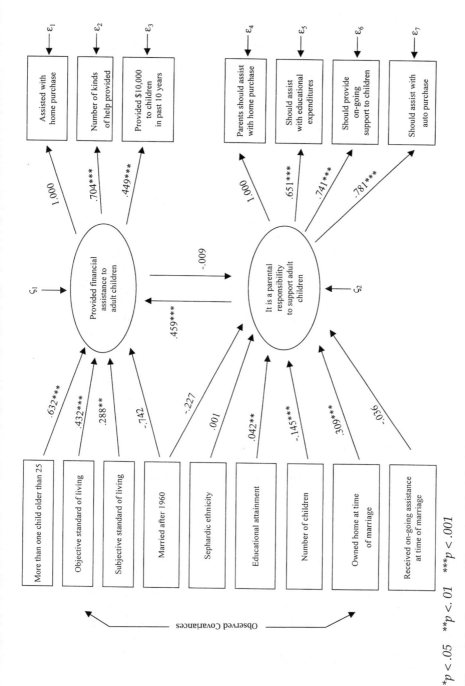

*p < .05 **p < .01 ***p < .001

Figure 9.1 Structural Equation Model of the Determination of Attitudes and Behavior (Unstandardized Coefficients)

long-term influence of this type of aid on transfer attitudes, but the variable for ongoing assistance in the early years of marriage is not significant. Nevertheless, since home acquisition is a central drama in the lives of young Israeli couples, it is quite possible that receipt of this sort of assistance has a dominating effect on attitude development.

CONCLUSIONS AND POLICY IMPLICATIONS

The importance of intergenerational transfers to the organization of society is threefold. First, private transfers of material resources play a critical role in the reproduction of inequality across generations. In Israel, the effect is heightened because of the absence of taxation on *inter vivos* gifts or bequests. Second, though not explored in this chapter, there is an evident interaction between the availability of public transfer programs and the provision of private family assistance. Though the usual assumption is that generous public programs crowd out private transfers (Cox, 1987), this view has recently been challenged by Kunemund and Rein (1999) and Attias-Donfut and Wolff (2000).

Third, since the bulk of transfers flow downward, from parents to children, critical decisions must be made by parents that carry a potential for generational conflict and can threaten family cohesion: how transfers are to be distributed over the life course of parents and how they are to be allocated when there are several children. In Israel, there are strong imperatives that influence the former decision. Because army service consumes much of a child's time from the completion of high school until marriage, and because the costs of establishing a new household are considerable, there is a need for substantial assistance early in adult life and a consequent reliance upon the resources of parents. One relevant matter, addressed in Spilerman (2003), concerns the differential availability of parental resources, especially the ethnic disparity in household wealth. A second issue, explored in this chapter, concerns the willingness of parents to provide substantial transfers at an early point in the life course.

In the first half of this study we examined attitude formation in terms of the background experiences of respondents. The amount of variation that can be explained with the objective background variables is limited, since we are attempting to account for a subtle psychological inclination. Nonetheless, we find evidence that receipt of parental assistance early in the marital career has a long-term effect on a respondent's disposition to provide financial support. We term this finding a "modeling effect." Net of this process, it is apparent that a higher standard of living—a proxy for household resource level—predisposes an individual to a more favorable view of assisting children. These findings replicate across domain areas, though they are stronger with respect to the more critical needs of a young couple—housing and education.

In the second part of the chapter we addressed the implications of the parental attitudes: Do they translate into transfer behavior? Restricting the sample to respondents with grown children and using different model formulations we obtain rather consistent results: Parental attitudes have a strong direct effect on behavior and this finding is net of parental resources, which also influence transfer decisions. This result about the impact of attitudes carries implications for future transfer behavior by Israeli parents, since the marriage year terms suggest a decline in attitudinal support for assistance. This finding is most clear in regard to support with a home purchase (column 2 of Table 9.3), which is, however, a central item in the constellation of material needs of young couples in Israel.

A particularly interesting "nonfinding" relates to the insignificance of the ethnic terms in all the tables. There is much evidence of ethnic inequality in Israel in educational attainment, labor market characteristics, home ownership, and standard of living (Cohen, 1998; Cohen and Haberfeld, 1998; Elmelech, 1992; Semyonov, Lewin-Epstein, and Spilerman, 1996; Smooha and Kraus, 1985). However, ethnic origin appears to play no role in determining transfer attitudes. This suggests that, contrary to the persistence of ethnic differences in economic attainment and living standards, ethnic-based cultural divisions are small, at least with respect to the matter of parental attitudes of responsibility for the welfare of adult children.

ACKNOWLEDGMENT

This research was supported by grants from the Ford Foundation (#1000-1729) and the Brill-Scheuer Foundation. The authors would like to thank Lawrence DeCarlo for helpful comments on an earlier draft. Initial work on the study was carried out when the first author was a Visiting Scholar at the Brookdale Institute, Jerusalem.

NOTES

1. Evidence for modeling behavior has been reported by Ribar and Wilhelm (2001) and by Stark (1995, p. 59). Different terminology is in use. Ribar and Wilhelm refer to "downward chain generalized exchange," whereas Stark speaks of a "demonstration effect"—the impact of a child's observations of parental behavior on the child's later behavior.

2. Ongoing assistance is measured by the item: "In the first three years of your marriage did you receive continuous assistance from either set of parents to help finance the living expenses of the household?" Home ownership at marriage is measured by whether the respondent owned an apartment or home within three years of marriage, in recognition of the possibly delay in completing a purchase or building a home even if parental assistance is available.

3. Receipt of ongoing assistance is indexed by the proportion of years since marriage in which the respondent received at least $1,000 in parental support.

4. Because of the reduced sample size, the ethnic terms have been collapsed into an Ashkenazi/Israeli category and a Sephardic category. The first is the omitted term. Similarly, the year-of-marriage terms have been collapsed into two categories—marriage before 1960 and after 1960. The first is the omitted term in the regressions.

REFERENCES

Attias-Donfut, C., and Wolff, F.-C. 2000. Complementarity between private and public transfers. In S. Arber and C. Attias-Donfut (eds.), *The myth of generational conflict* (pp. 47–68). London: Routledge.

Cohen, Y. 1998. Socioeconomic gaps between Mizrahim and Ashkenazim, 1975–1995. *Israel Sociology* 1(1):115–34.

Cohen, Y., and Haberfeld, Y. 1998. Second generation Jewish immigrants in Israel: Have the ethnic gaps in schooling and earnings declined? *Ethnic and Racial Studies* 21:507–28.

Cox, D. 1987. Motives for private income transfers. *Journal of Political Economy* 95:508–46.

Cox, D., and Rank, M. R. 1992. Inter-vivos transfers and intergenerational exchange. *Review of Economics and Statistics* 74:305–14.

Duncan, O. D. 1968. Inheritance of poverty or inheritance of race. In D. P. Moynihan (ed.), *On understanding poverty* (pp. 85–110). New York: Basic Books.

Duncan, O. D., Featherman, D., and Duncan, B. 1972. *Socioeconomic background and achievement*. New York: Seminar.

Elmelech, Y. 1992. *Immigrants, young couples and housing policy in Israel, 1948–1992.* Unpublished manuscript, Department of Sociology, Tel Aviv University.

Festinger, L. 1957. *A theory of cognitive dissonance*. Evanston, IL: Row Peterson.

Gale, W. G., and Scholz, J. K. 1994. Intergenerational transfers and the accumulation of wealth. *Journal of Economic Perspectives* 8:145–60.

Holtz-Eakin, D., and Smeeding, T. M. 1994. Income, wealth, and intergenerational economic relations of the aged. In L. G. Martin and S. H. Preston (eds.), *Demography of aging* (pp. 102–45). Washington, DC: National Academy Press.

Jencks, C., Smith, M., Acland, H., Bane, M. J., Cohen, D., Gintis, H., Heyns, B., and Michelson, S. 1972. *Inequality*. New York: Basic Books.

Joreskog, K. G., and Sorbom, D. 1993. *Lisrel 8 user's reference guide*. Chicago: Scientific Software International.

Kiecolt, K. J. 1988. Recent developments in attitudes and social structure. *Annual Review of Sociology* 14:381–403. Palo Alto, CA: Annual Reviews.

Kotlikoff, L. J., and Summers, L. H. 1981. The role of intergenerational transfers in aggregate capital accumulation. *Journal of Political Economy* 89:706–32.

Kotlikoff, L. J., and Summers, L. H. 1988. The contribution of intergenerational transfers to total wealth: A reply. In D. Kessler and A. Masson (eds.), *Modelling the accumulation and distribution of wealth* (pp. 53–67). Oxford: Clarendon.

Kunemund, H., and Rein, M. 1999. There is more to receiving than needing: Theoretical arguments and empirical explorations of crowding in and crowding out. *Aging and Society* 19(part 1):93–121.

McGarry, K., and Schoeni, R. 1997. Transfer behavior within the family: Results from the asset and health dynamics study. *Journal of Gerontology* 52B:82–92.

Modigliani, F. 1988. Measuring the contribution of intergenerational transfers to total wealth. In D. Kessler and A. Masson (eds.), *Modelling the accumulation and distribution of wealth* (pp. 21–52). Oxford: Clarendon.

Ribar, D., and Wilhelm, M. O. 2001. *The intergenerational transmission of exchange attitudes: Evidence of generalized exchange from three generations of Mexican-Americans.* Unpublished manuscript, Department of Economics, Indiana University.

Semyonov, M., Lewin-Epstein, N., and Spilerman, S. 1996. The material possessions of Israeli ethnic groups. *European Sociological Review* 12(3):389–402.

Sewell, W. H., and Hauser, R. M. 1975. *Education, occupation, and earnings.* New York: Academic Press.

Silver, C., and Muller, C. 1997. Effects of ascribed and achieved characteristics on social values in Japan and the United States. *Research in Social Stratification and Mobility*, 15:153–76. Greenwich: JAI.

Smooha, S., and Kraus, V. 1985. Ethnicity as a factor in status attainment in Israel. *Research in Social Stratification and Mobility* 4:151–75.

Spilerman, S. 2000. Wealth and stratification processes. *Annual Review of Sociology* 26:497–524. Palo Alto, CA: Annual Reviews.

Spilerman, S. 2003. Young couples in Israel: The impact of parental wealth on early living standards. *American Journal of Sociology* (forthcoming).

Stark, O. (1995). *Altruism and beyond.* Cambridge: Cambridge University Press.

|10|

Social Network Structure and Utilization of Formal Public Support in Israel

Howard Litwin

This chapter explores the association between the informal interpersonal environment of older people and their use of formal public assistance. The interpersonal environment is examined, in this case, by means of the construct of social network. A network is the meaningful collection of personal ties that individuals of all ages maintain, and which may include one's relations with family members, friends, neighbors, and others who might be significant in some way (Fischer, 1982; Mitchell, 1969). The use of formal public aid that is addressed in this analysis is the utilization of publicly funded home care assistance. Public assistance was chosen as the outcome variable of interest insofar as it clearly contrasts with the informal nature of assistance that may be provided by the social network. The question that is to be examined is whether there is a relationship between the kind of informal social network in which older people are embedded, and the use of formal support by them (Bass and Noelker, 1987; Bear, 1989; Logan and Spitze, 1994; Wan, 1987).

This is a relevant question at this time given that the continuing relative growth of elderly populations in many countries and the aging of their aged populations have led some societies to limit access to public assistance, or to cut back on its extent. Moreover, there is a current trend to encourage "back to the family" social policies, in which more and more of the long-term care that older people may require is expected to be provided to them at home by their family networks, rather than by public authorities (Walker, 1987). It is important to consider, therefore, whether informal social networks in general, and family networks in particular, impact upon the utilization of public support, and if so, in what way.

The analysis is based upon the results from a national survey of older adults in Israel. It explores the nature of the social networks of this population and examines the relationship of social network to receipt of publicly funded home care. As such, it provides insights into the relationship between informal and formal care, as well as additional understanding as to the strengths and limitations of the families of older people in this particular society.

OLDER PEOPLE AND SOCIAL NETWORKS

The social network is the primary interpersonal milieu in which people are located and the source from which they derive various and sundry supports (Fischer, 1982; Mitchell, 1969). For many older people, social network is synonymous with the notion of family, in that the members of their social network all come from their extended family system (Litwin, 1996, Wenger, 1984). Their network ties are, in essence, their multigenerational family relations. These family networks are often assumed to provide for all the elders' needs.

Other older persons tend to have more diversified social networks in which family members cofunction alongside other types of social ties. In these cases, it has been argued, family members can provide the kinds of supports for which they are uniquely capable, while other members augment the provision of support in ways uniquely suitable to their particular capabilities (Litwak, 1985). Thus, for example, family network members might provide long-term emotional support, while proximate neighbors might aid in instrumental matters that require immediate attention.

Still other older people may lack family members in their social networks, whether as a result of never having married or never having had children of their own, or whether as a result of estrangement from existing familial relations (Connidis and McMullin, 1994; Gironda, Lubben, and Atchison, 1999; Wenger, Scott, and Patterson, 2000). Their social networks are, thus, primarily nonkin-based, and may be comprised largely by friends, neighbors, and current acquaintances. It is believed that such nonkin social networks function in different ways from familial networks, especially in terms of the kinds and extent of support that is provided.

A social network measure of particular interest is the notion of network type. This construct encompasses a set of key network variables that collectively distinguish major groupings in a population of interest. Wenger (1991) discovered five major network types in Wales. Investigation indicates that network type may be predictive of various outcomes in later life

(Bond et al., 1998; Litwin, 1998; Wenger, 1997). Despite the progress in this line of inquiry, however, there is still relatively little research available on network types of older people.

Social networks are of particular interest not only for the support they provide their focal members, but for the role they play in regard to formal help-seeking (Hooyman, 1983; Litwin, 1997). Gourash (1978) has pointed out that social networks may encourage or discourage the seeking of formal help through the attitudes and the values they transmit to their members. They may also actively encourage utilization of formal assistance by performing advocacy and referral functions on behalf of their members. On the other hand, they may effectively prevent their members from utilizing formal assistance by providing the needed services themselves. Finally, they may obviate the need for services, by buffering the kinds of stress that create the sense of need in the first place.

There is currently very little known about the effect of social networks on the use of formal home care by older people. This may be due to the general lack of information on the determinants of home care use (Hanley and Wiener, 1991), or to lack of attention to social network variables in studies of professional home care utilization (Kempen and Suurmeijer, 1991). The following review summarizes the data available from the few studies that address this topic. As will be seen, a few common trends may be discerned, alongside some rather inconclusive findings.

Kempen and Suurmeijer (1991) distinguish between person-bound variables and environmental variables, such as social network, as predictors of home care utilization. In a study of home care clients in Holland, fifty-two elderly home care clients were compared to a matched sample of nonusers. The researchers considered the effect of (1) network size, (2) composition (family versus nonfamily), (3) travel time between network members and the elder respondent, and (4) the number of informal care providers on home care utilization. They found no significant differences between the two groups in regard to the first three network variables. The number of informal care providers, on the other hand, did show a difference. Nonusers of professional home care received more help from informal care providers than did the users.

A number of studies reinforce this finding. Soldo's (1985) study of dependent elderly persons in the United States, for example, shows that the absence of informal support was a strong predictor of the receipt of in-home services. Frederiks and colleagues (1992) also found the recipients of professional home care to be characterized by receipt of less informal care. Solomon and colleagues (1993) identified less accessible social support as one of four independent predictors of home health care use among 226 elderly patients who had been discharged from acute hospital care. However, other studies have found no significant relationship between informal support and professional home care utilization (McAully and Arling, 1984; Wan and Odell, 1981).

Hanley and Wiener (1991) raise serious reservations about the use of informal care as an indicator of social network influence on the use of formal care services. This is because the use of the two kinds of support may be confounded: an increase in need on the part of an elderly person may spur both increased informal care and utilization of formal assistance. Chappell (1985) found, in this regard, that despite having smaller networks, home care recipients in Manitoba had more assistance from informal sources than did nonrecipients.

Hanley and Wiener (1991) thus counsel against the use of measures of informal care—such as the number of informal helpers and whether the elderly person is living alone—as explanatory variables for predicting formal care. They recommend, instead, focusing on network factors not endogenously determined within the specific helping context. Structural network factors, such as being married and the number of children, are generally established before the need for home care develops, and thus are better indicators, in their opinion, of social network influence on utilization of formal home care services.

Using data from the 1982 National Long Term Care Survey in the United States, Hanley and Wiener (1991) performed a logistic regression of factors explanatory of paid home care among chronically disabled elderly persons. The analysis showed that in regard to social network factors, unmarried respondents and those with fewer sons and daughters were more likely to have formal home care. The researchers conclude, as a result, that family availability plays a major role in formal home care utilization. They clarify, at the same time, that having formal home care is not necessarily a substitute for informal care provided by the family (Hanley, Wiener and Harris, 1991).

The findings closest to consideration of network type as an influence on utilization of formal home care may be found in a study of one hundred clients of a statewide home care program in Illinois reported by Wilcox and Taber (1991). They found that most of the home care clients had some degree of informal help as well, but such help came from limited sources. Only 18 percent of them had a helping spouse, and only a half had more than one helper. Several had nonkin helpers only, and only a few had a coresiding informal helper. The researchers conclude that clients of formal home care have fragile social networks.

In regard to person-bound variables related to the use of formal home care, a prominent characteristic noted in the literature is physical or functional disability on the part of the elderly care-recipient. Quite logically, home care use is associated with measures of greater disability (Chappell, 1992; Hanley and Wiener, 1991; Solomon et al., 1993). A more specific study by Grabbe and colleagues (1995) utilized data from the 1986 National Mortality Followback Survey in the United States to estimate the relationship between functional status and the provision of formal home care during patients' last year of life. The findings confirmed that those with moderate and severe levels of physical impairment were most likely to use formal home care. However, the analysis also revealed that greater involvement of family caregivers was a "pivotal factor" in the lower use of formal home care, even in cases of severe impairment.

Much of the literature reports a relationship between gender and use of formal home care in old age. This finding emerges in multivariate examinations of the outcome variable. Specifically, the data underscore the greater use made of this formal service by women (Frederiks et al., 1992; Hanley and Wiener, 1991; Kempen and Suurmeijer, 1991).

Mutchler and Bullers (1994) specifically addressed the question of gender differences in an inquiry on the use of formal sources of home care among impaired older people. Drawing upon American panel data from 1984, they found that married women were indeed more likely to receive formal care than were married older men. This gender difference was not apparent, however, among the unmarried. The researchers conclude that the findings in their analysis underscore gendered expectations with regard to both caregiving and the receipt of formal care services within the marital unit.

Studies in a range of countries report a positive association between age and use of home care services, with the oldest cohorts making the greatest relative use of such formal care (Branch et al., 1981; Chappell, 1992; Frederiks et al., 1992; Kempen and Suurmeijer, 1991; Shapiro, 1986). An association between income and home care use is also reported, although the direction of this association is not always as clear. Grabbe and colleagues (1995):for example, cite a number of studies in which lower income elderly persons were found to be most likely to use home care (Evashwick, Rowe, Diehr, and Branch, 1984; Pawlson, 1989). Conversely, Branch and associates (1981) found that greater income significantly increased formal home care use. Soldo (1985), on the other hand, found no relationship between income level and utilization of home care.

The relationship between income and home care utilization may be affected by additional variables, such as issues of service availability, accessibility, and eligibility. Income-based eligibility for formal home care, for example, might encourage greater use among poorer impaired older persons. Lack of service availability, on the other hand, might lead to greater home care use among older people with the financial resources needed to overcome barriers of accessibility. Thus, Hanley and Wiener (1991) found both a strong inverse association between income and home care utilization, and a significant positive relationship between Medicaid enrollment and having paid home care. That is, low-income public health insurance enrollees had a higher probability of using home care than did nonenrollees.

This review underscores the potential impact of age, gender, income, disability, and social network on the utilization of formal home care services among elderly people. The analysis that unfolds in the following pages considers the effect of each of these variables upon receipt of publicly funded home care assistance in a national cohort of older Jewish adults in Israel. The analysis considers, in particular, whether there is an independent social network influence on the use of home care services, above and beyond the effects of the person-bound demographic and functional health variables.

RESEARCH METHODS

The analysis is based upon data compiled by the Israeli Central Bureau of Statistics (CBS) in a national survey of people age 60 and over. The study sample is comprised of older Jewish persons who resided in Israel from prior to 1990. Recent elderly Jewish immigrants and older Arab residents of Israel were both excluded from the current analysis, due to the unique social and cultural characteristics of these populations. Moreover, it should be noted that the CBS surveyors interviewed all persons age 60 and over in each of the sampled household units. In order to guarantee independent observations among respondents in the current analysis, random selection of one elder per household was performed. Thus, the present study sample includes 2079 people.

The sample includes a slightly greater proportion of men (51.6 percent). In terms of land of origin, a bit more than half the respondents were born in Europe or America (51.9 percent), more than a third were born in Asia or Africa, and about a tenth were born in Israel. The median age category of respondents is 70–74 years old. The median educational level is secondary school or less. Respondents' median income level is rated as fairly low.

Study Variables

The principal independent variable examined is social network type. The derivation of the network types in this analysis has been described at length elsewhere (Litwin, 2001). For purpose of understanding the measure, it is sufficient to note here that seven criterion variables reflecting the principal components of social networks of older people were selected (Berkman and Syme, 1979; Lubben, 1988; Wenger, 1991): (1) respondents' marital state, (2) the number of adult children residing in close proximity

(3) frequency of contact by respondents with their adult children, (4) frequency of contact with friends, (5) frequency of contact with neighbors, (6) frequency of attendance at a synagogue, and (7) frequency of attendance at a social club.

The social networks of older Jewish people in Israel almost always include a familial base (Fischer and Shavit, 1995). Nevertheless, variations beyond this familial base are evident. Five distinct network types were, thus, discovered in this analysis. They are termed: (1) the diverse network, (2) the friends network, (3) the neighbors network, (4) the family network, and (5) the restricted network.

The diverse network is the most relatively endowed in terms of the range of sources of contact and potential support present in this grouping. The majority of its members are married. They also reported having one proximate child on average, and very frequent contact with their children. In addition, they have a moderate degree of contact with friends and neighbors, and they attend synagogue occasionally. People in the diverse network attend a social club to a limited degree, but nevertheless, more frequently than the rest of the sample.

The friends network type is also quite endowed in its range of contacts and potential supports. The scores on most of the criterion variables for this grouping are quite similar to those of its predecessor. However, two major differences are evident. A slightly greater proportion of its members is currently married and, more importantly, the people in this network type report having almost no contacts whatsoever with their neighbors.

Older people in the neighbors network tend to be unmarried more frequently than the elders in the two preceding network types. Elders in this network type also report frequent contact with adult children and with neighbors. Their contact with friends, on the other hand, is minimal. They also report the lowest frequency of social club attendance among all the network types. It seems, therefore, that the neighbors network is a somewhat less endowed grouping in terms of contacts and support potential.

The fourth network type is a unique grouping in Israeli society. It is termed the family network, insofar as its members seem to rely principally upon their families. A majority of the people in this network type has a spouse. They also report having an average of five proximate children, as well as very frequent contact with at least one of them. The elders in the family network also have the most frequent synagogue attendance among the network types. On the other hand, they report having only minimal ties with neighbors and even fewer contacts with friends.

The last of the network types is termed the restricted network. On the whole, its members cite the most relatively limited degree of social contact and potential support among all the network groupings. The focal elders in this network type are the most frequently unmarried. They also have the least frequent contact with proximate adult children, and the lowest rate of synagogue attendance. More importantly, however, they report having virtually no contact at all with people who could be considered friends or neighbors.

The diverse network is the most prevalent among all the network types (30 percent). The friends network type is also quite prevalent (24 percent). Together, these two groupings characterize more than half of the elderly people in the sample. Persons in the restricted network type, on the other hand, make up about a fifth of all respondents. The neighbors network type is somewhat less prevalent (17 percent); and the family network type is the least prevalent of all the network types (9 percent).

The dependent variable addressed is utilization of publicly funded home care assistance. It is derived from the responses to four questions. Respondents were asked, first, whether they have a personal care aide to assist in tasks of bathing, dressing, eating, ambulating outside the house, and so on. They were then asked whether such services are funded totally, or in part, by a public authority. Another question asked the respondent whether he or she is in receipt of assistance by a housekeeper, for cleaning, laundry, and so on. Here too, respondents were asked whether such services are funded totally, or in part, by a public authority.

It is important to note that since 1988, the Long Term Care Insurance Law implemented in Israel provides persons in need with up to eighteen hours a week of home care. It is targeted to meeting the needs of the severely impaired elderly. As such, a relatively high disability score, as measured on an ADL assessment, is required for eligibility for this public insurance benefit (Morginstin, Baich-Moray, and Zipkin, 1992). Furthermore, additional discretionary home care benefits are offered through public welfare bureaus, health maintenance programs, and other sources.

The outcome measure derived for the current analysis is a dichotomous response reflecting receipt of publicly funded assistance (0 = no, 1 = yes). Respondents who answered positively to either of the two probes, that is, receipt of publicly funded personal care and/or housekeeping assistance received a score of one. The analysis also takes into account respondents' sociodemographic and health characteristics as background control variables. The sociodemographic variables of interest include gender, age, and income as a proxy measure for social class. The levels of measurement of each on the CBS survey instrument are spelled out below.

Gender is recorded as a simple nominal variable (men = 1, women = 2). Respondents' age was measured on the original survey instrument according to 5-year categories, from 60 to 64 through 85 to 89, and one additional category for people age 90 and over. The CBS officials explain that exact birth years were not solicited in order to prevent the possible identification of respondents by unauthorized individuals, and as such, to guarantee their privacy. The age data were recoded in the current analysis to reflect three major age groupings: 60–69, 70-79, and 80 and over.

Respondents' income levels were recorded on the CBS instrument on a nine-category scale, ranging from a minimal income level of about 4,200 to over 33,000 Israeli Shekels per year. For purpose of the present analysis, these categories were recoded into three groups of approximately equal size. The corresponding income levels of these groupings are termed very low, low to moderate, and moderate to high.

The health characteristic selected for consideration in this analysis is respondents' physical disability. It is measured on a physical capacity scale similar to the five-item Physical Activity Scale first employed in the Yale Health and Aging Project (Cornoni-Huntley et al., 1985). On this measure, respondents indicate the degree of difficulty they have in executing five different physical activities: pushing a large object, stooping, lifting, reaching, and using a delicate instrument. The measure in use by the CBS solicits a three-level response: (1) able to perform the task with no difficulty whatsoever, (2) able to perform the task, but with difficulty, and (3) unable to perform the task. Consequently, the total physical disability scores range from 5 to 15. For purpose of analysis, respondents in the current study were divided on this variable into three groups of approximately equal size. The corresponding physical disability levels of these groupings are termed low, moderate, and high.

Analysis

The analysis proceeds in three stages. First is a univariate description of the outcome variable—receipt of publicly funded home care assistance. Next is examination of the bivariate association between network type and the background variables, on the one hand, and the outcome variable, on the other. In order to identify the variables most associated with receipt of publicly funded home care, a final multivariate stage of analysis is performed using hierarchical logistic regression. This is the optimal statistical procedure given the dichotomous nature of the outcome variable and its unequal distribution. In the first stage, receipt of public assistance is regressed on the sociodemographic variables of gender, age, and income. In the next stage, the outcome measure is regressed on both physical disability and the sociodemographic characteristics. In the final stage, the network types are added to the analysis for examination of the full model. Given the nominal and ordinal level of measurement of the independent variables, a reference value was designated for each variable in the multivariate logistic regressions. The specific variable values serving as reference values are indicated in a table presented in the Results section.

RESULTS

Three hundred and forty three respondents reported being in receipt of publicly funded home care assistance (16.5 percent). These respondents clearly constitute a minority among the population of older adults in Israel. Identifying the factors most predictive of inclusion in this category, and particularly the role of social network type in such, is the focus of the results that are presented in the coming paragraphs.

The bivariate comparison reveals that close to a third of the elders in the restricted network are in receipt of publicly financed home care, and close to a quarter of the elders in the neighbors network. The corresponding percentage among respondents in the family network approaches a fifth of this grouping. Respondents in the diverse and friends networks, on the other hand, comprise only a tenth, or less, of the people in these network types. These differences are statistically significant.

Figure 10.1 presents this information from an additional point of view. The bar graphs show the percentage of all public aid recipients in relation to their network type compared to the percentage of all nonrecipients in these same networks. Here the differences are quite apparent. Outstanding in this regard is the dominant relative representation of elders from the restricted and neighbors networks among the recipients of publicly financed home care assistance.

As for the bivariate comparisons between the control variables and the outcome variable, all the associations are statistically significant. Women make more use of publicly funded home care than men. The youngest-old (60–69) make very limited use, the older-old (70-79) make about average use, and the oldest-old (80 and over) make the greatest use, almost 40 percent. In terms of income, respondents in the very low income group make the greatest use of publicly funded home care assistance. Respondents with low to moderate incomes make less relative use, and those in the moderate to high income group make little use. Finally, elders with a minimal degree of disability make almost no use of publicly funded home care, and only a tenth of those with moderate disability levels do so. On the other hand, more than 40 percent of elderly respondents with a high degree of physical disability are in receipt of publicly financed home care assistance.

In order to clarify the independent contribution of each variable in relation to the outcome measure, receipt of publicly funded home care assistance, multivariate analysis was performed. Table 10.1 presents the results of the logistic multiple regression procedure. As noted in the table, the variable values in parentheses are the reference variables in each case. The table presents the unstandardized regression coefficients (B), and the odds ratio (OR) for each variable.

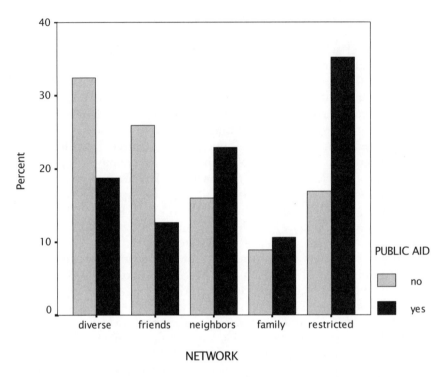

Figure 10.1   Percentage of respondents receiving publicly funded home care
assistance compared to the percentage of respondents not in receipt of
such assistance, by network type.

The first model examines the regression of receipt of publicly funded
home care on the sociodemographic variables only. As may be seen in the
table, all the sociodemographic variables are statistically significant at this
stage of the analysis. Women are more likely than men to receive publicly
funded home care, the older groups are more likely than the younger
group, and the lower income groups are more likely than the moderate to
high income group. Outstanding among the variable values in its predictive power is the 80+ age group, which at this stage is ten times more likely
to receive public home care assistance.

The situation changes somewhat with the addition of the physical disability variable in the second model. Here, the effect of gender disappears,
and the effect of income is minimized, with only the very low income
group retaining some predictive value. On the other hand, the physical
disability variable emerges as the strongest relative predictor, with the

Table 10.1 Factors associated with utilization of publicly funded home care
assistance: Hierarchical logistic regression

Variable	Model 1		Model 2		Model 3	
	B	OR	B	OR	B	OR
Gender						
(Men)						
Women	.56**	1.75	.19	1.21	.16	1.18
Age						
(60–69)						
70–79	1.23**	3.43	.95**	2.58	.96**	2.62
80+	2.33**	10.27	1.83**	6.21	1.82**	6.16
Income						
Very low	1.00**	2.72	.49*	1.63	.39	1.47
Low-moderate	.42*	1.52	.18	1.19	.11	1.11
(Moderate-high)						
Physical Disability						
(Low)						
Moderate			1.30**	3.66	1.28**	3.58
High			2.86**	17.46	2.76**	15.87
Network Type						
(Diverse)						
Friends					–.19	.82
Neighbors					.52	1.68
Family					.25	1.29
Restricted					.44*	1.55
Constant	–3.77**		–4.78**		–4.85**	
–2 log likelihood ratio	1566.45		1338.33		1311.20	
Model X^2	303.21**		511.83**		524.59**	
df	5		7		11	

*p < .05, **p < .001
Note: Reference groups in parentheses.

high disability group seventeen times more likely to be in receipt of public home care, and the moderate disability group almost four times as
likely. The age variable retains its effect, but its magnitude is somewhat
lessened.

Consideration of the network type variable is added in the final stage of
the logistic regression, in model 3. Here, the previously documented effect
of very low income disappears. On the other hand, the effect of two of the
network types becomes apparent. As can be seen, respondents in the
neighbors networks are almost twice as likely to be in receipt of public
home care, and those in the restricted network are one and a half times as
likely.

Looking at the final model as a whole, it is evident that the two major predictors of receipt of publicly funded home care assistance among respondents in this sample are the high disability group and the 80 and over age group, respectively. They are followed, in terms of relative predictive power, by the moderately disabled group and the 70–79 year olds, respectively. However, the model also underscores the additional effect of network type on the receipt of public home care. The neighbors network type and the restricted network type are significantly more likely to receive public home assistance even when controlling for the independent effects of age and disability.

DISCUSSION

The findings in this study reveal, first of all, that about 17 percent of older persons in Israel make use of some form of publicly funded home care assistance. Comparative figures in the United States show a wide range of such utilization, from as little as 4 to as much as 60 percent. This variation stems from both the nature of the samples considered in different studies and the means of measurement employed. When focusing on disabled elderly people living at home in the United States, for example, about 25 percent were found to be using paid in-home care on any given day (Hanley and Wiener, 1991). Given that the figures from the Israeli survey reflect a probability sample of all adults age 60 and over, and not just the frail or impaired, the reported utilization rate in the present sample is not unusually low.

The study findings also underscore the importance of two person-bound variables as major predictors of home care use: disability and age. The most physically impaired group and the oldest age group were the most likely to utilize public home care assistance. This is quite logical in that severe disability is a criterion for eligibility to Israel's largest public home care assistance program. The effect of age above and beyond that of disability, on the other hand, requires some additional consideration. People age 80 and over tend to have the most social care needs. Hence, it seems that there is an independent effect of age on public home care use. These same trends are repeated to a lesser degree for the moderately impaired group and for the middle old age group (70–79).

No influence on utilization was found in regard to respondents' gender and income. Unlike as in some studies in which women were found to make greater use of formal home care, the data from this study show that once disability and age are taken into account, there are no such differences in service utilization. The question that remains unanswered is whether older Jewish Israeli men and women are different in some significant way from other older people around the world, or whether the studies in the other settings had different analytical strategies that led to the different findings.

As for income, the findings from this analysis join those of selected other studies that show no direct relationship between personal wealth and use of paid home care (Soldo, 1985). The lack of clarity on this question is due, most likely, to such intervening factors as eligibility criteria and insurance coverage. In Israel, most of publicly funded home care assistance is given as a social insurance benefit. Only persons with monthly incomes above two and a half times the average are ineligible for this benefit. Thus, it is unlikely to find an income effect in relation to use of publicly funded home care assistance at this venue, and, indeed, none was found.

The question of primary interest to the current analysis, however, is the role of the social network in relation to formal home care use. Several findings are worth noting in this regard. First, it will be recalled that the greatest actual use and the greatest relative use of publicly funded home care assistance was made by people in restricted social networks. They are followed both in terms of actual and relative use by people located in neighbors networks. Taking into account the simultaneous effect of gender, age, income, and disability on the use of public home care, the two network types retain their previous bivariate influence. Interestingly, the extent of their respective influence in the multivariate analysis reverses itself. That is, when all else is considered, people in neighbors networks are a bit more likely to use formal home care. People in restricted networks are also more likely than the other network types to use formal home care, but to a slightly lesser degree than those in the neighbors network.

Both the neighbors and the restricted network types may be considered to be fragile network types, in that they reflect more limited sources of potential support. As such, the findings in this analysis support the contention that older people who belong to weaker network structures make greater use of formal public support (Wilcox and Taber, 1991). In addition, it was clarified earlier that persons in the restricted network are able to count on the possible help of one adult child only, on average. Their greater use of formal home care is, thus, in line with the findings of Hanley and Wiener (1991), who found that elderly people with fewer sons and daughters in the United States made greater use of paid home care.

Persons who count on their neighbors as the primary additional source of aid (beyond the help available from one child, on average), also find themselves in relatively weak networks. Among the three main categories of social ties—family, friends, and neighbors—the last is recognized as the most tenuous and time-limited source of long-term assistance (Litwak, 1985). Thus, being embedded in a neighbors network may not provide much hope for having significantly more support than that available in the restricted network. Indeed, as just mentioned, people in neighbors networks in the current study were slightly more likely than those in the restricted networks to use publicly funded home care assistance, when the person-bound characteristics were controlled for.

Respondents located in family networks in the current analysis present an interesting additional observation. They report the third highest probability of use of formal home care, among the five network types, after the people in restricted and neighbors networks. This higher than average utilization rate comes in spite of their having potential aid from five proximate adult children, on average. Even though the multivariate analysis showed that this trend toward greater use of formal care was not statistically significant when taking into account the effect of the person-bound variables, a few words on this finding are, nevertheless, in order.

Social policymakers have been seeking of late to encourage informal support, and particularly family support, as an alternative to public home care assistance (Walker, 1987). The research literature shows, however, that increased family-provided care is frequently accompanied by an increase in formal care as well. This is due, in all likelihood, to the increase in the extent of needed care of all kinds on the part of the elder in question. While the results from the current study cannot support this particular developmental dynamic, as they are drawn from a cross-sectional survey, they nevertheless show that networks with more available family support did not make less use of formal care, as policymakers might hope. On the contrary, they make more than average use of formal home care. Since this trend was not found to be statistically significant in the multivariate analysis, however, it cannot be ruled out that the greater use of home care is explained by another factor, namely, the high proportion of disabled people located in this network grouping.

The findings also reveal that older people in diverse and friends networks make less than average use of formal home care. This is not surprising given the wide availability of potential support from both family and friends in these two network groupings. Family and friends are particularly able to provide a variety of emotional supports that, in turn, may obviate the need for other kinds of assistance. The question of interest here is not why the people in diverse and friends networks make less use of formal public care, but why they make any use at all.

There are two possible explanations. First, the social insurance nature of home care assistance in Israel encourages utilization of this public benefit, regardless of the social status of the beneficiary. Second is the contribution of the social network toward securing the home care benefit. As noted earlier, social networks can function as advocates and as sources of referral for their members. It is quite likely that utilization of publicly funded home care assistance, in this case, was encouraged by the network members, in spite of their own ample helping resources.

It should be noted that, as in the previously discussed case of the family network, the findings regarding the diverse and friends networks were not statistically significant in the multivariate stage of the analysis. Thus, here too, there may be another factor that explains the rate of home care use among people in these network types, in this case, lower utilization. The very low proportion of disabled people reported in both of these groupings, and the greater proportion of younger elderly people in the friends network may be the primary explanatory factors of their lesser utilization of publicly funded home care.

In conclusion, this analysis found that a majority of elderly Jewish Israeli men and women are located in robust social network types that have the potential to provide informal aid if called upon to do so. A common element in these robust network types, moreover, is the connection of the focal elder with family and with friends. However, a substantial minority of older people in Israel is embedded in fragile network types. The elders in these networks make significantly greater use of publicly funded home care assistance. Moreover, the demonstrated influence of social network type on formal home care utilization remains, even when controlling for the sociodemographic and health characteristics of the elderly respondents in question.

REFERENCES

Bass, D. M., and Noelker, L. S. 1987. The influence of family caregivers on elders' use of in-home services: An expanded conceptual framework. *Journal of Health and Social Behavior* 28(2):184–96.

Bear, M. 1989. Network variables as determinants of the elderly entering adult residential care facilities. *Ageing and Society* 9(2):149–63.

Berkman, L. F., and Syme, S. L. 1979. Social networks, host resistance and mortality: A nine year follow-up study of Alameda county residents. *American Journal of Epidemiology* 109:186–204.

Bond, J., Gregson, B., Smith, M., Rousseau, N., Lecouturier, J., and Rodgers, H. 1998. Outcomes following acute hospital care for stroke or hip fracture: How useful is an assessment of anxiety or depression for older people? *International Journal of Geriatric Psychiatry* 13(9):601–10.

Branch, L., Jette, A., Evashwick, C., Polansky, M., Rowe, G., and Diehr, P. 1981. Toward understanding elders' health service utilization. *Journal of Community Health* 7(2):80–92.

Chappell, N. L. 1985. Social support and the receipt of home care services. *Gerontologist* 25:47–53.

———. 1992. Utilization of health and social services in Bermuda. *International Journal of Health Sciences* 3(2):91–103.

Connidis, I. A., and McMullin, J. A. 1994. Social support in older age: Assessing the impact of marital and parent status. *Canadian Journal on Aging/Revue Canadienne du Vieillissement* 13(4):510–27.

Cornoni-Huntley, J. C., Roley, D. F., White, L. R., Suzman, R., Berkman, L. F., Evans, D. A., et al. 1985. Epidemiology of disability in the oldest old: Methodological issues and preliminary findings. *Milbank Memorial Fund Quarterly/ Health and Society* 63:350–76.

Evashwick, C., Rowe, G., Diehr, P., and Branch, L. 1984. Factors explaining the use of health services by the elderly. *Health Services Research*, 19:357–82.

Fischer, C. S. 1982. *To dwell among friends: Personal networks in town and city.* Chicago: Chicago University Press.

Fischer, C. S., and Shavit, Y. 1995. National differences in network density: Israel and the United States. *Social Networks* 17:129–45.

Frederiks, C. M., Tewierik, M. J., Van-Rossum, H. J., Visser, A. P., Volovies, A., and Sturmans, F. 1992. Why do elderly people seek professional home care? Methodologies compared. *Journal of Community Health* 17(3):131–41.

Gironda, M., Lubben, J. E., and Atchison, K. A. 1999. Social networks of elders without children. *Journal of Gerontological Social Work* 31(1–2):63–84.

Gourash, N. 1978. Help seeking: A review of the literature. *American Journal of Community Psychology* 6:413–23.

Grabbe, L., Demi, A. S., Whittington, F., Janes, J. M., Branch, L. G., and Lambert, R. 1995. Functional status and the use of formal home care in the year before death. *Journal of Aging and Health* 7(3):339–64.

Hanley. R. S., and Wiener, J. M. 1991. Use of paid home care by the chronically disabled elderly. *Research on Aging* 31(3):310–22.

Hanley, R. S., Wiener, J. M., and Harris, K. A. 1991. Will paid home care erode informal support? *Journal of Health, Politics, Policy and Law* 16(3):507–21.

Hooyman, N. 1983. Social support networks in services to the elderly. In J. Whittaker and J. Garbarino (eds.), *Informal helping in the human services* (pp. 133–64). Hawthorne, NY: Aldine de Gruyter.

Kempen, G. I., and Suurmeijer, T. P. 1991. Factors influencing professional home care utilization among the elderly. *Social Science and Medicine*, 32(1):77–81.

Litwak, E. 1985. *Helping the elderly: The complementary roles of informal networks and formal systems.* New York: Guilford.

Litwin, H. (ed.) 1996. *The social networks of older people: A cross national analysis.* Westport, CT, and London: Praeger.

_____. 1997. Support network type and health service utilization. *Research on Aging* 19(3):274–99.

_____. 1998. Social network type and health status in a national sample of elderly Israelis. *Social Science and Medicine* 46(4–5):599–609.

_____. 2001. Social network type and morale in old age. *Gerontologist* 41 41(4):516–24.

Logan, J. R., and Spitze G. 1994. Informal support and the use of formal services by older Americans. *Journal of Gerontology: Social Sciences,* 49:S25-S34.

Lubben, J. E. 1988. Assessing social networks among elderly populations. *Journal of Family and Community Health* 8:42–51.

McAully, W. J., and Arling, G. 1984. Use of in-home care by very old people. *Journal of Health and Social Behavior* 25(1):54–64.

Mitchell, J. C. 1969. The concept and use of social networks. In J. C. Mitchell (ed.), *Social networks in urban situations.* London: Manchester University Press.

Morginstin, B., Baich-Moray, S., and Zipkin, A. 1992. Assessment of long-term care needs and the provision of services to the elderly in Israel: The impact of long-term care insurance. *Australian Journal on Ageing* 11(2):16–26.

Mutchler, J. E., and Bullers, S. 1994. Gender differences in formal care use in later life. *Research on Aging*, 16(3):235–50.

Pawlson, L. G. 1989. Financing long-term care: The growing dilemma. *Journal of the American Geriatric Society* 37(7):631–38.

Shapiro, E. 1986. Patterns and predictors of home care by the elderly when need is the sole basis for admission. *Home Health Care Services Quarterly* 71(1):29–44.

Soldo, B. T. 1985. In-home services for the dependent elderly. *Research on Aging* 7:381–94.

Solomon, D. H., Wagner, D. R., Mareberg, M. E., Acampora, D., and Cooney, L. M. 1993. Predictors of formal home health care use in elderly patients after hospitalization. *Journal of American Geriatric Society* 41(9):961–66.

Walker, A. 1987. Enlarging the caring capacity of the community: Informal support networks and the Welfare State. *International Journal of Health Services*, 17(3):369–86.

Wan, T. T. 1987. Functionally disabled elderly: Health status, social support, and use of health services. *Research on Aging* 9:61–78.

Wan, T. T. H., and Odell, B. G. 1981. Factors affecting the use of social and health services among the elderly. *Aging and Society* 1, 95–115.

Wenger, G. C. 1984. *The supportive network: Coping with old age.* London: Allen and Unwin.

_____. 1991. A network typology: From theory to practice. *Journal of Aging Studies*, 5(2):147–62.

_____. 1997. Social networks and the prediction of elderly people at risk. *Aging and Mental Health*, 1(4):311–20.

Wenger, G. C., Scott, A., and Patterson, N. 2000. How important is parenthood? Childlessness and support in old age in England. *Ageing and Society*, 20(2):161–82.

Wilcox, J. A., and Taber, M. A. 1991. Informal helpers of elderly home care clients. *Health and Social Work*, 10(4):258–65.

| 11 |

Family Transfers and Cultural Transmissions Between Three Generations in France

Claudine Attias-Donfut

The contemporary family is multigenerational. Each one of its generations belongs to a specific birth cohort whose destiny was shaped by a particular history, beliefs and values, level of economic growth, and stage of development regarding social welfare policies. This destiny is influenced by the prevailing social conditions encountered at the time of entry into professional life, notably concerning the educational system and the labor market. Successive cohorts do not have at the outset the same possibilities of employment or the same chances of social mobility. Research on cohorts, which represents a key to the understanding of social change (Riley, 1969), shows the evolution of beliefs, political behavior, social structures, and social mobility (e.g., Chauvel, 1998; Inglehart, 1993). It also shows the discontinuity of social destinies according to the period of history through which cohorts live. Family or kinship ties, which bond the cohorts, contribute in shaping the destiny of individuals, and reveal the deep interdependence of the generations (Hagestad, 1986; Hareven, 1996). Numerous research studies undertaken in Western countries (see among others Coenen-Huther, Kellerhals, and Von Allmen, 1994; Crenner, 1998; Lye, 1996; and other studies included in this volume) show the continuous bond between generations and the vitality of their solidarity, despite increasing individualization. What is the cement of such solidarity? What is the specificity of generational relations compared to other fundamental social relations such as class or gender? In line with Mannheim's thinking (1952), whose vision of generations was inspired by his Marxist conception of social classes, class stratification has often been placed in opposition to age or generation stratification, as if these divisions were mutually exclusive. As we know, there is, rather, an articulation between them. Then the question of what is specific to generational relations remains. We would like to contribute to such a debate by emphasizing the temporal dimension of these relations, in which their uniqueness lies. In order to do so, this chapter will analyze the dynamic of generational relations by dealing with economic transfers and cultural transmissions occurring between three generations. This perspective places families as "critical mediators between developing individuals and societies influx" (Hagestad, 2003), as well as the mediators between succeeding generations and those changing societies.

PRESENTATION OF THE TRIGENERATIONAL RESEARCH

Solidarity between generations has been studied using methodologies that entailed three generations. Among the most noteworthy studies are Mangen, Bengtson, and Landry (1988) and Rossi and Rossi (1990). In these studies, lineages are composed of persons from diverse age groups, which means that at a statistical level it is not possible to link a family generation to a social generation defined by birth cohort. The French three-generational study presented here was devised precisely to make this empirical link. It was focused on families comprised of at least three adult generations, anchored in the middle generation, subsequently referred to as the "pivots." A random sample of people aged 49 to 53 years was drawn from the population census in France. The birth cohort of the pivot generation was selected under demographic constraints in such a way as to have, for the majority of them, their children in the process of entering adult life and their parents still alive; this would make it possible to observe family-solidarity practices with the other two generations at key stages in their life courses. A preliminary telephone survey of 10,000 individuals belonging to this cohort aimed at identifying those who had at least one adult child and one living parent in order to constitute the final sample. It revealed that 67 percent had at least one living parent and 60 percent were members of a three-adult-generation family. Respondents provided the addresses of one of their parents and one of their adult children, who were then interviewed. In the end, about 5,000 individuals were interviewed.[1] By definition, all of the respondents were part of a three-adult-generation family, and many of them belonged to a four-generation family (45 percent of the pivots and 66 percent of their parents, the older generation). The methodology therefore allowed the same comprehensive questions to be put to a "pivot" generation member, a parent and an adult child, all of whom belonged to the same family. This sample had a feature that is of capital importance to the theoretical import and the objectives of the research: that is, a method for delimiting and defining the observed generations, which made it possible to operationalize the notion of generation in its various meanings, and to study private and public interactions.

At the Crossroads of Historical Generations, Family Generations, and "Welfare" Generations

All individuals have several, simultaneous generational identities: in reference to their position in the family, to their relationship to work and to the welfare state, and to their historical situation. These affiliations change as life progresses, and they make up a significant whole that has to be considered in all of its dimensions when examining intergenerational relations. This was made possible by the procedure used in this survey to isolate the three generations. By starting with the middle generation, selected from a cohort with a limited age variation, two other generations, the parents and the children, were defined within a relatively restricted age range: The pivots' parents, making up the older generation, are an average age of 77, with over 60 percent of them 72 to 82. The younger respondents were even more strongly concentrated within an age span: 80 percent were 19 to 29, and they ranged from age 19 to 36. For 80 percent of them, their children, that is, the pivots' grandchildren, were under 6 years of age (with the outstanding exception of one 19-year-old, whose grandfather, 52, had become a father at 14).

The age ranges in which the different generations are set, as well as their relative homogeneity, place them in a consistent relationship to work and social welfare: the younger generation at the start of their working life, the pivots at the peak of their working life, and the large majority of the older generation retired and exposed to the possibility of losing their physical abilities. They form three distinct *welfare generations,* according to the definition given by Martin Kohli (1996).

Each of these three generations has specific, identifiable historical experiences, clearly differentiated from one generation to the next. They form three distinct cohorts or historical generations, in the Mannheimian meaning. For some scholars, it is preferable to reserve the term "birth cohort" for this meaning and to apply "generation" only to family generations (Bengtson and Achenbaum, 1993; Kertzer, 1983; Marshall, 1983; Ryder, 1965). But I will apply the concept of generation to the social and historical context as well as the familial, thus enriching the symbolic import of the word, associating it to social change.[2]

The combination of the birth-reference cohort and the filiations proceeding from this cohort makes it possible to isolate within the population three generations that can be simultaneously defined, each in its position relative to the other two, in terms of the family, the sociohistorical context and the public-solidarity point of reference. On the basis of this construction, generational processes may therefore be studied in several of their interrelated dimensions, and particularly in an analysis of the interface between private and public spheres and that of social change interacting with family relations. In addition to this quantitative survey, a qualitative survey[3] was done on a subsample of thirty lineages, including ninety in-depth interviews with one member from each generation in each family. This study dealt with questions related to family relationships, transmissions, and exchanges between generations, as well as family history, gifts and reciprocity, norms, and values, among other themes.

Characteristics of the Three Generations

The members of the oldest generation (G1) had been mostly retired before the legal retirement age in France was brought down to the age of sixty (in 1982). The great majority of them therefore had long working lives, which took place during the so-called *trente glorieuses,* the thirty-year period between 1945 and 1975, which was characterized by continuous growth and nearly full employment. This is especially true for the men, as there tended to be more discontinuity in women's work. Their pensions constitute the essential part of their income, which is relatively modest compared to the income of younger retirees, but they are often, though very unevenly, complemented by an inheritance. No other generation before or after them will have had such a long working life characterized by full employment and the regular glorification of work. They could thus be called the *generation of labor.*

This *generation of labor* gave birth to a much wealthier generation, which is among those that got the most out of economic growth, full employment, and the increase in consumption: the pivot generation, which we could call the *generation of abundance,* whose income and inheritance are much larger than their parents' generation, receive less benefits from social transfers.

Its children, the young in our sample, spent their childhood in economic prosperity and were entering adult life in a period of recession with a shrinking labor market, where small jobs and precarious work constitute the narrow corridor into their working lives. They have a high level of education, much higher than their parents and *a fortiori* than their grandparents. Those who entered the labor market had, on average, a higher income than their grandparents but smaller than their parents. In the family, they are characterized by their late departure from the parental home. Thus, the generation of abundance is followed by a generation *under protection.* The image that might come to mind for it is a *kangaroo generation.* When looking

Table 11.1   Feelings of Social Accomplishment Compared with Parents

Feelings of social accomplishment compared with parents	Heading one	Heading two	Heading three
Greater (%)	59.3	59.9	32.6
Lesser (%)	5.3	5.6	8.3
Equal (%)	26.8	28.4	41.9

at the way the young define the main historical events that have marked their generation, they appear rather disenchanted. For the media, which emphasizes the magnitude of the difficulties involved in becoming part of the adult world, they are the *galley*[4] *generation*.

SOCIAL AND GEOGRAPHICAL CONTEXT OF THE RELATIONS

Before analyzing transmissions and transfers between these generations, some aspects of the contexts of their relations are described below, including social mobility, geographical distance, relational intensity—involving the frequency of contacts and family leisure activities—and the evolution of the relations after divorces and separations.

Social Mobility

Intergenerational social mobility is an important element in intergenerational relations and exchanges, the direction and content of which is partly conditioned by it. The next part of this chapter shows the significant influence of social mobility both in cultural transmissions and economic transfers between generations. Social mobility is made up of several elements: education level, life style, professional standing, and income compared to father's, mother's, paternal grandparents', and maternal grandparents'. A first approximation of it is established here on the basis of the subjective feeling of social success with respect to parents as it is expressed by the respondents of the two generations involved. This information turns out to be only partially relevant. For example, a comparison of the professional category of the respondent and his or her father's shows a positive correlation (see Table 11.1).

The same proportion of the elders to their own parents as that of the pivots to the elders demonstrates a strong feeling of social promotion. Each of the two generations experienced successive periods of strong growth during which the structure of the working population changed and generated a structural intergenerational mobility.

Table 11.2   Geographic Proximity of the Generations (Percentage of Total Number of Families)

	Same district	Same department	Same region[a]
Pivot-Young (N = 1.493)	32.8	65.2	76.8
Pivot-Elder (N = 1.217)	31	66.6	77.3
Young-Elder (N = 995)	18.4	51.9	64.2
Young-Pivots-Elder (N = 995)	14.5	49.2	62.3

[a]More or less the equivalent of an American state, comprising an average of four departments.

The results are different for the young, far fewer of whom position themselves higher than their parents on the social scale, and are not considered as such by the latter. Of course, they are still at the beginning of their careers, and these results testify more to their plans and perspectives as to actual situations. Such appraisals are also a reflection of the slow-down in growth and the restriction in future prospects.

Geographic Distance

In most cases, the three generations live close to each other, especially the elders and the pivots (see Table 11.2). The geographic distance between the pivots and their children living separately is somewhat larger than between the pivots and their parents. Among the elders, 49 percent have a child living less than one kilometer away and 90 percent at least one child less than fifty kilometers away; and if we consider all of their children (the pivots and their brothers and sisters), 63 percent of them live less than fifty kilometers away. The distance between the pivots and their children who have left home is greater, the latter two percentages being 69 and 56 percent, respectively. The three generations live in the same municipal district in 14 percent of the families and in the same department (more or less the French equivalent of a British or an American county) in almost half of them. In the generational topography, the pivots occupy a central position: They are close both to their parents and their children, the latter two generations living farther away from each other.

Measurement and Variations of Relational Intensity

To measure relational intensity, we built an index combining the frequency of the contacts, the leisure activities practiced together, and the holidays taken together, estimated for each of the generations in its relations

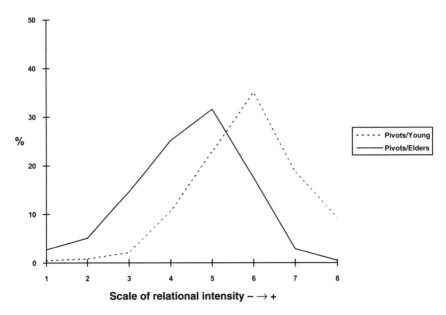

Figure 11.1 Comparison of relational intensity between Pivots/young and
Pivots/elders.

to the other two, not including those living together. Wherever relevant, the
relational intensity with the parents-in-law was also measured. Results
show that the pivots' households have much more frequent and varied
relations with their children than with their parents (Figure 11.1), and that
among their ascendants, the maternal lineage was given more importance
than the paternal lineage. They are somewhat closer, geographically, to the
woman's parents, and when the distance from the man's parents is equal
to that of the woman's, relational intensity is still greater with the latter.
Other factors can also interfere in these relations. For instance, when there
is upward mobility with respect to the parents, the intensity of the relations
is slightly less than with the parents-in-law. This suggests that of the two
lineages, the household favors the one with a higher social standing. The
intensity of the relations is therefore also a factor of social proximity, but not
very markedly. Professional categories do not appear to be discriminating
factors in relational intensity.

The stronger links between the pivots and their children compared to
those between themselves and their parents are confirmed by the answers
to the question, "Who would you call on first if you needed anything?"
When leaving the spouse aside, who in all generations is usually mentioned first, the pivots name their children as their main resort to meet a

Table 11.3   Differences between Generations

| | The generational difference is greater | | | |
As reported by	With parents	With children	No answer	Total
Elders (%)	38.8	54.9	7.3	100
Pivots (%)	58.7	38.8	2.5	100

practical or a emotional need, and their parents when the need is of a financial nature. The younger generation, by a large majority, say they would call on their parents to respond to needs relating to financial or health matters, and in cases of emotional problems, they name both their parents and their friends as recourses, primarily the former, and exceptionally mention their maternal grandparents. As for the elders, their first recourse for any type of need is always their children.

Elders turn to their children, who also turn more to their own children than to their parents, with some reciprocity on the part of the young to their parents. How will the young behave when their own children are adults? We can assume that they will then in turn redirect their solicitation to their children, following the pattern of generational stake according to which parents count more on their adult children than the latter do on the former (Bengtson and Kuypers, 1971).

This general trend in the evolution of parent-child relations during adult life varies in strength according to the historical period. The two ascendant generations do not fit into the generational sequence in the same way, the elders having been closer to their parents than their children are to them. To some extent, the pivot generation, who were young during the 1960s, broke with the previous family models, introducing far more radical changes than the previous generations had done, or for that matter, than the following generation has. The historical fracture of the 1960s and the 1970s is reflected in the intergenerational differences as they are perceived by the respective generations. The elders feel they have more differences with their children than with their parents, refuting the generational stake, while adults in their 50s feel they have less differences with their children than with their parents (see Table 11.3). This trend is accentuated among women, who went through more radical changes in their roles and therefore created a more fundamental rupture with their mothers' patterns.

Marriage Breakdowns and Relations between Generations

The instability of married life, the rising number of divorces and separations as well as of single-parent and reconstituted families, and the decreasing number of marriages, are often declared to affect the strength of intergenerational relations. In the Parsonian theory, the nuclear family, by withdrawing into the marriage unit, has loosened its bonds with the extended family, and therefore with the other generations. According to an opposite hypothesis, there would be an inverse relationship between the importance of marriage bonds and that of filiation bonds. Intergenerational relations would represent the very axis of family stability, having supposedly been reinforced precisely as a result of the weakening of marital bonds. These two propositions are both based on the assumption that marriage and filiation stand in competition, which remains to be proven.

Relations between divorced parents and their young children have been extensively studied. The French divorce rate today is higher than 30 percent, but the proportion of children of divorced couples is lower: In 1990, 15 percent of children under 19 did not live with both of their "biological parents" (or considered as such, for instance, in case of adoption) (Desplanques, 1993). In 90 percent of the cases, the mother was present, and there is often disinvolvement on the part of the father. One-fourth of the children in this situation never see one of their parents, usually the father (Meulders-Klein and Théry, 1993).

What happens to the children's relations with each of their separated parents once the former have become adults? What about their relations with their grandparents? This is a rather complicated question because of the great diversity of the situations and of their constant evolution over time. To get a general idea and identify the prevailing trend, the relations among the three adult generations were differentiated according to whether a separation in the parent couple had taken place, regardless of when the separation took place. The results do not in any way confirm that intergenerational bonds are strengthened to compensate for the couple's disassociation. On the contrary, it appears that there is relatively more distance between generations in these situations. In the pivot generation, divorced women or men have less intense relations with their children than married women or men, the difference in the marriage status being, however, much less of a factor among the women than among the men (see Figures 11.2 and 11.3).

Divorce not only affects relations with the children, it also has consequences for relations with ascendants: Relations with grandparents tend to taper off significantly, while with parents, there is only a mild added distance. This loosening of bonds can be explained by a variety of reasons, among which are parental disapproval, or the constitution of a new, nonlegalized couple (17.8 percent of divorced women and 45.6 percent of divorced men live with someone out of wedlock). Relational problems with children could also be due to other, less manifest phenomena, such as greater marriage difficulties within the parent couple: Among divorced women in their fifties, there is a much greater proportion whose parents

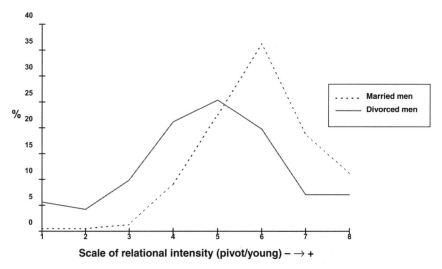

Figure 11.2 Comparison of relational intensity to their children among married and divorced men.

were divorced or separated when they were children (29.5 percent) than among those whose parents remained together (11.6 percent). This is also true for men (21 and 9.7 percent, respectively). Similarly, a childhood experience of parental dissension seems to increase the probability of a later divorce: 23 percent of the women and 24.6 percent of the men whose parents "did not get along" were divorced in the course of their life, in contrast to 11 and 9.7 percent, respectively, in the absence of declared parental discord. Parental influence on the chances of divorce is confirmed when the yardstick is no longer parental divorce or dissension, but whether the parents have been part of a couple more than once. Oddly enough, the three generations produce the same proportion: Some 13 percent of the elders, the pivots, and the young have had at least two marriage experiences. Of course, the young cannot be compared to their ascendants, as they are at the beginning of their family trajectory, but the pivots and the elders are more comparable, given that their chances of constituting a new couple are limited. Divorce is actually taking place among people of all ages, though at different rates, and the divorce index, which we know is increasing, leads to an underestimation among the general opinion of marriage instability in the older generations and to an overestimation of it in the younger ones. A certain measure of transmissibility of marriage instability can be inferred.

Divorces or separations have different effects on intergenerational relations, depending on whether or not they are followed by new unions.

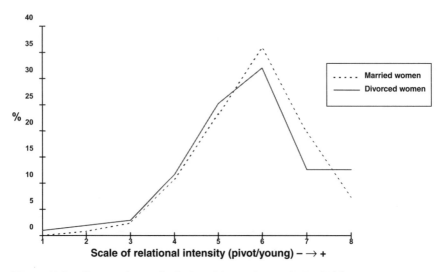

Figure 11.3   Comparison of relational intensity to their children among married and divorced women.

Among the elders, when there has been more than one marital union, relations with the children, as well as with the grandchildren, are somewhat looser; the same is true for the pivots, as much in their relations to their parents as to their children. When a new couple is not formed, things are slightly different: Single women, especially widows, have slightly more intense relations with their parents and their children than women who are part of a couple. Women resort to several means to adjust to being alone, and in certain cases they go back to living with their parents. Elderly parents thus go back to living with their children significantly more often with their divorced or widowed daughters. By contrast, men who have lost their spouse tend to loosen their relations with their children as well as with their parents, and rarely go back to living with their parents, while men who have remained single (and without any children) tend not to leave their parents' residence more than women with the same status.

Single men and single women of the pivot generation place more value on their relations with friends than those living as a couple. In answer to the question, "Generally speaking, do you maintain more relations with your family or your friends?" 51 percent of women who are part of a couple and 41 percent of single women mention the family, 11 and 20.5 percent, respectively, mention friends, the remainder declaring them to be equivalent. Only 27.7 percent of single men mention the family, in contrast to 47.8 percent of men who are part of a couple. These statements by members of the pivot generation confirm the family-centering role played by the marriage unit. This role is also confirmed by the fact that the elder and younger generations are less family-oriented because they are more often living alone.

As for the young, their relations with their disunited parents are often difficult, conflicted, or even broken off. Half of those who experienced their parents' separation express problems with one or the other, or with both. Many tell of changes in their relationships to their parents since the separation, with breakup and resumption periods, or changes in feelings toward the mother or the father.

The marital relationship does not compete with the intergenerational bond—on the contrary, it activates it. Only new unions following a breakup might partially distract the partners from their filiation bonds and compete with them. The dissolution of a marriage unit, when no new couple is formed, leads to very diverse situations in which extra-family relations enter more into competition, leading in turn to less turning toward the family, as much with men as with women. The current fragility of couples certainly does not destroy the filiation bond, but it definitely affects it and tends to dilute into a sociability that is less exclusively family-centered. This underscores the importance of the couple in the contemporary family, not only within the nuclear family, but also in the relations between generations, in which it is a catalyst.

THE MAIN FLOWS OF TRANSFERS

The Perceived Gift and the Actual Gift

When shifting the focus of the analysis from the relations among generations to the exchanges among them, a question arises: What are we referring to when speaking of solidarity, gift, and exchange? This is a vast theoretical question; however, it is also a specific research and methodology issue. Whatever is passed on between generations is evaluated on the basis of what is said to be given to the other and received from it, whether it is services, money, or goods. The same questions were put to the three generations, and we expected to find discrepancies in the answers that might indicate a different relationship to the act of giving than to that of receiving. Certain studies assume, for instance, that there is a tendency to lessen the value of what is received and to heighten the value of what is given, especially by parents to their children (De Singly, 1993; Stoller, 1985). The results only partially confirm this assumption, but they raise another fundamental problem.

What do we find? If we consider each generation separately, we observe, for most types of exchanges, remarkably concurring proportions of donors in one generation and receivers in the corresponding generation. For instance, 20.9 percent of the elders made a gift to their children and in

89 percent of the cases, it was equally distributed among all the children. Among the pivots, 19.9 percent say they received a gift from their parents. The results are in perfect conformity when comparing two generations as a whole, but things get complicated when we compare the answers given by the two generations by lineage. Then the correspondence only applies to part of the families. Thus, in the preceding example, the donors' answers agree with the receivers' only in 82.5 percent of the cases, and there are as many gifts made and not declared as received, as gifts received and not declared as made (i.e., close to 9 percent).

Another example is the help in shopping given by the pivots to their parents. When we limit the observation to single children in order to make sure that the parent's declaration regarding the help he or she receives from his or her child necessarily refers to the respondent pivot, and excluding cohabitation situations, we get the following results: 46.8 percent of the elders declare that their son or daughter helps them do the shopping, and 46 percent of the pivots declare that they help their parents with the shopping. Once again, the results concur almost totally. But when considering the results by family, a gap appears: in 16.4 percent of the families, the parents declare they get help while the children declare that they do not give it, and for 15.6 percent, on the contrary, the parents do not say they get help with the shopping while the children assure that they give it.

The following example relates to another type of exchange, gifts in kind made up of a variety of objects that the parents receive from the children (again, in cases of single children) outside of Christmas or birthday presents: 19.4 percent of the children declare they give such objects and 18.8 percent of the parents declare they receive them. These overall results are very close, showing a mere 0.6 percent difference. But the discrepancies by family in this area are significant. In 12.7 percent of the families, the pivots say they give their parents gifts, which are not reported by the latter, and in 13.4 percent of them, the pivots' children state they give things without their parents' mentioning their having received them. In all, only 6 percent of the pivot-parent dyads jointly declare the existence of these exchanges and 67.8 percent declare their absence.

This same pattern is repeated fairly regularly in many types of exchanges: it does not depend on specific types of pairs, since it is found among the three generations taken by twos, among the men as well as the women. The intrafamily discrepancy is less, but does not disappear altogether, when the service occurs "often" (as opposed to occasionally), as well as when there is reciprocity. This statistical regularity leads us to infer the existence of a general pattern, which is related to the very nature of a gift within families. The gift is a constituent element of the relationship and tends to be confused with it. The altruistic behavior that we, as observers, attempt to pinpoint, quantify, and even measure in terms of its economic value is, from the point of view of the people concerned, often spontaneous or obvious behavior that is not naturally differentiated from the relation itself.

According to Marcel Mauss (1923[1960]), gifts are materialized in the things, gifts, and presents that are passed from one person to another. The power of these things commands that a gift must necessarily be accepted, and returned later. In the new theoretical approach to gifts, exchanges of gifts are understood in a broader sense, the defining feature being essentially that they are not business dealings. Gifts are everywhere (Godbout, 2000); they are material or immaterial, ranging from the object offered, to words, or even a look or a smile. Their object is the transaction itself, in a sort of evidence that need not be specified.

One can wonder at what point a gift can be said to take place, and for whom—the observer, the donor, or the receiver. The somewhat disconcerting results obtained by comparing reports by the giver and the receiver, the fact that the thing or the act might not only have been given without being perceived by the receiver, but also received without having been perceived by the giver, forces us to make a distinction between the fact and the perception of it, the actual exchange and the perceived exchange.

The identification by those concerned of a gift in the relation implies a series of mental operations: feeling it, being aware of it, abstracting it from the relationship, and symbolizing it as a distinct element. When the exchange does not take place within a ritual, such as with Christmas presents or at family events where it is institutionalized by tradition, when it is part of daily life and its routine, the social references to support a cognitive elaboration such as this are absent. As a result, the gift is only partially perceived, which does not necessarily question the position of the donor or the receiver. Surveys only measure that which has been objectivized and expressed, the exchange that has been perceived by either or both of the people involved. This perceived exchange is only the visible part of an actual, much broader and more indiscernible exchange.

On the basis of this analysis, we considered the actual circulation between two people to cover any good or service declared as having been either given by one person or received by the other. Therefore, a more complete evaluation of the main exchange flows can be obtained by combining the answers given by the different generations.

Exchanges of Money, Time, and Home-Related Help

The following analyses mainly focus on the circulation of financial transfers and in-kind services (time transfers) between the three generations. They do not refer to the whole range of solidarity dimensions as defined by Roberts, Richards, and Bengtson (1991). The limits of measuring instrumental transfers within the family are often emphasized by sociologists and economists, but though the results undoubtedly give rise to an underestimated picture of private assistance, they show a large circulation of transfers among the three generations. The combination of responses simultaneously received from three generations of the same family makes possible a more realistic measurement of the different forms of support. When the data are presented in this way, among grandparents (the older generation) 33 percent give money to their adult children and 30 percent give money to their grandchildren (the younger generation). In total, almost one in two older people (49 percent) give money to either their adult children or grandchildren. As far as the pivot generation is concerned, the proportion of donor households is 64 percent for financial help to children and 9 percent for financial help to their parents. In contrast to these downward financial transfers, services are widely distributed between each generation, both downward and upward. For example, 89 percent of pivots provide at least one domestic service to their parents, and 49 percent of the older generation offer time assistance to their midlife children.

Figure 11.4 represents the total of these exchanges by distinguishing money transfers on one side and all kinds of services (time transfers) on the other and by combining the generations' declarations taken by pairs. There is no overall discrepancy between what the elderly declare as giving their children and what the pivots declare as getting from their parents. And almost as many of the pivots declare they provide their parents with one or more services as those elderly parents declaring they get one or more services from their children. By contrast, 77 percent of the young declare they provide their parents with one or more services, while only 60 percent of the parents declare getting them from their children. It can be assumed that the reciprocity of the young with regard to their parents is at stake in their relations; that it is probably a more-or-less latent point of contention or zone of conflict, finding expression in this discrepancy between the answers.

These results demonstrate some overall trends, which are both striking and significant. Private transfers among generations go in the opposite direction of the transfers of public resources that take place through the retirement pension system. This shows the existence of a circular mechanism generated by both the money flows from the elderly retirees to their children and by those that skip a generation from grandparents to adult grandchildren who have begun to face the world of labor.

The support provided by the family to a needy member is affected by public welfare policies. Social benefits do not crowd out family help, but on the contrary family support is stimulated by the possibility of receiving complementary public support. Our research has shown that the more the state provides support for a family member, the more support that mem-

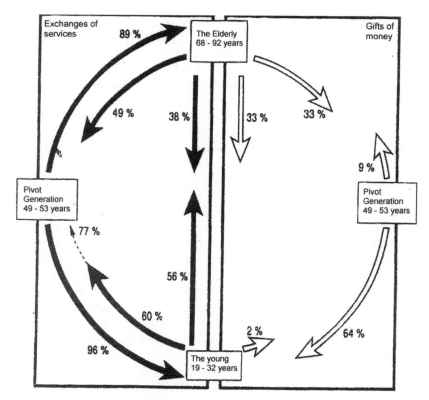

Example : 9 % of the pivot generation give money to their parents, and 64 % give money to their children.

Figure 11.4 Solidarity between three generations.

ber receives from his or her family (Attias-Donfut and Wolff, 2000). In addition, the impact of welfare benefits is not only a quantitative one, but also affects the quality of relations, the status of each generation, and the direction of the flow of transfers. A study done in Guadeloupe (Attias-Donfut and Lapierre, 2001) showed that the introduction of a generous system of social security has maintained and transformed family ties: In the span of one generation the conception of the child as a resource whose work served to support the family was transformed through the welfare state into the modern conception of a child, that is, as an investment for the future through education and prolonged studies. At the same time the economic status of the elderly changed as well. They used to be provided for by their children; they are now able to contribute financially to the well-being of the family. In this way, the norms of respect for the elderly, which always existed as a survival of African culture, could be maintained on a new basis.

The result is an inversion in the flow of family transfers, from formerly being directed toward the elderly to now being directed toward the young.

When the welfare state distributes social benefits, it also distributes through the same channels a set of values and representations that have a profound effect on family values and family life. It presents to the society a model of the generational contract, a strong symbol, having repercussions throughout. The welfare system in itself is able to create social bonds, even though each system is shaped by the cultural traditions of each society, as pointed out by Esping-Andersen (1990).

Care for Grandchildren versus Care for Elderly Parents

Half of the middle generation are grandparents. These young grandparents provide important help to their adult children by looking after their grandchildren. Two out of three give care (that is they spend time with their grandchildren in the absence of the parents)—whether on a regular basis or occasionally—during the entire year and also often during vacations. In addition, 18 percent of grandparents give care solely during vacations. In sum, 82 percent of grandparents provide some form of care to a grandchild. Help given by this group of young grandparents is more intensive than the help that was given in the past by the two previous generations[5] (Figure 11.5).

Figure 11.5 represents the amount of help received by young parents today compared to the help that their parents and grandparents received when their offspring were at an early age. An increase in the probability of being helped for the last generation is clear.

The main factors that explain such help have been evaluated by a regression analysis including both the characteristics of grandparents and the characteristics of young parents (Attias-Donfut and Wolff, 2000). The probability of childcare is the same whether the grandparent is employed or not. But the amount of time given is lower for employed grandparents. Concurrently, grandparenting is mainly directed toward full-time employed young mothers who need more help to look after their own progeny. It is noticeable that the employment participation of the young is more decisive than the paid employment of grandmothers regarding the existence of this type of care. Grandmothers in general arrange to spend time with their grandchildren whether they work or not. In addition, *this help is mainly given to young adults characterized by a higher social status than their parents.* The probability of the care of grandchildren increases by almost 7.6 percentage points in this case, while young respondents who consider that they have a lower social status than their parents receive significantly less informal assistance in the form of child care, with a fall of 11.6 percentage points. Generally, grandparents are closer to their daughters than to their

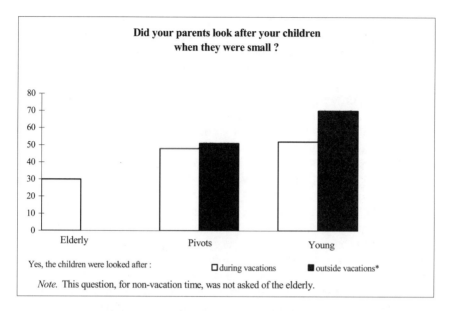

Figure 11.5 Comparison of help received by three generations from their parents in the care of their small children.

sons. This finding confirms the dominance of the female lineage, which highlights the privileged mother-daughter bond in families. Moreover, since this help benefits mostly young mothers, it is an expression of female intergenerational solidarity oriented to the promotion of the professional career for the new generation of women. This solidarity oriented toward the conquest of work did not exist in previous generations. It is the main factor in the increasing help given by grandmothers, despite the improvement of child care public systems in France.

Additionally, support is regularly provided to elders suffering from a handicap by 32 percent of the pivots and 6.6 percent of the young. The services of the pivot generation, in its role as a link, are significantly called upon by the other two generations. Since in these families generational age differences are not very large, loss of autonomy for the parents of this hinge-generation does not occur until the children have become adults and had children of their own, thus setting their grandparent role in competition with their role as helpers to their aging parents. Numerous studies have shown that women are more involved than men in caregiving to dependent parents. The role of caring is mainly ascribed to women. Even when men are involved in the support of their elderly parents, the kind of activities and care they give is different from that given by women. For example, they give less physical care, and support tends to be centered on activities such as shopping and banking. In addition, the act of caring for the elderly, according to the responses of caregivers, causes less emotional difficulty for men than for women.

Older women have more needs and greater levels of disability than men. Living alone is much more common for older women than for men, because women tend to marry men who are older and because women's life expectancy is longer. Women also receive more financial help from their children because of the lower level of pensions they receive in widowhood. Older women represent a larger percentage of the recipients of assistance than men. Therefore, caring (from both the caregiver's and the care receiver's perspective) appears to be mainly a female activity. In contrast with financial gifts, time-related assistance is not affected by differences in the donor's economic resources. In fact, most of the variables (except the geographical distance separating the generations) exert no significant impact on the probability of such help, which suggests that upstream transfers to older generations are associated with strong norms of obligation. This also probably affects the lack of substitutes for family support in the marketplace since the family provides an affectional solidarity (Bengtson, 1975) which can scarcely be replaced by a professional.[5]

While time transfers do not depend on the education level or the economic resources of older generation members, they do appear mainly directed toward elderly people with poor health who also receive some form of professional help. The lower their income, the more support they receive, and the support rate decreases from 50 percent among the first quartile of income to 21 percent among the fourth quartile. Again, upstream transfers are rooted in an intergenerational redistributive process of familial resources. Moreover, the empirical results show that elders who themselves cared for their own parents in the past are characterized by a greater probability of receipt of help from their own children.

Monetary Transfers

The importance of the circulation of money within the family demonstrates that the economic function has not disappeared from the modern family. In addition, the circulation of money also reveals some aspects of the dynamics of the generational bond. The following data include specific monetary gifts or loans that have taken place during the preceding five years and regularly *allocated* allowances. They do not include inheritances, and do not therefore fully account for all monetary flows. The determinants of family financial help have been analyzed using an econometric analysis, including both characteristics of the donors and of the receivers in Attias-Donfut and Wolff (2000). The uniqueness of our data makes possible an analysis including the income and the assets of each household. The following is a summary of the results.

Financial transfers from pivots are mainly directed toward well-educated noncoresident adult children. Having completed graduate or postgraduate studies is associated with an increased probability of the receipt of financial transfers by 12.3 and 14.5 percentage points, respectively. Financial gifts also are more often provided by higher-educated parents, and the results argue in favor of transfers expressed as human capital investments. The latter are more frequent in families characterized by a low number of children, and they are more often directed toward young female respondents.

In contrast with the redistribution of income, gifts and donations from the elderly to the pivots ensure the transmission of wealth between generations and are made later in the life cycle. In France, most of the donations are made by farmers and, to a lesser degree, by the self-employed, so as to give their professional assets to their children, even though they are made partially due to tax evasion incentives

Parental and child resources affect the pattern of downward cash gifts. In both cases, the diffusion of transfers is more likely to be directed from rich donors to poor recipients. A rise in the pivot's income or wealth significantly increases the probability of financial parental support. Conversely, the receipt of transfers is more frequent when they are directed toward children with a low level of resources (in terms of income and wealth). The results appear rather different when elderly-pivot pairs are examined, since the level of donor resources exerts no significant influence on the probability of gifts. The underlying transmission of wealth may explain the lack of significance for the income variable. *Inter vivos* donations and gifts from the older generation have redistributive effects and these transfers are higher for pivots with lower earnings.

Intergenerational social mobility has an impact on familial transfers. This intergenerational comparison gives information about the existence of two specific channels of redistribution within the extended family. Concerning young adults, individuals who expect to be at a lower social level of success compared to their parents are characterized by a greater probability of gift receipt, with 9.7 additional percentage points. Thus, private transfers to the young generation often act against descent mobility. In the same way, pivots who perceive a better position than their parents receive less in the way of financial transfers, with a fall of 6.6 percentage points.

Assistance from parents to children therefore seems the most widely used redistributive network within the family in France, a result attributable to the specific division of economic resources between the three coexisting generations. The trigenerational survey also indicates the existence of upstream transfers benefiting the older generation, with young adults providing very limited support to their parents. Middle-aged adults use two different types of assistance in order to improve the well-being of their parents, namely, financial support and the provision of services.

Financial support is mostly provided by rich pivots (as indicated by the positive effect of their level of income), and the probability of a gift is also higher when the donor is a middle manager and above. Financial difficulties encountered by donors in their youth give rise to an increased probability of upstream assistance, such that pivots who suffered in the past from financial difficulties have the desire to help their own parents in return. The intention to improve the financial position of recipients is also captured by the variable related to subjective social mobility. The probability of gifts slightly increases when middle-aged adults have a better social position compared to their parents, although the effect is insignificant at the 5 percent level. The results also show a gender gap in intergenerational assistance to parents. Men give financial help more often than women, whereas women more often give time-related and hands-on help, a finding that reflects the implicit gender contract.

Home-Related Exchanges

The importance of family mobilization around the place of residence has been underscored in many studies. Our data demonstrate that the development of home ownership is largely due to intergenerational assistance. These results have enabled us to observe this assistance regarding each generation: intergenerational solidarity in home-related matters is nothing new since in the elder generation, 43 percent benefited from a family contribution. And if we consider only those who own their main residence or some other real estate, 80 percent of them were helped in acquiring their property essentially by their ascendants through direct assistance, gift, or inheritance. Naturally, inheritance plays a greater role for this generation than for the descending generations, who have not yet fully benefited from their inheritance. As stated earlier, decapitalization is especially found among farmers and farmers' sons. Those who are still property owners are mainly executives, children of executives, and independent professionals. In this older generation, property was more limited to specific professional groups. It was not yet the status symbol among wage-earners that it was to become in the following generation.

Property ownership is greater among pivots than among the other two generations. Half of them received no contribution from their family. The development of property ownership in this generation was promoted by easy access to credit, inflation, and a variety of property-ownership incentives. Among the young, 76 percent of those owning property or in the process of become property owners benefited from a family contribution, essentially from the ascendant generations, mostly parents and parents-in-law, followed by grandparents. Home-related assistance is not limited to home ownership: much help is also provided to non–property owners in the form of accommodation, making a home available, and rental assistance. Many of the young, the least proportion of which are owners, receive these forms of assistance: 34 percent of those renting homes have been helped in one way or another, and 4 percent live in a home owned by their parents. In total, 44 percent of the younger generation who have left their parents' home have benefited from some form of housing assistance.

Time Giving and Reciprocity between Generations

The preceding results have shown that the circulation of money, goods, and assets within families flows mainly downward from the elder generations to the younger, unlike domestic and social services, or real time given by family members to each other, which circulate in both directions. We will now examine to what extent these transfers and help are reciprocal. In Table 11.4 we distinguish between three main kinds of transfers within the family. Financial help, including money given or lent, regularly or occasionally; domestic help including activities linked to cleaning and maintaining the house and caring for individuals; and social help, including doing administrative paperwork, banking, educational, or professional help, which implies that the giver has the "social capital" required, according to the expression of Pierre Bourdieu (1979). This table does not include help with residency (coresidency or any help given in securing a residence). The above transfers all have an economic dimension at their base and vary according to the social milieu and available resources. The biggest service dispensers are the pivots, in favor of both the young and the elders, but more to the young. Table 11.4 shows the frequency of reciprocity for the different kinds of services according to the generations and to the social status of the respondents. In every social category the domestic exchanges between the pivot and younger generation are largely reciprocal and balanced. Help between pivot and elderly parents follows another dynamic. There is no reciprocity, but the direction of transfers vary according to the kind of help required. For example, the pivot generation gives more domestic and social help than it receives but the elderly parents give more financial help. In this case, reciprocity does exist in the exchanges between these two generations, but each one has a different contribution to make. The exchanges between the two extreme generations—that is, the elderly and the younger generation—follow the same pattern. The young mainly give domestic services and the elderly give money or other kinds of gifts. But these transfers are less developed. The fact is that in one out of five families there are no exchanges whatsoever between them.

The norms of these transfers vary according to the social categories and the priority that is given either to the ascending or descending generation. For instance, the young receive more help of every kind in the upper classes while the elderly receive domestic support more often in the lower classes. It has been shown that these priorities are also culturally deter-

Table 11.4 Reciprocity in Exchanges Between Generations (%)

| | Occupational status of pivots | | | | | | | | | | | | |
| | Farmers | | Craftsmen, tradesmen, & small businessmen | | Middle managers | | Intermediate professionals | | Employees | | Workers | | Total | |
Exchanges with	Young	Elders	Young	Elders	Young	Elders	Young	Elders	Young	Elders	Young	Elders	Young	Elders
Domestic support														
Given & received	73.7	36.2	83.7	36.5	75.4	29.7	80.5	30.6	82.9	27.9	80.7	21.4	80.2	28.9
Given without receiving	10.5	56.9	7.1	49.0	15.2	47.8	10.9	51.4	10.4	55.5	14.4	64.8	12.2	54.7
Received without giving	13.2	5.2	7.1	3.1	6.5	8.7	4.8	6.1	3.9	4.7	3.7	3.8	5.0	5.2
Neither given nor received	2.6	1.7	2.0	11.5	2.9	13.8	3.8	11.9	2.9	11.9	1.2	10.0	2.6	11.2
Social forms of support														
Given & received	56.6	3.4	27.6	3.1	9.4	2.2	15.0	1.8	17.9	1.5	13.2	1.4	18.4	1.9
Given without receiving	22.4	62.1	53.1	53.1	77.5	55.8	59.4	57.9	56.3	62.0	52.3	62.9	56.3	59.1
Received without giving	13.2	8.6	7.1	2.1	2.2	3.6	4.1	2.9	3.6	0.6	7.8	0.5	5.3	2.1
Neither given nor received	7.9	25.9	12.2	41.7	10.9	38.4	21.5	37.4	22.2	35.9	26.7	35.2	20.0	37.0
Financial support														
Given & received	10.5	3.4	4.1	1.0	4.3	5.1	5.5	3.6	4.6	1.5	5.3	1.9	5.2	2.6
Given without receiving	43.4	10.3	66.3	8.3	83.3	8.7	66.9	5.8	52.9	5.3	53.9	4.8	59.6	6.2
Received without giving	3.9	19.0	5.1	31.3	0.7	37.7	1.4	30.9	1.9	30.3	1.6	27.6	2.3	30.4
Neither given nor received	42.1	67.2	24.5	59.4	11.6	48.6	26.3	59.7	40.6	62.9	39.1	65.7	32.9	60.8
All forms of support														
Given & received	92.1	48.3	91.8	55.2	82.6	54.3	86.7	48.6	86.0	44.5	86.0	38.6	86.2	46.8
Given without receiving	5.3	46.6	8.2	33.3	16.7	26.8	11.6	35.3	12.3	41.2	13.2	50.5	12.5	39.2
Received without giving	2.6	3.4	—	3.1	—	12.3	1.0	8.6	1.2	8.9	0.8	5.7	0.9	7.9
Neither given nor received	—	1.7	—	8.3	0.7	6.5	0.7	7.6	0.5	5.3	—	5.2	0.4	6.0

Base: Excluding cohabitants.

mined through cross-cultural comparisons. The differences are highest between Western and Asian countries, where filial piety is still very strong (Bengtson and Putney, 2000; Eun, 2001) but there are also significant differences between Western countries. For instance, the comparison between France and Germany shows that the French express much more closeness between generations in both directions, and mainly toward the elderly parents (Attias-Donfut, 2000).

The cement of solidarity is made up, to a large extent, of gifts, debts, and reciprocity. The debt toward the elder generation is in every respondent's discourse. It is a powerful norm, including the sense of duty and the feeling of gratitude. Between close relatives, the solidarity is taken for granted, and when it has to be explained by the interviewees, two reasons are always given: first the status, "because she is my mother," "my father," "my son," "my daughter," and so on. This evidence applies mostly to direct kinship, ascendant or descendent. The second reason is the debt: "what I owe to my parents," "what they did for me." The debt is mainly due to parents, or to ascendant or to other elders.

The power of reciprocity appears in all its strength through the family stories related by the elderly. These stories reconstitute the course of the relations and exchanges between generations, including the chain of giving and giving back all along the life span. They reveal the variety of exchanges, as studied by Marcel Mauss (1960), whether they be direct or indirect, delayed or not. Giving, receiving, and giving back creates a continuous debt across generations that links them to each other (Bloch and Buisson, 1994). The results of the quantitative survey statistically confirm the significance of reciprocity in several respects.

The elderly who cared in the past for their own parents have a greater probability of receiving help from their children. It is as if there is a transmission of solidarity patterns. It is also a kind of indirect reciprocity: I give to my parents and I receive back from my children. The care for grandchildren gives rise to multiple forms of reciprocity between the three generations involved. The grandchildren will keep a special bond with the grandparent who took care of them. The parents who benefited from the care given by their parents to their children will in the future have closer relations with their parents. They make, on average, ten additional visits to them a year, compared with those who did not benefit from this help. The coresidence between children and parents in their later life takes place mostly at the home of the daughter who received more help in the past. Since she succeeded in improving her own standard of living through the parental assistance, she gives back assistance in their old age and contributes, by the coresidency, to a higher living standard for her parents. Coresidency can therefore be seen in many cases as a return gift delayed in time from the children who received more parental help when they were younger.

However important the feeling of debt and obligation is, the cost of reciprocity is sometimes heavy. An example is given by one interviewee, a 50-year-old woman, who felt an inner constraint to spend every Sunday with her mother who devoted herself to the grandchildren, and allowed her daughter to go on working by taking care of the three of them. Now the middle-aged daughter perceives that obligation as a burden, since her mother was used to living only through her and her household. The load of the debt leans on both the creditors and the debtors. The obligation of giving back is called in with more or less insistence: "I reared you, you should assist me." It is difficult to escape. The pressure of the creditors takes place in several ways, direct or indirect, authoritarian or by eliciting feelings of guilt. And the frailty of old age and its misery contribute to that pressure by arousing compassion.

Reciprocity is also involved in past wounds. This is expressed through resentments, conflicts or even ruptures. The damage received must be undone. Failing that reparation, it should be returned, the same as a gift. It is rarely forgotten. Reciprocity often exerts a grasp from which it is difficult to be free. Family resentments are commonplace but they are not easily talked about because the norm is that family members should have good feelings between them.

Reciprocity, whether direct (one gives back to those from whom one receives) or indirect (one receives from the one and gives back to another), institutes a continuity across the generations and contributes to the transmission of values, behaviors or conflicts.

CULTURAL CONTINUITIES AND DISCONTINUITIES ACROSS THE GENERATIONS

Family stories across the generations are an illustration of the assumption that autonomy coexists with continuity between generations. From one generation to another one can observe the rise of independence without the breaking of the generational bond. There are marked differences between generations: from the eldest to the youngest, education patterns are less authoritarian, the practice of religion diminishes, and relations between couples move toward greater equality and more equitable division of household tasks.

The Smoothing Out of an Authoritarian Education

The severe education widely inculcated in the elderly is obviously no longer the norm among the youngest generation. Our data make it possible to trace the evolution of educational styles, from the one received by

Table 11.5 Evolution of Educational Styles (%)

Educational style	Elderly (G1)		Pivots (G2)		Young (G3)	
	Received	Given	Received	Given	Received	Given
Severe	62	44	61	34	39	25
Tolerant	38	56	39	66	61	75
Total	100	100	100	100	100	100

Table 11.6 Agreement and Discrepancy between Parents and Children in Judging Education Given and Received (%)*

	Agreement		Discrepancy	
	Severe	Tolerant	Severe given, tolerant received	Tolerant given, severe received
Between G1 and G2	14	24	18	43
Between G2 and G3	11	38	23	28

Note: The percentages are calculated based on the number of pairs of parent/child.

the elderly to the one given to the young. In each generation, education that is given to the children is less severe than the one that had been received by their parents. Across the generations there is the same trend toward the softening of the style of education. The most drastic change was brought about by the pivot generation (Tables 11.5 and 11.6). This confirms the greater proximity already shown between the two descending generations.

The discrepancy between the judgments of parents and children concerning the education given and received is striking. It is even stronger between the pivots and their parents than between the pivots and their children, a sign that they share more values with each other, according to the historical discontinuity already noted. Change in educational style occurs more often among women; it is also more frequent among individuals who have climbed the social ladder. Being a woman and having achieved an ascending social mobility are two of the main factors favoring social change. But as observed by Christian Baudelot and Roger Establet (2000), change in educational styles has been generally accepted by the elder generation and has not raised insurmountable generational conflicts or gaps.

Decline and Transmission of Religious Practices

The comparison of religious practices of the three generations confirms both the historical decline of religious observance and the strong influence

Table 11.7 Evolution of Religious Practices across Generations

	G1 (%)	G2 (%)	G3 (%)
Regular religious practices	34	15	5
Occasional religious practices	35	43	19
No practices	31	42	66
	100	100	100

Table 11.8 Passing on of Religious Practices within Families (Ascending to Descending Generations)

	Regular (%)	Regular or occasional (%)
G1 to G2	32	67
G2 to G3	22	45
G1 to G3	10	40

Table 11.9 Passing on of Religious Practices within Families (Descending from Ascending Generations)

	Regular (%)	Regular or occasional (%)
G2 from G1	72	79
G3 from G2	59	80
G3 from G1	66	81

of the family milieu. The rate of nonpracticing respondents more than doubles between G1 and G3. But among the young who do practice a religious faith, 80 percent are children of practicing parents, and 81 percent are grandchildren of those who practice. This underlines the weight of the continuity across the generations in the mechanisms of transmission. What has been inherited is more easily transmitted. The data show the active role of grandparents in passing on religious observance. In some families, transmission jumps over the middle generation, passing directly from the grandparent to the grandchild. Women are both more religious and the ones who break more often with family religious tradition. The data presented in Tables 11.7 to 11.9 are characteristic of this phenomenon in a situation of structural decline. They are comparable to the tables of mobility concerning the sector of agriculture in modern societies. Young farmers are almost exclusively originating from agricultural families, while the majority of the descendants of farmers are in the process of social mobility and only very few among them stay in agriculture. Here the family farm becomes the last preservation place. Generally speaking, structural decline leads to specific forms of family transmission and only within a small number of families. This phenomenon is occurring in numerous declining sectors, e.g., specialty crafts and small family stores.

Gendered Generations

One of the main points, now universally recognized, is the change in gender relations. This section deals with one of its consequences, the new relationship between female generations. The results of this survey confirm that there exists an interdependence between generational and gender relationships. The tendency toward equality between the genders is correlated with an increase in the closeness between generations. In order to test this hypothesis, we included in the questionnaires questions relating to styles of raising children, questions on attitudes concerning the education of sons and daughters, and questions about the division of household tasks among the couples. The main results from these questions can be summarized as follows:

The attitudes that were held by mothers and fathers toward the education of their sons and daughters were modified as a consequence of a simultaneous coming together of the genders and the generations: the most elderly women believed, more often than their partners, that it is more important to prepare a son than a daughter for a professional life. In contrast, in the next generation down, women are less likely than men to hold this view. This new pattern continues in the youngest generation. The preferential relationship between mothers and sons observed in the eldest generation has been replaced by the mother/daughter bond in the following generation. For both genders there is a drastic decline of those who give preference to their sons (46 percent for G1, 29 percent for G2, and 13 percent for G3). For the first time in history mothers are more supportive of the professional careers of their daughters than orienting them toward traditional female roles.

The ties between women of different generations change in line with changes that take place between couples, in particular the greater sharing of domestic tasks between spouses. These modifications have been explored through two series of questions. One series concerns attitudes relative to the desired division of labor, the other on the actual behavior of couples (or for those respondents who were separated or widowed, how this division functioned in the past). The responses were grouped according to two models, "traditional" and "modern." In the traditional category, sexual divisions of labor were very strong, with all the domestic tasks falling on women. Whereas men "earned money to keep the household," other activities—leisure, education—were the responsibility of women. In the second model, most of the activities are divided between partners

Table 11.10   Division of Domestic Tasks between Spouses: Evolution of Behavior and Values

	Behavior (%)		Values (%)	
	Traditional	Modern	Traditional	Modern
Older (G1, n = 1147)	77	23	75	25
Gender				
Men	68	32	79	21
Women	80	20	74	26
Occupational status				
Agriculture	79	21	84	16
Manual workers	79	21	73	27
Salaried workers	75	25	74	26
Management	66	34	65	35
Pivot (G2, n = 1711)	63	37	57	43
Gender				
Men	57	43	61	39
Women	67	33	53	47
Occupational status				
Agriculture	85	15	73	27
Manual workers	64	36	65	35
Salaried workers	62	38	57	43
Management	44	56	46	54
Young* (G3, n = 893)	42	58	38	62
Gender				
Men	40	60	43	57
Women	44	56	34	66
Occupational status (of the parents)				
Agriculture	47	53	53	47
Manual workers	42	58	39	61
Salaried workers	42	58	38	62
Management	41	59	30	70
Have children	51	49	41	59
Childless	31	69	33	64

Note: Only the youngest generation living in a couple is included.

(more or less equitably), but household tasks and above all, those concerned with laundry, remained mostly a woman's domain. From grandparents through to grandchildren, principles and practices move toward a more egalitarian model (See Table 11.10).

The rate of those who believe in the "modern couple" moves from 25 percent in G1 to 62 percent in G3, while those who practice this type of couple rises from 23 to 58 percent (Table 11.10). Men appear in principle a little more traditional than women in all generations, but the behavior they describe in the reality of their daily lives, in contrast, seems to be somewhat more egalitarian than those described by women, especially those in the pivot generation. Do they have a tendency to overestimate their engagement in domestic life? Or are women underestimating what their partners do? Among the youngest generation, the responses of men and women on actual domestic behavior are more evenly distributed but their normative models are still apart. In this generation, we can also see a clear division between couples with and without children. Parents have more traditional beliefs and practices and it seems that by becoming parents they align themselves more with tradition. Life cycle effects in these cases complicate the generational effect. This suggests that there is an evolution in young households toward more conformist relations through the birth of children. This pattern is reinforced by the influence of social class insofar as less educated young people have children earlier in life.

Social class differences at this stage in their life seem to have less impact on the younger generation than that of the parents. In fact, it is in generation G2 that social class is the strongest determinant of the model that the couple adopts; sexual division of labor is still very much in evidence in rural areas but it is less common among white-collar workers. There remains a certain distance between beliefs and behavior, particularly to the disadvantage of women in the two descending generations: the difference between the desire for more equality among couples and such equality actually taking place (or even partially) is 10 percentage points for young women, 15 points for their mothers, and only 8 points for their grandmothers.

The opposite situation is seen in the responses of men, where there is a difference between more traditional views of gender divisions and behavior that is less segregated than they wish. This can be seen most clearly among the eldest men, for whom there is an 18 percentage point difference in this direction. The influence of the life cycle (and retirement) certainly accentuates the generational effect as can be seen by the fact that this difference narrows to 3 percentage points among their children and grandchildren.

The contradictory attitudes of men and women, the persistence of traditional values in both sexes, and a certain inertia in the behavior of men and women explain the following, somewhat surprising finding: there is no correlation between the actual behavior of the parents and the behavior of their children, whether it is between the elderly and the pivot or the pivot and the young. However, there is a significant correlation between the opinions of parents and those of their children concerning the ideal model for couples. On this question, the transfer of values through the generations is gendered: women of the pivot generation are much more influenced by the values of their parents than men; their rate of adhesion to an egalitarian model rises 18 points where their parent that was interviewed holds the same view, whereas this is only 7 points for men in the same situation. Among the young, the difference becomes blurred with men and women having been equally influenced by their parents' values, although young men, as we have seen, remain more traditional than young women. We can therefore see a certain continuity at the level of normative models, but this continuity does not directly appear in behavior, contrary to analyses that have found the first source of resistance to gender equality is family heritage (Kaufman, 1992). Our data show that other factors are involved that are more in keeping with collective norms such as social class or the social networks of couples, rather than those norms transmitted within the family. Resistance also comes from the divergent position of men and women; the behavior of couples is the product of negotiation, and this tends to neutralize any inherited family traits.

Despite the lack of movement in the behavior of couples and the contradictory stances taken by men and women, relationships change in the same direction as changes between the generations, both tending toward the weakening of a hierarchical model. There is a slight correlation between educational norms and models of couples. A modern couple is more likely to give a tolerant education to their children, while a traditional couple is more likely to give a more severe education.

Women are achieving greater equality within couples because of the coming together of different generations of women and through the greater intergenerational solidarity between women in general that is occurring, as well as education systems that are less gender orientated. It needs to be stressed that this form of "complicity" between different generations of women is a new phenomenon. It is at the origin of the major changes occurring in the family. We can see it at work, for example, in the new model of grandmotherhood (Attias-Donfut, and Segalen, 1998), which supports the idea that there is a new contract between generations of women.

Generational Relations and Social Change

Beyond the dramatic changes occurring in society as a whole, the comparison of the answers of generations of the same family shows, at the same time, a strong transmission of values. Modern attitudes are transmitted, but also (although to a much lesser degree) traditional attitudes. The changes from one generation to the other only occur in some families. From this it is advisable to identify through whom and by what means changes and differences are introduced. Among the many factors and influences at play, one fact appears significant: the influence of intergenerational social mobility. Differences between generations are more marked in families of ascending social mobility. A change in social status facilitates or brings about the adoption of new values and new behavior. This demonstrates how the capacity of societies to change and the speed of this change is linked to the degree of openness of the social classes. The other main variable is gender: the changes occur more often among women in every domain. Women appear as the main actors in social change. It is particularly evident in the relationships between generations and between gender roles, both of which are deeply linked.

Mothers are still more receptive than fathers to their children's influence, which has been called "reversed socialization" (Allerbeck, Jennings, and Rosenmayr, 1979). The pivot generation was asked in the survey in which domains they had been influenced by their children: a minority of parents (29 percent of the mothers and 21 percent of the fathers) reported a strong influence exerted upon them in fundamental issues, like those of religion, politics, social problems, or education. This group of parents had children who experienced a higher degree of social mobility than the average. For a broader group of parents (38 percent of mothers and 37 percent of fathers), there nevertheless existed some form of influence, but weaker than the former group of parents and more linked to formal aspects of lifestyle such as dress appearance, house decoration, food, leisure activities, and style of education. Affective closeness and the quality of relationships facilitate this upward transmission. This takes place all the more so today because the colongevity of generations prolongs the length of time in which exchanges and influences take place, increasing probability of reciprocal influences between the generations. The age difference between parents and children symbolically contracts when the lifespan increases, which results in a shorter distance between them. The new models of relations that are more egalitarian bring about a greater closeness between parents and children and allow these exchanges of influences to occur.

These cultural transmissions favor the diffusion of social change, from the youngest adults to the oldest, leading the latter to change their values and behavior. This can be brought about by the prestige that accompanies their children's elevated social position and the pride that this inspires in the parents. This "rebound" effect of upward social mobility by children to their parents can clearly be seen for the most part in a rise in the standard of living and social capital of the latter, which has been demonstrated in the analyses of economic transfers within families (Attias-Donfut, 2000).

The confrontation between generations that have different values creates zones of influence in family life. New ideas are tested and there is a move toward their relative acceptance. This confrontation mediates and eases change. The changes introduced by the young thus slowly win through to other generations and extend outward socially through the mediation of the family. This supports the hypothesis of the linkage between generational relations and the nature of social change, as outlined by Mannheim, wherein he emphasized the importance of the problem of generations in understanding social change.

The pace of social change is related to generational relations in both directions. More communication and consensus between the generations have the effect of smoothing the change through the negotiations between them: their dialogue and their reciprocal influences bring their points of view closer and facilitate compromise. The rhythm of negotiated change becomes smoother. When the generations are opposing or less consensual, when there are barriers of communication between them, changes occur more abruptly. This has been noted, for instance, in the comparison between France and Germany, where French families have been found to be more consensual (Attias-Donfut, 2000). Reciprocally, a rapid social or political change increases the differences between the historical generations and limits their communication and the possibility for them to negotiate the forms and the rhythms of change, which can be seen nowadays in such countries as Spain (Tobio, 2001).

CONCLUSION

The respective positions of the generations in life and family cycles necessarily place them in asymmetrical positions in the system of exchanges. These positions are also conditioned by their own history, economic fluctuations, and the evolution of social welfare. Our results highlight some overall trends. Private transfers among generations go in the opposite direction of public transfers that take place through the retirement pension system. This shows the existence of a circular mechanism generated by both the money flows from elderly retirees to their children and by those that skip a generation from grandparents to adult grandchildren who have begun to face the world of work. Retirement pensions make it possible for elderly people to accumulate savings, putting them in a position of being providers with respect to their children as well as to their grandchildren, even when their income is low. They have in fact initiated a decapitalization process to the benefit of their descendants, as an advance against inheritance.

Between generations as well as within generations, income, savings, and patrimony are distributed very unevenly. When it is at work, family cooperation can partly compensate for the inequalities among generations as a consequence of social mobility and its return effects, and thanks as well to the extended parental support of adult children. The economic regulation resulting from this generational dynamic works in both directions, upwards and downwards. A large number of families, however, do not practice these forms of solidarity, which tend to be concentrated among the wealthiest. Family conflicts, misunderstandings, and breakups will also be obstacles to such exchanges. Thus, the fragility of unions and the problems they lead to in family relations can weaken solidarity between generations. By contrast, the improvement of relations between parents and children, which is the fruit of modern educational patterns, tends to strengthen it. The young receive important help from their parents in many forms, in the areas of housing and job-finding, when they need money or to have their children minded, or other sorts of everyday services. Moreover, in one-third of the families, their grandparents provide them with financial help. Two generations are therefore joining their efforts in helping the young. When they encounter difficulties, family economic support attenuates these difficulties and acts as a shock absorber on a macrosocial level during economic recessions. This private solidarity, however, is not always sufficient, given the inequalities between families. Despite these inequalities and despite the worsening of social marginalization, which are signs of a lack of solidarity both public and private, the overall picture can still be characterized by the vitality of exchanges and relations between the three generations.

Generational relations always involve more than two generations, whether in an actual or a symbolic meaning: each generation is located within a generational chain and is defined both by the preceding and the succeeding generations. Moreover the relation to each one is determined by the relation to the other, as shown by the various forms of reciprocity analyzed in this chapter. For instance, giving is related to what has been received and reciprocally. Therefore the study of relations between generations must include not only the two generations directly involved in these relations, but also the influence on these relations that either is or was played by a third or sometimes even a fourth generation, whether living or not.

The observation of these three generations highlights their twofold historical determination: on the one hand, that of the period each of them experienced and was marked by, and on the other, that time experienced by their predecessors or successors. Transfers between generations emphasize their economic interdependence. Successive accumulations and transmissions produce the never-ending movement of the past's returning in the form of property and money, as well as in the spheres of culture and ideas. Economic transfers are embedded in social and cultural transmissions from the oldest to the youngest, but also from the youngest to the oldest. There is a countervailing influence on the part of the young that cannot be underestimated and that participates in communicating social change to all generations.

ACKNOWLEDGMENT

Completion of this paper was supported by the Ford Foundation (Grant No. 1000-1729-1), which is gratefully acknowledged.

NOTES

1. When there were more than one child or two parents, the interviewee was randomly selected. The same technique—the submission of a questionnaire lasting about one-and-a-half hours at the respondent's home—was used for the three generations. Interviews were conducted with 1,958 persons in the pivot generation, 1,217 of their parents, and 1,493 of their children, amounting to a total of 4,668 individuals distributed according to 995 triads, 222 pivot-parent dyads, 498 pivot-child dyads, and 243 pivots alone.

2. In my perspective (Attias-Donfut, 1988), the notion of generation is a social construct, part of the social imagery and has a function of organizing "social time" in Durkheim's sense (Durkheim, 1915).

3. The qualitative survey was done in 1996, four years after the quantitative one. Its analysis is included in Attias-Donfut and Segalen (1998).

4. The French word for "galley" (galère) denotes, in its colloquial sense, a situation of constant, crippling obstacles and difficulties.

5. It appears that French grandparents are more involved in the care of grandchildren than, for example, British grandparents (Dench and Ogg, 2001).

REFERENCES

Allerbeck, K. R., Jennings, K. M., and Rosenmayr, L. 1979. Generations and families. In S. H. Barnes and M. Kaase (eds.), *Political action* (pp. 487–522). Beverly Hills, CA: Sage.

Attias-Donfut, C. 1988. *Sociologie des Générations. L'empreinte du temps.* Paris: PUF.

Attias-Donfut, C. 2000. Rapports de générations. Transferts intrafamilaux et dynamique macrosociale. *Revue Française de Sociologie* 41(4):643–84.

Attias-Donfut, C., and Lapierre, N. 2001. The welfare family: Three generations in Guadeloupe: The history of the family. *International Quarterly* 5(3):329–46.

Attias-Donfut, C., and Segalen, M. 1998. *Grands-Parents: La famille à travers les générations.* Paris: Odile Jacob.

Attias-Donfut, C., and Wolff, F. C. 2000. Complementarity between private and public transfers and the redistributive effects of generational transfers. In S. Arber and C. Attias-Donfut (eds.), *The myth of generational conflict: Family and state in ageing societies* (pp. 22–46, 47–68). London: Routledge.

Baudelot, C., and Establet, R. 2000. *Avoir trente ans en 1968 et en 1998.* Paris: Seuil.

Bengtson, V. L. 1975. Generation and family effects in value socialization. *American Sociological Review* 40(3):358–71.

Bengtson, V. L., and Achenbaum, W. A. (eds.). 1993. *The changing contract across generations.* Hawthorne, NY: Aldine de Gruyter.

Bengtson, V. L., and Kuypers, J. A. 1971. Generational difference and the developmental stake. *Aging and Human Development* 2, 249–60.

Bengtson, V. L., and Putney, N. 2000. Who will care for the elderly?: Consequences of population aging East and West. In V. L. Bengtson, K. D. Kim, G. C. Meyers, and K. S. Eun (eds.), *Aging in east and west: Families, states and the elderly* (pp. 3–16). New York: Springer.

Bloch, F., and Buisson, M. 1994. La circulation du don entre générations, ou comment reçoit-on? *Communications* 59, 55–72.

Bourdieu, P. 1979. *La distinction: Critique sociale du jugement.* Paris: Editions de Minuit.

Chauvel, L. 1998. *Le destin des générations.* Paris: Presses Universitaires de France.

Coenen-Huther, J., Kellerhals, J., and Von Allmen, M. 1994. *Les réseaux de solidarité dans la famille.* Paris: Réalités Sociales.

Crenner, E. 1998. La parenté: Un réseau de sociabilité actif mais concentré. *INSEE Première.* n. 600:juillet.

De Singly, F. 1993. *Sociologie de la famille contemporaine.* Paris: Nathan.

Dench, G., and Ogg, J. 2001. Grands-parents par le père, grands-parents par la mère. In C. Attias-Donfut and M. Segalen, *Le Siècle de Grands-Parents.* Paris: Autrement.

Desplanques, G. 1993. Les familles recomposées en 1990. In M. T. Meulders-Klein and I. Théry (eds.), *Les recompositions familiales* (pp. 81–96). Paris: Nathan.

Durkheim, E. 1915. *Les formes élémentaires de la vie religieuse: Le système totémique en Australie.* Paris: Presses Universitaires de France.

Esping-Andersen, G. 1990. *The three worlds of welfare capitalism.* Princeton, NJ: Princeton University Press.

Eun, K. S. 2001. Changing roles of the family and state for elderly care: a perspective of a Confucian Country. In *Conference on families, aging and social support* (pp. 17–21). Haifa: May.

Godbout, J. 2000. *Le don, la dette et l'identité: Homo donator vs. homo aeconomus.* Paris: La Découverte/Mauss.

Hagestad, G. 1986. Dimension of time and the family. *American Behavioral Scientist* 29(6):679–94.

————. 2003. Interdependent lives and relationships in changing times: A life-course view of families and aging. In R. Settersten (ed.), *Invitation to the life-course: Toward new understanding of later life.* Amityville, NY: Baywood.

Hareven, T. K. 1996. *Aging and generational relations: Life-course and cross-cultural perspectives.* Hawthorne, NY: Aldine de Gruyter.

Kaufman, J. C. 1992. *La trame conjugale.* Paris: Nathan.

Kertzer, D. I. 1983. Generation as a sociological problem. *American Sociological Review* 9:125–49.

Kohli, M. 1996. *The problem of generations: Family, economy, politics.* Public lecture series, Collegium, Budapest.

Lye, D. 1996. Adult child-parent relationships. *Annual Review of Sociology* 22:79–102.

Mangen, D. J. , Bengtson, V. L., and Landry, P. H., Jr. (eds.) (1988). *The measurement of intergenerational relations.* Beverly Hills, CA: Sage.

Mannheim, K. 1952. The problem of generations. In K. Mannheim, *Essays on the sociology of knowledge* (pp. 276–322). London: Routledge Kegan Paul.

Marshall, V. 1983. Generations, age groups and cohorts: Conceptual distinctions. *Canadian Journal on Aging* 2:51–61.

Mauss, M. 1960. Essai sur le don. In M. Mauss, *Sociologie et anthropologie* (pp. 145–312). Paris: Presses Universitaires de France.

Meulders-Klein, M. T., and Théry, I. (eds.) (1993). *Les recompositions familiales aujourd'hui.* Paris: Nathan.

Riley, M. W. (ed.) 1969. *Sociology of age stratification*. New York: Sage.

Roberts, R. E. L., Richards, L. N., and Bengtson, V. L. 1991. Intergenerational solidarity in families: Untangling the ties that bind. In S. K. Pfeifer and M. B. Sussman (eds.), *Marriage and Family Review. Families: Intergenerational Connections* (Vol. 16, pt. 1; pp. 11–46). Binghamton, NY: Haworth.

Rossi, A. F., and Rossi, P. H. 1990. *Of human bonding: Parent-child relations across the life course*. Hawthorne, NY: Aldine de Gruyter.

Ryder, N. 1965. The cohort as a concept in the study of social change. *American Sociological Review* 30:843–61.

Stoller, E. P. 1985. Exchanges patterns in the informal support networks of the elderly: The impact of reciprocity on male. *Journal of Marriage and the Family* 47:335–42.

Tobio, C. 2001. En Espagne, les grand-mères à la rescousse. In C. Attias-Donfut and M. Segalen (eds.), *Le siècle des grands-parents* (pp. x). Paris: Autrement.

IV

Intrasociety Changes in Intergenerational Support

|12|

Changing Roles of the Family and State for Elderly Care

A Confucian Perspective

Ki-Soo Eun

A Seoul newspaper article on April 6, 2001, reported that a municipal government ordered family members of nineteen elderly persons to repay what the government had provided for the elderly as welfare payments in Korea (*JoongAng Ilbo*, April 6, 2001). One of the nineteen welfare recipients, a 72-year-old mother of four adult children, had received 123,000 won ($95) every month under the National Basic Livelihood Protection Act (NBLPA) because she was not able to support herself. Two of her four children partially supported their mother by providing a small amount of money, although irregularly, so that they were judged to have carried out their duty to care for their mother. One daughter was herself so poor that she was exempted from the duty. However, the other daughter had not assisted her mother at all despite her monthly income of about three million won ($2,300). The mother would not have been eligible to receive welfare had the government known that she had a daughter who was able to support her. When the government found out about her daughter's income, the government ordered the daughter to repay what the government had already paid to her mother as a monthly allowance.

This was the first time that the government tried to retrieve a welfare allowance from those who were obligated to support their elderly parents, but had failed to fulfill their duty. Before this case was publicized, ordinary people had not heard of the National Basic Livelihood Protection Act (NBLPA), which was concerned with providing welfare allowance for the elderly poor. The article in *JoongAng Ilbo* brought the topic to the public's awareness: it is not a matter of choice, but a "duty" stipulated by law for adult children to support their elderly parents.

Enacted in September 1999, the NBLPA defines a welfare recipient as an elderly person who (a) does not have a person who has the "duty" to care for him/her, or (b) has a person who has the "duty" to care for him/her, but who cannot provide the needed assistance. The NBLPA clarifies who has the "duty" to care for the elderly. A supporter should be a direct descendant, spouse, or biologically close relative such as a brother or sister who lives with the welfare recipient.

Most public reactions were that the action was reasonable and acceptable in terms of filial piety toward elderly parents. One person further insisted that "the government should prohibit children from failing to support their parents by punishing those who do not take care of their own parents" (JoongAng Ilbo, April 6, 2001).

However, the action of the municipal government in the case cited led to fierce disputes regarding the relevancy of the action, the responsibility of adult children to support aged parents, and the philosophical foundations of the welfare policy. First, a debate arose with regard to the question of whether the state should intervene and regulate a private matter such as supporting the elderly. Second, the younger generation opposed the action of the municipal government, complaining that they would pay into the national pension for a much longer period than the older generation, and that it was the state's responsibility to support the older generation from fiscal revenue. It was further unacceptable for them that the state tried to confiscate personal assets or salaries for not supporting elderly parents. Third, some worried about the development of a new conflict between parents and adult children who did not provide care for parents. If adult children are condemned for neglecting their "duty," they should be shamed of losing face, an important value in Confucian teachings. They are then likely to attribute the shame to their parents, thereby worsening the relationship between parents and their adult children.

Due to this unusual official action, Koreans have had the opportunity to reflect on who has the responsibility to support the elderly in an aging society. Although most Koreans still take it for granted that the elderly are cared for by the family, they usually feel embarrassed to know that it is a "duty" stipulated by law. They feel harassed when the family is not only morally blamed for neglecting their "duty," but is also charged legally and ordered to compensate the state. Numerous questions regarding care for the elderly can be raised. Is the family is ultimately responsible for the care of the elderly in an aging society? Why is the family still in charge of caring for the aged as it did in the past? Will the younger generation within the family be the primary caregiver for the old generation? Does any intergenerational transfer between parents and children predict the possibility that the family will function as a primary caregiver to the aged? On what grounds does the state have the authority to impose on people the care of elderly parents? Can Confucian values legitimize the authority of the state to force the family to be a primary and last caregiver to the old in the twenty-first century? Does the state have to play a greater role in providing care for the old in the East while the family is permitted to retreat from their "duty"?

Rather than attempting to answer all the above questions in this chapter, I aim to explore how and why the roles of the family and the state are changing in caring for the elderly in Korea, a Confucian country. The West looks to the East for an alternative to the current welfare system. This chapter will provide an opportunity to think about the role of the family and social support in caring for an elderly population from a Confucian perspective. It will examine whether the Korean welfare system for the elderly is loading the family with too much responsibility as it enforces the Confucian principle, and whether the Eastern model can supplement the Western model.

CHANGES IN CONFUCIANISM AND FILIAL PIETY

Filial Piety in the Traditional Period

Asian societies have been well-known for sharing Confucian ethics of filial piety. Western scholars believe that Asian scholars on aging insist that a desirable social policy on aging should enforce Confucian values and customs. "Close and independent ties, responsibility and sacrifice, harmony, and viewing individuals in relation to the family" are characterized as the core contents of filial piety ingrained in the Confucian value system (Bengtson and Putney, 2000, p. 275). Researchers are likely to have the impression that Confucian teachings including filial piety have been the main value system in East Asian countries for over two thousand years. These perceptions are not accurate since the influence of Confucianism in Korea hasn't existed for two thousand years. Moreover, Confucianism is not the only value system that emphasizes filial piety as a principle of regulating parent-child relationships.

In fact, all social thought—in the East and the West—have taught the importance of respect toward the aged. Not only Confucianism, but also Moses' Ten Commandments and Buddhism include filial piety as a norm of practice in everyday life. In Korea, the influence of Buddhism has a longer history than that of Confucianism. When Neo-Confucianism was adopted as a ruling ideology in the Chosun Dynasty (1392–1910), most commoners still adhered to the teachings of Buddhism. Therefore, it is not true that filial piety only belongs to a Confucian legacy even in East Asian societies. Rather, it appears that all people in traditional times have lived with norms and values that promote respect and care for one's elderly parents. Even though the Chosun dynasty selected Neo-Confucianism as the ruling ideology at the beginning of the dynasty, it took a long time for Neo-Confucianism as a regulating force as well as a norm and value to penetrate into the lives of ordinary people. It was only in the late Chosun dynasty that the teachings of Neo-Confucianism prevailed among people regardless of social status. In the late Chosun period, filial piety was reinforced to regulate family relationships at the family level through rewards and negative sanctions. Those who practiced filial duty were given honor and material rewards. The person who carried out the filial duty and the lineage to which that person belonged were glorified by the state. Those who did not take care of their parents in an adequate manner were morally blamed for their neglect of filial responsibility. When parents were not cared for by their offspring, those adult children were punished by the community.

Filial piety toward parents was converted into loyalty toward a king at the societal level because the king was identified with the father in a family. As children ought to obey the parents, all people had to obey the king in a Confucian society. Loyalty to a king at the societal level was just an extension of filial piety at the family level. It was impossible for those who did not practice filial piety at home to achieve an official status, which was the highest goal for the literati and the elite. The literati and ruling class who did not care for parents materially as well as emotionally were denied government posts, and further were alienated from society. For the literati and ruling class, filial piety toward parents was not simply a family matter, but rather a necessary condition to maintain high social status in a Confucian society.

Where filial duty at the individual level was closely connected with rewards and negative sanctions in other social realms, the original good nature of filial duty degenerated in Confucian society. People, and especially the literati and ruling class, were eager to demonstrate in public that they were *hyojas* (a child who does filial duty sincerely) in everyday life. They strove at least not to lose face. Forms and manners for carrying out filial piety became too complicated to practice. In this situation, the literati and ruling class suffered from psychological oppression, which we can find in numerous old stories on *hyoja* written by the literati (U.-C. Jeong, 2000). Commoners, as opposed to the literati and ruling class, were relatively free from the burden of the complicated forms and manners of practicing filial duty. Because most commoners were illiterate and could not afford to spend too much, true intentions rather than complicated forms and manners were more valued in taking care of parents (Shin, 2000). Nevertheless, even commoners were not absolutely free from the obsession that they ought to obey parents and practice filial piety.

In sum, while filial piety in East Asian societies has a long history, it was not necessarily Confucian in character. It was not until the late Chosun dynasty that Confucian filial piety prevailed over society. Filial piety was not limited to a principle regulating family relationship, but rather it became a concomitant to the principle of loyalty to the king at the societal level. Both rewards and negative sanction were widely used by the state to force people to observe filial piety. The literati and ruling class clung to filial piety not because they were more empathic to parents but because it was necessary to maintain their honor and high social status. Although filial obligations toward parents were not written into law by the state, most people cast their behaviors to fit the minimal standard of filial responsibility in everyday life. Filial piety gradually degenerated, losing purity in character.

Confucianism and Filial Piety in the Contemporary Period

A recent book titled "Confucius Must Die for the Nation to Live" was published (Kim, 1999) strongly asserts that Confucianism has been an obstacle to the modern development of the Korean society, and that Koreans still are not free from the obsession of the authoritarian characters of Confucianism. Immediately, a counterbook appeared with the title "Confucius Must Live for the Nation to Live" (Choi, 1999). Disputes regarding the validity of Confucianism in contemporary Korean society followed the publication of these two books.

To explain the rapid industrial development that took place in East Asia, many Eastern and Western scholars looked to the cultural background of Confucianism. So-called Asian values have been praised as a significant factor that enabled East Asian countries to achieve a high level of capitalist industrial development within such a short period. The content of Asian values is mostly based on the Confucian value system. In this sense, Confucianism may be said to have a selective affinity with capitalist development in East Asia from the viewpoint of scholars favoring Asian values.

However, for those who have paid attention to the negative impact of Confucianism on Korean society, it is Confucianism, and Confucian values and customs, that should be eliminated as soon as possible for Korean society to become a modern civil society. Confucian practice has been criticized as too formalized for a long time. Even in the late Chosun dynasty, Chung Yak-Yong (1762–1836), a representative Confucian philosopher of the School of Practical Learning, criticized the formalized and complicated practice of filial piety by the literati and ruling class as violating the true teaching of Confucius (S.-B. Jeong, 2000, p. 43). Choi Jae-Suk, a Korean sociologist, looks for the cause of social problems in Korea in Confucianism and

Confucian values. In his book, published several decades ago, he criticizes the problems of Confucian values in the Korean society:

> The ideal attitude toward parents is still recognized as obedience to parents. Namely, children who listen to and follow parents' orders without any complaints are regarded as the ideal model. Those children who grow up under this circumstance are most likely to yield to [unjust] authority and lose autonomy. . . . While any individual must be able to express his/her own opinion freely, it is never permitted in society because of the oppressive principle of filial piety. . . . Personality cultivated under the influence of filial piety is likely to be exclusive in character. (Choi, 1963, pp. 144–46).

Choi attributes one of the main causes of social problems in Korean society to the principle of filial piety with an oppressive character.

Kim Kyong-Dong, a renowned sociologist, is also very harsh in evaluating Confucianism in contemporary Korean society. "Confucian ritualism has been very aptly used by the power elite for the purpose of legitimizing its rule and authority or by the clan, kinship group, or community to maintain social ties and hierarchical social order in the collectivity. . . . At any rate, the typical part of Confucian governance familiar to us today is that of authoritarian rule" (Kim, 1996, pp. 53–54). Kim asserts that the ruling class used Confucian social norms as a mechanism of social control. "The ruling elite in China and Korea almost blindly clung to the Confucian normative mechanism to maintain order, which was fast crumbling" (ibid.:61). Confucianism including filial piety functioned as a mechanism of social control at the societal level. Unlike Choi, who emphasizes the negative effect of Confucianism at the individual level, Kim warns of the abuse of Confucian values by the state and ruling class at the societal level.

In relation to care for the aged in contemporary society, Kim Kyong-Il, whose book led to disputes, indicates directly why elderly care based on filial piety is impossible in contemporary society:

> As we see from a number of books and articles, filial piety depends on *"jung"* [feeling of intimacy]. Filial piety was possible only in traditional times because parents and children lived together in the same place at the same time. However, diverse situations in housing, job, dual-income family and child education in contemporary society make it fundamentally impossible. As most Confucian teachings dictate, those teachings [of filial piety] depending on *"jung"* cannot effectively interpret the meaning of changes in diverse family matters, so that they cannot appropriately meet new problems caused by industrialization. (Kim, 1999, pp. 154–55)

These negative evaluations of the validity of Confucianism are fully understandable when viewed from a long history of authoritarian and military regimes in contemporary Korean society. In fact, illegitimate military regimes looked for their legitimacy to Confucian values and customs, namely *hyo* (filial piety) and *choong* (loyalty to the king). In the name of tradition, which is frequently glamorized and valorized even in the modern era, Confucianism and its values are repeatedly emphasized through the media, school textbooks, and various official and informal events. Various events that aim at promoting the practice of filial piety are regularly held by the state or by civil organizations. For example, a *hyobu* (a daughter-in-law who cares for parents-in-law earnestly) is sought and awarded for the practice of filial piety every year. A typical *hyobu* comes from a lower socioeconomic class in rural areas, and she is furthermore praised because she practices filial piety while overcoming severe hardship.

In fact, "typically in East Asia, Confucian social values and norms have, at different times, been selectively mobilized and effectively utilized by the ruling class or the power elite as a powerful mechanism of social control" (Kim, 1996, p. 54). Filial piety, which is ceaselessly mobilized as a means of social control, is a representative of those Confucian values and norms. In particular, it is frequently used as an effective way to legitimize the state's neglect of responsibility for elderly care.

Despite the harsh evaluation of Confucianism and Confucian values by critical scholars, general attitudes toward Confucian values by ordinary people are surprisingly positive and affirmative. According to the National Social Survey, conducted by the Academy of Korean Studies in 1999 (Academy of Korean Studies, 1999a), ordinary people regard Confucian values as effective leading values in the twenty-first century. Eighty-three percent of the respondents in the survey agree strongly that filial piety toward parents will be an effective leading value in the twenty-first century. Moreover, according to the General Survey for Graduates of Seoul National University (SNU), performed by the Academy of Korean Studies in 1999 (Academy of Korean Studies, 1999b), graduates of SNU also regard filial piety as a valuable Confucian heritage. Fifty-three and 40 percent of the graduates of SNU strongly agree and agree, respectively, that filial piety will play a leading role in reconstructing Korean society in the future. In addition, both ordinary people (99 percent) and former SNU students (89 percent) agree that the Confucian value of respect toward the elderly is a beautiful tradition and will be a good resource for development in the future. It is surprising that the reform-oriented SNU graduates favored the two Confucian core values despite their oppressive character.

Ordinary people regard other values such as loyalty to the state, trust and sacrifice for friends, and the trinity of king, teacher, and father as contributing to rebuilding the future Korean society. While the SNU graduates also agree that trust and sacrifice for friends will be important in the future, they demonstrate less favorable views toward the values of loyalty to the state, and to the trinity of king, teacher, and father. They particularly recognize the oppressive nature of this trinity.

The positive attitude toward filial piety and respect for the elderly is also reflected in the attitude toward the obligation to support elderly parents. Among 70,139 respondents in a general social survey conducted by the Korea National Statistical Office, 23 percent believe that the eldest son has the responsibility to care for elderly parents (Korea National Statistical Office, 1998). Forty-six percent agree that children who are able to support are responsible to support, and 22 percent suggest that all sons and daughters should be caregivers. In other words, 91 percent of the respondents view children as primary caregivers to elderly parents. Only 7 percent of the respondents think that parents should support themselves without depending on children or the state, and less than 2 percent of the respondents believe that the society or state is responsible for supporting old parents.

The older the respondents, the higher their tendency to attribute the responsibility to support old parents to the eldest son. Among respondents aged 60 and over, 41 percent answer that the final caregiver to old parents is the eldest son. By contrast, only 15 percent of the people aged 20–29 agree that the eldest son should support elderly parents. Most respondents under age 60 regard any children who are able to support as the primary caregiver. They do not want to give the burden of caregiver to the eldest son as was done in the past. This reflects a change of attitude toward filial duty in the contemporary period. However, it is still the family, not the state or society that has the primary responsibility of caring for elderly parents.

In summary, Koreans still evaluate the Confucian values of filial piety and respect toward the elderly very positively. They believe that those values can play a significant role in Korean society in the twenty-first century. Almost all Koreans, regardless of age and sex, regard the family as the primary caregiver to elderly parents. Although there is a slight difference in the attitude toward the eldest son as the primary caregiver between the younger and older generations, almost all respondents agree that the family is responsible for elderly parents. The state or society is not considered the subject in caring for the aged.

THE FAMILY AND THE STATE IN THE AGING KOREAN SOCIETY

Interaction within the Family

Contrary to Western societies where individualism is the basic value determining individual behavior and attitudes, familism or collectivism

Table 12.1 Patterns of Intergenerational Transfer between Parents and
Adult Children by Respondents' Age (%)

Pattern	Total	20–29	30–39	40–49	50–59
Parents ↔ Adult children	39.7	43.0	40.7	37.5	38.0
Parents → Adult children	24.5	32.3	29.7	20.6	8.5
Parents ← Adult children	13.8	7.6	10.1	17.8	22.5
Parents ≠ Adult children	22.0	17.1	19.4	24.1	31.0
Total	100.0	100.0	99.9	100.0	100.0
	(1113)	(158)	(464)	(349)	(142)

Source: National Family Survey (Korea Broadcasting System & Association of Family Studies, 2000).

dominates individual behavior in Korea. As there are close intergenerational interactions between parents and children in Korea, there are frequent intergenerational transfers. Based on the 2000 National Family Study, there are various intergenerational transfers between adult children and parents, most of whom live apart. More than half of adult children get diverse aid from parents after marriage. About 14 percent of the children get multiple forms of aid, including economic, instrumental, or emotional support from parents and parents-in-law. Twenty-five percent of the children only receive emotional support from their parents. More than 10 percent of adult children still receive financial support from parents and parents-in-law after marriage. If we consider multiple forms of aid to include financial support, we know that far more than 10 percent of adult children are assisted financially by their parents and parents-in-law after marriage.

Adult children also provide parents and parents-in-law with various forms of assistance. Twenty-five percent of adult children provide financial aid to their parents. Eighteen percent also give financial aid to parents-in-law. Children also think that they support parents and parents-in-law emotionally. Instrumental aid to parents by adult children is not much provided. The proportion of people who give any kind of assistance to parents and parents-in-law is higher than that of people who get something from parents. It is surprising that people report that they are receiving support from parents rather than giving something to parents even after marriage.

Patterns of intergenerational transfer between parents and married children are succinctly summarized in Table 12.1. Forty percent of the respondents report that their intergenerational transfer is mutual. Twenty-four percent of the respondents say that they only receive some aid from

Table 12.2   Distribution of the Elderly Aged 65 and Over by Type of Household, 1975–1995 (%)

Type of Household	1975	1980	1985	1990	1995
Household of one old person	0.1	0.2	0.3	9.6	13.8
Household headed by an old person	28.2	36.5	37.0	42.9	43.3
Household including at least one old person	71.7	63.2	62.8	47.5	42.8
Total	100.0	99.9	100.1	100.0	99.9

Source: Korean National Statistical Office (1975, 1980, 1985, 1990, 1995); Eun (2001, p. 97).

the parents without providing them with anything. Only 22 percent of the respondents report no intergenerational transfer.

While longitudinal data are needed, it appears that over time, mutual transfer between parents and children decreases. Furthermore, the transfer from parents to children decreases as one ages. On the contrary, the transfer from children to parents increases as time goes by. Interestingly, the percentage of no transfer between generations also increases as one ages. For those aged 50–59, 31 percent report that there is no transfer between their parents or parents-in-law and themselves.

In summary, intergenerational transfer is widespread in contemporary Korean society. There are very significant intergenerational transfers not only between children and parents but also between children and parents-in-law. The great extent of intergenerational transfer between adult children and parents-in-law implies that there is widespread solidarity beyond the nuclear family even in contemporary Korean society. It is also noteworthy that a considerable proportion of married children still depend financially on parents or parents-in-law. In Korea, parents usually help children buy or at least rent a house when they marry. However, we find that even after children marry and live apart from their parents, parents still provide financial support to their children. This indicates that the family in Korea includes more than just the nuclear family (Lee, 1999).

Living Arrangement of Parents

It has been documented that coresidence with the elderly is decreasing in Asia. However, decreasing coresidence does not necessarily mean a decline in support for the elderly (Mason, 1992). Table 12.2 shows the distribution of those 65 and over by type of household in 1975-1995.

In 1975, about 70 percent of the elderly lived in the family as dependents. Twenty-eight percent of the elderly were heads of household, and only 0.1 percent of the aged lived alone. Twenty years later, in 1995, the

Table 12.3   Living Arrangements That Respondents Want in Their Old Age by Age and Sex (%)

Sex	Age	Couple only	Any children who want to live with them	Eldest son	Others	Total
Male	20s	74.6	22.2	3.2	0.0	100.0 (63)
	30s	63.9	28.2	2.9	5.0	100.0 (241)
	40s	68.4	21.9	3.4	6.3	100.0 (237)
	50s	74.2	13.2	7.8	4.8	100.0 (128)
	60s	56.1	18.2	15.2	10.5	100.0 (66)
Female	20s	82.1	14.2	0.9	2.8	100.0 (106)
	30s	82.7	13.7	0.4	3.2	100.0 (271)
	40s	74.2	15.3	1.4	9.1	100.0 (209)
	50s	66.4	10.1	12.6	10.9	100.0 (119)
	60s	56.3	10.9	21.9	10.9	100.0 (64)

Source: National Family Survey (Korea Broadcasting System & Association of Family Studies, 2000).

distribution living arrangements of the elderly have greatly changed. The proportion of the elderly living as dependents has been greatly reduced to 43 percent. Forty-three percent of the elderly live as heads of household with any dependents, including a wife. The number of the elderly who live alone has greatly increased. Fourteen percent of the old lived alone in 1995 as opposed to only 0.1 percent in 1975. Table 12.3 shows that the living arrangement of the old has changed from coresidence with family members to independent residence. The increase in the number of the old who are heads of household with dependents indicates that the elderly are not just dependents but play a role supporting other family members in their old age. While a significant number of elderly currently live with the eldest son or other children, the attitude toward the most desirable living arrangement, as shown in Table 12.3, has changed from coresidence to independent living.

As shown in Table 12.3, most Koreans today want to live independently of their offspring when they are old. The most preferred living arrangement in old age for Koreans aged under 60 is to live in a couple. The second preferred living arrangement is to live with any children who want to live with the parents. However, a significant proportion of those aged 60 and over still prefers living with the eldest son. The figures in Table 12.3 reflect significant changes in the attitude toward living arrangements of the elderly. The traditional living arrangement preferred under the principle of filial piety was for children to coreside with and support their old parents. Although filial piety and respect for the elderly are still considered valu-

Table 12.4   Experience of Crisis in Various Family Affairs by Type of
Residence with Parents or Parents-in-Law (%)

Type of Family Crisis	Coresidence	Independent Residence
Extramarital affair	9.1	7.3
Gambling/addiction	3.9	7.0
Family violence	3.9	3.9
Unemployment/bankruptcy	2.7	18.3
Deviation of children	1.9	2.0
Conflict with parents or parents-in-law	19.2	15.0
Conspicuous consumption	5.8	4.4

Source: National Family Survey (Korea Broadcasting System & Association of Family Studies, 2000).

able, the attitude toward living arrangements of the elderly has remarkably changed in every age group. People may recognize that living independently is one of the best ways to reduce conflict between family members. Conflicts with parents or parents-in-law is the most frequent among conflicts in family relationship (see Table 12.4). Data from the National Family Study provide evidence that such conflict is more likely to occur when parents and adult children coreside. Nearly 20 percent of those who are living with parents or parents-in-law among the respondents of the National Family Study report that they experienced a severe conflict with their parents or parents-in-law. Among those who are not living with parents, only 15 percent reported that they had a serious conflict with parents or parents-in-law.

The State and Elderly Care

When compared with changes in the attitude toward elderly care and living arrangement at the individual and familial levels in an aging society, attitudes at the state level have not changed. The state always attributes the responsibility of elderly care to the family, or is likely to blame the nuclear family for neglecting its "duty" to care for the elderly (Chang, 1997a, 1997b, 1999).

The state accepted neo-Confucianism as a ruling ideology, and encouraged people to compete for the title of *hyoja* (a person who does filial piety sincerely) in the past. Children had to strive to support elderly parents regardless of their socioeconomic conditions. As for the literati and ruling class, practicing filial piety above all was taken for granted in everyday life. The state just fostered filial piety on the one hand by praising and awarding, and on the other hand by negative sanctions or punishment.

However, the state's attitude toward elderly care was contradictory to the teachings of orthodox Confucianism. According to Canda (2000), who interprets the teachings of Confucianism in the contemporary context, a Confucian state has the responsibility to care for the elderly. The constitution of the Republic of Korea declares that citizens who are not able to support themselves are protected by the state. But this does not mean that citizens have the right to require concrete welfare from the state. It is just significant in that the state set the standard for the future enactment.

Therefore, despite the stipulation in the constitution, various laws on the protection of livelihood are just supplementary to support by relatives (Kim, 1998, p. 425). The state, instead, stipulates the supporters in the law. According to the civil law in Korea, the supporter is determined in order of importance as spouse, direct descendants, direct ascendants, brothers and sisters, and elder brother of father (ibid.:428). In the tradition of Confucianism, the responsibility for elderly care is completely handed over to the family by law, and no one has questioned this arrangement. The order to return what the government already paid in the case, discussed in the beginning of this chapter, reiterated to ordinary people that the responsibility to support the elderly is in the hands of the family. By continuously mobilizing Confucian social values and norms including filial piety selectively on the one hand, and by stipulating the family's responsibility on the other hand, the state is completely free from the burden of the duty to protect citizens in need.

Table 12.5 shows how far the Korean government has distanced itself from welfare when compared with other advanced nations. Korea expends on social security much less than advanced countries in the West. It is far behind Mexico and Japan, yet spends more than Singapore and Thailand. Singapore scrutinizes the Confucian values much more, and Thailand is less developed than Korea in economic terms. But Korea, a member of the OECD, expends less on social security although it expends more on defense than other nations.

The State and Elderly Care after the Welfare Reform

There was no problem in family support for the elderly without any substantial welfare program by the state when the economic conditions of Korea were good. The financial crisis since late 1997, however, provided the opportunity to question fundamentally the state's policy of attributing the responsibility of elderly care to the family. With this economic crisis Koreans realized that the apparently successful economic development was no longer the case. As the number of people who were laid off increased, the unemployment rate soared within a very short time. It appeared as though the family, which

Table 12.5 Government Expenditure in Selected Countries (% of Government Expenditure)

Country	Year	Social security	Education	Economic affair	Defense	Gov't expenditure/ GDP
Australia	1998	39.8	13.6	6.8	7.8	21.7
Canada	1995	44.3	3.4	8.7	6.3	23.4
Chile	1998	33.9	20.4	13.9	8.3	22.7
Japan	1997	22.4	6.9	4.1	6.3	15.5
Korea	1998	10.9	14.9	26.9	12.1	25.3
Philippines	1997	2.5	20.3	22.1	7.9	19.4
Mexico	1997	18.5	2.3	18.0	3.6	15.9
Singapore	1997	1.1	12.0	10.9	18.4	26.1
Sweden	1998	43.5	6.8	10.6	5.5	41.1
United Kingdom	1998	36.3	4.0	4.5	7.1	36.8
United States	1998	28.7	1.8	5.1	15.3	19.8

Source: National Family Survey (Korea Broadcasting System & Association of Family Studies, 2000, p. 583).

had been seen as stable and strong before, began to dissolve rapidly. It was at that time that homelessness became a highly visible social problem in Korean society.

Faced with the economic crisis, the family completely lost its ability to protect the socially weak such as the elderly and the disabled. In fact, the family was not strong enough to be able to meet the needs of the socially weak even before the economic crisis. But under visible and invisible pressure by norms and values and legal regulations, the family had to cope with the burden of supporting the elderly. The economic crisis just revealed how weak the family as a social support.

Right after the crisis the state became aware of the need for at least a minimal welfare program to prevent society from collapsing. The Korean government introduced the concept of "productive welfare" in launching the new welfare programs. According to this concept, social assistance was directed toward education, job training, and massive public works. Also, the concept of balancing rights and responsibilities was introduced. Social assistance recipients can receive social assistance as a right. The National Basic Livelihood Protection Act (NBLPA) was enacted in 1999 as part of a series of welfare programs in accordance with the principle of balancing rights and responsibilities as a part of social assistance benefits. However, because the program covers so little, most beneficiaries do not escape poverty.

As far as elderly care is concerned, the effort of the government is neg-ligible. The government is still depending on mobilizing Confucian values in care for the elderly. According to the official report to the president by the Ministry of Health and Welfare, the government aims at promoting *hyo* (filial piety) in its contemporary meaning by consolidating the close rela-tionship among the family, society, and state (Ministry of Health and Wel-fare, 1999). Although the Korean government has revealed that it intends to pursue elderly care "through the family," there has been no substantial program to strengthen the family or for elderly care through the family. As the constitution clearly declares the right of the socially weak without any substantial benefits from the state, the family is always at the front line of elderly care without any substantial assistance from the state. The propor-tion of the budget for the elderly welfare was just 0.19 percent of the total government budget in 1997. It increased to 0.25 in 1998 and 1999. In 2000, it still remains at 0.32 percent of the total government budget.

In summary, a new phase of welfare system began in Korea after the 1997 economic crisis under the concept of "productive welfare." However, the benefits are small and the number of beneficiaries is small. The welfare programs are still far short of satisfactory. As far as elderly care is con-cerned, the state's welfare program is nearly negligible. This welfare for the aged "through the family" has not been carried out despite repeated promises by the state. The family still takes charge of elderly care, although it is on the verge of its own collapse.

SUMMARY AND DISCUSSION

The West looks to the East for an alternative to the current welfare system. A long history of care for the elderly by the family in the East is sure to attract the attention of Western observers. How is it possible for the fam-ily to be in charge of elderly care in the East? Western observers think that cultural traits, some of which come from Confucianism, are fundamental factors for family care to the elderly, and that no remarkable welfare pro-grams are needed in the East. Is it really so?

In this chapter I suggest that so-called Confucian values in the East, par-ticularly in Korea, are very hard to discern from other cultural and reli-gious traits. Neo-Confucian values played a great role for ordinary people as well as the literati and ruling class in accepting and internalizing filial piety and respect for the elderly in traditional Korean society. The state forced people, regardless of social status, to care for their elderly parents using both rewards and negative sanctions.

Critical intellectuals have criticized the validity of Confucian social val-ues and norms in the contemporary period. At the individual level they are criticized because they emphasize obedience to parents and authority even when they are not right. At the societal level, it is criticized for having served as a "fascist" mechanism of social order. The illegitimate military regimes in Korea mobilized selectively Confucian values and norms in order to acquire legitimacy.

Ordinary people, however, still regard the core Confucian values as effective values in Korea in the twenty-first century. Even the graduates of Seoul National University, who were very resistant to the military regimes, accepted the validity of Confucian values. In accordance with positive attitudes toward filial piety and respect for the elderly, people think that the family has the duty to support elderly parents. Instead of the traditional view of the sole responsibility of the eldest son, people think that any child who can and wants to support parents is suitable to care for them. People do not consider the state or society as the primary caregiver to the parents. This observation is very surprising in light of the increasing demand for welfare by the state.

Despite harsh criticism of Confucian values by intellectuals, Confucian values including filial piety and respect for the elderly still appear to be influential in the minds of ordinary people in Korea. This may be an example of Confucian "habits of the heart," a secularized version of Confucianism (Kim, 1994, p. 101),

Koreans have a very frequent interaction with close family members. Intergenerational transfers show that there is a significant proportion of mutual transfers between parents and married children. Parents are not limited to being the beneficiaries of intergenerational transfers. They are more likely to be the providers to children even after children marry. This type of intergenerational transfer is also found between children and parents-in-law. Although Korea is a patriarchal society, the intergenerational transfer between children and parents-in-law opens the possibility of an extended network of support beyond the nuclear family.

Living arrangements have changed significantly. While many Koreans aged 60 and above are living with their eldest sons, coresiding with the eldest son or any child is no longer a preferred living arrangement for Koreans aged under 60.

Contrary to the many changes in attitudes and behaviors of individuals, the state has not changed much. Depending on the Confucian authority on the one hand, and mobilizing Confucian values on the other hand, the state escapes from the burden of caring for the elderly. The family has managed to support the elderly without assistance from the state. Family care of the elderly was only possible while the economic conditions were better. When faced with the economic crisis after 1997, the myth of care for the elderly by the family began to collapse. With the increasing unemployment and dissolution of the family, the government had to implement a series of welfare programs including the support for the elderly. The welfare programs, however, have not worked well. Benefits are so small that most beneficiaries fail to escape poverty.

Ordinary Koreans do not insist on coresidence any more. Instead, they are likely to pursue independent living as Western elders do. But they keep close and frequent contacts with other family members. Intergenerational transfers between parents and adult children continue before and after children marry, and parents frequently support their married children financially. These practices make it possible for the family to be responsible for care of the elderly regardless of the lack of assistance from the state.

However, the family alone cannot care for the elderly without any outside assistance (C.-S. Kim, 2001; D.-S. Kim, 2001; Park, 2001). From the experience of hard times since the 1997 economic crisis, we know that the family in Korea is not stable and strong enough to be solely responsible for supporting the elderly. For the family to continue to be a primary caregiver to the old, the state must play a significant role through welfare programs. At least, the state has to make efforts to set up a social safety net as soon as possible. When the family fails to support the aged, a social safety net has to work to reduce difficulties in the elderly's experience. Without the expansion of the role of the state, it is now clear that the family cannot be a responsible caregiver in the future.

As aging of society proceeds with declining fertility and mortality rates, the capacity of the family to care for the elderly decreases. Moreover, as women increasingly take part in the labor force, and as their educational attainment increases, the availability of family caregivers is further reduced.

Korea represents a very unique situation, where a high reliance on Confucian values still enables the family to be the primary caregiver to the elderly without any substantial support from the state. We might expect to find a similar case in other societies that emphasized Confucian values for so long and that, as Korea, have utilized these values as mechanisms of social control. However, in Western societies, where individualism, not familism or collectivism, is a fundamental value, it is very hard to expect families to play a similar role to that of families in East Asian societies and particularly Korea. "The internal, sentimental life of the family" (Shorter, 2001, p. 181), which has continued for so long with few changes, under the Confucian values of filial piety and respect for the elderly, is related to the unique practice of family care for the elderly in Korea. In this respect, the "Eastern" model of family care for elderly, if any, is difficult to apply in the West.

REFERENCES

Academy of Korean Studies. 1999a. General survey for graduates of Seoul National University raw data.
_____. 1999b. National social survey raw data.
Bengtson, V. L., and Putney, N. M. 2000. Who will care for tomorrow's elderly? Consequences of population aging East and West. In V. L. Bengtson, K.-D. Kim, G. C. Myers, and K.-S. Eun (eds.), *Aging in east and west: Families, states, and the elderly.* New York: Springer.
Canda, E. 2000. Insights from classical Confucianism for contemporary social welfare: The book of rites and beyond. Paper presented at the 3rd colloquium, Academy of Korean Studies.
Chang, K.-S. 1997a. The Neo-Confucian right and family politics in South Korea: The nuclear family as an ideological construct. *Economy and Society* 26(1):22–42.
_____. 1997b. Modernity through the family: Familial foundations of Korean society. *International Review of Sociology* 7(1):51–64.
_____. 1999. Social ramifications of South Korea's economic fall: Neo-liberal antidote to compressed capitalist industrialization? *Development and Society* 28(1):49–91.
Choi, B.-C. 1999. *Confucius must live for the nation to live* (in Korean). Seoul: Sia.
Choi, J.-S. 1963. *Social attitude and characters of Koreans* (in Korean). Seoul: Hyuneumsa.
Jeong, S.-B. 2000. Hsiao in Confucianism and its significance in contemporary society. *Journal of Humanities* 34:33–49 (in Korean). Research Institute of Humanities. Kon-Kuk University, Seoul.
Jeong, U.-C. 2000. The psychology of sadaebu (the literati) in hyojajeon (stories of filial piety). *Journal of Humanities* 34:51–69 (in Korean). Research Institute of Humanities. Kon-Kuk University, Seoul.
JoongAng Ilbo. 2001. *JoongAng Daily,* April 6.
Kim, C.-S. 2001. The role of the old, family and state as subjects of elderly care. In D.-S. Kim (ed.), *Changing lives of the elderly and the aging welfare* (in Korean). Seoul: Hanyang University Press.
Kim, D.-S. 2001. Changes in Korean society and family relations in old ages. In D.-S. Kim (ed.). *Changing lives of the elderly and the aging welfare* (in Korean). Seoul: Hanyang University Press.
Kim, J.-S. 1998. *Civil law-family law* (5th ed.; in Korean). Seoul: Bupmoonsa.
Kim, K.-D. 1994. Confucianism and capitalist development in East Asia. In L. Sklair (ed.), *Capitalism and development.* London: Routledge.
_____. 1996. Confucianism and modernization in East Asia: theoretical explorations. In J. Kreiner (ed.). *The impact of traditional thought on present-day Japan.* Munich: Iudicium Verlag.
Kim, K.-I. 1999. *Confucius must die for the nation to live* (in Korean). Seoul: Bada.
Korea National Statistical Office (1998). General social survey raw data.
Lee, J.-K. 1999. A modern change of Korean family viewed from the experience of woman. *Journal of Korean Woman's Studies* 15(2):55–86 (in Korean).

Mason, K. O. (1992). Family change and support of the elderly in Asia: What do we know? *Asia-Pacific Population Journal* 7(3).

Ministry of Health and Welfare (1999). Official report of medium- and long-term development plan for the elderly welfare. Ministry of Health and Welfare, Seoul.

Park, K.-S. 2001. Aging of the labor market: Socioeconomic effect. In D.-S. Kim (ed.), *Changing lives of the elderly and the aging welfare* (in Korean). Seoul: Hanyang University Press.

Shin, D.-H. 2000. The concept of "hyo" of commoners in narrative legendary literature. *Journal of Humanities* 34:71–86 (in Korean). Research Institute of Humanities, Kon-Kuk University, Seoul.

Shorter, E. 2001 Review on Jack Goody's *The European family. Population and Development Review* 27(1):181–83.

|13|

Intergenerational Relationships of Japanese Seniors

Changing Patterns

Wataru Koyano

During the twentieth century, Japan experienced drastic social changes. As a results of these changes, the lives of today's Japanese are more Westernized and show a unique mixture of Oriental tradition and Westernized modernity. The family life of Japanese seniors has also changed and is still changing rapidly.

Before the end of World War II, the family was conceptualized as *ie* (lineage), and relationships among family members were normatively defined. Typically, seniors lived with their successors' nuclear family within the same household, and coresiding family members provided all the support needed. Therefore, even if seniors were completely dependent, and they often were, their lives seemed secured because the coresiding family members were "protective" (Hashimoto, 1996). The Confucian norm of filial piety was the normative factor that regulated intergenerational relationships.

Changes in the latter half of the twentieth century started when World War II ended and progressed along with Japan's remarkable economic growth. The ideal way of family life in prewar Japan was officially renounced, and the conception of *ie* and the Confucian norm of filial piety gradually disappeared from people's everyday life. Because of the maturation of public old-age pensions, the necessity for informal instrumental support was reduced. Coresidence with adult children became optional for Japanese seniors, and affection became the pivotal dimension of intergenerational solidarity. These changes in the family life of Japanese seniors provide an example for the old thesis of family sociology known as "from institution to affection."

In this chapter, I describe the changing patterns in family life of Japanese seniors that occurred in the twentieth century, as well as the currently observed patterns of intergenerational relationships in the Japanese society.

IDEAL WAYS OF FAMILY LIFE IN THE FIRST HALF OF THE TWENTIETH CENTURY

In the early half of the twentieth century, the ideal way of family life was clearly defined. The idea is now known as *ie* ideology. The *ie* ideology was established and propagated, through legislation and education, by the imperial government of Japan. The *ie* ideology consisted of two elements: conception of *ie* and paternalism within the family. The Japanese word *ie* has several meanings including family, lineage, home, and house. Within the context of the *ie* ideology, however, the word exclusively means lineage, which is conceptualized as continuously succeeding from generation to generation. Because each family was conceived as a small link in the long chain of lineage, family name, assets, social status, and occupation were inherited by the eldest son. Tombs and home Buddhist altars (in which the mortuary tablets of ancestors were placed) were also to pass to the eldest son in order to continue the ancestor worship of lineage. If there was no son, the adoption of a successor was undertaken through or not through marriage. If there was no son but daughters, adoption through marriage with the eldest daughter was arranged.

As typically found in the adoption of a successor, marriage was conceived as a means of continuation of lineage. Therefore, a marriage had to be carefully arranged in order to conform to the main purpose of marriage (i.e., maintenance of lineage), and should not be made freely by the couple without the permission of the heads of both families.

Inequality among family members—in terms of their importance, power, and privileges—was taken for granted. There was an order of importance and power among family members. Typically, the father was the household head and had the supreme position and legal power to predominate over other family members. The position, power, and privileges of the household head served as a means of fulfilling his obligations to maintain the family name, social status, and all assets of the lineage, and to pass them over to the next household head (ideally, his eldest son). The wife of the household head was expected to serve and obey her husband— the household head—but could have a superior position as a parent. Among children, the eldest son was given a superior position as the future household head.

The obedience of children to their parents or parents-in-law was regarded as an expression of filial piety. Filial piety was an extremely important moral virtue corresponding to the infinite grace of parents, including the grace of bearing children, nurturing them, and allowing them to marry. Filial piety was repeatedly taught in moral education and children were instructed to obey their parents and to never resist them.

The norm of filial piety was propagated by the imperial Japanese government in combination with loyalty to the emperor. Ideally, only the family and the nation were regarded as "formal" organizations, and the nation was conceptualized as a big family, consisting of real families, headed by the Emperor. Then, filial piety and loyalty to the Emperor were tightly interwoven in the imperial Japanese ideology.

Under the *ie* ideology, a senior was typically a retired household head, who had already transferred the headship to his eldest son, his wife, or his widow. Seniors lived with the successor's nuclear family within the same household and were provided with all types of support by the successor, his wife, and children. For the successor, coresiding and sharing all assets with elderly parents were legal, as well as moral, obligations. Furthermore, providing support to elderly parents was not only an obligation but also an actualization of filial piety. Therefore, the successor and his nuclear family were expected to provide support with gratitude and respect for the elderly parents. In moral education in prewar Japan, it was accepted and praiseworthy to serve parents while neglecting one's wife and children.

The above described ideal life of the elderly in prewar Japan was deduced from the *ie* ideology. There was no empirical datum indicating the actual lives and attitudes of people. Reality might have been different from this ideal type. However, it is important to note that the ideal way of family life in old age was normatively defined and legally institutionalized.

CHANGES DURING THE LATTER HALF OF THE TWENTIETH CENTURY

After World War II, as a part of the democratization of Japan, the *ie* ideology was officially renounced, and the conception of *ie* was completely removed from the constitution and civil law. The constitution declares that agreement between the couple is the only basis for marriage, and civil law gives the highest priority of support to the wife and children rather than to elderly parents. Filial piety was no longer taught in classrooms, at least not in the original and extreme form found in prewar Japan.

Instead of *ie* and the Confucian norms, American ways of family life became the new model (Miura, 1999). The nuclear family shown in American TV dramas, in which affectionate relations abounded, seemed fresh and happy and was accepted as an ideal goal. "American styles" were imitated in almost all facets of family life. People started to use refrigerators and washing machines. They started to use dining tables and chairs instead of *chabudai* (Japanese low table for dining) and *zabuton* (sitting mattress). *Tatami* (matting with grass) was partly replaced by wooden floors, and many parents made their children call them "papa" and "mama."

In terms of the structural aspects of the family, the population census shows that the nuclear family household rapidly increased from 52.6 percent in 1955 to 79.2 percent in 1995, and that the average number of household members significantly decreased from 4.97 in 1955 to 2.88 in 1995. For seniors aged 65 years and older, coresidence with adult children started to decrease in the 1960s. Because the concept of *ie* was eliminated, coresidence with elderly parents was no longer an obligation of children. Nevertheless, the percentage of seniors coresiding with adult children was very high for several decades. However, as shown in Table 13.1, from 1960 and during a 40-year period, the frequency of coresidence decreased from 86.8 to 50.5 percent, while that of living alone and living only with spouse increased from 3.8 to 13.8 percent and from 7.0 to 30.9 percent, respectively. The percentage of coresidence is generally lower in urban areas, among employees and members of the younger generation, and is expected to further decrease.

Changes in people's attitudes toward the conception of *ie* and support for elderly parents can be traced in opinion polls. Matsunari (1991) reviewed nationwide opinion polls and found a gradual decline in positive attitudes toward the *ie* ideology. For the adoption of a successor, the percentages of people showing positive attitudes decreased from 73 percent in 1953 to 28 percent in 1988, and for dependence on children in old age, the percentage decreased from 59 percent in 1950 to 18 percent in 1990. She commented that the percentages of people with positive and negative attitudes toward dependence on children reversed in the 1960s when the old-age pension became effective.

An opinion poll conducted in 1986 showed that a relatively small portion of people aged 20–59 years preferred to have economically close ties with children in their old age. The percentage of persons willing to have economically close but not emotionally close ties was only 4 percent, and 19 percent preferred to have both emotionally and economically close ties. The remaining 37 percent preferred to have emotionally close but not economically close ties, and 31 percent preferred to keep their independence.

The Japanese word used for describing the informal support provided by adult children to elderly parents is *fuyo*. Although *fuyo* may possibly include any type of support, the nuance of the word specifies instrumental support, especially financial aid and long-term care. It was the

Table 13.1   Changes (%) in Living Arrangement of Japanese Seniors

	Living Alone	Only with Spouse	With Children	Other[a]
1960	3.8	7.0	86.8	2.4
1965	4.6	9.1	83.8	2.5
1970	5.3	11.7	79.6	3.4
1975	6.6	15.1	74.4	3.9
1980	7.8	18.1	69.8	4.3
1985	9.2	20.6	65.5	4.7
1990	10.9	24.1	60.6	4.4
1995	12.1	27.8	55.9	4.3
2000	13.8	30.9	50.5	4.8
Men	8.0	41.8	46.8	3.3
Women	17.9	23.1	53.1	5.9

[a]Including institutionalized persons.
Source: Population Census.

instrumental support that was extremely stressed as the actualization of filial piety in prewar Japan. However, at the end of the twentieth century, while the majority of Japanese people preferred to keep emotionally close ties with their adult children in old age, they did not want to depend on them. Based on the opinion polls, it appears that the emotional closeness becomes the essential part or the basis for intergenerational relationships, while instrumental support has been reduced in importance.

RECENT PATTERNS OF INTERGENERATIONAL RELATIONSHIPS

Traditionally, most Japanese studies on families in later life focused mainly on the coresidence with adult children (for articles in English, see, for example, Hiroshima, 1987; Kojima, 1989; O'Leary, 1993; Tsuya and Martin, 1992). This emphasis was a result of several factors, including the high proportion of Japanese seniors coresiding with adult children, the central role of the family in the social support system of Japanese seniors (Koyano, Hashimoto, Fukawa, Shibata, and Gunji, 1994), and the sociological interest in the pervasiveness of Confucian norms. Coresidence was frequently viewed as an indicator of acceptance of the *ie* ideology and support provided by coresident children, because coresidence and support are only a portion of the *ie* ideology that is still accepted by Japanese today (Naoi, 2001; Takahashi, 1987), and actually, coresiding family members—being able to provide any type of support irrespective of situational factors such as health and socioeconomic status of parents—are the most dependable source of support (Koyano et al., 1994).

However, more recent empirical studies have challenged the focus on coresidence for the following reasons: (1) the percentage of seniors coresiding with adult children has been gradually decreasing and is especially lower in the new cohorts that enter old age; (2) coresidence with a child who is not the eldest son has become more common especially in urban areas (Koyano and Okamura, 1996; Naoi, 2001); (3) living arrangement are more strongly affected by situational factors, such as home ownership and occupation, than by the traditional norm of filial piety (Naoi, Okamura, and Hayashi, 1984; Sakamoto, 1996); (4) major parts of the *ie* ideology, such as the continuity of lineage and the inequality among family members, have become less accepted (Matsunari, 1991; Takahashi, 1987); (5) intergenerational exchanges are likely to take place irrespective of the lineage (Naoi, 2001; Sakamoto, 1996); and (6) coresidence does not indicate a single pattern of family life of seniors (Nishimura, Koyano, Ishibashi, and Yamada, 2001). From these research findings, the necessity to observe everyday interactions between elderly parents and their adult children, rather than coresidence or attitudes toward *ie*, becomes apparent. However, there are very few studies that focus on everyday interactions of seniors in Japan. The next section will briefly discuss two such studies.

Variety of Coresidence

Under the *ie* ideology in prewar Japan, sharing all assets with elderly parents and providing every type of support were the duty of the coresiding successor. Therefore, coresidence automatically meant one type of family life in which elderly parents and successors' family of procreation shared the same space, dined together, and shared financial expenses. At the end of the twentieth century, however, the pattern of intergenerational sharing of living becomes not uniform even among coresident households. Using a nationally representative sample of Japanese seniors, aged 65 years and over, coresiding with one married child under the same roof ($n = 732$), Nishimura et al. (2001) found that 74 percent shared the same living room, kitchen, bathroom, toilet, and entrance of the house with the child's nuclear family, 80 percent ate dinner with the child's family very frequently, and 78 percent shared economic expenses. Although these percentages are very high, the pattern of sharing was not identical: 56 percent shared space, dining, and household economy with the child's nuclear family; only 8 percent did not share at all; and the remaining one-third were mixtures. The percentage of seniors sharing all of the three was lower in urban areas, where the percentage of coresidence was also lower.

The results of this study confirm that coresidence generally implies some extent of intergenerational sharing of living. However, while over 50 percent of seniors coresiding with one married child are in the traditional pattern of coresidence (i.e., sharing all space, dining, and household economy), the pattern of sharing is not uniform. As long as coresidence does not indicate one single pattern of family lifestyle, coresidence itself is a very poor indicator of intergenerational relationships that can indicate merely a level of geographical distance. The variability of intergenerational sharing of living in the coresiding family should naturally turn our research from coresidence to dyadic interactions between seniors and their family members.

Everyday Interactions

A second study (Koyano, 1996) focused directly on the dyadic relationships of Japanese seniors. The survey was carried out in two distinctive areas: Setagaya Ward, Metropolitan Tokyo, and Yonezawa City, Yamagata Prefecture. Setagaya is a relatively affluent suburban area in Tokyo that has been at the forefront of social changes in Japan, while Yonezawa City is a more traditional provincial city, being a regional center for agriculture and light industry. Although the respondents ($n = 882$) were in the same age range, 65 to 79 years old, the frequency of coresidence with married children was significantly higher in Yonezawa (62 percent) than in Setagaya (25 percent). The difference in the percentages of coresidence suggest that the traditional pattern of family life established under the *ie* ideology is still alive more strongly in Yonezawa than in Setagaya.

In spite of the large differences in living arrangement, seniors' everyday interactions with others are almost identical. Table 13.2 shows the percentages of others who had the two types of interactions with the respondents: emotional closeness and enacted instrumental support. Further analysis of the data shows that emotional closeness and social support are interrelated yet distinctive dimensions of social relationships of Japanese seniors (Asakawa, Koyano, Ando, and Kodama, 1999). For emotional closeness ("make relaxed") felt by seniors, the highest percentage was found for wives, followed by husbands, daughters, sons, siblings, and friends. For instrumental support ("running errands") received by seniors, however, the order was different: the highest percentage was also found for wives, but was followed by daughters and daughters-in-law living together.

Both in Setagaya and Yonezawa, the sources of instrumental support were almost restricted to family members living together, followed by children living apart, but to a lesser degree. However, even among family members living together, husbands, wives, sons, daughters, and daughters-in-law have different social relationships with seniors. Spouses were emotionally close and well integrated in exchanges of instrumental support. Daughters and daughters-in-law living together were also well integrated in exchanges of instrumental support, but they were different in the

Table 13.2 Percentages of Others Having Two Types of Interactions with Seniors

	Setagaya		Yonezawa	
	Make Relaxed	Running Errands	Make Relaxed	Running Errands
Wife	94.1	81.6	88.4	55.5
Daughter living together	67.0	57.8	41.2	52.9
Daughter living apart	64.4	34.7	60.4	30.6
Daughter-in-law living together	31.6	53.2	33.1	44.8
Daughter-in-law living apart	33.1	18.4	23.3	8.8
Sister	53.7	12.8	41.7	10.3
Friend (women)	59.6	14.0	41.9	8.6
Neighbor (women)	40.8	12.2	37.5	9.2
Husband	77.6	44.8	83.8	48.0
Son living together	37.3	36.0	39.1	29.4
Son living apart	51.2	24.7	42.9	11.9
Son-in-law living together	26.5	23.5	15.6	20.0
Son-in-law living apart	20.3	9.7	18.2	7.8
Brother	45.1	7.8	37.0	9.3
Friend (men)	56.2	11.8	42.8	11.3
Neighbor (men)	37.2	11.2	35.1	8.9

Note: Figures are unweighted percentages.
Source: Koyano (1996).

degree of emotional closeness. Elderly parents did not feel emotionally close to their daughters-in-law living together, but they receive instrumental support from them. When the effects of characteristics of parents and children/children-in-law were controlled, those most likely to be felt emotionally close by elderly parents were daughters living far apart from them, followed by daughters living together (Koyano et al., 1995). However, those most likely to provide instrumental support were daughters living together with elderly parents. Daughters-in-law living together provided instrumental support as frequently as daughters living far apart, though they were far less likely to be felt emotionally close by elderly parents than daughters. Such unnatural relationships seem to indicate the difficult situation of daughters-in-law living together and to explain the well-known conflict between mothers and daughters-in-law.

Further analysis of the data demonstrates also that coresidence enhanced exchanges of instrumental support, but was inversely related to emotional closeness (Koyano et al., 1995). Coresidence with a married son, still the preferred living arrangement both in urban and provincial areas (Koyano and Okamura, 1996), is likely to bring harmful interactions with daughters-in-law living together characterized by the frequent exchanges of instrumental support without emotional closeness. Therefore, for seniors without immediate need for instrumental support, avoiding coresidence with children might be a beneficial choice.

INTERGENERATIONAL RELATIONSHIPS IN THE TWENTY-FIRST CENTURY

Rapid population aging is one of the most salient social changes in Japan today. It resulted from the population transition that occurred in the latter half of the twentieth century. During the five decades after World War II, the death rate decreased from 1.46 in 1947 to 0.77 in 2000; total fertility rate has declined from 4.54 to 1.36; and the life expectancy at birth has risen 1.5 times and marked the longest life expectancy in the world (in 2000, 77.72 years for men and 84.60 years for women).

The social changes brought about large generational differences. Especially the baby boomers, who will become seniors in the early half of the twenty-first century, are, in many ways, completely different from former generations. The baby boomers have made significant changes in lifestyle and social conditions throughout their life course, including an increase in higher education, increased labor force participation of women, growth of a new familism, and increased mass consumption. These changes will change the lifestyle of Japanese seniors when the baby boomers reach old age. They are the first generation that can foresee and intentionally prepare for their prolonged old age, though they are still uncertain as to what it will be like. When they enter the aged population, defined as the population aged 65 years and older, aging of the Japanese population will reach its peak and the images of seniors and of old age will drastically change.

Even among today's seniors, the young-old, who are one generation prior to the baby boomers, are already different from older generations. Compared with the old-old, they are much healthier, wealthier, better educated, and as a result also more functionally, economically, socially, and psychologically independent. The decrease of coresidence among seniors, observed in the latter half of the twentieth century (see Table 13.1), was brought about by such younger generations that entered the aged population. For them, filial piety and the conception of *ie* seem to sound somehow old-fashioned, feudalistic, and irrelevant to their everyday lives. Therefore, intergenerational relationships have become more affection-based, convenience-oriented, irrelevant to the *ie* ideology, and free from the norm of filial piety (see Naoi, 2001; Naoi et al., 1984; Sakamoto, 1996). For them, coresidence with children is optional, and avoiding it might be a beneficial choice.

The reasons leading to coresidence are complex. For example, the Confucian norm of filial piety, tradition of *ie*, affection between parents and children, and the shortage of housing may possibly contribute to the high percentage of coresidence of Japanese seniors. Among such potential factors, filial piety and the tradition of *ie* have attracted a great deal of research interest. In contrast, the frequently forgotten aspect is the necessity of informal instrumental support. As mentioned earlier, two types of instrumental support provided by adult children were greatly emphasized as the actualization of filial piety in prewar Japan. They were financial aid and long-term care for disabled parents. For most seniors at that time, coresidence was the only possible way to sustain their lives, by receiving financial aid and/or long-term care from children. Such conditions did not change for a few decades after the war. The situation started to change in the 1960s, the period of Japan's great economic growth, when the old age pension became effective and visible. In opinion polls, from the 1960s, the percentage of people with negative attitudes toward dependence on children in old age became higher than those with positive attitudes (Matsunari, 1991). In census data, the percentage of coresidence started to decrease in the 1960s.

While the need for informal financial aid decreased due to the old age pension, long-term family care has long remained important and necessary. Because of selectivism and the shortage of services under the traditional welfare service system, the vast majority of disabled seniors must be cared for by coresiding family members without any formal care services. This situation is widely known and causes anxiety about long-term care in old age to the average Japanese. However, the importance of family care may possibly be reduced by the introduction of a new long-term care system, named Insurance Against Care, enacted in 2000. This insurance acknowledges societal responsibility for long-term care (see Koyano, 1999). The insurance is a response to the changes in family life of seniors symbolized by the decrease of coresidence with adult children. At the same time, it may further stimulate the changes, which began in the 1960s, through reducing the importance and necessity of the instrumental support stressed in prewar Japan.

While the ideal way of family life in old age was clearly defined and institutionalized in the first half of the twentieth century, it is quite ambiguous now. Compared with necessity-based or norm-based relationships, affection-based intergenerational relationships are much more complex and variable in nature. Further, because of the drastic social changes in the last century, the ideal way of life in old age becomes uncertain in Japan. Kodama et al. (1995) found a persistence of the Oriental tradition and ambivalence in the preferred lifestyle in old age among Japanese middle-aged persons including the baby boomers. Although the theme of their study was general lifestyle in old age, the situation seems similar to family life and intergenerational relationships. At the beginning of the twenty-first century, groping for new ideal ways of family life in old age has just begun.

REFERENCES

Asakawa, T., Koyano, W., Ando, T., and Kodama, Y. 1999. The structure and the abundance of social relationships of the elderly. *Japanese Journal of Gerontology (Ronen Shakai Kagaku)* 21:329–88 (in Japanese with English abstract).

Hashimoto, A. 1996. *The gift of generations: Japanese and American perspectives on aging and the social contract.* New York: Cambridge University Press.

Hiroshima, K. 1987. Recent changes in prevalence of parent-child coresidence in Japan. *Journal of Population Research (Jinkogaku Kenkyu)* 10:33–41.

Kodama, Y., Koyano, W., Okamura, K., Ando, T., Hasegawa, M., and Asakawa, T. 1995. Preferred ways of living in old age among middle-aged persons in urban area. *Japanese Journal of Gerontology (Ronen Shakai Kagaku)* 17:66–73 (in Japanese with English abstract).

Kojima, H. 1989. Intergenerational household extension in Japan. In F. K. Goldscheider and C. Goldscheider (eds.), *Ethnicity and the new family economy.* Boulder, CO: Westview.

Koyano, W. 1996. Filial piety and intergenerational solidarity in Japan. *Australian Journal on Ageing* 15:51–56; *Hong Kong Journal of Gerontology* 10:3–10 (joint issue).

———. 1999. Population aging, changes in living arrangement, and the new long-term care system in Japan. *Journal of Sociology and Social Welfare* 26:155–67.

Koyano, W., Hashimoto, M., Fukawa, T., Shibata, H., and Gunji, A. 1994. The social support system of the Japanese elderly. *Journal of Cross-Cultural Gerontology* 9:323–33.

Koyano, W., and Okamura, K. 1996. Co-residence with married daughters and the tradition of *ie*: The percentage of elderly parents without son. *Indices of Health and Welfare (Kosei no Shihyo)* 43(3):23–26 (in Japanese).

Koyano, W., Okamura, K., Ando, T., Hasegawa, M., Asakawa, T., and Kodama, Y. 1995. Characteristics of children affecting the relationships between elderly parents and their children. *Japanese Journal of Gerontology (Ronen Shakai Kagaku)* 16:136–45 (in Japanese with English abstract).

Matsunari, M. 1991. Changes in family ideology in post-war Japan: Based on results of nation-wide public-opinion polls. *Japanese Journal of Family Sociology (Kazoku Shakaigaku Kenkyu)* 3:85–97 (in Japanese with English abstract).

Miura, A. 1999. *The history of "family" and "happiness" after the World War (Kazoku to Kohuku no Sengoshi)* (in Japanese). Tokyo: Kodansha.

Naoi, M. 2001. *To age successfully: Support of family and welfare system (Kofuku ni Oiru Tameni: Kazoku to Fukushi no Support)* (in Japanese). Tokyo: Keiso Shobo.

Naoi, M., Okamura, K., and Hayashi, H. 1984. Living arrangements of old people and some comments about future change. *Social Gerontology (Shakai Ronengaku)* 21:3–21 (in Japanese with English abstract).

Nishimura, M., Koyano, W., Ishibashi, T., and Yamada, Y. (2001). Share of living in the co-resident household. *Indices of Health and Welfare (Kosei no Shihyo)* 48(11):28–33 (in Japanese).

O'Leary, J. S. 1993. A new look at Japan's honorable elders. *Journal of Aging Studies* 7:1–24.

Sakamoto, K. 1996. Analyzing the relationship between the elderly and their children in Japan. In V. Minichiello, N. Chapell, A. Walker, and H. Kendig (eds.), *Sociology of aging: International perspectives.* 474–81. Melbourne: THOTH.

Takahashi, M. 1987. Family consciousness among urban elderly. *Japanese Journal of Gerontology (Ronen Shakai Kagaku)* 9:82–95 (in Japanese with English abstract).

Tsuya, N. O., and Martin, L. G. 1992. Living arrangements of elderly Japanese and attitudes toward inheritance. *Journal of Gerontology: Social Sciences* 47:45–54.

|14|

"Modernization" and Economic Strain

The Impact of Social Change on Material Family Support for Older People in Ghana

Isabella Aboderin

Material family support for older people in Ghana is declining, exposing increasing numbers to destitution and poverty and highlighting the urgent need for policy responses. A key requirement for such policy development, however—a solid understanding of the factors and processes that have underpinned this decline—is so far lacking. The two explanations put forward in the literature—blaming, on the one hand, "modernization" and weakening traditional norms and, on the other, the worsening economic situation in Ghana—are conceptually and epistemologically limited and fail to provide a sound understanding of why and how the decline has come about. Building on a detailed analysis of the existing explanations, and a brief illustration of the main findings of an empirical investigation undertaken in Accra, Ghana, this chapter develops a fuller understanding of the nature, causes, and consequences of the decline.

INTRODUCTION

In Ghana, as in other African countries, material support of older people has traditionally been the responsibility of the family. The dependence of the old on their relatives, especially their children, and the latter's duty to provide for them, are enshrined in the traditional moral code (Apt, 1996; Gyekye, 1996; Nukunya, 1992a). Although some formal systems of old-age security have existed for some time now, their coverage has remained minimal, restricted to former military and government employees. The vast majority of older people continue to rely on their family or their own work for their livelihood. Even among those receiving pensions, many remain partially reliant on family support because their annuities, eroded by inflation, are insufficient to meet their needs (Ahenkora, 1999); HelpAge International, 2000; U.S. Government, 1999). In the last two decades, however (beginning with the World Health Assembly on Ageing in Vienna, 1982), there has been increasing concern among observers of Ghanaian society that the traditional system of old-age family support in Ghana, as in other African countries, is eroding and no longer offering older people the "customary social protection" they once enjoyed (Aboderin, 2000; Apt, 1996, 1997; World Bank, 1994). While caution regarding wholesale claims of a "breakdown" of support is surely justified, there can be no doubt that the adequacy of support—in terms of the extent to which the support is able to meet older people's basic needs—has declined. The support that many older people receive from their families is often no longer sufficient to meet even their basic needs (Aboderin, 2000). The symptoms of this—growing poverty, neglect, and even abandonment of older people—are particularly visible in cities, where community-based charitable services such as HelpAge Ghana have emerged to respond to these problems (Aboderin, 2000; Apt, 2002). Apart from raising awareness and lobbying government, these services engage in running day-centers and income-generating schemes, and sporadically providing basic medicine, food, or household items for the neediest. The decline in family support for older people is occurring at the same time as the numbers and proportion of older people are set to sharply increase. Demographic projections indicate that as a result of reduced infectious, perinatal, and infant mortality and the consequent increases in life expectancy, the number of older people (aged 60 and over) will increase fivefold by 2050. The numbers of those aged 80 and over, meanwhile, will increase by a factor of more than eight (United Nations Population Division, 1999). In view of these trends, observers have feared an "imminent crisis in caring for the elderly" (Apt, 1996, p. 1), and have stressed the urgent need for policies to ensure the welfare of older people in the future (Apt, 1996, 1997; HelpAge International, 1999). Consequently, much if not all of the still relatively small body of research on aging in Ghana—mainly quantitative surveys on status and needs of older people—has been geared to providing an information base for policy development. However, the crucial question as to what factors and processes have led to the decline in support has not so far been addressed, despite its key importance for policy development. As a result, the nature and causes of the decline remain poorly understood.

EXPLANATIONS OF THE DECLINE IN THE LITERATURE

The accounts of the causes of decline in the Ghanaian or African geronto-logical literature (dominated by Professor Apt) put forward two kinds of explanation. The first, drawing on modernization and aging theory notions, argues that industrialization and urbanization have led to a weak-ening of traditional norms and values, and suggests that there is an increasing *unwillingness* on the part of younger people to support aged parents or relatives. In this vein it is argued that city living, urbanization, and access to world media have "weakened cultural ideas that pull the family together" and have thus "transform[ed] the aged into an unwanted stranger whilst the extended family fares poorly" (Apt, 1996, pp. 5, 40). As a result, the "burden" of supporting older people now rests solely on their spouse and children (Apt, 1993). The second explanation, in contrast, draws on local observations, and sees the decline as a consequence of Ghana's worsening economic situation. The argument is that growing material constraints—marked by widespread un- and underemployment and sharply rising costs of living—have led to an *incapacity* of younger people to care adequately for their elders (e.g., Apt, 1997). Both of these explanations undoubtedly capture some of the reality of the factors under-lying the decline in family support for older people. Neither of them, how-ever, is able to provide a solid understanding of how and why the decline has occurred.

"Modernization and Aging" Theory's Explanation

Modernization and aging theory—the notion that urbanization and industrialization cause a decline in status and family support of older peo-ple—emerged in the 1960s in the United States (Burgess, [1960] 1969; Cowgill, 1972, 1974).[1] It was, essentially, an attempt to interpret and explain the growing problems faced by older people in the postwar decades, and the earlier nineteenth-century decline in financial family support for older people that had led to the institution of state pensions. Though Burgess was the first to elaborate on it, the notion of a decline in support for older peo-ple had already been raised in earlier structural-functionalist analyses (e.g., Parsons, 1942). The idea of a declining status of older people went back even further, to eighteenth-century romantic writings (e.g., Smith, [1776] 1936) and Durkheim's *The Division of Labour* ([1893] 1964). The thrust of the theory's explanation, which crystallized strong prevailing popular con-ceptions, is that the young have become less and less willing to support their elders due to modernization in Western societies. This notion was solidly refuted during the 1960s and 1970s, by a series of studies (e.g., and Shanas et al., 1968), which showed that most older people were firmly integrated and involved in exchanges of support with their kin, and that where support was lacking it was not due to an abandonment but because the old person had no family at all or close by. At the same time, emerging historical evidence exposed as a romantic "golden past" myth the assumption that older people in preindustrial society had enjoyed full status and support from their families (Anderson, 1977; Fennell, Phillipson, and Evers, 1988; Laslett and Wall, 1972; Quadagno, 1982, 1999). A decade or so later, and despite the solid critique it had received in the Western literature, modernization and aging theory became the major underpinning of the emerging developing-world aging debate. It was taken as a prediction of the fate that awaited older people as countries continued to "modernize," and it was this concern that fuelled the debate. By the same token, the modernization model was (and continues to be) drawn on as an explanation for any inadequacies or declines in support that were actually observed. The first thing to note in examining the content of modernization and aging theory's explanation is that, apart from positing the decline in support as a corollary of the loss in status and roles of older people, none of the formulations give an explicit account of why, or by what mechanisms, the decline in family support could have come about. More recent literature has also not provided any further insights in this regard. However, a picture of the causal mechanisms inferred by modernization and aging theory can be gleaned through a careful examination of Burgess's and Cowgill's statements, and of some of the key sociological and anthropological sources they drew on (e.g., Burgess and Locke, 1945; Simmons, 1945, 1946). This reveals that modernization and aging theory essentially proposes a twofold mechanism by which "modernization" leads to a decline in family support for older people (Aboderin, 2000). On the one hand, increasing individualism and secularization weaken traditional norms of familism and filial obligation per se by emphasizing the value of independence in old age and implying, for the young, an increasing focus on their nuclear family (self, spouse, and children). What the origins or causes behind the shift toward individualistic values are, however, is not considered. On the other hand, and at the same time, "modernization" weakens younger people's *conformity* with filial obligation norms, by eroding older people's powers to wield the familial, economic, and religious sanctions that traditionally enforced the norms, and by eroding the resources they can offer in exchange for support. This erosion of powers and resources of the old is seen as a result of growing economic independence, education, and geographical migration of the young. As a result of these processes, so modernization theory argues, provision of support becomes dependent on the affective relationship between parents and children, that is, on the extent to which children feel love, gratitude, or sympathy and *wish* to help their parents. Evidently, this explanation is predicated upon classical structural-functionalist conceptions of support in "traditional" preindustrial society, which assume that it was compelled by binding filial obligation norms and sanctions and, additionally, by the receipt of services in exchange. The idea is that support was adequate because it was provided regardless of the affective relationship between parents and children.

Conceptual Limitations in Modernization and Aging Theory's Explanation

There are two major conceptual limitations to the essentially idealist explanation of decline in support that modernization and aging theory puts forward. First and most importantly, it fails to consider the role that material constraints (for example, the widespread poverty among the laboring classes during the nineteenth-century economic transition in the West, or currently in many developing countries) may play in bringing about the decline in family support. Second, though the explanation makes broad reference to declines in extended family support, the "explanation" only actually accounts for the decline in filial support. It leaves unclear what causal mechanisms underpin declines in support from relatives other than children.

Materialist Explanation

The second explanation of the decline in family support in Ghana, with its stress on economic constraints as the main cause, echoes materialist arguments that have been put forward to explain the historical shifts in financial family support for older people in the West (e.g., Anderson, 1971, 1977), and to explain declines in support in some other developing countries (e.g., DeLehr, 1992; Goldstein, Schuler, and Ross, 1983). Similar arguments focusing not on economic but on other (e.g., time) constraints have, moreover, been proposed by critical social gerontological perspectives to explain contemporary shifts in family support (e.g., the rising demand for formal old-age care in the United Kingdom) in the West (e.g., Clarke, 1995; Walker, 1995). In contrast to these arguments, which have typically been posited as critiques and counterarguments to the modernization model, the materialist accounts of the decline in Ghana (as in most general discussions of old-age support in developing countries (e.g., Foner, 1993; Hashimoto and Kendig, 1992), are simply put forward alongside the modernization model, as a second explanation. The causal mechanism implied by this materialist explanation of the decline is the following. Growing economic hardship and constraints (caused by macrolevel political, economic, and social factors) cause the young to be increasingly faced with difficult decisions as to how to allocate their meager resources between themselves, their children, and their older parents or relatives. In such a situation, the young give priority to the needs of self and children—at the expense of the old.

Conceptual Limitations in the Materialist Explanation

Like modernization theory, the materialist explanation of the decline in old-age family support is subject to two major conceptual limitations. First, it fails to consider the role of values and norms in underpinning the decline in support. Specifically, it fails to consider the norms and values that shape children's decisions to give priority to themselves and their children before the old, and how (if at all) these may be influenced by normative changes in society. Second, this explanation too fails to explicate whether the same or different mechanisms underpin the decline in support from children and from other relatives.

Epistemological Limitations in Both Explanations

The conceptual limitations in the existing explanations of the decline in support in Ghana—above all, their failure to illuminate what the interrelationships have been between material and normative changes in bringing the decline about—betray a fundamental, epistemological limitation inherent in both accounts. This is the fact that neither of them is based on a sound, interpretively grounded understanding of the basis of family support in the past and at present. A solid explanation of declines in family support would need to be based on an understanding of how and why people provided support to older parents and relatives in the past, and of how this basis of support has changed in the present. To be meaningful, this understanding (just as any explanation of social phenomena) would need to be grounded in evidence on individuals' perspectives—their values, motives and purposes, and their relationship to the wider economic and social context (Giddens, 1991; Guba and Lincoln, 1994). The existing accounts of the basis of family support to older people in the Ghanaian literature (e.g., Apt, 1996, 1997; Gyekye, 1996; Nukunya, 1992a) fail to provide such an interpretive understanding either of the past or the present basis of support. The latter is hardly discussed at all. Most accounts refer to the "traditional" basis of support, making no explicit reference to the situation at present. The assumption seems to be, though it is never discussed, that where support is given today, it is compelled by the same factors as in former times. The accounts of the "traditional" basis, meanwhile, which typically portray a very ideal picture of past support to the old, describe this support as having been compelled by three structural factors. First, a strong and binding *filial obligation*, rooted in reciprocity and enforced by familial and divine sanctions; second, *exchange* of domestic and economic services between old and young; and third, *economic coercion* by the old through the strategic use of inheritance options. How these three factors are interrelated in compelling support is, however, not discussed. Nor do these accounts provide evidence of the motives and perspectives of individuals in providing support. Rather, they echo the classical structural-functionalist anthropological interpretations of traditional society that also underpinned modernization theory and that were *etic* interpretations. That is, they were generated not from interpretative empirical evidence, but, in keeping with the positivistic research tradition (O'Brien, 1993), were based on a priori theoretical conceptions (typically, Durkheimian structuralist views of "mechanical solidarity" in kinship-based societies) about social life in preindustrial times (Craib, 1997; Durkheim, [1893] 1964; Lukes, 1973). The use of such a priori theories, and the influence that these early interpretations still have on African scholars' contemporary perceptions, have been strongly exposed and repeatedly critiqued in the literature (CODESRIA, 1988; Owusu, 1978; Prah, 1998; Stansfield, 1994).

DEVELOPING A FULLER UNDERSTANDING OF THE NATURE AND CAUSES OF THE DECLINE EMPIRICALLY

In view of the limitations in the existing explanations of the decline in support, an empirical investigation was embarked on in 1998, to provide a fuller understanding of the nature and causes of the decline. The specific aim was to develop an understanding that is grounded in the perspectives of individuals and that sheds light on the interrelationships between material and normative factors in bringing about the decline. Such an understanding was developed from the following: (a) an interpretively grounded understanding of the patterns, costs, and motivational basis of support in the past; (b) a similarly grounded appreciation of how this past basis differed from the attitudes, motives, and wider context that underpin the increasingly inadequate support today, and (c) people's own interpretations of the causes of decline and its current manifestations. The following sections will only briefly illustrate the major conclusions emerging from the investigation. The full evidence to support the conclusions is given in Aboderin (2000) and, in the future, will be presented in other papers as well as a book in this series.

METHODS AND APPROACH

The investigation, conducted over nine months in Accra, the capital of Ghana, employed an entirely qualitative methodology to examine the perspectives of a purposely selected, stratified sample ($N = 51$) of three linked generations—the oldest, the middle, and the youngest generation. In-depth interviews were used to explore each generation's past or present experiences of and attitudes to providing and receiving old-age support, as well as their interpretations of the diminished level of support today. The accounts of the oldest generation allow understanding of the basis of old-age support in the "past" (their combined recollections spanning, approximately, the period from the mid-1920s to the early 1960s), and the starting point for understanding the changes that have led to the decline in support. The views of the two younger generations complemented or qualified the older people's perspectives, and thus served to fully develop the understanding of the nature, causes, and consequences of the decline. Supplementary information was obtained through investigations of cases of abandoned older people, and through consultations with social welfare and nursing staff, HelpAge officials, and academics at Ghana University. Given the small, exclusively urban sample upon which they are based, the investigation's findings can clearly not make any claims to a greater generality. Rather they should be viewed as "working hypotheses" to guide further explorations.

Patterns and Costs of Support in the Past

The empirical findings reveal a clear picture of the patterns and costs of material family support to older people in Ghana in the past. Above all, though they clearly refute the ideal portrayals of past support in the literature by showing that rare cases of nonsupport from children did exist, they confirm that family support for older people in the past *was*, on the whole, adequate. It was sufficient to meet older people's basic material needs and requirements. The bulk of support came from adult children, typically in the form of money, foodstuffs, or provisions. Where children lived away from parents, contributions were usually sent on a regular basis. Often such support was provided although the older person had some resources of his or her own, signifying that support was also a symbol, a way of showing respect to the old. In addition to children's support, older people often received presents or food from other relatives, usually nieces, nephews, or siblings. Though usually supplementary, this support became vital in the rare cases where older people were childless or were not adequately supported by their children. The latter, usually, were older men who had reneged on their parental duties and whose children, in turn, "retaliated" by not supporting them, or older women who were accused of witchcraft and consequently were refused support.

The key feature of support to the old in the past was that it was affordable. The low price of the basic items of living (i.e., food, housing, and medical care), the relatively few "consumer needs" that people had, the resources that older people often had, and the shared responsibility often taken among relatives for expensive kinds of assistance—all meant that the young could afford to support older parents or relatives. It did not conflict with their material needs or aspirations, or with those of their offspring.

The Motivational Basis of Support

The Basis of Filial Support. Support to older parents was, above all, and as asserted in the literature, compelled by a binding, normative filial duty that required children to care for parents in old age. Exchange and economic coercion, however, were not important in motivating support. The duty to support parents was hedged by a range of grave family, community, and metaphysical sanctions. These threatened misfortune, withdrawal of family backing, neglect in old age, or even early death to those who reneged on providing family support. Conversely, fulfilling one's duty promised fortune and blessings from God. This binding filial duty had two distinct roots. On the one hand, as implied in the literature, it was rooted in the norm of reciprocity, the requirement to "help those who help them" (Gouldner, 1960). Children were obliged to repay parents for the care and support they had received from them in childhood, as was encapsulated in the traditional proverb: "If someone looks after you while you are cutting your teeth, you must look after then when they are losing their teeth."

Inherent in this reciprocal obligation was a clause of *conditionality*, which held that if parents had willingly failed to fulfill their parental duties (to feed, clothe, and set the children up for life), children in turn had no obligation to support them. If, however, parents had been *unable* to provide sufficiently, children's obligation to them remained. In other words, the conditionality operated on a key distinction between *unwillingness* and *incapacity*. In addition to the norm of reciprocity, and on the other hand, children's duty to support parents was rooted in an absolute, God-given "status-duty" (Gouldner, 1960), which required children to "honor" and support parents *regardless* of their past conduct, and which arose from the biblical fifth commandment, as presented in Exodus 20:12: "Honor thy father and thy mother that thy days may be long upon the land which the Lord thy God giveth thee." This duty to support and satisfy parents, no matter what, evidently overrode and invalidated the conditionality inherent in children's reciprocal obligation to repay parents. As a result, the normative "contract" between children and parents—a contract imposed by tradition and divine decree—was a contract on unequal terms. It was skewed by the absolute right of parents to support. Children, in this context, supported parents not out of any obvious sentiment of closeness, affection, or gratitude; parents were first and foremost feared, harsh authority figures (Aboderin, 2000, Azu, 1974; Nukunya, 1992b). They supported parents because it was their duty or, more precisely, because they feared the consequences of not doing so, in particular punishment from God. What ultimately drove children's support was thus an underlying self-interest. Children knew—given the graveness of the consequences—that supporting and "honoring" older parents was vital for their own future welfare and security. For the most part, children thus supported parents *irrespective* of the parents' past conduct and irrespective of their feelings toward or judgment of them. The rare exceptions to this were those cases where children, making use of the clause of conditionality, withheld support from parents (usually fathers) who had wholly neglected parental duties. Where mothers were accused of witchcraft and were consequently denied support, it seems, children's duty was simply suspended.

Support to Older Relatives. In contrast to the compulsion that underpinned support to aged parents, assistance to older relatives (who were usually not as harsh authority figures as parents) was much more voluntary in character. Rather than being compelled by a strict duty, it was provided out of a wish or felt obligation to help the older relative. Sometimes this was based simply on sympathy or the norm of beneficence, i.e., "to give to others such help as they need without making this contingent upon past benefits received" (Gouldner, 1973, p. 266). More often, however, it was based on a reciprocity—a sense of gratitude, affection, and obligation as a result of what the relative had done for one in the past. Thus, support to older relatives was driven mainly by motives arising from the history of the personal relationship between the old and young kin. At the same time, however, it too, was underpinned by an underlying self-interest. Though there were no harsh sanctions attached to not providing support, the young knew that assisting an older relative would bring them rewards (particularly blessings from God) that they would otherwise forgo.

Why Was Support in the Past Adequate? Together, the emerging picture of the patterns, costs, and motivational basis of support in the past gives a clear indication as to why, on the whole, material family support for older people was adequate. Simply put, it was adequate because (a) it was affordable—it did not conflict with the younger generations' own needs, and (b) it was in younger people's own self-interest—the young knew that providing support would bring rewards that were important for their own future welfare (see Figure 14.1).

Nature of the Decline in Support

The decline in material family support for older people over the past decades has occurred on two levels. On the one hand, support to older

294

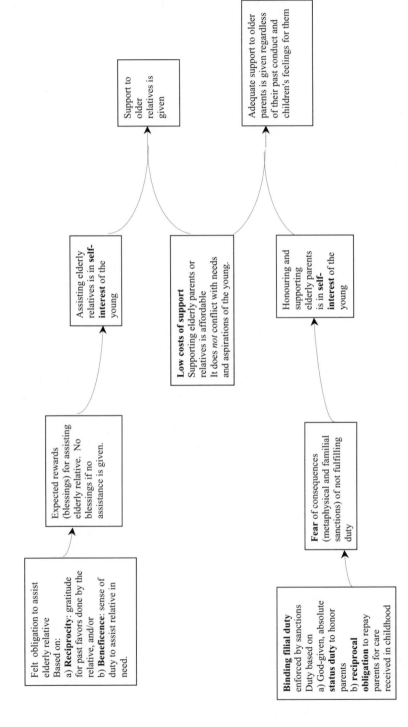

Figure 14.1 Motivational basis of past support to elderly parents and relatives in Ghana.

people from relatives other than adult children has become very rare (as has support generally between extended relatives). The result, as is also argued in the literature, is that the responsibility for the welfare of older people has shifted increasingly onto children and spouse alone. (By the same token younger individuals are increasingly alone responsible for their welfare and that of their children). On the other hand, and at the same time, the support from adult children itself has decreased. There has been a *general reduction* in the level or adequacy of filial support, i.e., in the extent to which it meets even the basic needs of the older person. In addition, there has been an increase in the incidence of children who do not support their parents *at all*.

Causes of the Decline in Support

These declines in material family support for older people, as the empirical findings clearly indicate, have emerged as a result of two main processes or shifts that have taken place over the recent decades.

Increasing Focus of Resources on Nuclear Family. The first and most important shift that has underpinned the decline in support from both adult children and other relatives is the fact that the young have increasingly begun to focus and spend their resources on their nuclear families (i.e., self, spouse, and children), at the expense of older parents or relatives. The cause of this narrowing focus, however, has not been, as modernization theory would imply, a growing individualism and weakening of familism. The general value of assisting older relatives and the obligation to support older parents clearly persist and are endorsed by the young. And, though there are indications of shifts in normative attitudes toward an increasing emphasis on self-reliance in old age, these have not caused, but are emerging in response to the decline. What has caused the increasing focus on the nuclear family, rather, is the worsening economic strain faced by the population. Increasing un- and underemployment and the drastic rises in the costs of living have meant, just as the materialist accounts in the literature propose, that people no longer have the resources or capacity to provide adequately for their elderly parents, let alone other relatives. This has been further exacerbated by an escalation of the needs of the young. The emergence of inescapable "modern" needs such as education and electricity, and of new consumer "needs" such as TVs, stereos, or fashion items, bolstered by a shift in status criteria toward an increasing importance of material possessions, has meant that the young have even less capacity to give to the old. The key factor that has underpinned this reduced capacity of the young to give to the old is an apparently fundamental normative hierarchy of needs that has crystallized as a result of the economic strain, and that holds that in situations of constrained resources, the needs of the young (self, spouse, and children) have priority over those of old parents, let alone other older relatives. The fundamental principle that this priority of the young expresses is that the old have no right to absorb resources that future generations need for their life. This principle, interestingly, is not just a Ghanaian conception. It is present also in other cultures—in the West for example in the notion of the "processional nature" or "transitive order" of justice between generations (Laslett, 1992; Moody, 1993), which has been raised in the contemporary debate on the "contract between generations" (see Bengtson and Achenbaum, 1993)—raising the empirical question of whether it perhaps may be an elemental component of all moral codes.

Shift in the Basis of Filial Support. The second process that has contributed to the decline specifically in the support from adult children has been a shift in the basis of filial support. As a result of this shift, this support has become increasingly dependent on parents' past conduct and the affective relationship that consequently exists between them and their children. Children have become increasingly ready to withhold some support from parents who themselves showed little concern in the past, and for whom they thus feel no particular sense of reciprocity or gratitude. In extreme cases, where parents (usually fathers) willfully neglected even their most basic parental duties, many children deny all support, arguing that they, in turn, have no duty to them. In withholding support from uncaring parents, children draw on the clause of conditionality that has always been inherent in their reciprocal obligation to support parents, but that in the past, given the overriding duty to honor parents, was rarely made use of.

Though this shift in the basis of filial support is precisely that posited by the modernization model, the main causes of it have not been the factors proposed by the model. First, the shift is not, as modernization theory would imply, a result of weakening filial obligation norms per se. The reciprocal obligation to support parents in return for them having fulfilled their duties clearly continues to be recognized and endorsed. What has weakened, however, is the absolute, God-given status duty that in the past required children to support and satisfy parents no matter what. That this status duty has weakened is not, as modernization theory assumes, a result of value changes such as a rising secularism. If anything, Christian practice has become even more fervent in the context of the economic crisis, as expressed in the phenomenal growth in charismatic and spiritual churches. Rather, the weakening of the status duty must be seen first as a result of the worsening economic situation. In a situation where support of an older parent has become very costly, and where the consequences of parents' earlier lack of concern (e.g., failure to provide good education or a professional training) have become so grave, children have become increasingly bitter. They have begun to judge parents and to question or reject a duty that requires them to do all they can for parents who failed to give them the necessary support. Their view is that these parents do not rightly deserve to be supported much or at all.

In this view children are increasingly supported by the growing emphasis that has been placed, in Ghana (as in other developing nations), on the rights of children, in particular vis-à-vis their parents. This "modern" notion, sparked by the UN convention on the rights of the child, increasingly propagated in the media, and introduced in legal provisions, has fostered an increasing empowerment of children and a greater accountability of parents. It has helped to foster a new, more equal order in the "contract" between parents and children in which parents receive support not according to fixed status rights but, in a sense, according to their merits.

The third factor that has contributed to the shift in the basis of filial support, in addition to the weakening of the absolute status duty itself, is a weakening of the sanctions that formerly enforced conformity with this duty. The young no longer fear, as much as their parents did, the familial and metaphysical consequences of not supporting or satisfying their parents. The main causes of this are not, as modernization theory would imply, geographical mobility, education, and economic independence of the young. Although these factors have played some role—by enabling the young to read for themselves of the forgiving nature of God, removing many from the sphere of family control, and making them "immune" to threats of withdrawal of family support—the most prominent causes of the recent weakening of sanctions have, again, been two effects of the economic crisis. The fear of family sanctions, specifically, has been weakened by the declining aid between extended relatives in general. This has meant that threats of withdrawal of family support have, in effect, become "empty threats." The fear of punishment from God, meanwhile, has been significantly undermined by an important shift in religious conceptions that has occurred in the context of economic crisis and the growing charismatic movement. This shift has changed the past view of God as a harsh punishing authority to one that sees God as a supportive friend whose aim it is to help one to achieve one's goals.

SUMMARY AND CONCLUSION

In response to the limitations in the existing "materialist" and "modernization theory" explanations in the literature, the empirical investigation I have drawn on but only briefly illustrated has sought to develop a fuller understanding of the nature and causes of the decline in material family support for older people in Ghana. It has done so by developing and building on an interpretively grounded understanding of the past and present basis and patterns of support. The findings show that the decline in support is the result of a complex interaction between the effects of the worsening economic situation in Ghana and some factors of "modernization." Together, these have led to an increasing focus of the young's resources on their nuclear families at the expense of the old, and to a shift in the basis of filial support toward an increasing dependence on parents' past conduct and their affective relationship with children (see Figure 14.2).

The dominant factor, just as materialist explanations suggest, has undoubtedly been the worsening economic situation. Most of its crucial effects, however—e.g., its weakening of the absolute duty to honor parents and its crystallization of a fundamental hierarchy of needs of young before old—are ones that have not so far been recognized in the literature. The role of "modernization" has mainly been to exacerbate the effects of the economic crisis, but again in ways—through the escalation of needs among the young, and the growing emphasis on children's rights vis-à-vis their parents—not hitherto addressed by modernization arguments. In contrast, the main causal factors that these arguments propose—rising individualism, secularization and a weakening of filial obligation norms per se—have clearly not played a major role.

Material Change Drives Normative Change?

The dominant role of material factors in driving change is further indicated by the shifts in normative expectations that are emerging in response to the decline in support. There is an arising stance that in the current economic difficulties it is no longer proper to expect and seek support from extended relatives. Similarly, there is a growing view that it is no longer "right" to expect material support from one's children in old age—the burden on them would be too great. Both these shifts, evidently, are responses first and foremost to the worsening material situation and, at least for this context, they illuminate the question of why and how old age family support norms change. The shifting norms regarding support from extended relatives (mainly expressed by those who are asked, but increasingly refuse to give such support), interestingly, indicate a mechanism akin to that identified by Anderson (1971) for nineteenth-century family support in Lancashire:

> If material conditions favour the establishment of new behaviour patterns which will better assist the actors involved to achieve their goals, then those who are able to disregard the prevailing normative system without serious

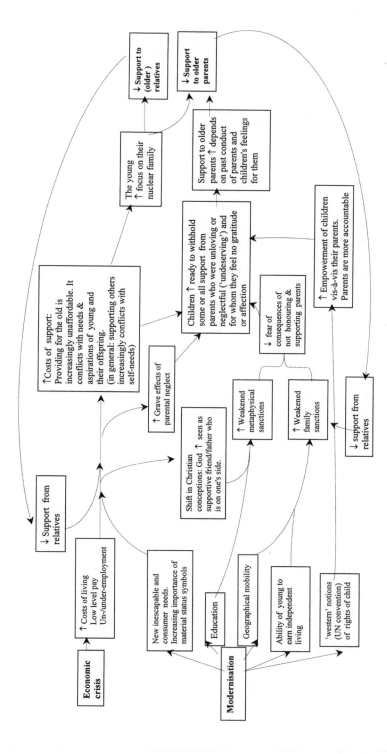

Figure 14.2 Causes of decline in family support for older people in Ghana: Dominant role of economic crisis reinforced by effects of modernization.

sanctions being imposed upon them will do so. Once new behaviour patterns are established new normative beliefs will then emerge to support them. (Qureshi and Walker, 1989, p. 117)

The changing normative expectations regarding filial support perhaps express a slightly different mechanism: if material conditions change to such an extent that fulfillment of a particular normative prescription becomes harmful to a significant part of the population (especially the future generations), and thus *necessitates* new behavior patterns, then the normative prescription is no longer tenable, and it must change.

Investigations into how the processes and factors that have shaped the shifts in material family support for older people in Ghana compare with those underpinning similar shifts in other societies or time periods, and to explore how, in future, family support norms in Ghana will respond to any new old-age income security systems that are developed will provide further valuable insights into the fundamental nature of intergenerational solidarity and support norms and their relationships to the wider structural context.

NOTE

1. As Quadagno (1982) notes, Cowgill's theory has been seen as a more extended and formalized version of Burgess's. A later, more elaborate defense of the theory (Cowgill, 1986) has been paid relatively little attention (Fennell, Phillipson, and Evers, 1988).

REFERENCES

Aboderin, I. 2000. Social change and the decline in family support for older people in Ghana: An investigation of the nature and causes of shifts in support. Ph.D. dissertation, School for Policy Studies, University of Bristol.

Ahenkora, K. 1999. *The contribution of older people to development. The Ghana study.* Accra, Ghana: HelpAge International and HelpAge.

Anderson, M. 1971. *Family structure in nineteenth century Lancashire.* London: Cambridge University Press.

_____. 1977. The impact on the family relationships of the elderly of changes since Victorian times in government income maintenance provisions. In E. Shanas and M. Sussman (eds.), *Family, bureaucracy, and the elderly* (pp. 36–59). Durham, NC: Duke University Press.

Apt, N. A. 1993. Care for the elderly in Ghana: An emerging issue. *Journal of Cross-Cultural Gerontology* 8:301–12.

_____. 1996. *Coping with old age in a changing Africa.* Aldershot: Avebury.

_____. 1997. *Ageing in Africa.* Geneva: World Health Organization.

_____. 2002. Ageing and the changing role of the family and the community: An African perspective. *Intenational Social Security Review* 55(1):39–47.

Azu, D. G. 1974. *The Ga family and social change. African social research documents* Volume 5. Cambridge: African Studies Centre.

Bengtson, V. L., and Achenbaum, W. A. (eds.) 1993. *The changing contract across generations.* Hawthorne, NY: Aldine de Gruyter.

Burgess, E. W. (ed.) [1960] 1969. *Ageing in Western societies.* Chicago: University of Chicago Press.

Burgess. E. W., and Locke, H. J. 1945. *The family.* New York: American Book Company.

Clarke, L. 1995. Family care and changing family structure: Bad news for the elderly? In I. Allen and E. Perkins (eds.), *The future of family care for older people* (pp. 19–50). London: HMSO.

Council for the Development of Social Science Research in Africa (CODESRIA) (1988). *A plea for an African anthropological renaissance.* CODESRIA Bulletin, No. 2.

Cowgill, D. O. 1972. A theory of aging in cross-cultural perspective. In D. O. Cowgill and L. D. Holmes (eds.), *Ageing and modernization* (pp. 1–14). New York: Appleton-Century-Crofts.

_____. 1974. Aging and modernization: A revision of the theory. In J. F. Gubrium (ed.), *Late life* (pp. 123–45). Springfield, IL: Thomas.

_____. 1986. *Aging around the world.* Belmont, CA: Wadsworth.

Craib, I. 1997. *Classical social theory.* Oxford: Oxford University Press.

DeLehr, E. C. 1992. Aging and family support in Mexico. In H. L. Kendig, L. C. Coppard, and A. Hashimoto (eds.), *Family support to the elderly. The International experience* (pp. 215–23). Oxford: Oxford University Press.

Durkheim, E. [1893] 1964. *The division of labour in society.* New York: Free Press.

Fennell, G., Phillipson, C., and Evers, H. 1988. *The sociology of old age.* Milton Keynes: Open University Press.

Foner, N. 1993. When the contract fails: Care for the elderly in nonindustrial cultures. In V. L. Bengtson and W. A. Achenbaum (eds.), *The changing contract across generations* (pp. 101–17). Hawthorne, NY: Aldine de Gruyter.

Giddens, A. 1991. *Modernity and self identity.* Oxford: Polity.

Goldstein, M. C., Schuler, S., and Ross, J. L. 1983. Social and economic forces affecting intergenerational relations in a third world country: A cautionary tale from south Asia. *Journal of Gerontology* 38:716–24.

Gouldner, A. W. 1960. The norm of reciprocity: A preliminary statement. *American Sociological Review* 25:161–78.

_____. 1973. *For sociology: Renewal and critique in sociology today.* London: Allen Lane.

Guba, E. G., and Lincoln Y. S. 1994. Competing paradigms in qualitative research. In N. K. Denzin and Y. S. Lincoln (eds.), *Handbook of qualitative research* (pp. 105–17). Thousand Oaks, CA: Sage.

Gyekye, K. 1996. *African cultural values. An introduction.* Accra: Sankofa.

Hashimoto, A., and Kendig, H. L. 1992. Aging in international perspective. In H. L. Kendig, L. C. Coppard, and A. Hashimoto (eds.), *Family support to the elderly. The international experience* (pp. 3–13). Oxford: Oxford University Press.

HelpAge International. 1999. *The ageing and development report.* London: Earthscan.
_____. 2000. Ageing issues in Africa. A summary. HelpAge International Africa Regional Development Centre, Nairobi, Kenya.
Laslett, P. 1992. Is there a generational contract? In P. Laslett and J. S. Fishkin (eds.), *Justice between age groups and generations* (pp. 24–47). New Haven, CT: Yale University Press.
Laslett, P., and Wall, R. 1972. *Household and family in past times.* Cambridge: Cambridge University Press.
Lukes, S. 1973. *Emile Durkheim.* Harmondsworth: Penguin
Moody, H. R. 1993. *Ethics in an aging society.* Baltimore, MD: Johns Hopkins University Press.
Nukunya, G. K. 1992a. *Tradition and change. The case of the family.* Accra: Ghana University Press.
_____. 1992b. *Tradition and social change in Ghana.* Accra: Ghana University Press.
Owusu, M. 1978. Ethnography of Africa: The usefulness of the useless. *American Anthropologist* 80:704–23.
O'Brien, M. 1993. Social research and sociology. In N. Gilbert (ed.), *Researching social life* (pp. 1–17). London: Sage.
Parsons, T. 1942. Age and sex in the social structure of the United States. *American Sociological Review* 7:604–17.
Prah, K. K. 1998. *Beyond the color line.* Trenton, NJ: Africa World Press.
Quadagno, J. S. 1982. *Aging in early industrial society: Work, family, and social policy in nineteenth-century England.* New York: Academic Press.
_____. 1999. *Aging and the life course. An introduction to social gerontology.* Boston: McGraw-Hill College.
Qureshi, H., and Walker, A. 1989. *The caring relationship. Elderly people and their families.* Basingstoke: Macmillan.
Shanas, E., Townsend,P., Wedderburn, D., Friis, H., Milhoj, P., and Stehouwer, J. 1968. *Old people in three industrial societies.* New York: Atherton.
Simmons, L. W. 1945. *The role of the aged in primitive societies.* New Haven, CT: Yale University Press.
_____. 1946. Attitudes toward aging and the aged: Primitive societies. *Journal of Gerontology* 1:72–95.
Smith, J. A. [1776] 1936. *An inquiry into the nature and causes of the wealth of nations.* Reprint. New York: Modern Library.
Stansfield, J. H. II 1994. Ethnic modelling in qualitative research. In N. K. Denzin and Y. S. Lincoln (eds.), *Handbook of qualitative research* (pp. 175–88). Thousand Oaks, CA: Sage.
U.S. Government, Social Security Agency 1999. *Social security programs throughout the world.* Washington: USGPO.
United Nations Population Division 1999. *The world population prospects: The 1998 revision.* New York: Author.
Walker, A. 1995. Integrating the family into a mixed economy of care. In I. Allen and E. Perkins (eds.), *The future of family care for older people* (pp. 201–20) London: HMSO.
World Bank 1994. *Averting the old age crisis.* New York: World Bank.

V

Intra- and Intersociety Differences
and Social Change

|15|

Family Norms and Preferences in Intergenerational Relations

A Comparative Perspective

R. Katz, S. O. Daatland, A. Lowenstein, M. T. Bazo, I. Ancizu,
K. Herlofson, D. Mehlhausen-Hassoen, and D. Prilutzky

INTRODUCTION

The purpose of this chapter is to review theoretical perspectives on family norms and preferences regarding intergenerational obligations and to present empirical findings from a cross-national five-country study: four European countries (Germany, Norway, Spain, and the United Kingdom) and Israel. The five countries represent different family cultures and different welfare regimes.

Population aging and social changes in modern societies have led to a growing concern about the social cohesion between generations. These concerns refer to generations at both the family (micro-) and the societal (macro-) levels. Do family norms still include the older generation(s), or is the isolated nuclear family model expanding? Are intergenerational tensions on the societal level growing—in response to the changing population balance—leading to growing conflicts over scarce resources?

Quite a few studies have proven the family pessimists false. Intergenerational norms seem strong and attract general support among the old and young alike (Bengtson and Roberts, 1991; Walker 1993a, 1993b). The family is still carrying the major load in the care for the elderly—even in most modern welfare states (Chappell and Blandford, 1991; Sussman, 1985) with the possible exception of Scandinavian countries, which are characterized by more generous services and benefits to elders (Daatland and Herlofson, 2001; Lingsom, 1997). The concern for the generational contract on the societal level seems also exaggerated (Walker, 1990; Ward 2001). The generational equity debate, which focuses on the issue of whether more public resources are allocated to the elderly and thus the younger generations receive less, has mainly been a media phenomenon. In fact, public opinion has until now been supportive of policies and benefits for the elderly (Walker, 1993a; Bay, 1998). This support might be partially because people in general think that older people are weaker and worse off than they in fact are (Bay 1998, Lubomudrow 1997), and therefore adopt a sympathetic, but condescending attitude. Such an attitude was termed by Robert Binstock (1983) "compassionate ageism."

The continued aging of populations, the increase in longevity, and the late modernity trends toward increased individualism may, however, add pressure and tension to the preferred balance between the family and the state. This is even more the case, as the global political and economic climate seems to point toward less government responsibility for elder care and increased pressure on families. There are, therefore, good reasons to continue to monitor how intergenerational solidarity patterns develop, and in particular under what conditions solidarity is supported or threatened.

Families may choose different coping strategies, based on family values and preferences, in response to similar problems and pressures. Likewise, countries may adopt different welfare policies to meet the needs of elders and their families. We therefore need to study these issues in various cultural contexts and in a comparative perspective. This is part of the rationale behind the OASIS (Old Age and Autonomy: The Role of Intergenerational Solidarity and Service Systems) study, where family norms and preferences regarding intergenerational relations and the proper expected balance between family and state responsibilities are among the questions studied in five countries with different family and social policy traditions.

Some of the major research questions in the OASIS study address these issues: What are the normative ideals of intergenerational care and living arrangements in these countries, and what is the actual and preferred balance between families and service systems? The assumption is that social policies have an impact on family solidarity and vice versa. We assume that families and service systems will tend to relate to problems of modernization in different ways, because of path dependency on the already established traditions (Alber, 1995; Daatland, 2001). However similar the challenge of population aging is, there will be room for different ways of relating to these challenges. Each family—and country—may be expected to place their idiosyncratic mark on their solutions. For example, although general family norms may be strong, there may be considerable variation in how these norms are enacted (Daatland, 1990; Finch and Mason, 1993; Katz and Lowenstein, 1999; Lowenstein and Katz, 2000; Rossi and Rossi, 1990). To borrow a more general phrase by Inglehart and Baker, "The broad cultural heritage of a society . . . leaves an imprint on values that endure despite modernization" (2000, p. 19).

The focus of this chapter is on *attitudes* to intergenerational responsibilities. More specifically, the beliefs, intentions, and preferences of intergenerational solidarity will be addressed, not if and how such beliefs and intentions are acted out. The relationship between attitudes and behavior—between normative and functional solidarity to stay within the intergenerational solidarity paradigm (Bengtson and Roberts, 1991)—is a large research theme in its own right, which we shall return to in later analysis.

Intergenerational solidarity, and conflict are manifested at two different levels, as suggested by Bengtson and Murray (1993), the macro-public-arena level and the micro-intergenerational-family level. On the macro-level, attention should be given to the larger social context where social norms are created and activated and where state policies and responses of various welfare regimes to the needs of the growing elderly populations are shaped. On the micro–family level, attention should be given to issues of filial obligations, expectations of different generations in the family, and the actual flow of help and support between the generations.

In the OASIS study we address both these levels, focusing on the relationship between (adult) generations in families—primarily from the perspective of filial obligations—and the responsibility of adult children toward older parents. Do attitudes to filial obligations differ between countries? Do we find characteristic attitudinal differences between the countries, or are the within-country variation more prominent? We also look at solidarity between "generations," or rather age groups, on the societal level, through attitudes to policies and benefits for the elderly. And finally, the personal preferences for housing and care in old age are reviewed. While the beliefs about filial obligations represent an input to general attitudes to family solidarity, the personal preferences may be beliefs and intentions related more closely to one's own family. The latter represent what Stein et al. (1998) call the relational approach, the former what they call the attitudinal approach. They view the relational approach as "obligation to kin as negotiated commitments that emerge between family members when they decide what things they do and do not do in their relationships" (ibid.:612). The attitudinal approach is presented as the "filial responsibility that emphasizes the larger social context in which duties between adults and their parents may unfold" (ibid.).

Let us first review earlier studies in the field, and then focus on theoretical and conceptual perspectives, before we turn to the OASIS study and data.

REVIEW OF EARLIER STUDIES

Filial Responsibility Norms and Expectations

Filial responsibility represents the extent to which adult children feel obligated to meet the basic needs of their aging parents. Filial responsibility can be viewed as a component of normative solidarity that has been defined as "strength of commitment to performance of familial roles and to competing familial obligations" (Bengtson and Roberts, 1991).

A number of studies have concluded that filial responsibility norms and expectations are still strong and shared across class, gender, ethnicity, and age (Burr and Mutchler, 1999; Hamon and Blieszner, 1990; Lee, Peek, and Coward, 1998; Logan and Spitze, 1995). There are, however, mixed evidence and conflicting explanations on how and why these norms and attitudes vary.

Gender differences in attitudes to filial obligations (normative solidarity) seem small or nonexistent, but women (daughters) are more inclined to act out their obligations in actual help and caring (Hamon and Blieszner, 1990). On the other hand, Finley, Roberts, and Banahan (1988) found that factors most salient to the development of filial responsibility varied by the gender of the respondents and were different, depending on whether the recipients of care were mothers, fathers, or in-laws.

Several studies have focused on racial differences in filial norms (Hanson, Sauer, and Seelbach, 1983; andLee et al., 1998). Lee et al. (1998) find blacks to be more supportive to filial obligations than whites, and attribute this to socialization to more collectivistic values in the black relative to the white U.S. community. They also find that filial obligations among blacks do not reduce interest in formal services. Services and family care are hence not seen as alternatives but as complementary. Burr and Mutchler (1999) also find blacks (and Hispanics) to be more supportive of filial responsibility norms than whites, but not generally so. They were more in favor of coresidence between generations than whites, but no difference in attitudes to financial help and support were found. Such a mixed picture is also presented by Hanson et al. (1983), who found that white respondents demonstrated stronger support for filial norms than black and, in general, that filial norms are rather weak. The latter conclusion is in contrast to most other studies in the field.

There are also reports about filial norms being stronger in rural versus urban areas, and among the working class more than in the middle class, but then there are also studies that conclude the opposite.

The only (nearly) consistent finding reported—in addition to the general high consensus on filial norms—is the inverse relationship between age and support for filial obligations. The younger are more inclined to support strong filial responsibility than the older (Hamon and Blieszner,

1990; Hanson et al., 1983; Logan and Spitze, 1995). The decline in obligation level is progressive across age groups, with no striking drop among the oldest old. One explanation is that the younger generation is more dependent today on their parents (Connidis, 2001, pp. 148–58; McGarry and Schoeni, 1997). This trend could press in the direction of recent cohorts of young adults feeling more obligation to parents than in the past and, as a ripple-out effect, more obligation toward other kin than was the case for earlier cohorts (Rossi and Rossi, 1990). Seelbach (1978, 1984) devised a scale of filial responsibility expectations—the degree to which adult children feel normatively obligated to assist their aging parents—and several more studies have analyzed similar scales (Finley et al., 1988; Hamon and Blieszner, 1990). These studies generally find that older persons are slightly less supportive of filial responsibility norms than are younger persons. This is of interest because it is elders who benefit from filial responsibility and younger persons who sustain the costs. Adult children generally express a greater degree of filial responsibility than their parents expect of them (Cicirelli, 1981).

Because many roles are age-structured, they lend themselves to explaining differences in attitudes concerning filial responsibility between various age groups. Findings from a study by Logan and Spitze (1995) illustrate these contentions. Their findings reveal that age differences in the attitudes highlight intergenerational solidarity: older people's attitudes seem to give greater weight to the needs of younger generations and vice versa. Relations across age groups apparently have an altruistic character. This pattern may have many sources. The social norms evinced by older people may reflect their desire for autonomy and self-reliance, their sense that the proper roles of parents is to be givers rather than receivers, and their wish not to become a burden to the younger generation. The views of middle-aged respondents may be based partly on self-interest: several observes have noted that these people can anticipate their own aging and that younger persons with aging parents may benefit immediately from public programs for the elderly (Pampel and Williamson, 1989).

Corresponding age differences are reported in preferences for care and services. The older tend to favor help from services over family care, and more so the more available services are and the more disabled one is (Daatland, 1990). Similar findings are reported on preferences for housing, where both the younger and older generations favor independent living, and the older seem even more reluctant than the younger to think about coresidence with children when in need for care. Whether or not this should be seen as a positively chosen preference or rather a negatively forced choice is more unclear (Connidis, 1983). Furthermore, these attitudes probably vary across countries and cultures, and findings from specific studies and countries can hardly be generalized directly to other settings.

For Europe as a whole there is a lack of good data on preferences for care, and where research has been undertaken it has generally failed to set stated preferences in the existing cultural/ideological context. It has been suggested that, while elderly people in Southern Europe appear to prefer family care, Northern European elderly people are more likely to favor formal service provision (OECD, 1992). In a Norwegian study it was found that preferences for care varied with the amount and type of help needed. When long-term care and especially long-term personal care would be needed, the majority would first turn to public services. However, there was a small group who would always turn to children, even for long-term personal care. The author concludes that the elderly had invested more in the adult child–parent relationship and are the most concerned about it and would like to be as independent as possible, thus trying to impose less responsibility on the children (Daatland, 1990).

Intergenerational Attitudes on the Societal Level

The shifting responsibility of elder care toward the welfare state, with the ensuing economic costs, has raised public policy concern around issues of generational equity.

Intergenerational relations on the societal level are a recurrent issue in anthropology and social science, but are added a new momentum through the generational equity debate of the last two decades. The idea that a growing population of elders is consuming ever larger portions of the common resources at the expense of the younger and coming generations (Johnson, Conrad, and Thompson, 1989; Preston, 1984) has been challenged and rejected by a number of studies. Public opinion is in general very supportive to policies and benefits for older people, and the younger more so than the older (Walker, 1993a; Ward, 2001).

Part of the background for the generational equity issue is the fact that while elders have gained better levels of living during the last decades, a growing number of children are in some countries, for example the United States, left behind in poverty. On the other hand, U.S. studies also indicate that each new cohort has until now experienced better (material) levels of living than the cohorts preceding them (Easterlin, Macunovich, and Crimmins, 1993). Relative deprivation may, however, be higher among the young, because while the older have done better than they expected, the younger may have done worse.

How these attitudes may be shaped by social policy is indicated by Marshall, Cook, and Marshall (1993) . They find the intergenerational equity debate to be much more prominent in the United States than in Canada, and attribute this to the universality of the Canadian system and the built-in differences and sources of tensions in the U.S. system, where older people are better covered by social policies than are children and young people.

Quite a few countries have social policies that are relatively friendlier to their older than their younger populations, and the bias to the favor of elders may in fact have grown in the later years (Esping-Andersen, 1997). When people in general are still so supportive to services and benefits for older people, and the younger seemingly more so than the older, this may at least partly be due to the "compassionate agism" we have already mentioned. People seem to believe that elders are more victims in modern society, and worse off, than they in actual fact are. Gerontology may have contributed to this image by its focus on the decline and discriminations associated with aging. Older people's associations and lobbyists are also cultivating such images in an effort to attract further support. Older people may in fact be more self-centered, and less concerned about the welfare of younger people than the other way around, as for example indicated by the relatively low support for investments in schooling among elders that was reported in a recent U.S. study (Vinovskis, 1993).

Conceptual Approaches

A substantial amount of data about filial responsibility and intergenerational relations have been accumulated, but the data are mixed, we lack good comparative studies, and there is little consensus on how patterns and variations should be explained. Four lines of theorizing about these issues can be identified, according to the direction of suggested explanations: retrospective, situational, prospective, and mixed theories.

Retrospective theories are those that highlight early socialization and cultural patterns, as these can be expressed in normative variations according to race, ethnicity, and for that matter gender. A specific variant of this paradigm is represented by role theory—mainly related to gender roles, and to the roles of parents versus the role of children. Modernization theory and the changing role of families (from instrumental to emotional) also belong to this paradigm. So also does attachment theory, but then as microlevel experiences and commitments established early in life and carried over into adulthood and old age.

Other explanations are here-and-now, or *situational,* and refer to characteristics that are barriers or motivators for solidarity. Conflicting role obligations in work and family life, or between children on the one hand and older parents on the other, may serve as illustrations. More practical barriers are geographical distance and poor health. Included in this line of theorizing is the interest in what represent legitimate excuses for not acting out intergenerational obligations.

Prospective theories seek explanations in expected future consequences of present actions and choices. The role and impact of self-interest and other forms of utility arguments belong here, including how people more or less rationally relate to perceived norms. The theory of reasoned action

(Ajzen, 1988) adapted to the relationship between norms, attitudes, intentions, and actual behavior could serve as an example.

Finally are those we may call the *mixed theories*, which integrate the possible impact of past, present, and future directed factors. Exchange theory belongs to this paradigm, as it looks partly back to reciprocal obligations for earlier contributions, and partly to the present attractiveness of an exchange partner in terms of his or her resources for exchange now or in the future. The social exchange framework may for example provide a venue for understanding why individuals choose to sustain long-term stressful caregiving situations with minimal formal assistance, and why some families find it reasonable to involve formal networks early in the caregiving experience.

The role of self-interest versus altruism or solidarity for intergenerational relationships has received particular attention. Do people hold attitudes that protect their stage of life interests, or are they rather motivated by concern for others? Most studies support the latter explanation, as illustrated by the already reported finding that older parents are less inclined to support filial norms than are their adult children. Role theory may have particular relevance here in order to understand how filial norms in families, and public opinion about benefits for elders, are constructed. As a parent one may be more concerned about the welfare of one's children than the other way around. One may therefore be afraid to burden children and be instead guided by a norm of independence. Parental roles and norms are, however, varying across cultures, and the present body of literature is dominated by studies from modern, Western societies. We need data from other cultures and traditions in order to test this and other explanations.

The intergenerational solidarity framework of Bengtson and colleagues (Bengtson and Roberts, 1991) also belongs to the mixed paradigm, as it integrates exchange theory and role theory. This framework also allows testing the role of personal attraction and identifications in the construction of solidarity norms and practices. The intergenerational family solidarity model is, however, as of today more a theory of how solidarity (and conflicts) are expressed, than how such bonds are created.

One need not expect that filial norms, personal preferences, and intergenerational relations on the societal level have been formed by the same factors. They do, however, influence each other, which is a theme that is often addressed through studies of the impact of welfare state arrangements on the family. The expansion of the welfare state into areas that in the past were the responsibility of the family moves the boundaries between public and private. The limits between the state and the family become uncertain and there is a multiplicity of relationships and circumstances that do not fall completely within either the public or the private sphere. State and family merge into one another. Accordingly, the family ethic is changing. Although the family still accomplishes a broad series of tasks of care and maintenance of its members, some of the responsibility of caring for the elderly is now entrusted to the welfare state. This applies in particular to the duties of children toward elderly parents (Sgritta, 1997). Social care has come to mean both formal and informal caregiving networks existing side by side (Cantor, 1989, 1991).

Among the attitudes to intergenerational responsibility are those relating to this very balance between family and state responsibility for the welfare of older people. A basic limitation of the aging policies of most countries is, according to Hooyman (1992), that families and service systems are seen as alternatives that tend to counteract (substitute), not complement each other. Public opinion also tends to support the substitution idea (Daatland, 1990), while most research supports the complementarity hypothesis (Chappell and Blandford, 1991; Lingsom, 1997; Litwak, 1985).

The complementarity thesis takes two slightly different forms. Family support theory leans on social exchange theory, and suggests that families will be more willing to provide help—and elders more willing to accept it—when burdens are not too heavy. Services may then strengthen family solidarity by sharing these burdens. Chappell and Blandford (1991) support this thesis on the basis of a Canadian study. Attias-Donfut andand Wolff (2000) do likewise in a French study, while Lingsom (1997) finds mixed support for this position in Norway. Kohli (1999) and Künemund and Rein (1999) add to the support from a different angle. They find that generous pensions enable the older generation to reciprocate support from the younger generation. The elders' position in the family is thus strengthened and more balanced, which in turn strengthens intergenerational solidarity.

The dual specialization or complementary model (Litwak, 1985) is based on the notion that formal and informal networks have certain kinds of caregiving responsibilities and abilities that are best suited to each particular network structure. According to this model, the highly specialized nature of the networks has the potential to cause friction and precipitate conflict. Therefore, formal and informal networks work best when the amount of contact or level of involvement between them is minimized. A criticism of this approach is that it is increasingly difficult to differentiate between formal and informal responsibilities in contemporary caregiving situations (Soldo, Wolf, and Agree, 1990).

An alternative form of complementarity is represented by family specialization theory, where the access to services allows families to concentrate on emotional support rather than instrumental help. Modern families are then not deprived of functions by the welfare state, but have changed focus.

There is, however, still no consensus in these matters, and we need to study what circumstances will pull in this or that direction, rather than to study substitution or complementarity as simple contrasts along one dimension only. And while most researchers support the conclusion that intergenerational solidarity is still strong—even when (or because) services are available—people in general seem to have little faith in family solidarity. The majority seems to be of the opinion that family members were more willing to care for their elders earlier than they are now. Many blame the welfare state for this, and this is the case in universalistic welfare states like the Scandinavian as well as the conservative or residual welfare states in Central and Southern Europe (Daatland, 1997). It may then be something of a paradox that public opinion is at the same time very supportive to develop services for the elderly, which in its opinion should reduce family solidarity even more.

In sum, the empirical findings and theoretical approaches presented above outline the central issues regarding intergenerational solidarity, filial responsibility norms, and expectations and preferences for care, on the familial and societal levels. The OASIS study attempts to contribute to the existing knowledge base regarding the interplay between personal, familial, and social service factors, and their impact on quality of life of the elderly population in a cross-national perspective.

THE OASIS PROJECT

The OASIS study is based on the conceptual model illustrated in Figure 15.1. As can be seen from the model, family norms and ideals are one of the core concepts. They are linked to the three clusters of the independent variables (individual, familial and societal levels) and they impact on intergenerational solidarity and quality of life of elders and their caregivers.

The OASIS study covers a diverse range of welfare regimes and familial cultures in five different countries: Germany, Norway, Spain, the United Kingdom, and Israel. The research focuses on three prominent dimensions that influence healthy aging and coping of family caregivers: mixes of informal (family) and formal (services) care, family norms and transfers, and coping with beginning dependency.

The study adopts a cross-national, cross-generational perspective using a multimethod design. It combines quantitative and qualitative methods and cross-sectional and a longitudinal approach. The cross-sectional survey collected information from 1,200 respondents (800 aged 25–74 and 400 aged 75+) in larger urban areas in each country (totaling 6,000). These data will allow identification of elders at risk (of becoming dependent), and selection of a sample of dyads of elders and their "primary adult child care person" in each country. Data from the dyads are collected through in-depth interviews.

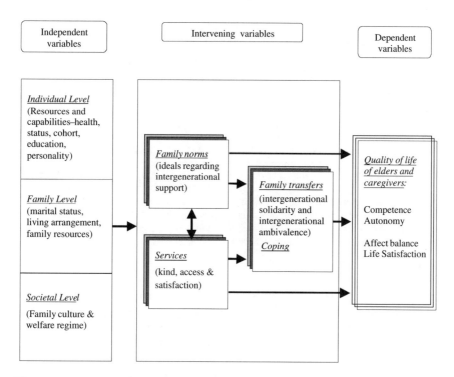

Figure 15.1 Conceptual model.

A major question in the OASIS study relates to the substitutive or complementary function of the mix in care provision between the family and the state. Answers are sought to the differential impact of this mix on autonomy and quality of life by exploring norms and expectations of family care and the perceived role of public services of different age groups in the participating countries. The data presented here are preliminary and illustrative, and refer to the issue of norms and expectations, seen from an attitudinal as well as a relational perspective (Stein et al., 1998).

The Attitudinal Component

As outlined in the introductory section, the attitudinal approach applies to the filial responsibility that emphasizes the larger macrosocial context and refers to the preferred balance between state care and family care. In the OASIS study this component was measured by questions about filial obligations and questions probing the respondents' perceptions about filial versus state responsibility for assistance to elderly persons.

Table 15.1   Percentage (*n*) in Agreement with Filial Obligation Norms[a] among Persons Aged 75+ by Country

	Norway	UK	Germany	Spain	Israel
Live close	35	25	51	72	58
Sacrifice	41	39	41	51	34
Depend on	65	32	64	62	42
Return for	27	45	37	60	52
n	394–402	373–382	433–443	358–361	353–359

[a]Filial obligation scale items: (1) Adult children should live close to their older parents so that they can help them if needed. (2) Adult children should be willing to sacrifice some of the things they want for their own children in order to support their aging parents. (3) Older people should be able to depend on their adult children to help them do the things they need to do. (4) Parents are entitled to some return for the sacrifices they have made for their children. *Source:* Lee et al. (1998).

Filial Obligations.   Filial obligations were measured with a four-item scale developed by Lee et al. (1998). Among the items are for example, "Adult children should live close to their older parents so that they can help them if needed," and "Parents are entitled to some return for the sacrifices they have made for their children." Responses were given along a five-graded Likert type scale from 1, strongly agree, to 5, strongly disagree.

Table 15.1 gives an overview of the percentages of respondents in agreement (agree or strongly agree) with each of the four statements in the oldest age group (75+) in each of the five countries. The proportion in support of filial obligation norms is in general highest in Spain and lowest in Norway and the UK, which was to be expected, but this is not uniform.

The obligation of adult children to live close to their old parents follows the general pattern: About three-quarters (72 percent) of Spanish elders agree, but only one-quarter of UK elders, and one-third (35 percent) of Norwegian elders. Germans and Israelis are in in-between positions (51–58 percent). More or less the same pattern emerges as far as the support for the reciprocity norm is concerned (parents are entitled to returns for their sacrifices). The proportion in agreement here varies between 60 (Spain) and 27 (Norway).

The variation between countries is, however, much less along the other two items of the scale. Norwegian elders are, for example, equally supportive to the idea that older people should be able to depend upon their children for help as the Spanish and German (62–65 percent agree). The United Kingdom is here the odd case (only 32 percent agree).

Hence, norms and attitudes may cluster differently from country to country. While for example the Spanish are seemingly relating the obliga-

Table 15.2   Percentage (*n*) with Familistic, Ambivalent, and Nonfamilistic Attitudes[a] According to Age and Country

Age 75+	Norway	UK	Germany	Spain	Israel
Familistic	30	22	40	54	36
Ambivalent	42	41	44	39	41
Nonfamilistic	28	37	16	8	23
n	382	353	416	344	338
Percentage (*n*) with familistic attitudes					
25–49	28 (492)	37 (327)	29 (385)	44 (435)	44 (491)
50–74	29 (271)	26 (417)	28 (331)	42 (338)	41 (319)
75+	30 (382)	22 (353)	40 (416)	54 (344)	36 (338)

[a]Familistic: in agreement with three or four filial obligation items (see Table 15.1). Nonfamilistic: in disagreement with three or four filial obligation items. Ambivalent: all other combinations.

tion of children to help old parents to the reciprocity norm, Norwegians and Germans are equally likely to expect help, but not necessarily linked to reciprocity. We need further and more sophisticated analysis to test out this and other hypotheses.

The overall picture is that Spain is the most "familistic" country as far as the norms of filial obligations are concerned. The United Kingdom and Norway are in the other extreme, while Germany and Israel occupy in-between positions. This is even better illustrated in Table 15.2, presenting the distribution on an index of filial obligations based on the four items. The respondents included in the "familistic" category are those who agreed on at least three of the four statements, whereas the "nonfamilistic" category includes those who disagreed on at least three statements. The in-between group, which is the larger group in most of the countries, could be described as more or less ambivalent as far as filial obligations are concerned.

The lower section of Table 15.2 shows that age differences in attitudes to filial obligations are modest or nonexistent in Israel and Norway, while the older are more supportive to filial obligations in Germany and in particular in Spain. This is seemingly in contrast to earlier studies in the field (see the review section), which have usually reported an inverse relationship between age and filial obligation norms, as seems to be the case for the United Kingdom.

Attitudes to the Family-State Balance.   Respondents were asked to state how much responsibility families on one hand, and the welfare state on the other, have to provide for three kinds of support to elders in need:

financial support, help in household chores, and personal care. Responses were given along a five-graded Likert type scale: 1, totally family responsibility; 2, mainly family; 3, both equally; 4, mainly welfare state; 5, totally welfare state responsibility.

The welfare state is by the great majority in Norway (65–83 percent in the different age groups) perceived as having the main (or total) responsibility in all three domains, and by a majority—although a smaller majority—also in Israel (47–68 percent). The role of the welfare state is less in Spain, Germany, and the United Kingdom. In these three countries there are minorities that place the main responsibility for practical help and personal care with the welfare state. The state is, however, perceived as more responsible for financial support to elders than for care in Spain and Germany. There are only small variations in ascribed responsibility across domains in Norway and Israel (Figure 15.2).

The oldest age group (aged 75+) is in general more inclined to favor a welfare state responsibility than the younger age groups. Spain is an exception, with the middle age group (50–74) being the most supportive for ascribing the responsibility to the welfare state. Due to technical reasons, UK respondents were given only a four-graded response scale, leaving out the "totally welfare state responsibility" option. The comparably low support for welfare state in the United Kingdom should be interpreted on this background.

Another side of the picture is the responsibility ascribed to the family. Norwegians and Israelis assign less responsibility to families than do the Spaniards and Germans, and they assign less responsibility to families than to the welfare state in all three domains. Respondents from Germany are more inclined than the respondents from the other three countries to support the idea of an equal split of responsibility between the family and the state.

Another finding that is not evident from Figure 15.2 is that most people indicate that there should be some mix of responsibility—some partnership—between the welfare state and the family (Herlofson and Daatland, 2001). Very few indeed favor a total family responsibility in any of the three domains. A total welfare state responsibility is favored by more, in particular in Norway and Israel, but still only by a minority. The great majority of the respondents seem to favor some form of complementarity and partnership. This complementarity, however, takes different forms in the four countries. Most Germans and Spaniards either support an equal share of responsibility between the family and the state, or the idea that the major responsibility should rest with the family and the welfare state in a supportive role. In Norway and Israel in contrast, the welfare state is seen as the main responsible agent, with the family in a supportive role.

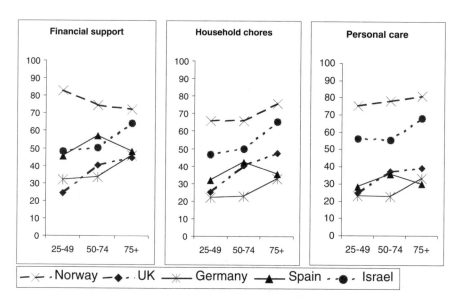

Figure 15.2 Percentage in favor of total or mainly welfare state responsibility by age and country. Respondents were asked: About how much responsibility should in your opinion the family on the one hand, and the welfare state on the other, have: (1) To provide financial support for older persons who are in need? (2) To provide help with household chores for older persons who are in need such as help with cleaning, washing? (3) To provide personal care for older persons who are in need, such as nursing or help with bathing or dressing? Responses were given along a five-graded Likert type scale from 1, totally family, to 5, totally welfare state, and an additional category 6, none of these apply.

Attitudes to Future Responsibility

Do people expect families—or governments—to take the major responsibility for the growing needs of elder care in the years to come?

Nine out of ten elderly (75+) Norwegians place the primary responsibility with the welfare state, compared to three out of four in Israel and nearly two out of three in Germany. Spanish elders are more or less equally split between the welfare state and the family, while the United Kingdom is a distinct case. Only a few elders in the United Kingdom place the responsibility with the family, as is the case in Norway, but responsibilities outside the family are then split between several parties, not only the public

Table 15.3   Who Has the Primary Responsibility for the Increasing Need for
              Elder Care in the Years to Come? Percentage among Respondents Aged 75+
              by Country

	Norway	UK	Germany	Spain	Israel
Family	3.8	8.6	26.4	48.8	16.4
Public services	93.4	38.9	65.1	49.4	76.7
Voluntary organizations	0.8	17.7	2.9	0.3	3.0
Private sector	1.8	22.0	4.8	0.9	2.7
Others	0.3	12.9	1.0	0.6	1.2
Total	100.1	100.1	100.2	100.0	100.0
n	396	350	421	338	330

services, but also the voluntary and the commercial sector. The latter two
are hardly mentioned in the other four countries (Table 15.3).

Age group differences are in general modest, and substantially less than
the differences between countries, but in all countries except Spain the
younger are more inclined to favor family responsibility than the older.

THE RELATIONAL COMPONENT

The relational component is expressed through personal preferences that
reflect beliefs and intentions related more closely to one's own family. In
the OASIS study this component was measured by questions probing the
respondents' answers to two statements relating to intergenerational preferences. One question asks about personal preferences in case of long-term
care needs: preference for one's own family, services, or others like friends
or neighbors. The second question asks about preferred housing arrangements if one could no longer live by oneself—to move in with a child or to
move into a residential setting.

Preferences for long-term help among those 75+ are in all countries,
except Spain, in the direction of services (Table 15.3). Norway in particular, and next Israel, have great majorities with a preference for services.
Germans and Britons are more or less split in half, while Spain is the only
country with a majority stating a preference for family help.

The childless are naturally more inclined to state a preference for services over family (or other informal) care, but Norway and Israel have substantial majorities preferring services also among those with children
(Table 15.4). Preference for services tend to increase with age, except in
Spain. The younger are in this sense the more traditional and family-
oriented, while experiences may have made the older adapt their attitudes

Table 15.4 Preferences for Long-Term Help from Services[a] According to Age and Parenthood (Percentage Stating a Preference for Services)

	Norway	*UK*	*Germany*	*Spain*	*Israel*
25–49	67.8	30.6	43.5	35.0	56.0
50–74	79.6	49.5	47.6	31.7	57.3
75+	87.2	51.4	52.4	24.9	69.0
n	1151	1060	1152	1092	1144
Of the 75+					
with children	86.2	45.9	41.3	22.1	68.3
childless	91.5	78.7	82.8	42.9	78.3
n	398	366	456	361	338

[a]Suppose you should come to need long-term help on a regular basis with household chores like cleaning, washing clothes, etc., from whom would you prefer such help? From family, from organized services, or from others?

to real life circumstances. The older may also be concerned about not becoming a burden to their families. Preferences anyway vary with age, but seemingly less so than by country, which indicates that national differences are more salient for these attitudes than differences between age groups.

Preferences for housing follow a similar pattern, as indicated in Table 15.5. Three of the countries, and Norway in particular, have majorities stating a preference for residential care over shared living with children. The older are less inclined to prefer the family solution in Norway, while there are small and unsubstantial age differences as to these attitudes in the other four countries.

CONCLUDING REMARKS

The preliminary analysis and findings illustrate that the picture is quite complicated when comparing the five countries, and the results might reflect the mix between different family cultures and welfare regimes. For example, the centrality of the family in Israel is well-documented (Lavee and Katz, forthcoming), but Israel is also a very developed welfare state with regard to the elderly, and this duality is reflected in filial obligation norms, on the one hand, and in the preferences for services, on the other. In Spain the family plays a major and central role regarding elder care, more so than in the other three countries. The reform in the welfare services for the elderly reflects this family culture, where the reform is in "the

Table 15.5   Percentage with a Preference[a] for Residential Care among Those with Children (Percentage Stating a Preference for Residential Care)

	Norway	UK	Germany	Spain	Israel
25–49	66.4	58.1	51.1	52.4	72.0
50–74	79.1	65.9	53.4	45.8	76.4
75+	90.0	54.6	54.8	25.9	66.5
n	793	806	687	684	711

[a]If you could no longer live by yourself in older years, and had to choose between living with a child or in residential or institutional care, what would you prefer? With a child, in residential care, don't know, not relevant?

way that they try to reinforce the traditional emphasis on family care" (Twigg, 1996, p. 163).

The data from Norway reflect basically the notion of this country being a representative of what Esping-Andersen calls the social democratic welfare regime, with high levels of services, and an active role of the state. This is supported by data from other Scandinavian studies, which also find that a majority of elders now prefer help from services (Daatland, 1990). In the case of Norway, the inclination of respondents toward the use of welfare services over family care is taken as a direct consequence of the expanding welfare state (Daatland, 1997). In Germany, on many of the attitudinal aspects regarding state-family balance, the respondents chose the option of coresponsibility between the two. In general, family policy developments in Germany are characterized by "programmatic uncertainties and strong discontinuities and, despite an explicit family policy, [Germany] has a social welfare system that remains unfavorable to the family" (Kaufmann, 1997, p. 91). The UK picture is rather varied, partly leaning toward Norway as to the attitudes to family responsibility, but partly also toward Germany in the smaller role and responsibility attributed to the welfare state.

Judged on the basis of these preliminary data, it can be concluded that the respondents in the OASIS project do not have a clear-cut preference for family care, nor are they reluctantly pushed over to services as a secondary option, as implied in the substitution argument. The attitudinal aspects follow more or less the same pattern as general societal attitudes, but seem to favor welfare state arrangements. It seems reasonable, then, to say that a welfare state containment policy does not seem to have support in any of the five countries.

In sum, we found similarities as well as differences between the countries that might reflect variations in family norms and patterns of behaviors, and social policy traditions of the participating countries. While comparing the OASIS data on norms and preferences for care, and the balance between state support and family responsibility between the various age groups, differences were found to be greater among the oldest age groups than among the youngest. This might reflect the process of "familistic" states converging toward the individualistic welfare regimes. On the other hand, country differences were found to be larger than the variations between age groups within each country, implying that there are national and cultural idiosyncrasies that have to be further explored.

ACKNOWLEDGMENT

The OASIS study is supported by the European Commission, Quality of Life and Management of Living Resources Programme (1998-2002), Fifth Framework Programme, Contract number: QLK6-CT1999-02182.

REFERENCES

Ajzen, I. 1988. *Attitudes, personality and behavior.* London: Open University Press.

Alber, J. 1995. A framework for the comparative study of social services. *Journal of European Social Policy* 5:131–49.

Attias-Donfut, C., and Wolff, F. C. 2000. Complementarity between private and public transfers. In S. Arber, and C. Attias-Donfut (eds.), *The myth of generational conflict: The family and the state in ageing societies* (pp. 47–68). London: Routledge.

Bay, A. H. 1998. *Opinionen og eldrepolitikken,* report 24-1998. Oslo: NOVA.

Bengtson, V. L., and Murray, T. M. 1993. "Justice" across generations (and cohorts): Sociological perspectives on the life course and reciprocities over time. In L. M. Cohen (ed.), *The changing contract across generations* (pp. 111–38). Hawthorne, NY: Aldine de Gruyter.

Bengtson, V. L., and Roberts, R. E. L. 1991. Intergenerational solidarity in aging families: An example of formal theory construction. *Journal of Marriage and the Family* 53, 856–70.

Binstock, R. H. 1983. The aged as scapegoat. *Gerontologist, 23,* 136–43.

Burr, J. A., and Mutchler, J. E. (eds.) 1999. Race and ethnic variation in norms of filial responsibility among older persons. *Journal of Marriage and the Family* 61, 674–87.

Cantor, M. H. 1989. Social care: Family and community support systems. *Annals of the American Academy of Political and Social Sciences* 503, 99–112.

———. 1991. Family and community: Changing roles in an aging society. *Gerontologist* 31, 337–46.

Chappell, N., and Blandford, A. 1991. Informal and formal care: Exploring the complementarity. *Ageing and Society* 11, 299–317.

Cicirelli, V. G. 1981. Kin relationships of childless and one-child elderly in relation to social services. *Journal of Gerontological Social Work* 4(1):19–33.

Connidis, I. 1983. Living arrangement choices of older residents: Assessing quantitative results with qualitative data. *Canadian Journal of Sociology* 8(4):359–75.

Connidis, I. 2001. *Family ties and aging*. Thousand Oaks, CA: Sage.

Daatland, S. O. 1990. What are families for? On family solidarity and preferences for help. *Ageing and Society* 10:1–15.

_____. 1997. Family solidarity, public opinion and the elderly. *Ageing International* 1, 51–62.

_____. 2001. Ageing, families and welfare systems. *Zeitschrift für Gerontologie und Geriatrie* 34, 16–20.

Daatland, S. O., and Herlofson, K. 2001. Service systems and family care–substitution or complementarity? In S. O. Daatland and K. Herlofson (eds.), *Ageing, intergenerational relations, care systems and quality of life. An introduction to the OASIS project* Report 14-2001. Oslo: NOVA.

Easterlin, R. A., Macunovich, D. J., and Crimmins, E. M. 1993. Economic status of the young and old in the working-age population, 1964 and 1987. In V. L. Bengtson, V. L. and W. A. Achenbaum (eds.), *The changing contract across generations*. Hawthorne, NY: Aldine de Gruyter.

Esping-Andersen, G. 1997. Welfare states at the end of the century: The impact of labour market, family and demographic change. In P. Hennesy and M. Pearson (eds.), *Family, market and community: Equity and efficiency in social policy*. Social Policy Studies no. 21. Paris: OECD.

Finch, J., and Mason, J. 1993. *Negotiating family responsibilities*. London: Tavistock/Routledge.

Finley, N. J., Roberts, M. D., and Banahan, B. F. 1988. Motivators and inhibitors of attitudes of filial obligation toward aging parents. *Gerontologist* 28:73–78.

Hamon, R. R., and Blieszner, R. 1990. Filial responsibility expectations among adult child–older parents pairs. *Journal of Gerontology* 45(3):P110–12.

Hanson, S. L., Sauer, W. J., and Seelbach, W. C. 1983. Racial and cohort variations in filial responsibility norms. *Gerontologist* 23(6):626–31.

Herlofson, K., and Daatland, S. V. 2001. The limits of intergenerational responsibility: Values and preferences towards elder care in a comparative perspective. Paper presented at the 5th conference of the European Sociological Association, Helsinki, Finland, August.

Hooyman, N. R. 1992. Social policy and gender inequities in caregiving. In J. W. Dwyer and R. T. Coward (eds.), *Gender, families, and elder care*. Newbury Park, CA: Sage.

Inglehart, R., and Baker, W. E. 2000. Modernization, cultural change, and the persistence of traditional values. *American Sociological Review* 65:19–51.

Johnson, P., Conrad, C. and Thompson, D. (eds.) 1989. *Workers versus pensioners*. Manchester: Manchester University Press.

Katz, R., and Lowenstein, A. 1999. Adjustment of older Soviet immigrant parents and their adult children residing in shared households: An intergenerational comparison. *Family Relations* 48(1):43–50.

Kaufmann, F. X. 1997. European welfare states in their relation to the family. In J. Commaille and F. de Singly (eds.), *The European family* (pp. 91–102). The Netherlands: Kluwer Academic.

Kohli, M. 1999. Private and public transfers between generations: Linking the family and the state. *European Societies* 1.

Künemund, H., and Rein, M. 1999. There is more to receiving than needing: Theoretical arguments and empirical explorations of crowding in and crowding out. *Ageing and Society* 19:93–121.

Lavee, Y., and Katz, R. (in press). The family in Israel between tradition and modernity. *Marriage and Family Review*, 34(1 and 2).

Lee, G. R., Peek, C. W., and Coward, R. T. 1998. Race differences in filial responsibility expectations among older parents. *Journal of Marriage and the Family* 60:404–12

Lingsom, S. 1997. *The substitution issue. Care policies and their consequences for family care* report 6-1997. Oslo: NOVA.

Litwak, E. 1985. *Helping the elderly: The complementary roles of informal networks and formal systems.* New York: Guilford.

Logan, J. R., and Spitze, G. D. 1995. Self–interest and altruism in intergenerational relations. *Demography* 32(3):353–64.

Lowenstein, A., and Katz, R. 2000. Coping with caregiving in the rural Arab family in Israel. *Marriage and Family Review* 30(1):179–97.

Lubomudrow, S. 1997. Congressional perceptions of the elderly: the use of stereotypes in the legislative process. *Gerontologist* 27:77–81.

Marshall, V. W., Cook, F. L., and Marshall, J. G. 1993. Conflict over ingergenerational equity: Rhetoric and reality in a comparative context. In V. L. Bengston and W. A. Achenbaum (eds.), *The changing contract across generations* (pp. 101–40). New York: Aldine de Gruyter.

McGarry, K., and Schoeni, R. F. 1997. Transfer behavior within the family: Results from the asset and health dynamics study. *Journal of Gerontology* Series B, 52B, Special issues, 82–92.

Organisation for Economic Co-operation and Development. 1992. *Urban policies for ageing populations.* Paris: OECD.

Pampel, F. C., and Williamson, J. B. 1989. *Age, class, politics, and the welfare state.* New York: Cambridge University Press.

Preston, S. 1984. Children and the elderly. Divergent paths for America's elderly. *Demography* 21, 435–57.

Rossi, A. S., and Rossi, P. H. 1990. *Of human bonding: Parent-child relations across the life course.* Hawthorne, NY: Aldine de Gruyter.

Seelbach, W. C. 1978. Correlates of aged parents' filial responsibility expectations and realizations. *Family Coordinator* 27:341–50.

———. 1984. Filial responsibility and the care of aging family members. In W. H. Quinn and G. A. Hughston (eds.), *Independent aging: Family and social system perspectives* (pp. 92–105). Rockville, MD: Aspen Systems.

Sgritta, G. B. 1997. The generation question: State solidarity versus family solidarity. In J. Commaille and F. de Singly, *The European Family* (pp. 151–66). Dordrecht, The Netherlands: Kluwer Academic.

Soldo, B. J., Wolf, D. A., and Agree, E. M. 1990. Family, households, and care arrangements of frail older women: A structural analysis. *Journal of Gerontology: Social Sciences* 45:S238–49.

Stein, C. H., Wemmerus, V. A., Ward, M, Gaines, M. E., Freeberg, A. L., and Jewell, T. C. (1998). Because they are my parents: An intergenerational study of felt obligation and parental caregiving. *Journal of Marriage and the Family,* 60:611–22.

Sussman, M. B. 1985. The family life of old people. In R. H. Binstock and E. Shanas (eds.), *Handbook of aging and the social sciences.* New York: Van Nostrand Reinhold.

Twigg, J. 1996. Issues in informal care. In OECD, *Caring for frail elderly people: Policies in evolution* (pp. 81–92). Social Policy Studies No. 19. Paris: OECD.

Vinovskis, M. A. 1993. An historical perspective on support for schooling by different age cohorts. In V. L Bengtson, and W. A. Achenbaum, (eds.), *The changing contract across generations.* Hawthorne, NY: Aldine de Gruyter.

Walker, A. 1990. The economic 'burden' of ageing and the prospects of intergenerational conflict. *Ageing and Society* 10:377–96.

Walker, A. 1993a. Intergenerational relations and welfare restructuring: The social construction of an intergenerational problem. In V. L. Bengtson and W. A. Achenbaum (eds.), *The changing contract across generations.* Hawthorne, NY: Aldine de Gruyter.

Walker, A. 1993b. Community care policy: From consensus to conflict. In J. C. Bormat, D. Perieva, D. Pilgrim, and F. Williams (eds.), *Community care: A reader* (pp. 204–26). Basingstoke: Macmillan,.

Ward, R. A. 2001. Linkages between family and societal-level intergenerational attitudes. *Research on Aging, 23*(2):179–208.

|16|

The Role of Family for Quality of Life in Old Age

A Comparative Perspective

Andreas Motel-Klingebiel, Clemens Tesch-Roemer, and
Hans-Joachim von Kondratowitz

INTRODUCTION

This chapter explores the role of the family and its contribution to quality of life in old age under a comparative perspective, looking at different European welfare states. The literature demonstrates a consistent association between well-being and social networks in old age. Intergenerational family relations seem to be of special relevance in their contribution to health and well-being of older family members (Antonucci, Sherman, and Akiyama, 1996). Key features of intergenerational relationships include association, help, and support but also conflicts and the manner in which conflicts are dealt with (Bengtson, Rosenthal, and Burton, 1996). However, in modern welfare states certain tasks traditionally performed by families are covered by services.

To assess the relative impact of families and the welfare state and to understand the interaction between both we take a comparative perspective, analyzing diverse cultures and welfare regimes. It is our contention that cultural and societal contexts are of central importance in exploring and understanding the complex association between family relations and the quality of life of the elderly. Such a perspective implies an empirical analysis concerning structure and culture of different welfare state settings. The countries to be included in our analyses will be Norway, the United Kingdom, Germany, Spain, and Israel.

This chapter will address the issue of the role of the family for quality of life in old age by:

- Reviewing key theoretical arguments concerning family structure and relations, welfare regimes, and quality of life in older age and the association between them.
- Providing a short overview of the project "OASIS—Old Age and Autonomy: The Role of Service Systems and Intergenerational Family Solidarity" and the database being used for analyses.
- Presenting descriptive and theoretically guided analyses based on empirical data from the OASIS project.

THEORETICAL PERSPECTIVES

Family Structure and Relations

A crisis of the family is often diagnosed in the sociological debate on the family. Historically, weakening generational ties were discussed as the cause of increasing social isolation of elderly people in contemporary modern societies (Parsons 1943). Modernization theory offers a hypothesis that attributes the crisis of the family to the development of the welfare state and to the progressive tendency toward individualization.

Empirical data on family and household structures in modern societies show indeed a strong decline in the number of multigenerational households, a decline in the number of persons with three or more children, and an increase in the number of unmarried persons over time (e.g., Phillipson, Bernard, Phillips, and Ogg, 2000). However, these statistical trends do not of themselves constitute a compelling confirmation of the breakdown of the family as an institution. While the cited analysis seems to confirm the traditional thesis of the decay of the nuclear family, this can be criticized using a more elaborated empirical analysis. Kohli, Künemund, Motel, and Szydlik (2000) using the data of the German Aging Survey can show that, on the one hand, the average numbers of children and the proportion of multigenerational households decline within successive cohorts. On the other hand, however, most elderly are still embedded in a strong family network. Families often live in different households under one roof or in the immediate or a close neighborhood with high levels of intrafamilial support, close relations, and attachment. Data from the German Aging Survey show that nearly 50 percent of Germans 55 years and older have at least one child living in the neighborhood or even closer. The family obviously has changed from a household-based structure into a neighborhood-based structure without a severe loss of familial support, close relations, and attachment to family members. Clearly, intergenerational relationships alter and evolve at the microlevel. Norms and expectations as well as individual behavior patterns regarding intergenerational support, relationships, and care are all factors influenced by structural factors and evolving social constructions. It is essential, however, to move beyond analysis of sociodemographic factors like household structure and geographical proximity and approach a more thorough analysis of family relations.

Basic dimensions of family relations are on the one hand positively identified as help and support, proximity, affect, association, consensus, and normative agreement [aspects that are interpreted by Bengtson and Roberts (1991) as components of "intergenerational solidarity"]. However, family relations cannot always be characterized as harmonious. Disagreement, arguments, tensions, and abuse (summarized as conflict) and polarized emotions, thoughts, relations, and structures (marked as ambivalence) are important aspects of relations within families (Lüscher and Pillemer, 1998). Hence, the term "family relation" is defined in the current context as a complex multidimensional construct.

In behavioral and practical terms support behavior can be shown in diverse ways. To give an example: elderly people give substantial payments and transfers to the younger generation—mainly within their own family (Attias-Donfut, 2000; Motel and Szydlik, 1999). Instrumental support is statistically more likely to be provided by younger family members to older members although, however, grandparents quite often provide practical care, emotional support, and assistance to their grandchildren (Kohli, Künemund, Motel, and Szydlik, 2000; Thompson, 1999). When analyzing the preferences of elderly people for sources of support, family help is often identified as the preferred type of support (Künemund and Hollstein, 2000)[1] but these patterns may vary between societies.

Conflicts within the family are an important, but often neglected aspect of family relations. Such conflicts may manifest in diverse ways. Family culture, history, and normative expectations are likely to be essential components in understanding the ways in which conflicts may be caused and subsequently managed. In order to capture the complexity of the different dimensions of family relations, the concept of "intergenerational ambivalence" has only recently been revisited by family sociologists (Lüscher and Pillemer, 1998; Lüscher and Pajung-Bilger, 1998). The concept of ambivalence refers to the "double valence" of social phenomena. In the words of Kurt Lüscher and Frank Lettke: "We speak of ambivalences if polarizations of (simultaneous) emotions, thoughts, social relations and structures, which are considered relevant for the constitution of individual and collective identities, are (or can be) interpreted as temporarily or permanently irreconcilable" (2000, p. 15). Those ambivalences play a particularly important role in aging families, for example, with regard to conflicts over the compatibility of employment and caregiving (Phillips, 1994) and in the dynamics of intergenerational relations, where one has to deal with ambivalences as an essential quality of these relations. However, ambivalence is not to be understood as claiming a universal or "ontological feature" of such relations, but rather as an empirical characteristic that may be experienced in some, but not necessarily in all cases.

In the following paragraphs we will concentrate on the connection between family structure, welfare state, and the quality of life in old age. A first step in this direction will be to consider the impact of welfare state on families in a comparative perspective.

Family and the Welfare State

We have already cited some empirical evidence of the ways in which family structures are influenced by social changes and by the developing welfare state. We will extend this debate further by shedding light on two key debates about the relationship between families and welfare state: the economic debate about "crowding out" the family by the means of welfare state transfers, and the sociological debate about stabilizing effects between welfare state and family transfers. Finally, we will consider the characteristics of the welfare states represented in the project OASIS.

When analyzing familial and societal transfer systems, economists introduced the criterion of efficiency in order to evaluate the outcomes of those mixed (support) systems. Within economic modeling this finally came down to a debate as to whether the provision of state intervention would crowd out or replace familial assistance.

This obviously can only—and from a sociological point of view insufficiently—be analyzed by an indirect measurement of the motives for private transfers. Those analyses rest on the premise that family support is more efficient than welfare state services. The rationale for this assumption is the underlying idea of higher distribution costs within societal transfer systems. However this leads to an inconsistent and therefore unsatisfactory analysis. On the one hand, several studies have supported the idea of crowding out between family and society transfers. This results in the conclusion that welfare state intervention turns out to be inefficient. On the other hand a lot of studies have shown quite the opposite (see Altonji, Hayashi, and Kotlikoff, 1992; Altonji et al., 1996; Andreoni, 1989; Cox, 1987; Cox and Jakubson, 1995; Cox and Stark, 1994; Schoeni, 1994, 1997; Stark, 1995; for summaries see Künemund and Rein, 1999; Motel and Spieß, 1995; Soldo and Hill, 1993).

In the sociological debate of the mid- and late nineties it was primarily argued that family and state intervention have stabilized each other, allowing for both a degree of complementarity and functional differentiation. While the combination of both institutions leads to changes in the role of the modern family, these changes do not necessarily contribute to decline or decay of the family because more societal transfers correspond with increasing family transfers (Attias-Donfut, 2000; Motel-Klingebiel, 2000; Künemund and Rein, 1999). This seems to be the case when one compares the resources of transfer givers within the family and the probabilities of transfers in culture-specific studies (e.g. Künemund and Motel, 2000; Motel-Klingebiel, 2000) or the distributions and predictors of transfers between different welfare regimes (Künemund and Rein, 1999). Therefore, before we devote more attention to the outcome of such combined transfer systems we should explore the implications of the use of the term "welfare regime" with respect to family policies.

In project OASIS, five countries with different types of welfare state regimes are represented: Norway, Great Britain, Germany, Spain, and Israel. The notion of a "welfare regime" as defined by Esping-Andersen (1990) refers to the institutional arrangements adopted by societies in the pursuit of work and welfare. Three of these countries can typically stand for a regime type: the British welfare state represents the "market liberal" model, the German welfare state stands for the "conservative-corporatist" model, while the Norwegian welfare state is a representative of the "social democratic" model.

While this differentiation of welfare regimes undoubtedly has driven comparative research on welfare states in general, the concept itself has been criticized by several researchers as being too much centered on employment and not taking into consideration historical changes and differentiation within societies. Highly relevant is the critique that this concept neglects the impact of family cultures and family provision as well as the changing position of women in the family and employment market. This has brought some feminist researchers to recommend the model of "caring regimes" instead of "welfare regimes" (cf. Sainsbury, 1994). Indeed, in order to reflect the social determinants of the family situation within welfare states, the model of welfare regimes has to be complemented by bringing to mind legal regulations and latent sociopolitical norms, which give the management of child and elder care the respective societal framework.

Table 16.1 provides a comparison of some central policy determinants concerning the family position in the welfare states of the OASIS project: strategies of improving the economic situation of families and of enabling a higher degree of compatibility of family work and employment. Additionally, these welfare states can be differentiated regarding the existence of legal obligation for families to care for their elders.

This first contrast of policy determinants clarifies that the concept of "welfare regime" does not exhaust the existing variety of welfare state

332

Table 16.1 Family Policy Determinants in the Countries of the OASIS Project

	Norway	United Kingdom	Germany	Spain	Israel
Welfare state regime according to Esping-Andersen	social democratic	market liberal	conservative-corporatist	(southern European?)	—
Sociopolitical points of reference I: Improving the economic situation of families	yes	yes (concentrating on families in need)	yes (balancing of burdens within family)	no (but recently more developed)	yes
Sociopolitical points of reference II: Compatibility of family work and employment for women	yes (as a national policy objective)	yes	yes (recently more prominent in public discourse)	no (recently more moves toward compatibility)	yes
Legal obligation to give family support to elderly	no	no	yes (but long-term care insurance)	yes (but attempts to develop long-term care insurance)	yes (but long-term care insurance)

strategies. Most of these countries seem to be in transitional stages illustrated by mixtures of policy orientations rather than representing one single model. For comparisons it is necessary, to take into account the ongoing change with respect to each of the determinants within these countries. Nevertheless, Germany and Spain seem to be specific "latecomers" with respect to the implementation of policies of allowing compatibility between family and employment for women, thereby giving room for family care activities. And while these two countries (together with Israel) are comparable with respect to the obligation of family support to elders, the implementation of long-term care insurance schemes in Israel and Germany (including the first debates in Spain about such a perspective) seem to direct attention to the possibility of new service offers complementing and qualifying family care work. Thus, the relation between an enabling welfare state allowing for transfers and services to qualify care work and their consequence for family dynamics seems to be a crucial point to be studied more carefully using the data of OASIS.

Quality of Life: Reflections on the Concept

A criterion to evaluate the outcome of combined transfer systems under the condition of differentiated models of welfare regimes has not been introduced so far. The concept of "quality of life" might be used in this context (see also Tesch-Römer, Motel-Klingebiel, and von Kondratowitz, 2001). Quality of life can serve as an indicator of the success of different help and support mixes. Moreover it traditionally serves as a benchmark for results of welfare state intervention in the analyses of welfare states. The chosen comparative perspective in project OASIS allows us to differentiate the effects of support mixes under the conditions of different welfare regimes and family cultures as well as the effects of the analyzed welfare regimes and family cultures themselves. Of course from a methodological point of view it does not make much sense to compare absolute levels of quality of life expressed by individuals in each country but rather the connection between family and welfare state support on the one hand and welfare or quality of life on the other hand.

"Quality of life" is a multidimensional concept and includes material and nonmaterial, objective and subjective, individual and collective aspects of welfare. Historically, there are two traditions regarding conceptualization and measuring welfare and quality of life (Noll, 1999). In the Scandinavian tradition the "level of living approach" is based on the concept of resources. Quality of life is defined as "an individual's command over . . . mobilizable resources with whose help s/he can control and consciously direct her/his living conditions" (Erikson, 1974). Individuals are seen as active and creative beings who strive toward autonomy in reaching goals. In this sense resources are seen as means to reach those goals and increase individual agency.

However, one can argue that not the objective conditions, but rather the individual's subjective interpretations of these conditions are "real" in their consequences. This basic assumption has been expressed in the American "quality of life research." It has been argued that subjective well-being at least consists of cognitive and emotional aspects (Smith et al., 1996), that negative and positive aspects of well-being might be independent dimensions (Diener, 1994), and that therefore psychological well-being is more than life satisfaction, e.g., personal growth, meaning in life, self-acceptance, and positive relationships (Ryff, 1989.

A first approach to integrate objective and subjective aspects of quality of life can be seen in the description of welfare positions, which is based on a classification according to the dimensions of objective and subjective quality of life (Zapf, 1984). The combination of good living conditions and good subjective well-being can be simply called "well-being"; this is the intended outcome of political intervention. Going beyond such an elementary 2*2 classification means analyzing the relationship between objective and subjective aspects of quality of life (e.g., Smith et al., 1996).

In the case of comparative research it is important to rely on instruments that can be used in cross-cultural research, taking appropriate account of diverse cultures and societies. Moreover, this instrument should go beyond the measurement of general life satisfaction. For this reason, the project OASIS chose an instrument developed by a group within WHO consisting of fifteen culturally diverse research centers from Europe, Asia, North and South America, Australia, and Africa (WHOQOL Group, 1994a, 1994b). This group defined quality of life as "individuals' perception of their position in life in the context of the culture and value systems in which they live and in relation to their goals, expectations, standards and concerns"(WHO, 1999, p. 3). Four dimensions are measured by the short version of the WHOQOL, used by OASIS.

- physical health,
- psychological health,
- social relationships, and
- environment.

These four domains of the WHOQOL-BREF instrument cover twenty-four facets of quality of life by single indicators. Hence, one can use this instrument to look at domain-specific effects of family support under the conditions of various welfare states. As one can see, the chosen definitions concern dimensions of subjective well-being, while objective living conditions such as income, receipt of transfer income from welfare state sources, marital status, or the housing situation are treated more or less as independent variables within the OASIS model—independent from the influence of families and their behavior.

Family Structures and Quality of Life: Hypotheses

Figure 16.1 gives a description of two alternative models that will be used in the statistical analyses: The circles represent the predictor variables, i.e., family structure and family relations on the one hand and transfers and services of the welfare state on the other. The square represents the dependent variables, i.e., several dimensions of quality of life.

Model (a) points to an additional impact of family relations and welfare state support on quality of life. This leads to the hypothesis that family support and welfare state transfers independently and additively influence the quality of life of elderly people. Model (b) however, conceptualizes a moderating effect of the welfare state. This model would imply that the relationship between family structure/family relations and quality of life depends on the type of welfare state and welfare state transfers and services. Hence, this leads to the hypothesis that the relationship between quality of life and family support is strong only in those cases where welfare state transfers are low. However, according to Table 1 there are also other cultural dimensions of the welfare state which might moderate the relations.

The main focus of this chapter is concerned with the relationship between family support and welfare state transfers on a macrolevel involving comparisons between welfare states. The two alternative models will be tested. For the time being, intergenerational family structures will be considered only. Hence, existence and number of children will be used as independent variables. First, descriptive analyses regarding family structures and quality of life in a comparative perspective will be presented. Second, theory-guided analyses regarding the combined relationship between family structure, welfare state systems, and quality of life will be described. Theory-guided analyses will be based on the data of the eldest participants, i.e., those persons 75+ years of age.

METHOD

The OASIS project uses a cross-cultural, cross-generational approach, comparing five European societies (Norway, United Kingdom, Germany, Spain, and Israel). Representative samples were drawn from two age

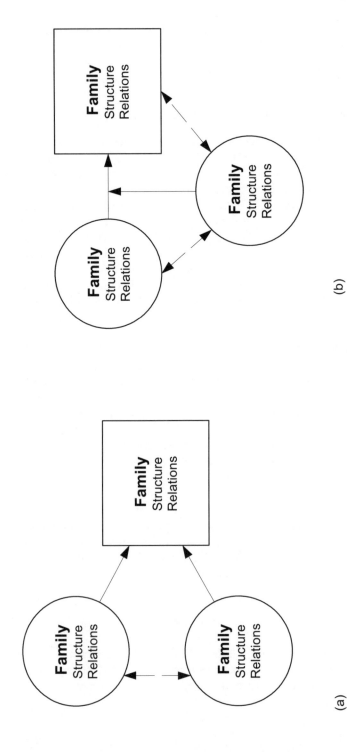

(a)

(b)

Figure 16.1 Basic theoretical model. (a) Additive impact of predictors, (b) Interaction effects of predictors.

Table 16.2   Sample Structure (*n*) of the OASIS Project

	Norway	UK	Germany	Spain	Israel	Total
25–74	790	799	798	816	839	4,042
75+	413	398	499	385	369	2,064
Total	1,203	1,197	1,297	1,201	1,208	6,106

groups: 25 to 74 years of age (*n* = 4,042) and 75 years and older (*n* = 2,064). The total sample size is *n* = 6,106 for all participating countries (see Table 16.2). The samples for the survey were either drawn from population or electoral registers or randomly selected by random-route procedures. The samples are representative for the population dwelling in urban settlements and residing in private households. Additionally, respondents must be able to give informed consent to participate in the study. In the following analyses we will mainly use the data from the 75+ years old participants.

Data collection was performed through a standardized survey in all five countries. The survey addressed the following subject areas: sociodemographic information; living conditions and environment; work status and income; subjective and functional health; health and care services; children, grandchildren, and other family members; social integration; values and preferences; coping. Quality of life was measured by the WHOQOL-BREF (WHOQOL Group, 1994b). Therefore we define four dimensions of quality of life: Physical health, psychological health, social relationships, and environment. All four scales are defined as mean of the items.

The WHOQOL-BREF offers two global single-item indicators of quality of life: "subjective quality of life" and "global life satisfaction." The correlation between them is $r = .50$, $p < .001$, in the OASIS dataset (including all age groups). Hence, although there is a substantial correlation between the two indicators, none of them is redundant. The correlation between age and life satisfaction ($r = -.15$, $p > .001$) is lower than the correlation between age and subjective quality of life ($r = -.20$, $p < .001$). The correlation between the domains described above and subjective quality of life ranges between $r = .37$, $p < .001$, and $r = .68$, $p < .001$. Hence, for the current analyses, the single-item indicator "subjective quality of life" will be used as dependent variable.

As independent variables we are using information about the existence and number of children, and as control variables health, gender, and age. In addition, for comparative reasons we are looking at the existence of grandchildren, too. Apart from age and gender, an indicator of self-rated

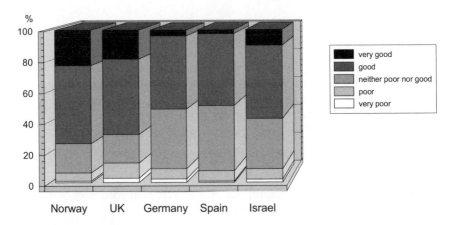

Figure 16.2 Overall quality of life of the elderly (75+). *Source:* OASIS 2000, n = 2040.

health was included in the analyses as a control variable, based on the physical health status scale of the SF36.

RESULTS

Descriptive Results

Figure 16.2 gives an impression of the subjective quality of life in the highest age group (75+ years) of the OASIS sample. According to the overall single-item indicator, at least 50 percent of the 75+ persons rate the quality of their life as good or—rarely—as very good in each country. In Norway this proportion is highest (reaching nearly 75 percent) while Spain obviously has the lowest rates with Germany and Israel close behind. About 10 percent in each society rated their quality of life as poor or very poor. This proportion is nearly the same in every country—differences in the overall quality of life between societies can be found mainly in the upper and middle ranges of the scale.

More impressive differences can be found when analyzing the domain-specific quality of life as discussed above (Figure 16.3). Here the four columns show the results of the four domains, which can be compared with the overall measure given in Figure 16.2. The Norwegian and German data look quite similar on a high level, the United Kingdom shows moderate values, the Israeli mean levels are significantly lower, and the

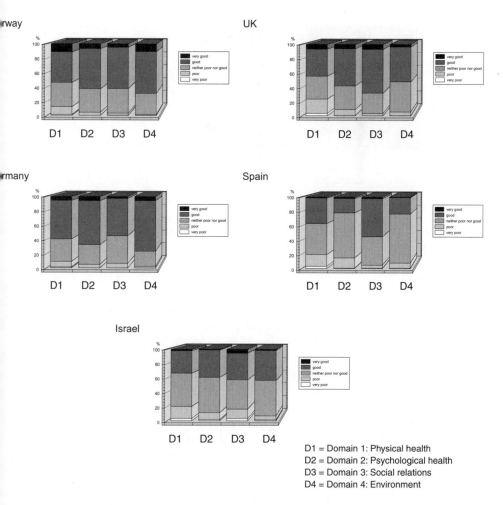

Figure 16.3 Domain-specific and overall quality of life of the elderly (75+).
Source: OASIS 2000, n_N = 399-404, n_{UK} = 384-394, n_D = 493-498, n_E = 355-374, n_{IL} = 271-338.

Spanish data show considerable internal variation (with rather low values in the dimensions "psychological health" and "environment"). Hence, the distribution of domain-specific quality of life differs significantly from overall quality of life.

Figure 16.4 shows the percentage of persons 75 years and older in each country with children or grandchildren, while Figure 16.5 gives percentages for the whole age range starting at age 25 in each of the participating

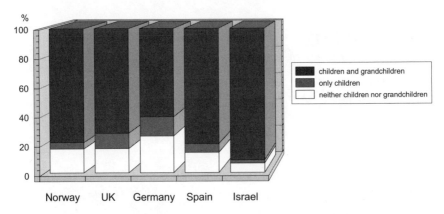

Figure 16.4 Living children and grandchildren of the elderly (75+). *Source:*
OASIS 2000, $n = 2,053$.

societies. Childlessness in old age is highest in Germany and lowest in
Israel, where the elderly without children are a small minority.[2] Norway,
Great Britain and Spain are in the middle range. When it comes to the distributions over all cohorts we observe a slightly different situation. Figure
5 gives overall percentages of persons with offspring by age groups 25–49,
50–74, and 75+ years of age. As can be expected, the percentage of persons
with children or grandchildren increases with age. In the oldest age group
by far most persons in each country have children and grandchildren.
Nevertheless, it can be shown that the distributions of (grand)parenthood
over age groups differ substantially between countries. While Norway,
Israel, and Germany have nearly the same proportions of parents and
nearly no grandparents in the youngest age group, the United Kingdom
has a significantly higher proportion of young parents while Spain has a
significantly higher proportion of childless persons in this group than the
other countries. The problems of young parents are often reported for
the contemporary society in the United Kingdom. For Spain this can be a
result of three different effects: In the first place, the age at birth of first
child may be higher in Spain; second, we may find a cohort effect in the
sense that rapid modernization of the Spanish society shows its effects on
the urban population; and third, it can be a result of sample selection in
Spain. The second explanation seems to be the most plausible while we
find no evidence for either of the other alternatives. However, this differs
from what we observe in the oldest group, where Germany shows the lowest proportions of parents and grandparents. It should be noted, however,
that in four of the countries (with the exception of Israel) the percentage of

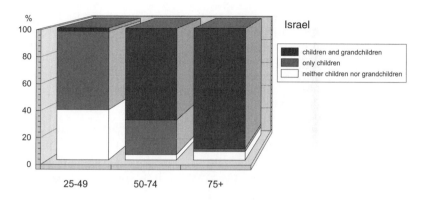

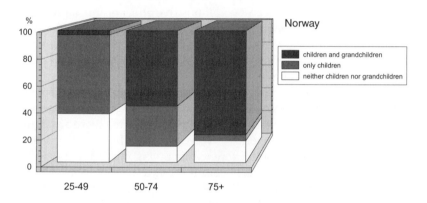

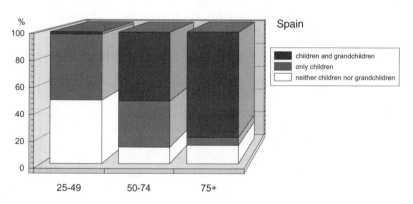

Figure 16.5 Living children and grandchildren by age of parents. *Source:* OASIS 2000, n_N = 1,203, n_{UK} = 1,195, n_D = 1,285, n_E = 1,199, n_{IL} = 1,114.

persons without children is comparably high. This is due to the sampling criterion of OASIS project: Only inhabitants of urban centers were included in the study. Hence, rural populations with higher fertility rates are not represented in the OASIS sample.

Theory-Driven Analyses

After having presented separate descriptive analyses on quality of life on the one hand and the existence of offspring on the other, the relationship between family structures and quality of life in different societies is analyzed. The analyses of the OASIS data show the differences of overall subjective quality of life between persons with and without children as well as for persons with and without grandchildren in each of the participating countries. There is an overall positive effect of "social integration" by the family: Those persons who have children or grandchildren show on average higher subjective quality of life ratings. Additional analyses show that this is not only the case for children but also for close friends and other network members. Interestingly, there seems to be no additive effect of grandchildren: The overall subjective quality of life does not seem to be higher for persons with grandchildren than for persons with children only. There are distinct differences between societies. While there are significant effects of (grand)parenthood in Norway, Great Britain, Germany, and Israel we cannot find mean differences in Spain. Instead, in Spain having children results in lower rates of very positive and lower rates of very negative answers. Hence, there is less variance in the Spanish (grand)parent population than in the Spanish nonparent population. This is equally the case for children and grandchildren. Having children results in a more equal distribution of overall quality of life in Spain while in the other countries it mainly results in higher values.

In the following we will concentrate on the effect of children on quality of life, using the number of living children as a continuous variable. Figure 16.6 shows the distribution of children for the age group 75+ in Norway, Great Britain, Germany, Spain, and Israel. While Germany has not only the highest rates of nonparents and parents with only one child but also the lowest rates of those with three or more children, the opposite is the case for Israel. In Israel we find low rates of childlessness combined with a high proportion of large families with three or even more children. Norway, Great Britain, and Spain are somewhere in between with Spain having high proportions in the group with three and more children. There are differences in the average number of children in the different societies: While Israeli (urban) elderly have the highest number of children on average (2.6), Spain follows closely (2.4), which is due to the higher proportion of those having much more than three children. Norwegian and British elderly have fewer children (1.9), and German elderly only have 1.4 children on average.

343

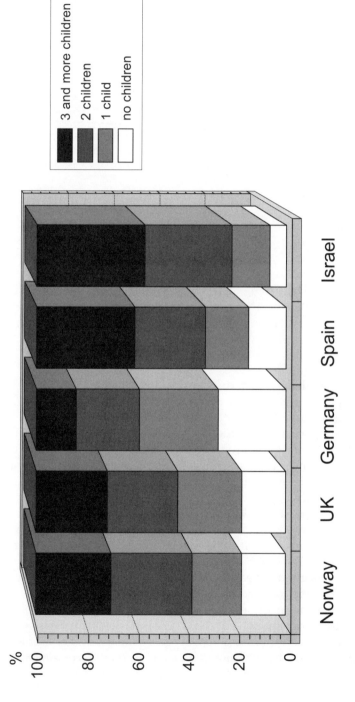

Figure 16.6 Number of children of the elderly (75+) *Source:* OASIS 2000, n = 2,058.

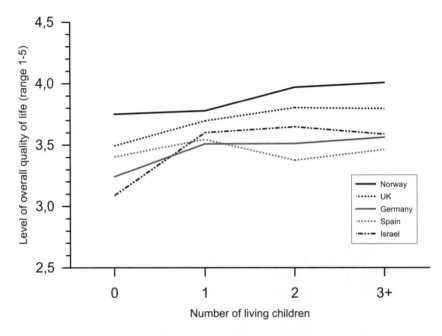

Figure 16.7   Levels of overall quality of life of the elderly (75+) by the number of children. *Source:* OASIS 2000, *n* = 2,034.

This difference is strong and, of course, highly significant (F = 36,164, $p < .001$).

Figure 16.7 shows that the effect of children on quality of life in old age is neither simply linear nor can it simply be reduced to a single dummy effect. Instead we find a strong impact of being a parent and a weaker effect of the number of children itself (the Norwegian data tell a slightly different story—here the threshold is between having none or one and two or more children).[3]

The positive effect of children on the quality of life of elderly parents may be different for those who are physically impaired in contrast to those who are not, if we assume specific needs to be an additional important moderating dimension. In a subsequent step of our analysis we differentiated between the extent of impairment in each country measured by the SF36 physical health status (Gladman 1998; Radoschewski and Bellach 1999) (Figure 16.8). One can argue that—besides an expected higher quality of life in the healthier population—for the handicapped elderly potential helpers may have a greater importance. As can be seen there is higher average overall quality of life in the healthier groups for all countries (except Spain). In Germany and Norway the moderate importance of children seems to be

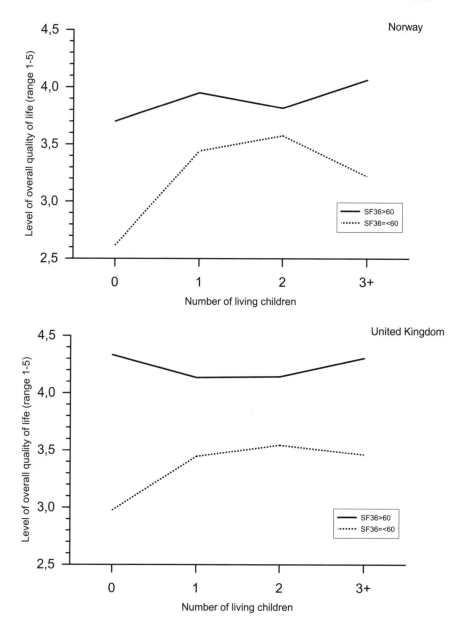

Figure 16.8 Levels of overall quality of life by the number of children and physical health status of the elderly (75+). *Source:* OASIS 2000, $n_N = 397$, $n_{UK} = 389$, $n_D = 493$, $n_E = 372$, $n_{IL} = 345$.

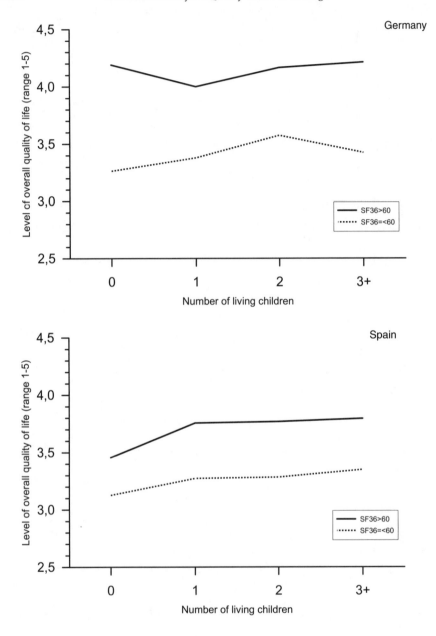

Figure 16.8   Continued from p. 345.

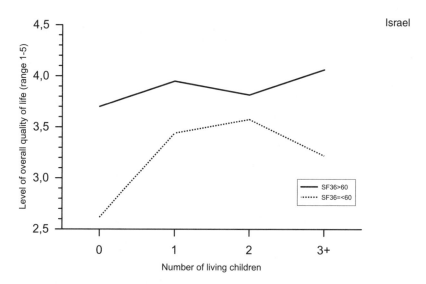

Figure 16.8 Continued from p. 345.

independent of the physical health status. In Israel there is a much stronger effect of children for the physically impaired elderly, while in the United Kingdom we can only find a weak nonlinear effect for the healthy elderly (which is similar to the results for Norway) but a strong and significant association between the number of children and the overall quality of life of those reporting severe physical health problems. Spain is an outlier in these results because here a higher quality of life of the healthier elderly can only be found for those having no children or only one child. Those healthy elderly in Spain having more than two children show a significant reduction of quality of life. However, a positive effect of having children can be shown for those in need of help and assistance. Hence, in Spain having children has positive effects only when parents are in need. Otherwise adult children seem to be a burden for their elderly parents. This seems to be plausible in the context of rapid modernization, especially in the Spanish urban areas.

In a last step a regression model was estimated to directly test the two models outlined above (cf. Figure 16.1). The two alternative models suggested additive effects of both family and welfare state (model a) versus an interaction effect between family and welfare state, i.e., family relations have a lower impact on quality of life under generous welfare regimes (model b). Norway should be an example of such a generous system. The opposite should be the case in a society with a less giving system like in

Table 16.3 Overall Quality of Life of the Elderly (75+, OLS Regression)

		Model 1	*Model 2*
Norway	1 child[a]	0.01	0.00
	2 children[a]	0.12	0.11
	3 and more children[a]	0.13	0.07
	Gender: female[b]		0.13**
	Age		0.14**
	Physical health status		0.55**
	n	397	397
	R_2/adjusted R_2	0.02/0.01	0.29/0.28
UK	1 child[a]	0.08	0.07
	2 children[a]	0.12	0.08
	3 and more children[a]	0.14*	0.10
	Gender: female[b]		−0.03
	Age		0.06
	Physical health status		0.49*
	n	389	389
	R_2/adjusted R_2	0.01/0.00	0.24/0.22
Germany	1 child[a]	0.17**	0.13**
	2 children[a]	0.14**	0.11*
	3 and more children[a]	0.16**	0.11*
	Gender: female[b]		−0.01
	Age		0.05
	Physical health status		0.44**
	n	483	483
	R_2/adjusted R_2	0.03/0.02	0.21/0.20
Spain	1 child[a]	0.07	0.07
	2 children[a]	−0.03	−0.06
	3 and more children[a]	0.02	0.03
	Gender: female[b]		0.01
	Age		0.01
	Physical health status		0.26**
	n	372	372
	R_2/adjusted R_2	0.01/0.00	0.07/0.06
Israel	1 child[a]	0.24**	0.20*
	2 children[a]	0.33**	0.27**
	3 and more children[a]	0.30**	0.26**
	Gender: female[b]		−0.04
	Age		0.01
	Physical health status		0.43**
	n	345	345
	R_2/adjusted R_2	0.03/0.02	0.22/0.21

*, $p < .05$; **, $p < 001$.
[a]Reference: no children; [b]reference: male.
Source: OASIS 2000.

the United Kingdom or in a less developed welfare state and a more accentuated family culture like Spain. In these cases the existence of children should show the largest effects on quality of life. For Israel and Germany similar and moderate effects are expected with higher family obligations in Israel and therefore higher coefficients.

Simple two-step OLS regression models are estimated separately for each country to allow complete interaction between country and the respective effects of the predictor variables (see Table 16.3). In a first step the number of children was used a predictor variable, entering a set of dummy variables that tested against a reference group (having no children at all). This strategy has been chosen because the descriptive analyses presented have already shown that there are no straightforward linear effects of children. In a second step, age and gender are introduced as well as functional status measured by the physical health scale taken from SF36. This was mainly done to analyze whether there are simple effects of need for help behind the influence of the existence of children or whether the effects are not influenced by this.

The analyses show low effects of the existence of children and their number on overall quality of life in Norway, which are statistically not significant (this was theoretically predicted). For Germany we find moderate but significant effects, while for Israel the model shows strong effects. For all these countries the models reproduce the descriptive results of nonlinear effects of the number of children: the main effect is parenthood (having children at all) while the number of children is of minor importance.

So far the models confirm the theoretical assumptions regarding the impact of children on quality of life under different welfare regimes—even under the restriction of looking at the structural dimension of family relations only (existence of children). Stronger effects can be expected when using more elaborated measures in future analyses, considering indicators of family relations such as measures of help and support, conflict, or ambivalence.

Major exceptions are the Spanish and the British cases. The existence of children had no clear effect on the well-being of parents in both societies. This is contrary to the theoretical assumptions made before. Strong effects had been expected as Spain has traditional roots in terms of family culture and a relatively weaker welfare state system in comparison to the other countries. Similar to this we expected strong effects of the family structure under the conditions of the less generous British welfare state system. Further analyses show that such effects can indeed be found when modeling quality of life of the physically impaired elderly separately in both countries. Descriptive results shown above indicate that children are only of the expected importance if there is some need for help in Spain and the United Kingdom. Otherwise one has to understand children as a factor that leads to lower quality of life in Spanish and ambiguous results in British old age.

Both effects work against each other so no significant effects of the family structure can be found in the overall model (see Table 16.3).

The models confirm our theoretical assumptions of welfare state regime dependence of the children's effect on the elder's quality of life only partly. Three out of the five analyzed OASIS countries show results that strongly support the hypothesis of an intervening effect of welfare state systems on the connecting between family and overall quality of life in old age. The data of Spain and Great Britain do not fit the overall theoretical assumptions. Hence, further analyses are needed. First, more sensitive indicators of parent-child relations have to be used. Second, needs and their intervening effects on the direct linkages between children and quality of life have to be taken into account in more complex analyses. Third, more elaborated indicators of "quality of life" should be used in future analyses.

CONCLUSIONS

This chapter has explored the role of the family and its contribution to quality of life in old age under the perspective of welfare state infrastructure. The analyses basically support the idea of an interaction between family relations and welfare state support, but also raise new questions. The existence of living children is positively related to overall (subjective) quality of life. However, the Spanish and the British data did not confirm the overall theoretical assumptions.

However, this relationship has to be explored in future analyses more thoroughly. The weaknesses of the present analysis are easy to point at: First, only a rough indicator of intergenerational family relations has been used in the analyses. Moreover, also the indicators of the welfare state systems are missing so that the differentiation by country is not sufficient and awaits a more elaborated operationalization of the macro- and mesolevel. The following guidelines could lead to a more appropriate analysis of the interactions between intergenerational family support and welfare state infrastructure.

A first line of analysis would be to further explore the models described above. This could be done generally speaking by relating and connecting quality of life to the extent of family solidarity in each country as well as between countries. In addition, problematic facets of family life could also be taken into account (i.e., conflicts). Another additional step of analysis would be reached by performing multiple regression with indicators of family solidarity and indicators of service use as predictors, the product of family solidarity and service use as moderators, and quality of life as dependent variable. A second perspective to be explored independently would open up the comparison more to the critical aspects of welfare regimes mentioned above. This would imply going beyond the mere classification into society-specific regimes and to distinguish between the microlevel characteristic patterns of support and care, mesolevel measures like indicators of local infrastructure, which may differ between regions especially in the larger ones of societies such as Spain or Germany, and macrodimensions of different welfare regimes. This leads directly into more complex analyses taking into account the hierarchical structure of the comparative data. Further research activities of the OASIS project will include this perspective.

Another intriguing perspective would have to integrate the content of the qualitative interviews to be conducted as part of the OASIS study. This promises some deeper insights into individual decision-making processes in the context of families, social infrastructure, and overall welfare regimes. However, these analyses demonstrate how useful it is to integrate aspects of family relations with the infrastructure provided by modern welfare states in order to explain the variations in quality of life in old age.

NOTES

1. These data allow a discussion of the theses of "substitution" or "hierarchical compensation" (Cantor, 1979) and "functional specificity" (Litwak, 1985; Messeri et al., 1993) of such relations. Data like the German Aging Survey suggest that there is not necessarily a conflict between both poles as there is only little variation in the hierarchy of helpers if different types of help (emotional, cognitive, and instrumental) are compared (Künemund and Hollstein, 2000). This is a strong argument against functional specificity. The substitution thesis also becomes problematic if one considers the meaning of friends for elderly people with and without children. For the childless, friends do not play the same role as children for their parents. Additionally, friends are highly important even for elderly with children. However, detailed analyses on the situation of elders in need of care—these are people with a high and very specific need—show a strong functional specificity (Blinkert/Klie, 1999).

2. Persons with grandchildren but without living children are a negligible minority of less than 0.5 percent of the whole population in each country. Therefore the percentages are not shown in Figure 3.

3. Further analyses show that the effect reverses slightly when it comes to having five and more children. This can be an effect of other factors such as social strata and socioeconomic resources.

REFERENCES

Altonji, J. G., Hayashi, F., and Kotlikoff, L. J. 1992. Is the extended family altruistically linked? Direct tests using micro data. *American Economic Review* 82: 1177–98.

Altonji, J. G., Hayashi, F., and Kotlikoff, L. J. 1996. *The effects of income and wealth on time and money transfers between parents and children* (Working Paper 5522). Cambridge: National Bureau of Economic Research.

Andreoni, J. 1989. Giving with impure altruism: Applications to charity and Ricardian equivalence. *Journal of Political Economy*, 97:1447–58.

Antonucci, T. C., Sherman, A. M., and Akiyama, H. 1996. Social networks, support, and integration. In J. E. Birren (ed.), *Encyclopedia of gerontology* 2:505–15. San Diego, CA: Academic Press.

Attias-Donfut, C. 2000. Familialer Austausch und soziale Sicherung. In M. Kohli and M. Szydlik (eds.), *Generationen in Familie und Gesellschaft* (pp. 222–44). Opladen: Leske and Budrich.

Bengtson, V. L., and Roberts, R. E. 1991. Intergenerational solidarity in aging families: An example of formal theory construction. *Journal of Marriage and the Family* 53:856–70.

Bengtson, V. L., Rosenthal, C., and Burton, L. 1996. Paradoxes of families and aging. In R. H. Binstock, and L. K. George (eds.), *Handbook of aging and the social sciences* (4th ed.), pp. 253–82. San Diego, CA: Academic Press.

Blinkert, B., and Klie, T. 1999. Pflege im socialen Wandel. Studie zur Situation Häuslich versorgter Pflegebedürftiger. (Social care and societal change. A study about the frail elderly at home.) Hannover: Vincentz.

Cantor, M. H. 1979. The informal support system of New York's inner city elderly: Is ethnicity a factor? In D. Gelfand and A. Kutzik (eds.), *Ethnicity and aging*, 153–74. New York: Springer,

Cox, D. 1987. Motives for private income transfers. *Journal of Political Economy* 95:508–46.

Cox, D., and Jakubson, G. 1995. The connection between public transfers and private interfamily transfers. *Journal of Public Economics* 57:129–67.

Cox, D., and Stark, O. 1994. *Intergenerational transfers and the demonstration effect. NIA Workshop on Cross-National Issues in Aging.* Syracuse, New York: Syracuse University.

Diener, E. 1994. Assessing subjective well-being: progress and opportunities. *Social Indicators Research* 31:103–57.

Erikson, R. 1974. Welfare as a planning goal. *Acta Sociologica* 17:273–78.

Esping-Andersen, G. 1990. *The three worlds of welfare capitalism*. Princeton: Princeton University Press.

Gladman, J. R. F. 1998. Assessing health status with the SF-36. *Age and Ageing* (3):27:3.

Kohli, M., Künemund, H., Motel, A., and Szydlik, M. 2000. *Grunddaten zur Lebenssituation der 40–85 jährigen deutschen Bevölkerung*. Berlin: Weißensee Verlag.

Künemund, H., and Hollstein, B. 2000. Soziale Beziehungen und Unterstützungsnetzwerke. In M. Kohli, and H. Künemund (eds.), *Die zweite Lebenshälfte: Gesellschaftliche Lage und Partizipation im Spiegel des Alters-Survey* (pp. 212–76). Opladen: Leske and Budrich.

Künemund, H., and Motel, A. 2000. Verbreitung, Motivation und Entwicklungsperspektiven privater intergenerationaler Hilfeleistungen und Transfers. In M. Kohli and M. Szydlik (eds.), *Generationen in Familie und Gesellschaft* (pp. 122–37). Opladen: Leske and Budrich.

Künemund, H., and Rein, M. 1999. There is more to receiving than needing: theoretical arguments and empirical explorations of crowding in and crowding out. *Ageing and Society*, 19:93–121.

Litwak, E. 1985. *Helping the elderly: The complementary roles of informal networks and formal systems.* New York: Guilford Press.

Lüscher, K., and Lettke, F. 2000. Dealing with ambivalences: Toward a new perspective for the study of intergenerational relations among adults. Arbeitspapier 36, Part 1, Universität Konstanz-Humboldt TransCOOP Network on Intergenerational Ambivalences.

Lüscher, K., and Pajung-Bilger, B. 1998. *Forcierte Ambivalenzen.* Konstanz: UVK Universitätsverlag Konstanz.

Lüscher, K., and Pillemer, K. 1998. Intergenerational ambivalence: A new approach to the study of parent-child relations in later life. *Journal of Marriage and the Family* 60:413–25.

Messeri, P., Silverstein, M., and Litwak, E. 1993. Choosing optimal support groups: A review and reformulation. *Journal of Health and Social Behavior Sociological* 34(2):122–37.

Motel, A., and Spieß, K. 1995. Finanzielle Unterstützungsleistungen alter Menschen an ihre Kinder. Ergebnisse der Berliner Altersstudie (BASE). *Forum: Demographie und Politik* 7:133–54.

Motel, A., and Szydlik, M. 1999. Private transfers zwischen den Generationen. *Zeitschrift für Soziologie*, 28(1):22.

Motel-Klingebiel, A. 2000. *Alter und Generationenvertrag im Wandel des Sozialstaats. Alterssicherung und private Generationenbeziehungen in der zweiten Lebenshälfte.* Berlin: Weißensee Verlag.

Noll, H. 1999. *Konzepte der Wohlfahrtsentwicklung: Lebensqualität und "neue" Wohlfahrtskonzepte.* No. 3. Mannheim: Centre for Survey Research and Methodology.

Parsons, T. 1943. The kinship system of the contemporary United States. *American Anthropologist* 45:22–38.

Phillips, J. E. 1994. The employment consequences of caring for older people. *Health and Social Care* 2:143–52.

Phillipson, C., Bernard, M., Phillips, J., and Ogg, J. 2000. *The family and community life of older people.* London: Routledge.

Radoschewski, M., and Bellach, B. M. 1999. Der SF-36 im Bundesgesundheits-Survey: Möglichkeiten und Anforderungen der Nutzung auf der Bevölkerungsebene. *Gesundheitswesen (Sonderheft 2)* 61:191–99.

Ryff, C. D., 1989. Beyond Ponce de Leon and lie satisfaction: New directions in quet of successful aging. *International Journal of Behavioral Development* 12(1): 35–55.

Sainsbury, D. 1994. *Gendering welfare states.* London: Sage

Schoeni, R. F. 1994. *Does aid to families with dependent children (AFDC) displace familial assistance?* Santa Monica, CA: RAND.

Schoeni, R. F. 1997. private interhousehold transfers of money and time: New empirical evidence. *Review on Income and Wealth* 43:423–48.

Smith, J., Fleeson, W., Geiselmann, B., Settersten, R., and Kunzmann, U. 1996. Wohlbefinden im hohen Alter: Vorhersagen aufgrund objektiver Lebensbedingungen und subjektiver Bewertung. In K. U. Mayer and P. B. Baltes (eds.), *Die Berliner Altersstudie* (pp. 497–523). Berlin: Akademie Verlag.

Soldo, B. J., and Hill, M. S. 1993. Intergenerational transfers: economic, demographic, and social perspectives. *Annual Review of Gerontology and Geriatrics* 13:187–216.

Stark, O. 1995. *Altruism and beyond. An economic analysis of transfers and exchanges within families and groups.* Cambridge: Cambridge University Press.

Tesch-Römer, C., Motel-Klingebiel, A., and von Kondratowitz, H.-J. 2001. Intergenerational Cohesion. In Bundesministerium für Familie, Senioren, Frauen und Jugend [Federal Ministry for Family Affairs, Senior Citizens, Women and Youth] (eds.), *The ageing of society as a global challenge: German impulses. Integrated Report on German Expert Contributions* (pp. 131–48). Berlin: Bundesministerium für Familie, Senioren, Frauen und Jugend.

Thompson, P. 1999. The role of grandparents when parents part or die: Some reflections on the mythical decline of the extended family. *Ageing and Society* 19 471–503.

World Health Organization 1999. WHOQOL—Annotated bibliography. Geneve: World Health Organization, Department of Mental Health.

WHOQOL Group 1994a. Development of the WHOQOL: Rationale and current status. *International Journal of Mental Health* 23:24–56.

_____. 1994b. The development of the World Health Organization quality of life assessment instrument (WHOQOL). In J. Orley and W. Kuyken (eds.), *Quality of life assessments: International perspectives* (pp. 41–57). Berlin: Springer.

Zapf, W. 1984. Individuelle Wohlfahrt: Lebensbedingungen und wahrgenommene Lebensqualität. In W. Glatzer and W. Zapf (eds.), *Lebensqualität in der Bundesrepublik Deutschland. Objektive Lebensbedingungen und subjektives Wohlbefinden* (pp. 13–26). Frankfurt/M., New York: Campus.

|17|

Ethnic and Cultural Differences in Intergenerational Social Support

Toni C. Antonucci and James S. Jackson

ETHNIC AND CULTURAL DIFFERENCES IN
INTERGENERATIONAL SOCIAL SUPPORT

The concept of generations is ancient. It is well-documented in the Bible, in both the Old and the New Testaments, and the Koran. In many ways, however, the definition and experience of generations is changing significantly. In this chapter we consider a variety of matters that are important to the practical issue of understanding generations. We consider how generations are defined, how they are perceived, and how they critically affect the lives of generation members. We begin with a consideration of theoretical, definitional, and design elements. Generational issues as global phenomena are considered next, recognizing that different population trends, economic and geographical realities, practically and fundamentally influence the experiences of generation members. We also consider the nature and expectations of generational transfers, both affective and instrumental, and how these exchanges influence the health and well-being of family members.

DEFINING GENERATIONS

The definition and characteristics of generations vary considerably. Data from different countries, cultures, and racial and ethnic groups suggest similarities in structure and expectations of social relations but also unique characteristics among different groups. The importance by age, birth, and period cohorts should not be underestimated. In addition, within-family generation structures are also affected by generational spacing. As the figure (Figure 17.1) from Jackson and Antonucci (1994) illustrates, there are many factors that can influence the nature of generations and how generational relations are experienced. The convention is that the oldest generation is Generation 1. In Figure 17.1, which illustrates potential generational structures in 1980, for example, Generation 1 could have been born any time from 1880 to 1940! This means that the Generation 1 member of the family could be 100 or 40. One needs to superimpose upon this the additional fact that the life expectancy in 1880 was less than 30 years, even in the most developed countries, whereas by 1940 it had increased to 50, and in many parts of the world is now over 70 years of age. The complexity does not end there. The family with the 100-year-old could have produced new generation members every 40 years while the family of the Generation 1 person who is 40 may have had only 20 years spacing between the generations. Realistically, in fact, the trend is likely to have been the opposite, that is, generation spacing among people from earlier cohorts would have been generally shorter than among people from later cohorts.

Generational spacing has implications for cross-generational transmission of values, transfers of assets, social contacts, and social support including care giving and care receiving. The 40-year-old G1 will have the opportunity for significant, close relationships with her child, grandchild, and probably her great-grandchild. But the 80-year-old G1 with a 40-year-old G1 daughter will have little opportunity (in terms of years likely to still be alive) to develop a significant relationship with her grandchild and even less of likelihood to have a relationship with a great-grandchild.

As one can see, there is nothing to suggest or mandate that these generation spacings will be the same across each generation. We know, for example, that in the United States, regardless of the fact that the birth control pill had not yet been invented, the years after the 1929 stock market crash saw the birth of very few children, while the years after World War II, often called the years of prosperity in the United States, marked an unprecedented baby boom. It is not much of an extension to recognize that each country with its own individual history has similar factors that influence the creation and spacing of generations within its borders. While an almost complete universal is the joy experienced with the introduction of a new generation, individual issues of history, culture, and ethnicity influence each generation. Thus war, famine, disease, religion, cultural values, and other historical events all influence the introduction or creation of the next generation. The number of children born during war is almost always fewer, although wartime polices, such as ethnic cleansing, may uniquely affect this trend. Similarly, the number of children born during economic affluence is almost always greater. Famine and disease both reduce the

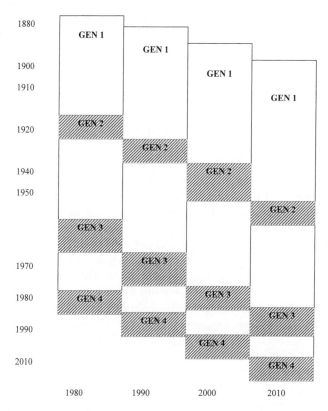

Figure 17.1 Factors influencing the nature of generations and how generational relations are experienced.

number of children born as well as the number who survive. Religious,
cultural, and ethnic patterns influence the age at which people marry, and
when and how many children they are expected to have. Some religions
mandate or encourage early or multiple marriages, some proscribe the
replenishing of the race, ethnic, or religious group through multiple births,
and others effect similar outcomes by forbidding the use of any or specific
types of birth control. All of these patterns influence the generational
structures found in various societies. These patterns are identifiable across
Europe, Asia, Australia, and Africa.

Returning to Figure 17.1, it should also be noted that in addition to age,
history affects the individual experience. Let us take one example from a
single family. A few years ago, in 1996, the first author (Antonucci) had a
96-year-old grandmother, a 75-year-old mother and was herself 47. Her
maternal grandmother while born in the United States was the child of

immigrants from southern Italy. She was the second of seven children, born and raised in Connecticut. Her paternal grandmother was Italian born, immigrating before her marriage to another teenage immigrant from the same village in central Italy. She was the baby girl of the family with three older brothers. They all immigrated to the Lower East Side of New York. After her paternal grandparents married, her grandfather moved the family out to the country, Brooklyn, because a doctor said the sea air would be good for the new sickly baby. In a coincidence across generations, that sickly baby was also the baby sister of three older brothers. Her father and mother were American born, both very influenced by Italian Catholic traditions. As the joke goes, in her parents' family a mixed marriage was one between northern and southern Italians. Now she has teenage daughters who have a 52-year-old mother and an 80-year-old grandmother. We live in the Midwestern portion of the United States. Her husband's family (Jackson) were also immigrants, though the patterns of migration in his family are quite different. His family can trace their ancestry back several generations in the southern United States where life was mostly agricultural. His grandmother, her children's great-grandmother, moved up north with her young daughter to get work in the booming car factories of the Midwest. That daughter grew up in Detroit, married her high school sweetheart, and had three sons, and later adopted a daughter. The second author is the first-born son. Their heritage is Southern Baptist and African-American. There is an obituary of his great-great-grandmother recounting her death at age 101, having been born a slave and been granted freedom during her lifetime. Needless to say the second author's teenage daughters have a history across generations, cohorts, culture, race, religion, and ethnicity that has uniquely influenced them.

As the above example illustrates, ethnic and cultural traditions are transmitted and experienced in a variety of ways. These include significant immigration histories, ethnic traditions, as well as individual family histories. In the first author's Italian family everyone immigrated within the last two or three generations, everyone came seeking a "better" life, everyone came through Ellis Island. There are family stories of who made the trip, who was left behind, what the first jobs were like and where, who went back or sent for others. In the second author's family there is also a shared tradition but it is very different. Most family members have only a vague knowledge about the immigration patterns of their ancestors, no one voluntarily came from Africa, and very few have any information about the family they left behind. No one came to America seeking a better life; everyone has a difficult history within the last several generations in the United States. The transmission of values, customs, and religion was often forbidden by law and, therefore, had to be accomplished surreptitiously.

As these examples are meant to illustrate, to understand why generations are important and how they affect exchanges among generation members, it is critical to understand the diversity within and across generations. In the rest of this chapter we focus on how the experiences of each individual influences his or her development as a person as well as his or her development as a generational member.

WORLDWIDE GENERATIONAL ISSUES

It is critical to note that generational concerns, especially as they pertain to family relationships, and the provision of social support, are a worldwide issue. Clearly, the United Nations recognized this fact when it adopted "A Society for All Ages" as the theme for its International Year of the Older Person. Older people live in families and societies that consist of generational members, often members of different age groups. In order for the older person to live well, all generational members of all age groups must also live well. There is no doubt that the quality of life of one generation is firmly linked to the quality of life of other generation members.

As we recognize the universality of generations, it is also critical to note the ways in which history, culture, and experience influence generations differently around the world. In fact, the people of Israel have witnessed this, though perhaps not recognizing the issue as such. In Israel not only is different generational membership recognized, special names designate people who are first-generation Israeli born—*sabra*. People are given this special designation because it is thought to be something special to have been the first generation born on Israel soil. What is the reason? No doubt this has to do with the unique history of the people of Israel. Given the events of World War II, to have been born in the newly created Israel marks a special generational beginning and is so noted by a newly created term. Of course, this is a uniquely Jewish experience. But, Jews born in Israel are not the first or only to name generations distinctively. The Japanese in the United States have special names, e.g., *nisei and sansei,* to designate first- and second-generation American born. One might argue that there is not much similarity in the experiences of the Israeli-born Jew and the American-born Japanese, but clearly there is something about their generational membership that warrants these unique labels.

As we turn to other parts of the world, it is clear that unique historical events are shaping generational identity, membership, and even role expectation. In Africa, the devastation of the AIDS epidemic has resulted in a totally different set of generational issues. Here the oldest generation, G1, who we might note is not very old, with a life expectancy of approximately 50 years, has found itself caring for the youngest generation, G3, because the middle, G2, generation has either already succumbed to the illness or is overwhelmed with the demands of coping with it. These problems supersede the previously recognized generational issues being faced in Africa with young people leaving rural areas and their families seeking work in urban industrialized cities. At one time, generational researchers wondered who would care for the young while their parents worked in the cities and had no elders to care for their children. Then we worried who would care for the elders as they got old and had no children to look after them. And now we worry, as we are losing the generation in the middle, who will care for both the children and their elders.

Moving to the Eastern world, including places like Japan and China, we see very different circumstances. Japan is perhaps the most intriguing case because it is part Eastern in traditions, expectations, goals, and aspirations, and yet it is also part Western in its industrialization, its technology, its economy, and its interactions with the West. In Japan, this confluence of circumstances yields a population in flux. While the young do respect their elders, there is no "norm of reciprocity" as we know it in the Western world (Gouldner, 1960). Younger generations are seen as eternally indebted to their elders, that is, it is impossible to achieve reciprocity because one owes one's elders so much. One can only seek to reduce the debt. There is a clear pattern of expectation concerning care for elders and generational transfers. But, simultaneously, times do seem to be changing. The young are often seen to be rebelling against traditions that impose limited options about what they can do with their lives and how they will live those lives. In addition, since Japan has been so successful in modernizing, they can look forward to experiencing the longest life expectancy in the world. Hence, while the sense of traditional responsibility for the care of elders may be changing, the increased life expectancy means that many Japanese families will experience not only three generations, but often four and five generations as well. Fortunately, these generations are also healthier than in times past, but with four and five generations within a family, it is clear that there will be some caregiving needs to be met.

China, while also an Eastern country, is facing these problems of industrialization much more slowly. The sheer numbers of Chinese, however, place the issue of generational membership, expectations, and transfers on a more massive scale. For example, studies of centenarians in the United States are considered large if they include one or two hundred people. A recent study of the elderly in China, using only half of the Chinese provinces, includes over 2000 centenarians! While China is not at the same economic or industrial level, the Cultural Revolution and the one-child policy have placed a totally different burden on generational structures and relations. With the one-child family, there are fewer children to be cared for but also fewer children to care for their elders. We can only imagine the impact of this policy mandate on intergenerational relations of the future.

In Japan, the tradition is for the eldest son to live with his parents in his parents' house. The daughter-in-law cares for her in-laws and the son

inherits his parents' wealth. Data we have collected on generational relations in Japan reveal that the most stressed adult in the family is the adult
son. This man is often torn between intergenerational relations with his
mother (his father likely to have predeceased her) and his wife. On the
other hand, in China we have only children who will potentially find
themselves at the center of their parents', grandparents', and potentially
great-grandparents' world. It is clear that generation relations, expectations, and transfers in both these countries will have to change. The question remains how these changes will affect individuals, families, and
society more globally.

SOCIAL SUPPORT ACROSS CULTURES, RACE, ETHNIC GROUPS, AND GENERATIONS

Research over the last several decades has provided important information about the structure and nature of social support. We now recognize
that support relations are critical to well-being at all ages (Antonucci, 2001;
Levitt, 1991). In this section we turn to a consideration of how social support is experienced across cultures, racial and ethnic groups, and generations. We draw on data available in the field and in our own research
programs. Our purpose is to point to both the similarities and differences
in social support across different groups. We consider two areas: structure
of support relations and quality of support relations. These examples are,
of course, illustrative rather than exhaustive.

In recent years, increasingly high quality data from representative samples have become available in the United States and other countries
around the world. This is important because numerical ethnic minority
group data have either been nonexistent or based on specialized, nonrep-
resentative samples. These data have offered interesting insights but can
in no way be considered representative. Examples of this early social network research literature include Elizabeth Bott's (1957) study of family
and social networks in urban London, Barbara Myeroff's (1979) study of
Russian immigrant Jews in Los Angeles, and Carol Stack's (1974) study
of African-Americans in a small, rural town in the American South. All
of these studies offer insights into the global and specific characteristics of
the people they studied, but they are not able to offer the broad understanding provided by representative samples. There are now studies available from the United States, Europe, and Asia, including the Middle East,
as well as some smaller studies from Africa and South America. In the
paragraphs below we draw from these findings.

Wenger (1997), using data from a number of European countries, reports
that there are several social network and social relationship characteristics
that appear to be relatively universal. Family members are almost always

among the closest social relations reported by people, and, apropos of our interest in generations, most studies find that people have and feel quite close to multigenerational family members. Thus, people speak of their parents, spouse, and children as the people to whom they feel closest.

We believe this finding, while perhaps not revolutionary, is important to emphasize because it reinforces the belief that people feel strong ties to intrafamily, intergeneration relatives. At the same time, increasingly available data provides us with information about how these close relationships are influenced by subgroup memberships, i.e., by racial, ethnic, cultural, and historical differences. In the United States we recognize that ethnic minorities, in addition to what might be considered universal support characteristics, also have specific ones. Among African-Americans it has been documented that kin and nonkin, as well as the church, are important sources of support (Taylor and Chatters, 1986). While this is true for other groups in the United States, unique characteristics of this population influence the availability of these relationships. Thus, African-Americans are more likely than many other groups to be never married, separated, divorced, or widowed (Taylor, Chatters, and Jackson, 1997). These demographic differences explain the findings of Ajrouch, Antonucci, and Janevic (2001). Their study of a representative sample of African-Americans in the Detroit metropolitan area indicates that compared to whites in the same city, African-Americans have smaller networks that consist of more family with whom they have more contact. On the other hand, comparisons of age and race differences in social relations indicated that age was a stronger predictor of the structure of social networks than race; older people of both races were more likely than younger people to have smaller networks, with a higher proportion of family members who lived in less proximity and were seen less frequently than those of younger people. Silverstein and Waite (1993) reported a similar confound of age and race. They suggest that while age and race may affect the exchange of support, a critical explanatory factor is specific or individual life circumstances.

Wenger's (1997) examination of available data from Western European countries suggests that there are considerable similarities in the size and structure of social network across countries. Thus, in addition to the same people or relationships being nominated as close support network members, she reports that people also generally report an average of three to seven people to whom they feel especially close. It does not appear that variation within this range is the most important influence on the individual's well being. That is to say, people with seven social network members are not more than twice as happy as people with only three social network members. It appears that it is quality, rather than size of support networks that is most important both to physical and mental health (see also Antonucci, Fuhrer, and Dartigues, 1997; George, Blazer, Hughes, and Fowler, 1989; Oxman, Berkman, Kasl, Freeman, and Barrett, 1992). These findings are replicated in the data that are thus far available from Asian countries, most notably Japan and China (Chen and Silverstein, 2000; Matsuda et al., 1993). Very few data are yet available from African and South American countries.

Turning away from studies in different parts of the world to those in the United States, an interesting study by Kim and McKenry (1999) examined multiple ethnic groups, African-Americans, Asian-Americans, Caucasian-Americans, and Hispanic-Americans within the United States. These authors report more similarities than differences across ethnic groups in social relations. Of particular interest is the fact that socioeconomic and education differences accounted for more social relations differences than did ethnic group membership. This finding demonstrates that what might be considered an ethnic difference may, in fact, be more accurately attributable to other causes. Thus, they found significant reliance on close family members, especially children, for help in times of need among some ethnic groups, but once financial resources were available members of these same ethnic groups relied less on their children, more on other family, nonkin, and even formal services for which they now could afford to pay. It is important to note that who people feel close to does not change, but the availability of other resources appears to alter the nature and content of support exchanges. Families who can afford to pay for noncrisis services may be able to focus their support exchanges on emotional and affective support and crisis support rather than on the provision of custodial services. Given what is known about the experienced burden of chronic and demanding caregiving, this paid alternative may serve the important function of relieving family members from physical care so that they can provide more optimal emotional care.

Support provision is certainly affected by expectation and need. Differences in expectation and need clearly vary by subgroup characteristics. Much of this may be obvious but should be noted because it profoundly influences supportive exchanges. As the examples above illustrate, needs across ethnic, cultural, or racial subgroups may be affected by characteristics correlated with these subgroups in different ways in different societies. The status of being a minority, of being impoverished, of being discriminated against can all influence the support needs of the individual, but are not inherent to the subgroup to which that person belongs. These "needs" may not always be the result of something negative. Minority group members of very wealthy families, for example, may have unique expectations of preserving family wealth, maintaining family traditions of philanthropy or politics. Persons in these circumstance would not be expected necessarily to provide hands-on care for a needy family member, but more likely may be expected to arrange to make the needed care available. These differences transcend ethnic, racial, and cultural groups. For example, the eldest Japanese son is responsible for the care of his parents but it is actually his wife, the daughter-in-law, who provides hands-on care.

Events and holidays are often a special manifestation of group membership. Some will be extremely important to the family, others unimportant. These might be religious events, the Jewish High Holidays, Christmas, specific rites of passage, e.g., baptisms, bar mitzvahs. They may be civic holidays, e.g., Bastille Day in France, the Fourth of July in the United States. Each of these events has special meaning, but only to the groups for whom they are important. Those who have ever tried to negotiate whose family will host the holiday, or explain why they will not be present at an important family event, have felt the unique importance of these events. They often take months to plan, last only one day, and are evaluated or discussed for months, even years, afterward.

We have considered differences in network structure and to some smaller degree how networks might vary by structure or group circumstance. As family structures change, e.g., a recent newspaper headline in the United States claimed that the nuclear family structure, i.e., mother, father, and children living in one household, is now less than 25 percent of the U.S. population, it becomes increasingly important to recognize what is core and what is flexible about social relations. Clearly structure varies by group and population circumstance, but it is also clear that individuals are readily able to adapt to these changes.

While structure identifies who are the network people significant in the individual's life, also critically important is the quality of these relationships. While all people have parents, and most have a spouse, siblings, or children, it is not equally universal that these relationships are all of high quality. Social relationships can be positive, negative, or some combination of the two. Positive relationships are those that can provide the individual with a firm base of support. These relations have been conceptualized by Kahn and Antonucci (1980) as convoys of social support. Ideally support network members socialize, protect, educate, and provide for their support relations or convoy members. Over their lifetime, positive associations and interactions accumulate to mold, shape, and enhance the individual's development. This is the most optimistic case.

The opposite, unfortunately, can also occur. Individuals can be surrounded by a convoy that provides what has been termed negative support; negative either because it is nonsupportive, or lacking in positive affect or because it supports negative interactions, choices, or behaviors. As the individual who enjoys high-quality positive support relationships is benefited by these relationships in a cumulative manner, individuals with negative support are disadvantaged by these relationships, and rather than accumulating a sense of security and confidence about themselves and their life goals, either embrace negative goals, or do not have the confidence to achieve the positive goals that they set for themselves.

Once again, the effect is cumulative. With the help of a positive, support-ive convoy, one might aspire to go to school, get good grades in school, go to college. However, a negatively supportive convoy might either ridicule the goal of college or the individual's ability to successfully complete a col-lege program (Antonucci, 1994).

There are several aspects of supportive relationships that are important. One is the fundamental role of the quality of these social relations. Psy-chologists have documented rather convincingly the degree to which indi-viduals are influenced by those who are close and important to them (Ainsworth, Blehar, Waters, and Wall, 1978; Bowlby, 1973; Freud, 1935). For example, while many might think that the critical variable in seeking a college education is basic intelligence, we would argue that although a certain basic intelligence is necessary, the emotional confidence that one acquires through the support of significant others is also very important. But this, too, is influenced by traditions, customs, and circumstances. In some groups, girls are not expected to get a college education; in others only the oldest or youngest members of the family can go to college. In still others, it depends on financial resources, whether the family has the wealth or the individual has obtained scholarships.

As this example illustrates, achieving any goal is influenced by a multi-tude of factors. These operate at the individual, group, and societal levels. To best understand how any individual meets or attains a goal, these mul-tiple factors must be considered. In this chapter we have highlighted each of these layers and emphasized the bidirectionality and reciprocity of influences. Thus, certain psychological characteristics such as sense of con-trol or self-esteem are known to influence the probability of success (Krause, 1997; Lachman and Weaver, 1998a, 1998b). On the other hand, group membership and circumstance influence the expectations and envi-ronment to which the individual is exposed and hence the sense of control or self-esteem that is developed (Bisconti and Bergeman, 1999).

This is just as true of the aspiring college student as it is of the aging individual. Thus, an 80-year-old recently widowed woman who has never been an independent person may be significantly incapacitated by wid-owhood if her family and friends do not anticipate her inability to cope even though she is physically quite healthy. The data on learned helpless-ness and learned dependency illustrate this point (Baltes and Baltes, 1986). At the same time, another 80-year-old, also a recent widow, but one who has always felt that she was an independent soul, the backbone and tower of strength upon whom her husband depended, may now feel that with the support of her children and grandchildren, she can maintain a useful and productive life. She is much more likely than the first widow to set goals of enjoying activities with family and friends and of maintaining a healthy lifestyle. It is not that the two women were of different ages, cohorts, or of different health or wealth, but simply that they had different visions of their future, of what they would individually be able to accomplish. Both women recognize that with age will come health challenges; one is willing to give in and give up right now, while the other wants to view life as still having many opportunities for enjoyment, success, and fulfillment. It is a complex web of individual, group, and societal characteristics that produces these differences.

Before leaving this topic there is one more point that should be raised and that is differences in the expression of support. While the examples noted above highlight group differences in expectation or experience, as psychologists we would be remiss if we did not note that the expression of support can and does vary by individual as well as group membership. We know that some groups are considered expressive, others not. One favorite example is the French versus the British. One group takes pride in being emotional, expressive, warm, and friendly. The other takes equal pride in being rational, reserved, cold (stiff upper lip), and formal. With these very different self-definitions, one can extrapolate to expected differences in expressed support. Though it is the case that the British and the French identify the same people as close and important to them (i.e., parents, spouse, children), there is no doubt that how they commonly express that support is significantly different. Each of us can recognize similar differences in groups we know and/or with whom we identify.

A LIFE-SPAN MULTIGENERATIONAL VIEW OF RECIPROCITY

An important concept in intergenerational relations is that of reciprocity. All societies and cultures appear to have this concept, although different groups conceptualized it in different ways (Gouldner, 1960). As we consider how best to understand intergenerational relations, we suggest that the notion of reciprocity is particularly useful. This give and take of emotional and instrumental support helps explain much of how people perceive their role within families and is useful in understanding both behaviors and expectations. As we consider how best to assure ourselves that all generational members are supported and cared for, we believe the notion of life-span and multigenerational reciprocity is especially useful. Of special interest is the appropriateness of this conceptualization of reciprocity across racial, ethnic, or cultural differences.

Basic social psychological research suggests that people feel best about their relationships when they do not feel indebted (Greenberg and Shapiro, 1971). There are, however, clearly racial, ethnic, and cultural specifics to this notion. We propose that for this reason people construe their relationships in such a way as to make themselves not feel indebted. Generational transfers might be seen as a manifestation of this. Reciprocity can be seen as both a contemporaneous and longitudinal concept

(Antonucci and Jackson, 1990). One might strive to achieve reciprocity immediately, i.e., contemporaneously; or one might strive to maintain relationships that are nonreciprocal, specifically overbenefiting or under-benefiting so that at some point in the future when support is needed, reciprocity might be maintained by drawing on these support reserves. Lending someone money this week and borrowing some the next; or driving someone to the store and having them bake you a cake might both be seen as contemporaneous support. However, providing support to one's parents when they are old may be seen as reciprocating support that they provided when you were young. Babysitting your grandchildren while your daughter works might be considered a multigenerational reciprocal act when conceptualized as an act of reciprocity for the support your mother gave you, the grandmother, when you were a working mother. Receiving support when you are ill or disabled may also be experienced as reciprocal support if it is evaluated as support being provided in exchange for support that was provided at an earlier point in time.

The notion of reciprocity allows people to avoid a sense of indebtedness that might be psychologically unhealthy. We have been able to explore this conceptualization empirically and have found interesting support for this perspective. Antonucci and Jackson (1990) examined the support exchanges of American whites and blacks and French elders. These data indicate that whites were less likely to report reciprocal relationships than blacks and that whites were more likely to report that they provide more support across all ages. As people age, all groups were less likely to report providing more support than they received and more likely to report receiving more support then they provided. Our data indicate that increased resources, financial or educational, especially among older people also increase the likelihood of relationships being considered reciprocal and decrease the likelihood of individuals reporting that they receive more support than they provide. This effect is stronger for whites than blacks, perhaps related to the fact that whites in the United States tend to have more resources than blacks. Generally speaking, reciprocity of relationships is associated with higher levels of life satisfaction and family satisfaction (Antonucci and Jackson, 1990).

We have also examined the effects of functional capacity on the exchange of support (Antonucci and Jackson, 1990). Among blacks, though not among whites, the most important predictor of reciprocity was disability. For the most part, this represented a change from providing more than one received to reciprocal relationships. This, too, might best be understood within the context of resources available. Once a functional impairment occurred, the individual had fewer resources with which to provide support to others but, nevertheless, was still able to report reciprocally supportive relationships. This reciprocity might have been achieved by asking for less, by interacting with fewer people, or by incorporating previously provided support to balance the current receipt of support.

One final point on cultural differences should be noted. Although completely comparable data were not available, we were able to contrast French elders' with American white and black elders' responses on the percentage of support they viewed as reciprocal. The French were least likely to indicate that they received less support than they provided (<4 percent), compared to American blacks (30 percent) or whites (55 percent) in the same category. Discussing these differences with me, a French colleague argued that the French simply found overindebtedness unacceptable and were therefore not very likely to report it. Here there may be an overriding cultural perspective that prevents the French from indicating that they receive more support than they provide under any circumstances. For the French, the longitudinal, rather than contemporaneous assessment of reciprocity may be used for this purpose, in contrast to the late-life disability apparently used by Americans. We should note that initially we considered the differences between blacks and whites to be significant. However, this difference paled when compared with the responses of the French elderly. Nevertheless, we believe that this concept of reciprocity, and particularly how different groups conceptualize the provision and receipt of support over time, relationships, and generations, may provide important insights into how to best maximize the lifetime benefits of multigenerational support relationships (Bengtson, 1996, 2001; Silverstein and Bengtson, 1993).

SUMMARY AND CONCLUSIONS

Tempered by historical time, major national and international events, and cultural practices, generations are represented by birth cohorts and family-linked structures moving through time together. These structures, reflecting reciprocal influences, change through the losses and additions of new members, and the historical and period events that affect both inter- and intragenerational relations across and within families. Intrageneration family structures exist within sociohistorical, ethnic, geographical, and geopolitical contexts. These contexts have important implications for the content of beliefs, values, and attitudes within generations, and the process and products of familial and generation cohort socialization. While we noted the universal joy associated with the arrival of new generations, both collectively and within families, across the globe, it is clear that what transpires as communication, socialization, social, and tangible exchanges, are historically, ethnically, and culturally conditioned. The challenge to intergenerational researchers will be to specify how, and with what results, these contexts affect the quality and quantity of intergenerational relationships.

REFERENCES

Ainsworth, M. D. S., Blehar, M. C., Waters, E., and Wall, S. 1978. *Patterns of attachment*. Hillsdale, NJ: Lawrence Erlbaum.

Ajrouch, K. J., Antonucci, T. C., and Janevic, M. R. 2001. Social networks among blacks and whites: The interaction between race and age. *Journal of Gerontology: Social Sciences* 56b(2):112–18.

Antonucci, T. C. 1994. A life-span view of women's social relations. In B. F. Turner and L. E. Troll (eds.), *Women growing older: Psychological perspectives* (pp. 239–69). Thousand Oaks, CA: Sage.

_____. 2001. Social Relations: An examination of social networks, social support and sense of control. In J. E. Birren and K. W. Schaie (eds.), *Handbook of the Psychology of Aging* (5th ed.), pp. 427–53. New York: Academic Press.

Antonucci, T. C., Fuhrer, R., and Dartigues, J.-F. 1997. Social relations and depressive symptomatology in a sample of community-dwelling French older adults. *Psychology and Aging, 12* 189–95.

Antonucci, T. C., and Jackson, J. S. 1990. The role of reciprocity in social support. In I. G. Sarason, B. R. Sarason, and G. R. Pierce (eds.), *Social Support: An interactional view* (pp. 173–98). New York: John Wiley and Sons.

Baltes, P. B., and Baltes, M. M. 1986. *The psychology of control and aging*. Ann Arbor, MI: Books on Demand.

Bengtson, V. L. 1996. Continuities and discontinuities in intergenerational relationships over time. In V. L. Bengtson (ed.), *Adulthood and aging: Research on continuities and discontinuities* (pp. 271–303). New York: Springer.

_____. 2001. Beyond the nuclear family: The increasing importance of multigenerational bonds (The Burgess Award Lecture). *Journal of Marriage and the Family* 63(1):1–16.

Bisconti, T. L., and Bergeman, C. S. 1999. Perceived social control as a mediator of the relationships among social support, psychological well-being and perceived health. *Gerontologist* 39:94–101.

Bott, E. 1957. *Family and social network*. London: Tavistock.

Bowlby, J. 1973. *Attachment and loss* (Vol. 2). New York: Basic Books.

Chen, X., and Silverstein, M. 2000. Intergenerational social support and the psychological well-being of older parents in China. *Research on Aging* 22(1):43–65.

Freud, A. 1935. Psychoanalysis and the training of the young child. *Psychoanalytic Quarterly* 4:15–24.

George, L. K., Blazer, D. G., Hughes, D. C., and Fowler, N. 1989. Social support and the outcome of major depression. *British Journal of Psychiatry* 154:478–85

Gouldner, A. W. 1960. The norm of reciprocity: A preliminary statement. *American Sociological Review* 25:161–78.

Greenberg, M. S., and Shapiro, S. P. 1971. Indebtedness: An adverse aspect of asking for and receiving help. *Sociometry* 34:290–301.

Jackson, J. S., and Antonucci, T. C. 1994. Survey methodology in life-span human development research. In S. H. Cohen and H. W. Reese (eds.), *Life-span developmental psychology: Methodological contributions* (pp. 65–94). Hillsdale, NJ: Lawrence Erlbaum.

Kahn, R. L., and Antonucci, T. C. 1980. Convoys over the life course: Attachment, roles, and social support. In P. B. Baltes and O. Brim (eds.), *Life-span development and behavior* (pp. 253–86). New York: Academic Press.

Kim, H. K., and McKenry, P. C. 1999. Social networks and support: A comparison of African Americans, Asian Americans, Caucasians, and Hispanics. *Journal of Comparative Family Studies* 29(2):313–34.

Krause, N. 1997. Social support and feelings of personal control in later life. In G. R. Pierce, B. Lakey, I. G. Sarason, and B. R. Sarason (eds.), *Sourcebook of social support and personality* (pp. 335–55). New York: Plenum.

Lachman, M. E., and Weaver, S. L. 1998a. Sociodemographic variations in the sense of control by domain: Findings from the MacArthur studies of midlife. *Psychology of Aging* 13:553–62.

_____. 1998b. The sense of control as a moderator of social class differences in health and well-being. *Journal of Personality and Social Psychology* 74(3):763–73.

Levitt, M. J. 1991. Attachment and close relationships: A life-span perspective. In J. L. Gewirtz and W. Kurtines, *Intersections with attachment* (pp. 183–206). Hillsdale, NJ: Lawrence Erlbaum.

Matsuda, T., Ando, T., Okamura, K., Yokoyama, H., Yatomi, N., and Noguchi, W. 1993. Social support and depressive symptoms among the middle-aged and aged: Moderating effects of gender and marital status. Paper presented at the International Congress of Health Psychology, Tokyo, Japan, July.

Myeroff, B. G. 1979. *Number our days*. New York: E. P. Dutton.

Oxman, T. C., Berkman, L. F., Kasl, S., Freeman, D. H., and Barrett, J. 1992. Social support and depressive symptoms in the elderly. *American Journal of Epidemiology* 135:356–68.

Silverstein, M., and Bengtson V. L. 1993. Does intergenerational social support influence the psychological well-being of older parents? The contingencies of declining health and widowhood. *Social Science and Medicine* 38:943–57.

Silverstein, M., and Waite, L. J. 1993. Are blacks more likely than whites to receive and provide social support in middle and old age? Yes, no, and maybe so. *Journal of Gerontology: Social Sciences* 48:212–22.

Stack, C. 1974. *All our kin: Strategies for survival in the black community*. New York: Harper and Row.

Taylor, R. J., and Chatters, L. M. 1986. Patterns of informal support to elderly adults: Family, friends, and church members. *Social Work*, 31:432–438.

Taylor, R. J., Chatters, L. M., and Jackson, J. S. 1997. Changes over time in support network involvement among black Americans. In R. J. Taylor, J. S. Jackson, and L. M. Chatters (eds.), *Family life in Black America* (pp. 293–316). Thousand Oaks, CA: Sage.

Wenger, G. C. 1997. Review of findings on support networks of older Europeans. *Journal of Cross-Cultural Gerontology* 12:1–21.

|18|

Challenges of Global Aging to Families in the Twenty-First Century

Ariela Lowenstein and Vern Bengtson

The new millennium and the twenty-first century confront us with numerous challenges related to the aging of societies in the modern world. Population projections for the year 2020 show that in much of Western Europe, including the Scandinavian countries, the United Kingdom, and Spain, the age group of 65+ will constitute 17–18 percent of the population, and the 80+ age group will be about 4 percent (OECD, 1996). In the United States, the projections are similar to those for Western Europe (Treas, 1995). Japan may be one of the most rapidly aging societies in the modern world. In 2000, the 65+ age group already constituted 17.2 percent of the population, but it is projected that by 2050 the 65+ group will be about a third of the total population and the 75+ age group will be close to 19 percent of Japan's population (Kojima, 2000).

Thus, the phenomenon of aging populations is a broad, global one, even though it is happening gradually in some countries and more rapidly in others. This global phenomenon raises questions about the definition of old age, the microexperiences of older people and their families, and the macroresponses of societies to the needs of these older people and their families. In addition to the aging of populations, marked changes are being seen in family forms. These include a collapse in fertility (for example, in most EU countries); changes in the timing of family transitions, especially marriage and parenthood, that have resulted in two distinct family forms based on the timing of fertility: age-condensed and age-gapped family forms (Bengtson, Rosenthal, and Burton, 1995); changes in patterns of family formation and dissolution and the ensuing diversification of family forms that have led to more complex and "atypical" families. This diversity of family forms creates uncertainty in intergenerational relations and expectations and has specific effects on life course role transitions (e.g., from parenthood to grandparenthood). Diverse family forms have evolved in different population groups and cultural contexts. This diversity is related to what Stacey (1990) has labeled the postmodern family, characterized by "structural fragility" and a greater dependence on the voluntary commitment of its members.

Added to these factors are societal trends such as changing employment patterns—especially of women—that impact family relationships and caregiving and that are forcing us to look seriously at the more traditional patterns of living arrangements and family intergenerational solidarity. Other structural changes affecting the lives of the elderly include the growing number of elderly single households and the increased mobility of adult children. Along with these transformations in family structure and family life, we are witnessing the impact of broader social and technological changes involving such things as internal and external migration, shifts in social policies, and changing trends in families' preference for care.

Yet, despite this situation of flux in modern societies, the couple and family orientation of social life and the value attached to sociability make the family a main reference point in the aging process, and the needs of the elderly are best understood within the context of the family. Solidarity between generations has long been at the forefront as an enduring characteristic of families (Brubaker, 1990). As presented in this volume, and in much of the research literature during the past decade, intergenerational bonds among adult family members may be even more important today than in earlier decades because individuals live longer and thus can share more years and experiences with other generations (Antonucci, Sherman and Akiyama, 1995; Bengtson, Giarrusso, Silverstein, and Wang, 2000; Connidis, 2001; Domingo and Asis, 1995; Lowenstein, Katz, Mehlhausen-Hassoen, and Pritlutsky, 2003; and Lowenstein, Katz, Prilutzky, and Mehlhausen-Hassoen, 2001). Nonetheless, some basic questions must be addressed. They include: (1) How much help and support is really exchanged between family generations? (2) How strong are the bonds of obligation and expectation between generations? (3) What accounts for the differences in contact and closeness and the similarities in opinions, expectations, and exchanges of help? (4) Is there a potential for intergenerational family ambivalence? (5) What is the economic value of the intergenerational transfers that occur within families? (6) What is the role of society, with its elaborate service system, with regard to the enhancement of family relations?

In this book, prominent scholars and researchers from different parts of the globe have made an attempt to address the above questions and issues and to examine similarities and differences between cultures and social structures. The authors are mostly from developed, industrialized countries, including Europe, the United States, Israel, and Japan, but there is also a perspective from South Korea and one from a developing country, Ghana. This group of scholars represents countries with diverse social, cultural, and familial norms and values, as well as different welfare responses to the phenomena of aging and changing family relationships. Thus, their contribution enriches and extends our knowledge base on how families in the twenty-first century will meet the challenges of global aging.

The studies in this volume present a picture of intergenerational family relations taking on diverse forms in response to individual, familial, and social structural characteristics. These characteristics serve as markers for differences in socialization, personal role identities, cultures, values, and individuals' access to resources, and as such they shape intergenerational family solidarity. On the individual level, two main variables are especially important: age and gender. The age of family members is important because with age come changes in roles and responsibilities. Gender is important because women and men undergo different socialization processes and because women tend to maintain social relationships between family members more than men and are more inclined to act as the primary caregivers (Aldous, 1987; Lowenstein, 1999). Family characteristics refer to the positions that family members hold within the family structure, depending upon whether they are married, divorced, widowed, etc. The third significant level of variables includes social structural characteristics such as race and ethnicity, because ethnic and racial groups have been found to differ in terms of their members' willingness to assume various family roles (see Chapter 17 in this volume).

The research presented here is based primarily on the theoretical perspectives of the life course and modernization. Thus, the focus of the volume is on the outcomes of the changes described above—in demography and in family forms, households, and behaviors—and their impact on the personal and familial life course of elders and their families and the quality of life of all concerned. Throughout the discussions of intergenerational relationships presented in the book, several key themes emerge. Even though family forms have changed from "pyramids" to "beanpoles," with an increased availability of extended intergenerational kin as family resources, the data in the different chapters point to the following themes. The first is the continued importance of the family and the strength of intergenerational family solidarity, as revealed particularly in the Longitudinal Study of Generations (LSOG) data over a period of 30 years (Bengtson et al., 2000). The main conclusion in this regard is that families, while taking on new and diverse forms, will continue to be important in the lives of individuals in the twenty-first century, even though they will face more and newer challenges. The second important theme is greater longevity, which means longer periods of shared experiences but also a growing number of disabled elderly (WHO, 2002). In addition, this situation indicates that more years of caregiving will be required for dependent elders. Finally, it might also mean more potential conflicts between generations, especially in step-kin families.

A third theme that emerged from the data in this volume is that intergenerational and family relations are becoming more and more varied and complex, which is having and will continue to have important impacts on family expectations, family transfers, and family support. One example is cases of divorce and remarriage (Connidis, 2001; Kaufman and Uhlenberg, 1998; Lowenstein and Ron, 1999), in which a new "latent kin matrix" is formed (Riley and Riley, 1996). Another example is grandparent-grandchild relations, as presented in this volume by Silverstein, Giarrusso, and Bengtson.

A fourth theme that arose is the importance of attitudes, motivations, and expectations regarding intergenerational transfers and caregiving. Chapters 15 and 16 present data at the national and cross-national levels (from the OASIS five-country study) on the consequences of current trends for the quality of life of elders and their families. In this case, however, the data appear to be equivocal, and thus more studies are needed to help us identify and understand the important factors that will affect the relationship between parental expectations of children and filial behavior. It is obvious that this relationship is changing even in more traditional societies and in societies that are in a transition state from traditional to modern, such as South Korea and Japan (see Chapters 12 and 13). Yet, we still know too little about the organizing principles and values that shape families' responses—or nonresponses—to elder care needs. Also, we do not know much about the effects of such care transfers. In the future, emphasis should be on the study of the family network, with the goal of developing a theory of family caregiving (Cicirelli, 1992). In the family caregiving literature there is still considerable ambiguity about three significant questions: (1) What is caregiving? (2) What are the positive and negative outcomes of caregiving? and (3) What are the relations between formal and informal caregiving?

The last theme addressed in the book is the interrelations between the micro- and macrosystems or, in other words, family solidarity versus state solidarity. It has become evident that the care of the aged is a mix of public and private resources, with the characteristics of this mix varying from one country to another. The specific mix is related to three factors: (1) the norms and preferences of families with regard to care, (2) the family culture that guides the level of readiness to use public services, and (3) the availability, accessibility, quality, and cost of those public services. Even though the debate regarding the substitution model versus the complementarity model is still continuing (see Chapter 15) it is well established in the literature that family care (i.e., care of the elderly by families) is substantial and that collective responsibility through available public services has not discouraged family care (Daatland, 1997; Katan and Lowenstein, 1999). However, it has been pointed out that the needs and interests of caregivers need to be incorporated into public policy debates. In addition, data show that as a result of the increased availability and social acceptability of public services, there is more willingness by the elderly and their families to use public services when dependency starts (Daatland, 1997).

In the future, rising levels of affluence and the introduction of state welfare provisions will allow the operation of choice in family relationships. Thus, sentiment rather than obligation might increasingly govern ties between elderly parents and younger generations. Not many role models of caregiving have existed until now, and there is a need to develop new models.

This volume establishes the idea that in modern aging societies quality of life in old age is dependent upon both relationships of intergenerational family solidarity and the responses of societies' formal service systems. To help families cope with the challenges of global aging, we must find ways to assess what is considered good quality care, from both the familial perspective and that of the formal service systems. In addition, we must continue to study the relationships between family networks and governmental family policy.

It is evident from the research presented here that current assumptions about the family, caregiving, and the work life cycle appear to be inadequate in the context of newly emerging individual and family life cycle patterns. Also, further analyses—on the national as well as the regional and local levels—of demographic trends and changing family forms and their consequences are crucial in order to allow us to describe and better understand the diversity of families as they cope with aging and with changes in family behaviors, support, and caregiving.

Without doubt, the institutions of marriage and the family will continue to be popular, but family forms in the future will also be characterized by divorce, remarriage, and other types of family arrangements. These social trends will have important implications for the elderly in families, which will lead to further developments in intergenerational ties and caregiving patterns and styles.

It can be expected that new generations of the elderly will be better educated and will have higher incomes than past generations, and many families in the future may well be composed of four or five generations—a situation that will involve a continuing evolution in care demands and responses in the twenty-first century. There will be more elderly and more very old people—two-generation geriatric families—who will need care and assistance. At the same time, these elderly will demand better care and will be able to purchase many in-home and community services. In short, the responses of both families and governments will be vitally important. Yet, in the end, if history tells us anything, the quality of life of elders and families is unlikely to improve unless, as Maddox (1985) says, "the revolution of possibilities and hope" takes place. Given the current and projected significance of the family for societies of all kinds, the issues addressed by the authors in this book loom as some of the most critical and challenging in all of human affairs.

REFERENCES

Aldous, J. 1987. New views on the family life of the elderly and the near-elderly. *Journal of Marriage and the Family* 49(2):227–34.

Antonucci, T. C., Sherman, A. M., and Akiyama, H. 1996. Social networks, support, and integration. In J. E. Birren (ed.), *Encyclopedia of Gerontology* 41:408–16.

Bengtson, V. L., Giarrusso, R., Silverstein, M., and Wang, H. 2000. Families and intergenerational relationships in aging societies. *Hallym International Journal of Aging* 2:3–10.

Bengtson, V. L., Rosenthal, C. J., and Burton, L. M. 1995. Paradoxes of families and aging. In R. H. Binstock and L. K. George (eds.), *Handbook of aging and the social sciences* (4th ed.; pp. 253–82). San Diego, CA: Academic Press.

Brubaker, T. H. 1990. Families in later life: A burgeoning research area. *Journal of Marriage and the Family* 52:959–81.

Cicirelli, V. G. 1992. Children's sibling relationships: Developmental and clinical issues. *Journal of Marriage and the Family* 54(4):1004–5

Connidis, I. 2001. *Family ties and aging.* Thousand Oaks, CA: Sage.

Daatland, S. O. 1997. Family solidarity, public opinion and the elderly. *Ageing International* 1:51–62.

Domingo, L. J., and Asis, M. M. B. 1995. Living arrangements and the flow of support between generations in the Philippines. *Journal of Cross-Cultural Gerontology Special Issue: Focus Group Research on the Living Arrangements of Elderly in Asia* 10(1–2):21–51.

Katan, J. and Lowenstein, A. 1999. *A decade of the implementation of the long-term Care Insurance Law.* Jerusalem: The Center for Policy Research (in Hebrew).

Kaufman, G., and Uhlenberg, P. 1998. Effects of life course transitions on the quality of relationships between adult children and their parents. *Journal of Marriage and the Family* 60:924–38.

Kojima, H. 2000. Japan: Hyper-aging and its policy implications. In V. L. Bengtson, Kim, K.-D., Myers, G, C., and Eun, K.-S. 2000. *Aging in East and West: Families, states and the elderly* (pp. 95–120). New York: Springer.

Lowenstein, A. 1999. Intergenerational family relations and social support. *Gerontologie und Geriatrie.* Key Note Lectures, Fifth European Congress of Gerontology (pp. 398–407). Darmstadt: Steinkopff.

Lowenstein, A., Katz, R., Mehlhausen-Hassoen, D., and Pritlutsky, D. 2003. A comparative cross-national perspective on intergenerational solidarity. *Retraite et Societe* 38:52–80.

Lowenstein, A., Katz, R., Prilutzky, D., and Melhousen-Hassoen, D. 2001. *The intergenerational* solidarity *paradigm.* In S. O. Daatland and K. Herlofson (eds.), *Ageing, intergenerational relations, care systems and quality of life: An introduction to the OASIS project* (pp. 11–30). Oslo: NOVA—Norwegian Social Research.

Lowenstein, A., and Ron, P. 1999. Tension and conflict factors in spousal abuse in second marriages of the widowed elderly. *Journal of Elder Abuse and Neglect* 11(1):23–45.

Maddox, G. L. 1985. Constructing the future of aging. In M. T. Coleman, B. K. Smith, and C. Warner (eds.), *Looking forward: Texas and its elderly* (pp. 43–5). Austin, TX: University of Texas.

OECD. 1996. Social Policy Studies No. 19. *Caring for frail elderly people. Policies in evolution.* Paris: OECD.

Riley, M. W., and Riley, J. W. 1996. Generational relations: A future perspective. In T. K. Hareven (ed.), *Aging and generational relations: Life-course and cross-cultural perspectives* (pp. 283–91). Hawthorne, NY: Aldine de Gruyter.

Stacey, J. 1991. *Brave new families.* New York: Basic Books.

Treas, J. 1995. Older Americans in the 1990s and beyond. *Population Bulletin,* 50(2):2–46.

World Health Organization. 2002. *Active ageing: A policy framework.* Madrid, Spain: Second United National World Assembly on Ageing.

Index